CLAUDIA RAPP is Associate Professor of History at the University of California, Los Angeles. She is the coeditor of *Elites in Late Antiquity* (2000) and *Bosphorus: Essays in Honour of Cyril Mango* (1995).

# Holy Bishops in Late Antiquity

# THE TRANSFORMATION OF THE CLASSICAL HERITAGE

*Peter Brown, General Editor*

# Holy Bishops in Late Antiquity

*The Nature of Christian Leadership*
*in an Age of Transition*

Claudia Rapp

UNIVERSITY OF CALIFORNIA PRESS
*Berkeley   Los Angeles   London*

ꞌ

Frontispiece: *Saint Demetrius with the Bishop of Thessalonike and the Eparch Leo*. Seventh-century mosaic from the Church of Ayios Dimitrios, Thessaloniki, Greece. Courtesy of the Museum of Byzantine Culture, Thessaloniki, Greece.

University of California Press
Berkeley and Los Angeles, California

University of California Press, Ltd.
London, England

© 2005 by the Regents of the University of California

Library of Congress Cataloging-in-Publication Data
Rapp, Claudia.
   Holy bishops in late antiquity : the nature of Christian leadership in an age of transition / Claudia Rapp.
       p.   cm. — (The transformation of the classical heritage ; 37)
   Includes bibliographical references and index.
   ISBN 0–520–24296–3 (alk. paper)
   1. Bishops—Rome.   2. Church history—Primitive and early church, ca. 30–600.   I. Title.   II. Series.
   BR166.R36   2005
   262'.1214—dc22
   2004013430

Manufactured in Canada

13   12   11   10   09   08   07   06   05   04
10   9   8   7   6   5   4   3   2   1

This book is printed on New Leaf EcoBook 60, containing 60% post-consumer waste, processed chlorine free; 30% de-inked recycled fiber, elemental chlorine free; and 10% FSC-certified virgin fiber, totally chlorine free. EcoBook 60 is acid-free and meets the minimum requirements of ANSI/ASTM D5634-01 *(Permanence of Paper)*.

In memoriam
*Edeltraud Rapp, geb. Ebert*
*Bromberg, 2.*
*März 1931–Dortmund, 30. Dezember 1985*

# CONTENTS

# ACKNOWLEDGMENTS

This book has been long in the making, and it is a pleasant duty to acknowledge my debts of gratitude, which are considerable, as they reach back to the early days of my academic life. In Berlin, the late Paul Speck taught me how to read hagiography, and Ralph-Johannes Lilie how to think like a historian. In Oxford, Cyril Mango's erudition and wisdom provided guidance during the dissertation writing process and beyond, while James Howard-Johnston's inspiring direction and Michael Whitby's tough dialectic made me understand that research is hard—and enjoyable—work. My parents, Edeltraud and Friedrich Rapp, supported me through it all.

Many other friends and colleagues, both in the United States and in Europe, have contributed to the shape of this book, even if they may not recognize their contributions on the following pages. Without the inspiration, sustained interest, and persistent encouragement of Peter Brown, this book would not have been written. I will never be able to adequately express my gratitude to him. Many others have been helpful in a myriad of different ways. The following deserve to be singled out: Clifford Ando, Glen Bowersock, Wolfram Brandes, Averil Cameron, Daniel Caner, Patricia Crone, Harold Drake, Susanna Elm, Michael Gaddis, Sharon Gerstel, John Haldon, Paul Halsall, Judith Herrin, Jennifer Hevelone-Harper, John Langdon, J. H. W. G. Liebeschuetz, Michael Maas, Ralph Mathisen, Neil McLynn, Michele Salzman, Andrea Sterk, Alice-Mary Talbot, Tim Vivian, and Mary Whitby.

At the University of California, Los Angeles, I am grateful to my colleagues for many stimulating conversations about issues of religion and power, especially Michael Cooperson, Patrick Geary, Bariša Krekiá, Gail Lenhoff, Michael Morony, and Kathryn Morgan. Many graduate students, past and present, have acted as sounding boards and, in some instances, provided research assistance; they include Elizabeth Goldfarb, Scott McDonough, Maged Mikhail, Jason Moralee, Daniel Schwartz, Boris Todorov, Julia Verkholantsev, and Cynthia Villagomez. Several undergraduate students have also been research assistants: James Brusuelas, Natalie Esteban, Benjamin Kang, and Cindy Le. The ever-patient staff of the Young Research Library at UCLA, and especially its Interlibrary Loan department, were of invaluable help. The team at University of California Press accompanied the publication process from the beginning, and I am grateful for their professionalism and expertise: Kate Toll, Cindy Fulton, and, last but not least, Marian Rogers, who turned copy editing into an art.

I was fortunate to be able to jump-start this project as a member of the Institute for Advanced Study in Princeton during 1997–98, with additional support from a UC President's Fellowship in the Humanities. The serene surroundings of the Institute offered the concentration that was necessary to make this book become a reality. I dedicate it to the memory of my mother, who did not live even to see its inception.

# PART ONE

# CHAPTER ONE

# The Nature of Leadership in Late Antiquity

The emperor, the holy man, and the bishop. These were the most powerful and evocative figures in late antiquity. They provided practical leadership, moral guidance, and the dispensation of favors. Their important position in society is illustrated by artistic representations such as the seventh-century mosaic from St. Demetrius in Thessalonike on the frontispiece of this book, which shows the youthful saint flanked by the bishop of the city and a civic dignitary as representative of the emperor. Emperors, bishops, and holy men also occupy center stage in the literary production of late antiquity. The ancient genre of panegyric in praise of emperors flourished on an unprecedented scale, the writing of church history where bishops were the protagonists was a new, pioneering effort, and various forms of hagiographical writing, especially saints' *Lives,* were created to extol the virtues of holy men and women.

The interaction of emperor, holy man, and bishop can be seen in the *Life of Daniel the Stylite.* Inspired by the example of Symeon the Stylite, whose reputation as an exceptional ascetic and miracle worker attracted large crowds to his pillar near Antioch, Daniel established himself in a suburb of Constantinople in the mid-fifth century. The local priests reacted with resentment and jealousy to the presence of this stranger from Syria, whose decision to take up residence in an abandoned temple, and later on top of a pillar, seemed to generate a great deal of interest and admiration among the local population. In response to their complaints, the archbishop of Constantinople looked into the matter. In a personal meeting, he recognized Daniel's spiritual strength and then convinced the clergy that their suspicions were groundless. The popular local cult of the holy man thus received the stamp of approval from the highest ecclesiastical authority.

Over the following years, the *Life* explains, Daniel became something like a personal saint for Emperor Leo I (457–474) and for his successor, Zeno (474–491), who depended upon Daniel to soothe restless crowds on the verge of rebellion, to predict the outcome of imperial initiatives, and to quell heretical stirrings. Leo rewarded Daniel's cooperation with public gestures of recognition, especially by donating a large pillar, topped by an enclosed platform, on which Daniel would live. The holy man was, quite literally, put on a pedestal, so that his extraordinary ascetic stamina—his motionless stance on the small platform, his exposure to the elements—was visible even from afar. To express his gratitude for Daniel's efficacious prayers, Leo also instigated Daniel's ordination to the priesthood at the hands of the archbishop of Constantinople. Archbishop Gennadius willingly complied with this request, apparently unperturbed by the prospect of violating a number of church canons that regulate priestly appointments. But when the archbishop asked Daniel to descend from his pillar in order to receive his ordination, the latter refused—most likely because he did not want to be seen as coveting the priesthood. Thus, instead of consecrating the new priest through the customary imposition of hands, Gennadius decided to perform the ordination rite from the bottom of the pillar where he stood. In describing this unconventional procedure, the hagiographer reveals his own awkwardness when he has Gennadius explain to Daniel that during his prayer of consecration "God laid His hand upon you from above."[1] Daniel's ordination had no effect on his way of life or daily routine, since he never exercised any priestly duties. His ordination to the priesthood served the exclusive purpose of recognizing, confirming, and enhancing Daniel's position as a holy man, and it took place at the initiative not of the highest representative of the church, but of the highest secular authority in the empire.

Daniel's influence in Constantinople and among his followers was considerable. But it is not easy to pinpoint its origin and to establish whether it derived from his reputation as a holy man, his ordination to the priesthood, or his close association with the emperor. In fact, his contemporaries are reported to have had an equally blurry view of the nature of his authority. An episode during the rebellion of Basiliscus, a supporter of Monophysitism, against the emperor Zeno illustrates this. While the efforts of the new archbishop Acacius to force Basiliscus to embrace orthodoxy remained fruitless and resulted only in stirring up the potential for unrest in the capital, Daniel came to the rescue, restored order in the city, and reaffirmed orthodoxy. This was one of the few occasions when, yielding to popular pressure, he descended from his pillar and entered Constantinople. There, he was acclaimed by the people as "high priest," while a Goth, presumably

---

1. *Life of Daniel the Stylite* 43.

an Arian, mockingly referred to him as "the new consul."[2] This vignette in the *Life* shows the Constantinopolitans and the Goth in agreement in their appreciation of Daniel's authority, even as they conceptualize its origin in different ways, the former as deriving from the institution of the church, the latter from that of the empire. Daniel's triumphant presence in Constantinople culminated in his visit to the cathedral church of Saint Sophia, where both the rebel emperor Basiliscus and the archbishop Acacius demonstrated their submission to the holy man who had succeeded where they had failed, in bringing unity to a divided population on the brink of civil unrest. They fell at his feet and, while laying prostrate on the ground, were formally reconciled by Daniel, a gesture that derived its particular poignancy from the fact that his feet were crippled and worn down to the bone—a tangible token of his ascetic achievement.[3] Thanks to Daniel's intervention, Basiliscus also gave a formal profession of orthodoxy, which ended his antagonism with Acacius. Shortly before describing Daniel's death, the hagiographer is at pains to reinforce the notion of Daniel's position as a "priest," complete with quasi-liturgical prerogatives. In a vision, the story goes, he saw the saints in heaven asking him to celebrate the eucharistic liturgy. Upon awakening, he asked to receive communion, and his disciples partook of it also. The hagiographer, who claims to have been one of the disciples present on that occasion, explains that it was "just as if he had been administering to us the holy sacrament."[4]

This extraordinary story illustrates the ambiguous and fluctuating relation between Christian priesthood and personal holiness: Daniel's "virtual priesthood" was bestowed on him as a confirmation of his sanctity, at the behest of the secular ruler, by the highest representative of the church. At a time of crisis and political instability, both emperor and archbishop submitted to Daniel's higher authority. He was recognized by the people as their true priest and preserver of doctrinal unity, and his followers even experienced him in the role of a priest consecrating the eucharist. Daniel's story, as it was narrated for the benefit of his admirers, exemplifies the complex relation between the possession of spiritual gifts, visible evidence of ascetic living, and concrete authority within the institution of the Christian church.

To the modern reader, this story may seem strangely over the top. In our view, the emperor and the holy man embody the contrasting principles of secular and religious leadership. The Enlightenment and its heritage, from the ideals of the French Revolution to the work of Edward Gibbon, have

2. Ibid.,73 and 75. Cf. also 71, where the people of Constantinople call him "the priest of orthodoxy."
3. *Life of Daniel the Stylite* 83.
4. Ibid., 96.

taught us not only to make a sharp distinction between the secular and the religious, but also to consider this distinction as an essential precondition for modern statehood.[5] Yet the notion of the association of imperial authority with the divine that guided, protected, and guaranteed the emperor's rule was pervasive in the Roman Empire and was passed on—in Christian guise—to the Byzantine Empire and the medieval West. Just as imperial authority was intricately linked to the divine, the religious authority of holy men had overtones of secular power. The appreciation by his contemporaries of an individual as a holy man depended to a large extent on his ability to bestow on them benefactions of a very concrete, worldly kind: healing from illness, relief of famine, and restoration of social order. To assume that in the later Roman Empire the secular and the religious were perceived as separate and that our view of this period should adhere to this dichotomy is a misleading result of modern thinking. It is more fruitful to conceive of secular and religious authority as the opposing ends of a sliding scale, where each individual, whether emperor, holy man, or bishop, has his own place, depending on his role in society and his own personal conduct.

It is, in fact, the bishop who occupies the middle ground between the two poles of secular and religious leadership. His responsibilities as administrator of a diocese involve him in very mundane matters from financial administration to building works, while his duties as the shepherd of his flock entail such religious obligations as pastoral care, the preservation of doctrinal unity, and the celebration of the liturgy and other Christian rites. The nature of episcopal leadership during the third to sixth centuries is the central theme of this book. This is the formative period during which the church was propelled to assume an ever-increasing role in the public life of the later Roman Empire, and its representatives, the bishops, were saddled with ever-increasing public duties. It is my contention that a proper understanding of the role of the bishops during this time of transition can be accomplished only once we rid ourselves of the anachronistic baggage of a supposed secular-religious dichotomy. This is an artificial distinction that would have been completely incomprehensible to the men and women of late antiquity. In an extended sense, then, this study hopes to contribute to a more nuanced understanding of the nature of authority in late antiquity in general.

## PREVIOUS SCHOLARSHIP ON THE ROLE OF BISHOPS IN LATE ANTIQUITY

No single figure seems to encapsulate the changes and transformations of late antiquity better than the Christian bishop. Bishops figure prominently

5. On this, see the incisive remarks by W. Wischmeyer, "M. Iulius Eugenius: Eine Fallstudie zum Thema 'Christen und Gesellschaft im 3. und 4. Jahrhundert,'" *ZNW* 81 (1990): 227–29.

in the scholarly literature about this period. They are often invoked in overview treatments of church history, social structure, and urbanism as the focal point on which significant transformations hinge. The common underlying assumption of such studies tends to be that the rise of Christianity goes hand in hand with the rise of the bishop to political prominence, a rise whose lasting consequences reverberate into the Middle Ages and beyond. Bishops were actively involved in the defense of their cities, acted as judges in civil cases, amassed great wealth, became important building patrons, and on more than one occasion usurped or challenged civil authorities. These are just a few of the litany of examples that are commonly adduced to illustrate the rise of the shepherd of the Christian flock to unprecedented political power.

Studies of the growth of Christianity tend to idealize the Christian communities of the apostolic and subapostolic age, where social differentiations were forcefully rejected, the gifts of the spirit were shared by all, and several *episkopoi* fulfilled the function of overseers. The subsequent departures from this ideal are noted, from the hindsight of the historian, with sadness and alarm. The first significant step in this decline was the stratification and formalization of relationships within the Christian community through the development of a hierarchy of offices within the clergy, combined with the notion that only one bishop should stand at the head of each large urban community. This monarchic episcopate arose at a time when the unity and integrity of the church were threatened by persecution and heresy. Ignatius of Antioch in the late second century and Cyprian of Carthage in the mid-third century responded to this challenge by advocating strong episcopal leadership as a guarantee for the cohesion of the church. The second step in the development of the episcopate, which signaled a further departure from the apostolic ideal—so the conventional narrative goes—occurred when the emperor Constantine began to champion Christianity and showered the bishops with privileges and benefactions. At the same time, he charged them with certain tasks and duties that have been interpreted as extending far beyond the bishops' original reach—a notion that will be challenged in the chapter titled "Empire." During the age of persecutions, the church had defined itself in opposition to the state; now it was put in a position to cooperate with it. Later developments did not essentially alter this relationship; they merely intensified it. The bishops' public role and their political power increased over time, especially in those regions where the existing social order was disrupted by invasions and central government had become ineffectual, obsolete, or nonexistent.

Continental historians of early Christianity, in particular, tend to blame the progressive institutionalization of the church for the attendant loss of spirituality of the early times. The extreme position in this approach was taken by Theodor Klauser who regarded Constantine's ecclesiastical policy as an unprecedented and dangerously successful attempt by the state to absorb the church and its representatives into its administrative apparatus.[6] Klauser based his argument on the observation that certain adjectives, such as *glorio-sissimus*, which signaled high status at the top of a social hierarchy of imperial offices, were also used to address bishops. His thesis was proposed over half a century ago and has since then repeatedly come under criticism from different angles. Hans Ulrich Instinsky pointed out that martyrs had been honored with this adjective long before the reign of Constantine. His study of the titulature and other elements of episcopal and imperial ceremonial emphasized the similarities and possible mutual influence between the two.[7] In response to Klauser and Instinsky, Santo Mazzarino noted that in late antiquity episcopal and imperial authority were thought to have a common origin in the supreme divinity as the source of all power and glory.[8] Ernst Jerg's systematic study of the variety of forms of address used by secular authorities for bishops settled the issue once and for all by demonstrating that bishops were never formally integrated into the administrative apparatus of the empire.[9] The recent book by Harold Drake, *Constantine and the Bishops*, goes a long way to inject a healthy dose of realpolitik into the evaluation of the emperor's religious politics and his treatment of bishops as uneasy allies, moral and spiritual superiors, and subject citizens.[10] Scholarly debate, however, continues to be occupied with the central question that Klauser raised: How are the public activities of a bishop to be interpreted?

French and Italian scholars, many of them rooted in the Catholic tradition, tend to adopt a teleological perspective and welcome the new, public role of bishops after Constantine as paving the way for the rise of the papacy. This is often evident in the anachronistic use of the term "pope" by these scholars for the bishop of Rome, even though the sources they use clearly speak of the *episcopus* and were written at a time when the primacy of the see of Rome was not yet taken for granted. Not surprisingly, French scholars have also been in the forefront of the study of early canon law, beginning with the fourth century, which provides valuable insight into episcopal self-definition.[11]

---

6. T. Klauser, *Der Ursprung der bischöflichen Insignien und Ehrenrechte*, Bonner Akademische Reden 1 (Krefeld, 1949).

7. H. U. Instinsky, *Bischofsstuhl und Kaiserthron* (Munich, 1955).

8. S. Mazzarino, "Costantino e l'episcopato," *Iura* 7 (1956): 345–52, repr. in his *Antico, tardoantico ed era costantiniana*, vol. 1 (n.p., 1974).

9. E. Jerg, *Vir venerabilis: Untersuchungen zur Titulatur der Bischöfe in den ausserkirchlichen Texten der Spätantike als Beitrag zur Deutung ihrer öffentlichen Stellung*, Wiener Beiträge zur Theologie 26 (Vienna, 1970).

10. H. A. Drake, *Constantine and the Bishops: The Politics of Intolerance* (Baltimore and London, 2000).

11. J. Gaudemet, *L'église et l'état au IV^e siècle* (Milan, 1981); id., *Église et cité: Histoire du droit canonique* (Paris, 1994).

While the work of church historians especially until the mid-twentieth century is often colored by their own Christian confession, the approach of social and political historians of a more recent generation is marked by a noticeable neglect of the religious or even ecclesiastical dimension of the episcopate. The recent trend in late antique studies to regard the period largely in terms of urban transformations, coupled with the desire to counterbalance the literary record with archaeological findings, has focused attention on the role of bishops not within the empire, or even within the larger structure of the church, but within the context of their own cities. But although the picture that emerges from such studies is more nuanced, the verdict remains the same: bishops are seen as political actors whose power derives from their social position and wealth.

Peter Brown in *Power and Persuasion,* for example, studies the rising power of the bishop against the background of the transformation of urban culture in late antiquity. In the post-Diocletianic empire, he argues, the bishops gained greater prominence as part of a tighter administrative web that extended a closer grip on cities and individuals than ever before. In this context, the bishop's ability to become an advocate for his community, including its poor, is explained as having its basis in the common cultural "language" of *paideia*—a mode of comportment and a form of expression based on a thorough education in the classical tradition—that is shared by bishops and prominent town councilors, provincial governors, and imperial administrators alike.[12] According to this model, the power of bishops has the same root and is measured by their late antique contemporaries with the same yardstick as that of other prominent men.

There is much to be said for this approach, as the city was the primary stage on which the bishop's role was played out.[13] The Roman Empire, especially along the coast of the Mediterranean, was dotted with cities, each a microcosm of different social groups, each a cultural hub, and each a focal center for the economy and administration of its rural hinterland. The decline of the traditional markers of city life brought to light by the archaeological record—the disappearance of the grid system of streets, the crumbling of theatres, and the shrinking of the walls that enclosed the city territory—has long been taken as evidence for a widespread, simultaneous, and steady decline of urban culture that marks the end of the Roman Empire. The research of the last decades, however, especially the recent synthesis by Wolfgang Liebeschuetz,[14] has challenged this view as being too schematic.

12. P. L. R. Brown, *Power and Persuasion in Late Antiquity: Towards a Christian Empire* (Madison, 1992).

13. See, for example, E. Rebillard and C. Sotinel, eds., *L'évêque dans la cité du IV^e au V^e siècle: Image et autorité,* Collection de l'École Française de Rome 248 (Rome, 1998).

14. J. H. W. G. Liebeschuetz, *The Decline and Fall of the Roman City* (Oxford, 2001).

Greater attention is now being paid to regional differences. While in northern Gaul the few existing cities disappeared altogether by the fifth century, the commercial centers in the eastern Mediterranean were thriving well into the seventh century.[15] The excavations at Aphrodisias, for example, have shown the continued vitality of this large city, with its theatre and other public buildings intact.[16] A more nuanced view has also been taken with regard to urban building activity. We now know that the neglect of public structures was offset by an increase in private and ecclesiastical building. The structures associated with the old, pagan way of life—theatre, hippodrome, forum, public bath—were replaced in their function as social centers by the churches that were now increasingly erected in prominent spots, often with the active encouragement and financial support of bishops.

As the outward appearance of cities changed, so did their demographic profile. Beginning in the fourth century, the various regions of Gaul had to accommodate Visigoths, Franks, and Burgundians. The northern part of the Italian peninsula became home to the Ostrogoths in the fifth century; a century later the Lombards settled primarily in the center and the south. Although these immigrants established themselves mostly in the countryside, their presence necessitated adjustments in the economy, political mechanisms, and social structure of these regions. After the end of imperial rule in Italy, the aristocrats of the Latin West were deprived of the opportunity to enhance their profile through appointment in the imperial service and found a new outlet for their ambitions by joining the episcopate.

Several studies have explored these developments in Gaul[17] and Italy,[18] with a special emphasis on the role of the bishop in providing political leadership as well as much-needed social services in times of crisis and transition. In this respect, the late antique bishop in Gaul and Italy has been seen as an early incarnation of his medieval counterpart, who exercised complete control over his city. The prototypes of such episcopal activity were Martin of Tours and Ambrose of Milan. We are exceptionally well informed about them through

15. A useful overview is provided by the articles in J. Rich, ed., *The City in Late Antiquity* (London, 1992).
16. C. Roueché, *Aphrodisias in Late Antiquity: The Late Roman and Byzantine Inscriptions* (London, 1989).
17. M. Heinzelmann, *Bischofsherrschaft in Gallien: Zur Kontinuität römischer Führungsschichten vom 4. bis zum 7. Jahrhundert: Soziale, prosopographische und bildungsgeschichtliche Aspekte* (Munich, 1976); F. E. Consolino, *Ascesi e mondanità nella Gallia tardoantica: Studi sulla figura del vescovo nei secoli IV–VI* (Naples, 1979); R. W. Mathisen, *Roman Aristocrats in Barbarian Gaul: Strategies for Survival in an Age of Transition* (Austin, 1993).
18. R. Lizzi, *Vescovi e strutture ecclesiastiche nella città tardoantica: L'Italia Annonaria nel IV–V secolo d.C.* (Como, 1989). A useful tool for demographic studies of ecclesiastical officeholders in Italy is C. Pietri and L. Pietri, eds., *Prosopographie chrétienne du Bas-Empire: Italie (303–604)*, 2 vols. (Rome, 2000).

their hagiographers, and in the case of Ambrose also through his own writings, including his letters. Not surprisingly, both Martin and Ambrose have become the subject of several self-contained studies.[19] Similarly, the sheer number of hagiographies of later bishops in Gaul and Italy, such as those of Caesarius of Arles, Germanus of Auxerre, Epiphanius of Pavia, Leo the Great, and Gregory the Great, has contributed to the fact that the bishops of these regions, whether individually or collectively, have received more scholarly attention than those of other areas of the later Roman Empire.[20]

A related strand of studies has tried to uncover the late antique roots of the *Stadtherrschaft* of bishops. As the absence of an English translation of this term indicates, this is a particular concern in German scholarship. The beginnings of this phenomenon can be attributed to the dwindling local powers and the absence of a strong central government in the Merovingian period, although it reached its full extent in the tenth to twelfth centuries, when the bishops of large cities in Germany and Gaul held all the reins of civic administration, complemented by legal and financial independence, thus acting as veritable "lords of their cities."[21] This form of *Stadtherrschaft* of bishops is a later, medieval development, however, that did not necessarily follow from the role of bishops in the later Roman Empire alone but resulted from a combination of other factors specific to Gaul and Germany. In other regions of the Roman Empire, bishops of the fourth to sixth centuries fulfilled the same functions as representatives of their cities and providers of humanitarian help in times of crisis, yet this did not lead to the autonomous episcopal governance of cities in later centuries. Dietrich Claude attempted to apply this Gallic model to early Byzantium in order to show that bishops in the Eastern Roman Empire also exercised a veritable *Stadtherrschaft,* but the limitations of this approach have long been recognized, at least by Byzantinists.[22] More recent studies of the transformation of cities in Asia Minor have emphasized the stabilizing role of bishops in up-

19. Sulpicius Severus, *Vita Martini,* ed. and trans. J. Fontaine, 3 vols., SCh 133–35 (Paris, 1967); C. Stancliffe, *St. Martin and His Hagiographer: History and Miracle in Sulpicius Severus* (Oxford and New York, 1983); R. van Dam, *Leadership and Community in Late Antique Gaul* (Berkeley, 1985); N. B. McLynn, *Ambrose of Milan: Church and Court in a Christian Capital* (Berkeley and Los Angeles, 1994).

20. W. E. Klingshirn, *Caesarius of Arles: The Making of a Christian Community in Late Antique Gaul* (Cambridge and New York, 1994); R. A. Markus, *Gregory the Great and His World* (Cambridge, 1997).

21. R. Kaiser, "Bischofsstadt," in *Lexikon des Mittelalters* (Munich and Zurich, 1983): 2: cols. 239–45. For a descriptive overview of the range of episcopal activities in late antique Gaul, see N. Gauthier, "Le réseau de pouvoirs de l'évêque dans la Gaule du haut moyen-âge," in *Towns and Their Territories between Late Antiquity and the Early Middle Ages,* ed. G. P. Broglio, N. Gauthier, and N. Christie, 191–95 (Leiden, 2000).

22. D. Claude, *Die byzantinische Stadt im 6. Jahrhundert* (Munich, 1969). See the critical remarks by A. Hohlweg, "Bischof und Stadtherr im frühen Byzanz," *JÖB* 20 (1971): 51–62.

holding and perpetuating the existing social order as they operated in conjunction with the people and the leading men of their cities.[23] The writings of the Cappadocian fathers, Basil of Caesarea, Gregory of Nazianzus, and Gregory of Nyssa, have generated several scholarly treatments of their views of the episcopate and their own exercise of this office.[24] Studies of the role of bishops along the southern shore of the Mediterranean have centered on issues such as the patterns of urbanization, the structure of civic life, the presence of dissenting Christian groups, and the nature of the surviving evidence. Since Egypt spawned the thriving monastic movement that attracted pilgrims and followers from all over the empire, monasticism in all its forms is the focus of most studies of Christian life in this region,[25] while less energy has been devoted to the discussion of dissenting movements within the church, such as Arianism and Monophysitism.[26] As a consequence, modern studies concentrating on this region accord only a marginal role to bishops within their urban setting. An exception is Athanasius of Alexandria, whose prolific literary output has given rise to several studies of his dogmatic stance, political maneuvering, and ascetic outlook.[27] Apart from the bishop of Alexandria, bishops do not dominate the picture, while the papyri often show village priests in a uniquely prominent role. Because of the wealth of the surviving documentary evidence, scholars have been able to investigate the ecclesiastical and economic administration of Egypt as an organic entity in which the bishops were firmly embedded.[28]

The nature of the available sources has also influenced the studies of Christianity in North Africa. Here Augustine of Hippo is the towering figure, not so much because of the saint's *Life* written by his disciple

23. W. Brandes, *Die Städte Kleinasiens im 7. und 8. Jahrhundert* (Berlin, 1989); M. Whittow, "Ruling the Late Roman and Early Byzantine City: A Continuous History," *Past and Present* 129 (1990): 3–29.

24. P. Rousseau, *Basil of Caesarea* (Berkeley and Los Angeles, 1994); R. van Dam, *Kingdom of Snow: Roman Rule and Greek Culture in Cappadocia* (Philadelphia, 2002); id., *Families and Friends in Late Roman Cappadocia* (Philadelphia, 2003). See also the forthcoming monographs on Gregory of Nazianzus by Susanna Elm and Neil McLynn.

25. D. H. Chitty, *The Desert a City* (Oxford, 1966); J. E. Goehring, *Ascetics, Society, and the Desert: Studies in Early Egyptian Monasticism* (Harrisburg, 1999).

26. W. H. C. Frend, *The Rise of the Monophysite Movement: Chapters in the History of the Church in the Fifth and Six Centuries* (London, 1972).

27. T. D. Barnes, *Athanasius and Constantius: Theology and Politics in the Constantinian Empire* (Cambridge, Mass., 1993); D. Brakke, *Athanasius and the Politics of Asceticism* (Oxford, 1995); A. Martin, *Athanase d'Alexandrie et l'église d'Égypte au IV^e siècle (328–373)*, Collection de l'École Française de Rome 216 (Rome, 1996); C. Haas, *Alexandria in Late Antiquity: Topography and Social Conflict* (Baltimore and London, 1997).

28. E. Wipszycka, *Les ressources et les activités économiques des églises en Égypte du IV^e au VIII^e siècle* (Brussels, 1972); R. S. Bagnall, *Egypt in Late Antiquity* (Princeton, 1993).

Possidius, but because of the numerous works that survive from his pen, especially his extensive epistolographical collection, which has been augmented in recent years by Johannes Divjak's discovery of additional letters.[29] North Africa was also a densely urbanized region that enjoyed great economic prosperity until the Vandal invasion of the late 430s and beyond. The archaeological work, and especially the epigraphic record, provide a mine of information about the life of the North African cities and the bishops' participation in it.[30]

Previous studies of bishops in late antiquity thus fall into three distinct groups: histories of the development of the episcopal office within the church, which usually end with the reign of Constantine; investigations of the public role of bishops within their urban or regional context, which usually begin with Constantine's legislation in favor of the clergy; and biographies of important men of the church, based to no small extent on their own literary record. Each of these areas of study has considerable merit in contributing important insights into specific aspects of the role of bishops in late antiquity. But at the core of these studies are two underlying assumptions, one chronological, the other ideological. The chronological assumption consists in highlighting the reign of Constantine as a radical turning point when the idealized, charismatic age of early Christianity came to an end and the church became tainted through its exposure to the empire, a decline that is thought to be accompanied, as if in a seesaw, by the rise of the bishops. What has been lacking is a study that deemphasizes the reign of Constantine and that, instead of treating it as a watershed in the history of the institutional development of the church, follows the continuous flow of developments, both in Christian culture and in the Roman Empire, in the centuries before and after Constantine's reign. The present study is intended as a first step in this direction, as its chronological range extends from the third to the sixth century.

The general ideological assumption upon which most studies of the episcopate have rested until about two decades ago is that of a strict division between the religious and the secular aspects of the role of bishops, in order to concentrate on the bishops' social prominence and political power. Yet there are some notable exceptions of scholars who have chosen a more integrative approach, in an effort to link the bishops' public activities within their cities with their religious position as Christian leaders. Thus Henry

29. P. Brown, *Augustine of Hippo: A Biography* (London, 1967; rev. ed., Berkeley, 2000); Augustine, *Epistolae ex duobus codicibus nuper in lucem prolatae,* ed. J. Divjak (Vienna, 1981); Augustine, *Lettres 1–29,* rev. ed., ed. and trans. (into French) J. Divjak (Paris, 1987).

30. C. Lepelley, *Les cités de l'Afrique romaine au Bas-Empire,* 2 vols. (Paris, 1979–81); A. Mandouze, *Prosopographie chrétienne du Bas-Empire: Prosopographie de l'Afrique chrétienne (303–533)* (Paris, 1982).

Chadwick[31] and Philip Rousseau[32] explore the interconnection between the roles of monks and those of bishops. In a similar vein, Rosemarie Nürnberg acknowledges that asceticism provides the foundation and justification for episcopal power in late antique Gaul, and Andrea Sterk has undertaken a similar study for Cappadocia.[33] Bernhard Jussen, by contrast, pursues the notion of the survival of elites in changing political circumstances and points out that the new prominence of aristocratic bishops in Gaul since the fifth century goes hand in hand with their ceremonial self-representation as charismatic leaders through the performance of the liturgy in its various forms.[34] An entire volume of essays was dedicated to the interconnection of episcopal power and pastoral care in 1997.[35] Rita Lizzi has investigated the role of bishops, especially prominent bishops, in the East and highlights what she calls the "process of moralization" that characterizes their interaction with secular authorities and its representation in the sources.[36] Recent articles by Susanna Elm and Rebecca Lyman draw attention to the importance of the ascetic stance in the assertion of episcopal authority.[37] Conrad Leyser explores the connection between interpretations of asceticism, the formation and internal structure of monastic communities, and leadership within those communities.[38] In a similar vein, the latest monograph by Peter

31. H. Chadwick, "Bishops and Monks," *Studia Patristica* 24 (1993): 45–61.

32. P. Rousseau, "The Spiritual Authority of the 'Monk-Bishop': Eastern Elements in Some Western Hagiography of the Fourth and Fifth Centuries," *JThS* n.s. 22 (1971): 380–419.

33. R. Nürnberg, *Askese als sozialer Impuls: Monastisch-asketische Spiritualität als Wurzel und Triebfeder sozialer Ideen und Aktivitäten der Kirche in Südgallien im 5. Jahrhundert* (Bonn, 1988); A. Sterk, *Renouncing the World Yet Leading the Church: The Monk-Bishop in Late Antiquity* (Cambridge, Mass., and London, 2004).

34. B. Jussen, "Über 'Bischofsherrschaften' und die Prozeduren politisch-sozialer Umordnung in Gallien zwischen 'Antike' und 'Mittelalter,'" *HZ* 260 (1995): 673–718; id., "Liturgie und Legitimation, oder Wie die Gallo-Romanen das römische Reich beendeten," in *Institutionen und Ereignis: Über historische Praktiken und Vorstellungen gesellschaftlichen Ordnens*, ed. R. Blänkner and B. Jussen, 75–136 (Göttingen, 1998).

35. *Vescovi e pastori in epoca teodosiana*, vol. 2 (Rome, 1997).

36. R. Lizzi, *Il potere episcopale nell' Oriente romano: Rappresentazione ideological e realtà politica (IV–V sec. d. C.)* (Rome, 1987); id., "I vescovi e i potentes della terra: Definizione e limite del ruolo episcopale nelle due *partes imperii* fra IV e V secolo d.C.," in *L'évêque dans la cité du IV^e au V^e siècle: Image et autorité*, ed. E. Rebillard and C. Sotinel, Collection de l'École Française de Rome 248 (Rome, 1998), 95. A smilar argument has been made for clergy in general by G. Demacopoulos, "A Monk in Shepherd's Clothing: Pope Gregory I and the Asceticizing of Pastoral Direction" (PhD diss., University of North Carolina, Chapel Hill, 2001).

37. S. Elm, "The Diagnostic Gaze: Gregory of Nazianzus' Theory of Orthodox Priesthood in His Orations 6 *De pace* and 2 *Apologia de fuga sua*," in *Orthodoxie, Christianisme, Histoire/Orthodoxy, Christianity, History*, ed. S. Elm, E. Rebillard, and A. Romano, Collection de l'École Française de Rome 270 (Rome, 2000); J. R. Lyman, "Ascetics and Bishops: Epiphanius on Orthodoxy," in *Orthodoxie, Christianisme, Histoire/Orthodoxy, Christianity, History*, ed. Elm, Rebillard, and Romano.

38. C. Leyser, *Authority and Asceticism from Augustine to Gregory the Great* (Oxford, 2000).

Brown, *Poverty and Leadership in the Later Roman Empire*,[39] focuses on the role of the bishop in his city as the "lover of the poor," with all the social and political consequences this entails, and at the same time seeks the roots of the bishop's advocacy for the poor in the religious traditions of Judaism and Christianity. Brown argues that the Judeo-Christian tradition of the distribution of the offerings of the community through its appointed officers prepares the ground for the concrete exercise of Christian charity, while the radically new, Christian idea of a deep-rooted solidarity among fellow humans as a result of the incarnation of Christ provides additional motivation for its practice among Christians. On the whole, there is a noticeable trend, especially in Anglophone scholarship since the late 1980s, to treat episcopal power not as an isolated social or political phenomenon, but as a complex construct of secular and religious elements that come to bear in ever-shifting constellations.

The study of the role of holy men has evolved according to the same pattern. Initial emphasis on the single criterion of personal sanctity has given way to a more integrative interpretation that takes into account additional socioeconomic factors. The important studies by German scholars of the late nineteenth and early twentieth centuries, especially the seminal works of Karl Holl[40] and Hans von Campenhausen, isolated the charismatic element as crucial in the establishment of personal holiness.[41] A second wave of scholarship set in with Peter Brown's foundational 1971 article "The Rise and Function of the Holy Man in Late Antiquity,"[42] which explained the activities of holy men, especially in fifth- and sixth-century Syria, with reference to the socioeconomic context in which they operated. In this article, Brown explored the holy man's public role as a *patronus* and its connection to asceticism, but to the neglect of the spiritual element. Brown has since then added further facets to the interpretation of the functions of the holy man by drawing attention to his role as philosopher-sage and as exemplar, while others have suggested that holy men were at the center of prayer communities that were also linked by common economic enterprises.[43] In the

39. P. L. R. Brown, *Poverty and Leadership in the Later Roman Empire* (Hanover, N.H., 2002).

40. K. Holl, *Enthusiasmus und Bussgewalt beim griechischen Mönchtum: Eine Studie zu Symeon dem Neuen Theologen* (Leipzig, 1898; repr., Hildesheim, 1969).

41. H. v. Campenhausen, *Kirchliches Amt und geistliche Vollmacht in den ersten drei Jahrhunderten* (Göttingen, 1953); translated as *Ecclesiastical Authority and Spiritual Power in the Church of the First Three Centuries* (London, 1969).

42. P. L. R. Brown, "The Rise and Function of the Holy Man in Late Antiquity," *JRS* 61 (1971): 80–101, repr. in his *Society and the Holy* (Berkeley and Los Angeles, 1982). See now also the important retrospective article by P. Brown, "The Rise and Function of Holy Man in Late Antiquity, 1971–1997," *JECS* 6 (1998): 353–76.

43. P. L. R. Brown, "The Philosopher and Society in Late Antiquity," in *Protocol of the Thirty-Fourth Colloquy of the Center for Hermeneutical Studies in Hellenistic and Modern Culture*, (Berkeley,

study of holy men, as in the study of bishops, the tendency in recent years has been to obliterate the earlier perception of a dividing line between the religious and the secular and to abandon the stark dichotomy of charisma versus institution, mysticism versus politics, and prayer versus power.

The present book builds on these trends in two ways. First, it takes as its central theme late antique attitudes regarding the compatibility and interrelation of personal holiness and episcopal office, thereby combining the study of the role of the bishop with that of the holy man. And second, it consciously departs from the established binary opposition of religious and secular power and introduces a new interpretive model of three kinds of authority.

### A NEW EXPLANATORY MODEL: SPIRITUAL, ASCETIC, AND PRAGMATIC AUTHORITY

The authority of the bishop is a multifaceted and ever-mutating construct that continued to change as individuals adapted, necessity dictated, and circumstances permitted. The office itself underwent a process of growth and change over time during which certain aspects and tasks gained in importance, while others receded into the shadows.

The main components that define episcopal authority, however, remained the same. What changed was the relative weight of these components, or the way in which they were combined. In order to facilitate the understanding of the role of bishops in late antiquity, I wish to introduce the following three categories: spiritual authority, ascetic authority, and pragmatic authority.

Spiritual authority indicates that its bearer has received the *pneuma,* the Spirit from God. Spiritual authority has its source outside the individual. It is given by God, as a gift. Spiritual authority is personal. It is given directly to a specific individual, without personal participation or preparation by its recipient. Finally, spiritual authority is self-sufficient. It can exist in the individual independent of its recognition by others. In highlighting the concept of spiritual authority, I follow the lead of the Christian writers of the later Roman Empire who acknowledged God as the source of all gifts of the spirit.[44]

The public recognition of "charismatic" abilities, so important to Max

---

1980); id., "The Saint as Exemplar in Late Antiquity," *Representations* 1 (1983): 1–25; C. Rapp, "'For Next to God, You Are My Salvation': Reflections on the Rise of the Holy Man in Late Antiquity," in *The Cult of Saints in Late Antiquity and the Middle Ages: Essays on the Contribution of Peter Brown,* ed. J. Howard-Johnston and P. A. Hayward (Oxford, 1999).

44. See especially the material assembled by R. Reitzenstein, *Historia Monachorum und Historia Lausiaca: Eine Studie zur Geschichte des Mönchtums und der frühchristlichen Begriffe Gnostiker und Pneumatiker* (Göttingen, 1916).

Weber, is encompassed in what I call ascetic authority. Ascetic authority derives its name from *askēsis*, meaning "practice." It has its source in the personal efforts of the individual. It is achieved by subduing the body and by practicing virtuous behavior. These efforts are centered on the self, in the hopes of attaining a certain ideal of personal perfection. Ascetic authority is accessible to all. Anyone who chooses to do so can engage in the requisite practices. Finally, ascetic authority is visible. It depends on recognition by others, as it is made evident in the individual's appearance, lifestyle, and conduct.

I refrain from using the term "charismatic" in this context, because it has been given a very specific meaning in Weber's influential theory of charisma. Charisma, in his view, can exist only inasmuch as it is recognized by others and generates discipleship. It emerges through the interplay between the charismatic leader and his followers.[45] Weber's notion of charismatic authority functions in specific contradistinction to institutionalized authority, a dichotomization that this study hopes to transcend by introducing a model that embraces three types of authority: spiritual, ascetic, and pragmatic.

The third member of this triad, pragmatic authority, is based on actions (from *prattō*, meaning "to do"). It arises from the actions of the individual, but in distinction from ascetic authority, these actions are directed not toward the shaping of the self, but to the benefit of others. Access to pragmatic authority is restricted. Its achievement depends on the individual's wherewithal, in terms of social position and wealth, to perform these actions. Pragmatic authority is always public. The actions are carried out in full public view. The recognition of pragmatic authority by others depends on the extent and success of the actions that are undertaken on their behalf.

These definitions are, of course, schematic and serve merely to isolate the most important distinctions between the three types of authority. The usefulness of this tripartite scheme lies in the fact that it accords a special place of relevance to ascetic authority as the vital link to the other two. The personal practice of asceticism prepares the individual for the receipt of the gifts of the spirit, and thus of spiritual authority, from God. Since ascetic authority is founded on the regulation of lifestyle and behavior, this is a path open to all. In fact, it is the only path by which an individual can hope to

---

45. M. Weber, "Charismatic Authority," from his *Theory of Social and Economic Organization*, trans. A. R. Henderson and T. Pasons (London, 1947), quoted in *Max Weber on Charisma and Institution Building: Selected Papers*, ed. S. N. Eisenstadt (Chicago and London, 1968), 48: "The term 'charisma' will be applied to certain qualities of an individual personality by virtue of which he is set apart from ordinary men and *treated* as endowed with supernatural, super-human, or at least specifically exceptional powers or qualities. These are such as are not accessible to the ordinary person, but *are regarded* as of divine origin or as exemplary, and on the basis of them the individual concerned is *treated* as a leader" (emphasis mine).

bring down God's grace on his or her own initiative. Yet at the same time, asceticism is a gauge of the presence of spiritual authority. Nobody can walk the difficult and thorny road of ever more demanding ascetic practices unless he or she receives the help of God. To observers and bystanders, ascetic accomplishments are thus the outward face of spiritual authority. In other words, ascetic authority is simultaneously the humanly and freely accessible precondition for spiritual authority and its openly visible confirmation.

At the same time, ascetic authority is also the motivation and legitimation of pragmatic authority. This feature is essential to the understanding of the public activities of bishops in late antiquity. It allows us to perceive a crucial distinction between bishops and civic leaders. Bishops are always held to a higher code of conduct, and their ability to exercise leadership is conditional on their adherence to that code. In contrast to civic leaders, the bishops' pragmatic actions on behalf of the community are considered to be a manifestation of their ascetic authority, so much so that the successful exercise of the former is believed to be a direct consequence of the latter.

The emphasis on the ascetic component distinguishes this model from previous work on the authority of bishops, while the identification of pragmatic authority as an independent component facilitates the study of the public role of holy men. The combination of these three kinds of authority—spiritual, ascetic, and pragmatic—provides the analytical tools that allow the study of bishops and holy men within the same cultural, religious, social, and political context.

·   ·   ·

This book aims to assert and explain the importance of ascetic authority as the focal point at the intersection between spiritual and pragmatic authority. It owes its inspiration to both the German and the Anglophone strands of scholarship, as is perhaps inevitable for an author who moved from Germany to England and then to the United States in the course of her academic and intellectual formation. I became aware of the importance of the spiritual-ascetic-pragmatic nexus while working on my doctoral dissertation on the *Vita* of Epiphanius, bishop of Salamis in Cyprus. This well-known champion of orthodoxy and author of antiheretical works died in 402; his *Life* was composed sometime between 430 and 475. Epiphanius is thus one of the earliest bishops who was considered holy and who was honored and immortalized in a saint's *Life*. He is joined by a few others: Martin of Tours, who died in 397 and was celebrated in a saint's *Life* by Sulpicius Severus; Ambrose of Milan, who died the same year and whose *Life* was written by his disciple Paulinus; Porphyry of Gaza in Palestine, who died in 420 and whose *Life* poses particular historical problems; and Augustine of Hippo, who died in 430 and was honored in a *Life* by his disciple Possidius. The *Lives* of these bishops were composed around the middle of the fifth century. They were not the last bishops to be honored in this manner. From this time, bishops became the subject of hagiographical literature, where previously only martyrs and ascetics had received such treatment. In contrast to the glorification of those who had attained their spiritual perfection through rejection or avoidance of the world, the *Lives* of bishops propagate a very different ideal. They celebrate the attainment of holiness by ecclesiastical officeholders in an urban setting and in continued exposure to worldly affairs. How can this new direction in the appreciation of what "makes" a holy man be explained? And how do the hagiographers respond to the challenge posed by the novelty of their topic? These are the central questions that form the undercurrent of the present study.

The book is divided into two major parts. The first part juxtaposes bishops and holy men and deals with the nature of Christian authority and its spiritual roots. The second part compares bishops and civic leaders and addresses the realities of the episcopal office. Following these treatments of what it meant to be "holy" and what it meant to be a "bishop," an epilogue discusses the hagiographical treatment of "holy bishops." The chronological framework of this inquiry extends from the third to the sixth century. This time frame was chosen to bracket the reign of Constantine and to allow a thorough reassessment of its consequences for the leadership role of bishops in their cities. The geographical scope expands and contracts depending on the demands of the subject matter, and on the spread of the available source material. The more theoretical analysis includes relevant texts from the Latin West and the Greek East, while the in-depth historical study of the bishop's activities in the urban context is centered on the cities of the Levant, where the evidence for our period is more plentiful and only occasionally draws on supplementary evidence from the West.

Part 1 is largely based on the writings generated by men of the church. Its subdivisions follow the explanatory model outlined above, discussing pragmatic, spiritual, and ascetic authority in turn. The second chapter serves as an introduction to the history and development of the idea of the episcopate. It shows how the concrete or pragmatic authority of bishops within the church has its roots in an appreciation of a bishop's spiritual abilities. It begins with an overview of the early church orders that describe the various tasks of the bishop within the community. These texts also emphasize that it was the most outstanding Christian in the community who should be elected to the episcopate. This nexus between pragmatic authority and its justification by ascetic authority is pursued further in a detailed study of the late antique comments on the only passage in the New Testament that describes the role of the bishop in detail, 1 Timothy 3:1–7. Chapter 3 illustrates the concept of spiritual authority with reference to its most eloquent postapostolic spokesmen, Clement of Alexandria and Origen, and their remarks on bearers of the Spirit *(pneumatophoroi)* and bearers of Christ *(christophoroi)*. The next segment gives a direct snapshot of spiritual authority at work. Exclusively based on documentary, not literary, sources, it shows how spiritual men were appreciated by their contemporaries for the power of their intercessory prayer. This kind of prayer is then investigated further, as it was performed on behalf of sinners by martyrs and holy men as much as by priests and bishops, all of whom could make claims to spiritual authority. Ascetic authority is the subject of chapter 4. It is addressed only inasmuch as it has particular bearing on our understanding of the episcopal role. Special emphasis is placed on the importance of the desert—a symbol of total withdrawal and rejection of the world—as a training ground for those who aspire to ascetic authority. The insistence on the physical desert setting as most beneficial for spiritual progress, it is argued, was soon augmented by the notion that the soul could achieve complete inner detachment regardless of its surroundings. This expanded understanding of the significance of the desert as an internalized state of mind made the monastic ideal accessible to those who, like bishops, lived in cities and were active in the public life. The biblical model for bishops who follow the desert ideal while being active on behalf of others is Moses, as discussed in the following section of chapter 4. He was the divinely appointed leader who proved himself worthy through his deeds to hold pragmatic authority over the people of Israel. The complex nature of episcopal leadership as a combination of pragmatic, spiritual, and ascetic authority provides an explanation for the frequent rejection of ordination by monks, which is investigated next. This rejection is occasioned by the notion that ordination is a confirmation of personal virtue and thus should not be coveted by a truly humble person. Yet there was a growing trend to validate the ascetic ideal through honorific ordination, or indeed to attract monks to active service in the clergy. Ascetic authority was the supreme qualification for obtaining the pragmatic authority of office and, for those who lacked ascetic training, the best validation for a successful tenure in office.

Part 2 deals with the realities of episcopal office and is mainly based on historical writing and legal and epigraphic sources. The problematic relation of worldly criteria and spiritual qualifications in the appointment of bishops and in their discharge of office is exemplified in chapter 5, which begins with a comparison between the episcopal careers of Synesius of Cyrene and Theodore of Sykeon, the former a pagan man of leisure in the late fourth century, the latter a seventh-century monk given to ascetic excesses. As these examples show, late antique bishops had ample leeway to define their role and range of activities. Contemporary attitudes were opaque, and theologians sensed the need to defend the nature of the episcopate as work and service, not as an honor.

Chapter 6 offers a detailed overview of the patterns of recruitment to the episcopate, which reveals that wealthy and locally prominent men were increasingly at an advantage as candidates for this ministry. Not surprisingly, many status-conscious urban citizens were eager to attain the episcopate as an additional distinction at the end of their careers.

Chapter 7 examines the role of the bishop within the context of his city. It aims to bring out the concrete manifestations of the pragmatic authority of bishops, which was often determined by their elevated social origin prior to their election. This is followed by treatments of three aspects of the pragmatic authority of the bishop that invite comparison with the activities of prominent citizens and of holy men—namely, the bishop's residence, his access to wealth, and his distribution of wealth.

Constantine's laws granting bishops extensive administrative rights and obligations are traditionally regarded as the touchstone of church-state relations in this formative period. Chapter 8 proposes a critical reassessment of Constantine's measures in order to show that, rather than absorbing the bishops into the apparatus of imperial administration, they merely confirmed the existing episcopal oversight over practical matters that were considered to be of particular concern to Christians in general. A more significant change that was heralded by the reign of Constantine was the open access to the imperial court that the bishops now enjoyed. But holy men of ascetic or monastic distinction enjoyed the same privilege, and thus this chapter concludes with a comparison of the different manifestations of the *parrhēsia* of bishops and of holy men with the emperor.

The last chapter of part 2 takes issue with the oft-repeated view that the bishop steps into a power vacuum created by the decline of the *curiales*, the wealthy city councilors, and argues that instead of being integrated into existing structures, he fulfills a new role that derives its authority precisely from the idealized status that adheres to his ecclesiastical rank. A comparison of the treatment of bishops in the Theodosian Code and in the Justinianic Code and Novellae shows that in the interval between these two codifications, bishops who had in the fourth century been regarded and revered as model Christians were in the sixth century treated as dependable model citizens. I then go on to argue that the bishop was never absorbed into the *curia* but instead joined the new ruling group of leading citizens that was crystallizing at the time, forming a new urban and Christian elite.

The brief epilogue gives a synthetic overview of the literary representation of bishops in hagiographical works to the seventh century. It is the nature of those texts to extol the personal holiness of their protagonists in order to celebrate them as saints. The subtle shifts in emphasis on the spiritual authority of bishops that can be traced in these texts over time confirm the general trends and developments in the exercise of the bishops' pragmatic authority that have been identified in the previous, historical chapter.

The hagiographical treatment of holy bishops shows them increasingly engaged in activities and duties that resemble those of civic functionaries. At the same time, these *Lives* are an attempt to vindicate the bishops by pointing to the spiritual origin of their authority and by elaborating on the divine powers that are at their disposal in the discharge of all aspects of their office and that are especially present in their celebration of the eucharistic liturgy.

This is the moment to make a full disclosure of what this book does not attempt: it does not provide a complete and detailed treatment of the development of the episcopal office within the framework of the church as an institution, nor does it deal in any detail with issues connected to the bishops' liturgical role at baptism, ordination, and the celebration of the eucharist. It does not treat the role of bishops in the theological debates that threatened the doctrinal unity of the church, nor does it investigate specific moments of friction between episcopal and imperial power. Finally, it deliberately avoids the treatment of highly prominent bishops, such as the Cappadocian fathers, aiming instead to draw a composite picture of the bishop as a leadership figure in late antique society.[46] If the pattern that emerges helps to reinsert into their contemporary conceptual framework the thousands of bishops who were discharging their duties, for better or for worse, throughout late antiquity, my purpose will have been served.

46. This is also the place to acknowledge previously published work that has served as the basis for some of the discussion here. Chapter 3 contains a revised version of " 'For Next to God, You Are My Salvation': Reflections on the Rise of the Holy Man in Late Antiquity," in *The Cult of Saints in Late Antiquity and the Early Middle Ages: Essays on the Contribution of Peter Brown*, ed. J. Howard-Johnston and P. A. Hayward (Oxford, 1999), 63–81. Chapter 4 incorporates some of the discussion from "Comparison, Paradigm, and the Case of Moses in Panegyric and Hagiography," in *The Propaganda of Power: The Role of Panegyric in Late Antiquity*, ed. Mary Whitby (Leiden, 1998), 277–98, and "Imperial Ideology in the Making: Eusebius of Caesarea on Constantine as 'Bishop,'" *JThS* 49 (1998): 685–95. Chapter 6 covers much of the same material as "Bishops in Late Antiquity: A New Social and Urban Elite?" in *Late Antiquity and Early Islam*, vol. 6, ed. J. Haldon and L. Conrad (forthcoming), 144–73.

CHAPTER TWO

# Pragmatic Authority

The average bishop of a large city in the later Roman Empire fulfilled a number of different roles: he was a preacher to his community; a teacher to the catechumens; administered baptism to neophytes; celebrated the eucharist and other liturgical occasions; and admonished and, if necessary, reprimanded Christians who had stumbled. He was responsible for the charitable works of his congregation, the care of consecrated virgins, widows and orphans, prisoners, travelers, and the poor. In addition, he was in charge of the discipline and proper discharge of office of the clergy under his authority, the priests, deacons, and perhaps *chorepiskopoi*, and—if he was metropolitan or patriarch—of the other bishops within his region. Once Christianity had gained a stronger foothold in society, beginning in the fourth century, bishops also gradually became involved on a hitherto unknown scale in the administration of their cities and in regional politics. As a consequence of the process of Christianization set in motion by Constantine, bishops would eventually enjoy unrivalled power in their cities in the European Middle Ages.

It is all too easy to neglect the slow historical evolution of the episcopate and to project modern notions of the episcopal office onto the formative period of late antiquity, when definitions of the episcopate were just beginning to be formulated. The danger of such historical anachronism lies in treating the office of a bishop as if it consisted of a predetermined portfolio of tasks and obligations, and in assuming that the episcopal officeholder had to meet an unchanging set of personal requirements. But this was not the case. In this chapter, I wish to draw attention to the fluidity of the definition of the episcopal role in late antiquity by examining the normative texts that were generated within the church to describe and define ecclesiastical leadership. Of particular interest is the way in which these texts set spiritual, ascetic, and pragmatic authority in relation to one another.

In the apostolic age, the *episkopos* was nothing more than an administrative officer. Beginning in the second century, as he increasingly took on teaching and preaching duties, he was also expected to be inspired by the Holy Spirit. This relation between pragmatic and spiritual authority is explained in the first part of this chapter. For the discharge of his pastoral obligations, the bishop needed to set an example of moral and virtuous conduct to his congregation. The development of this line of thought can be traced in the patristic comments on the passage in the First Letter to Timothy, which gives a catalog of episcopal virtues. This is the subject of the second part of this chapter. Beginning with Ambrose and John Chrysostom, separate treatises devoted to ecclesiastical leadership were composed; these are discussed in the third and last part of this chapter.

### THE EARLY CHURCH ORDERS

The episcopal office, as it developed over the first three centuries, was in essence a hybrid creation the original administrative function of which was uncomfortably juxtaposed to the demand for spiritual leadership that was added to it by the second century.[1] These two components of the office could be held together only by adding a third: personal virtues (or, as I call it, ascetic authority).

The bishop's original administrative function is encapsulated in the history of the Greek word *episkopos*, whose Latinized adaptation *episcopus* is the root of the English word *bishop*. Derived from the Greek verb meaning "to oversee" *(episkopein)*, the *episkopos* is literally an "overseer." The word *episkopos* thus originally refers to an activity or a function that could be performed in various situations and by various people. It could then also denote the person who fulfilled this function on a regular basis within a group, and in this way became a title.[2] The Christians were not the first to employ this designation. In classical antiquity, the highest officers of corporations, including *collegia* of pagan priests, were also called *episkopoi*.[3] The oscillation between the function and the title of *episkopos* could still give occasion for amusing puns in the early fifth century. A pious monk, who was also the cook for his monastery, was once told that he would one day become *episkopos*, that is, hold the office of a bishop. He rejected this prospect, cheerily

1. For a well-documented study of the development of ecclesiastical offices in the first six centuries, see A. Faivre, *Naissance d'une hiérarchie*, Théologie Historique 40 (Paris, 1977).

2. For the development from the original sense of "watchman" to *episcopus* as a title in Christian Latin, see C. Mohrmann, "Episkopos—Speculator," in *Études sur le latin des chrétiens* (Rome, 1977), 4: 231–52.

3. H. W. Beyer and H. Karpp, "Bischof," *RAC* 2 (1954): cols. 394–407.

announcing that he was already an *episkopos*: he held the function of over-seer, over the pots and pans in his kitchen.[4]

It is striking that the word *episkopos* and its cognates appear only rarely in the New Testament. It is entirely absent from the Gospels, surfaces in Acts only as a quotation from a psalm,[5] and appears in the letters of the apostle Paul for a total of seven times. Paul met with the elders *(presbyteroi)* of the community of Ephesus and admonished them to fulfill their responsibility with zeal and watchfulness: "Keep watch over yourselves and over all the flock, of which the Holy Spirit has made you overseers *(episkopous)*, to shep-herd the church of God that he obtained with the blood of his own Son" (Acts 20:28). The same image of the shepherd who, as an *episkopos,* watches over those entrusted to him is evoked in the First Letter of Peter (1 Pet. 2:25), but this time with reference to Christ, who has gathered the lost souls into his flock. Paul's Letter to the Philippians begins with his greetings to the Christian community, including the *episkopoi* and deacons (Phil. 1:1).

In the most significant passage, to which I will return below, Paul advised his disciple and close associate Timothy on how to regulate the internal structure of the Christian communities (1 Tim. 3:1–7). Paul's lengthy expo-sition of the qualifications to be expected from an *episkopos* is followed by similar instructions regarding deacons. These words of Paul would become the yardstick of all subsequent pronouncements on the personal qualifi-cations of bishops. Paul repeated several of these injunctions in his Letter to Titus, who was in the process of setting in order the affairs of the commu-nity in Crete. The context of this passage reveals the absence of any clear distinction between the presbyterate and the episcopate. Paul begins by en-couraging the appointment of elders *(presbyteroi)* in every town and then re-capitulates his list of moral qualifications by referring to the same men as *episkopoi* (Titus 1:5–9, esp. verse 7).

These Pauline passages show that the earliest Christian communities were led by a group of elders or, in Greek, *presbyteroi.* In some, but not all, communities, the group of elders was headed by *episkopoi.* Their tasks were of an administrative nature: keeping an eye on the incoming gifts of food or money brought by the wealthier members of the community and watching over their distribution to the needy, especially the widows who depended on this kind of support. These early passages refer to *episkopoi* in the plural, indicating that more than one man was entrusted with these tasks. *Diakonoi,* or deacons, are frequently mentioned in the same context as their assistants.

It is paramount to bear in mind that throughout the period that con-

4. Palladius, *HL* 35.10–11.
5. Acts 1:20, "Let another one take his position as overseer," is a quotation of Psalm 108 (109):8.

cerns us here, the distinction between the priesthood and the episcopate remains blurry.[6] The Greek term *hierosynē* or the Latin *sacerdotium* simply refers to higher ecclesiastical office, no matter whether it was held by a priest or by a bishop. This poses some problems in the interpretation of sources. Even after the monepiscopate is firmly established, the haze of indistinction between the episcopate and the presbyterate will remain well into the fourth century. Every *episkopos* is also a presbyter, but not every presbyter is an *episkopos*. As late as the fourth century, Pseudo-Augustine declares that the bishop is essentially, a priest, but that among the priests he holds the highest position:

> For what is the bishop, if not the first presbyter, that is, the highest priest? Indeed, he calls them nothing else but fellow presbyters and fellow priests. And does the bishop ever call the ministers his fellow deacons? Not so, for they are inferior by far, and it is foolish to call the judge a secretary.[7]

The oldest surviving church order, the *Didache*, was probably compiled in Syria or Palestine at the beginning of the second century, but the individual regulations it contains may well reflect earlier stages in the development of the life of the church. The *Didache* encourages the Christian communities to appoint for themselves *episkopoi* and deacons. They are to be held in the same honor as the prophets and teachers who are visiting and sometimes taking up residence in the communities.[8] With its omission of presbyters, the *Didache* reflects a time before the development of the tripartite hierarchy of deacons-presbyters-bishop. In mentioning deacons in the same breath as *episkopoi*, the *Didache* also draws attention to the administrative function that both fulfilled. The spiritual and pastoral care of the congregations, by contrast, fell to the prophets and teachers.[9]

The earliest evidence for the existence of only one *episkopos* for each community comes from the letters of Ignatius of Antioch. On his way to be martyred in Rome during the reign of the emperor Trajan (98–117), Ignatius wrote seven letters that offer insight into the life and organization of the Christian communities at this time. Ignatius was the third bishop of Antioch, which was the foremost city in Syria and had a long and venerable Christian tradition reaching back to the days of the apostles Barnabas and Paul. This position, enhanced by the special grace that he held as a martyr-to-be, gave him the authority to address the communities of Asia Minor—

---

6. J. Ysebaert, *Die Amtsterminologie im Neuen Testament und in der Alten Kirche: Eine lexikographische Untersuchung* (Breda, 1994).

7. Ambrosiaster, *Questions on the Old and New Testament* 101.5.

8. *Didache* 15.1–2.

9. For commentaries, see K. Niederwimmer, *Die Didache* (Göttingen, 1989), 241–43; A. von Harnack, *Die Lehre der zwölf Apostel* (Leipzig, 1884), 56–59.

Ephesus, Magnesia, Tralles, Philadelphia, and Smyrna—with words of encouragement and advice. Ignatius regarded the monarchic episcopate simultaneously as a reflection of the One God and as a guarantor of the doctrinal unity of the church. Harmony and cohesion within each community can be accomplished, he said, only if the congregation is united under the authority of the deacons, the presbyters, and the bishop.[10] Nothing should be done without the bishop.[11] The bishop is the sacral center of his congregation because of his liturgical functions. His presence ensures the validity of the celebration of the eucharist and of baptism.[12] He represents the One God to his congregation, and hence he is owed the same obedience.[13] In comparison to the *Didache*, Ignatius's *Letters* reflect a new stage in the development of church organization. The ecclesiastical hierarchy now includes priests, and it is one *episkopos* who presides over the priests and deacons below him. From now on, it is appropriate to abandon the word *episkopos*, and to employ the word *bishop* with its connotation of the monepiscopate at the head of a structured ecclesiastical hierarchy.

Ignatius makes a bishop's effective pastoral care dependent on his personal conduct. He should be constant in his prayer, asking especially for the gift of understanding.[14] He must oppose heterodox teaching[15] and win over the unruly elements in the congregation through his gentleness.[16] In fact, the most distinguishing virtue of a bishop should be his meekness. He should constantly exercise his care for his congregation, he should look after the widows,[17] and he should admonish the slaves[18] and the married men and women to be content with their station in life.[19] The bishop's ability to serve as a model to his congregation was of great importance to Ignatius. In order to emphasize this point, he adopted the Greek neologism *exemplarion*, derived from the Latin *exemplum* or *exemplarium*. The Latin word was most commonly used in the context of book production, where it referred to the original from which a manuscript was copied. The word is very rare in Greek. It is attested in a papyrus from Oxyrhynchus, where it refers to a model pattern

---

10. *Letter to the Magnesians* 6.1–2; *Letter to the Trallians* 3.1, 7.1–2; *Letter to the Philadelphians*, introductory greetings.

11. *Letter to the Ephesisans* 4.1–2; *Letter to the Trallians* 2.1–2; *Letter to the Philadelphians* 3.2, 7.2, 8.1; *Letter to the Smyrnaeans* 8.1–2.

12. *Letter to the Philadelphians* 4; *Letter to the Smyrnaeans* 8.1–2.

13. *Letter to the Ephesians* 6.1; *Letter to the Magnesians* 3.1–2; *Leter to the Trallians* 2.1; *Letter to Polycarp* 6.1.

14. *Letter to Polycarp* 1.3.

15. Ibid., 3.1.

16. Ibid., 1.3, 2.1–2.

17. Ibid., 4.1.

18. Ibid., 4.3.

19. Ibid., 5.1–2.

in textile production,[20] and in a number of very peculiar pagan inscriptions from Phrygia, of the second and third centuries A.D., where it has the sense of negative example or deterrent. These inscriptions were set up by individuals who had been punished for offending the deity by blindness, paralysis, or in other concrete ways but were given the opportunity to redeem themselves through sacrifices and offerings. These inscriptions are now known as confession inscriptions. Their declared purpose was to warn others so that they might learn from the painful experience of their authors.[21] The word *exemplarion* also appears in a spurious sermon of John Chrysostom.[22] The only later author to use it is the seventh-century theologian Maximus Confessor, who refers to Christ as *exemplarion* and elsewhere talks about men who make their own life an *exemplarion* of virtue.[23] Even though Ignatius's use of the word *exemplarion* did not catch on among Greek authors after him, his insistence that the bishop be of such character that his conduct invite imitation by others would continue to be a major theme in Christian writing about the episcopate.

Ignatius also notes that the bishops' ministry is bestowed on him in the love of God, not because others wanted to appoint him or because he sought this distinction for himself.[24] For this reason, the selection of a bishop should not depend on external criteria such as seniority. Ignatius has high praise for Damas, for example, who had become bishop of Magnesia despite his youthful age.[25] In this way, episcopal appointment is regarded as a gift from God that may sometimes be granted to unlikely candidates. Ignatius was the first to give voice to two ideas that would become the prevalent view in the centuries that followed: (1) the bishop's tasks are not only administrative, but also pastoral and liturgical; (2) in order to maintain the respect and cooperation of his flock, the bishop must be an exemplar of Christian conduct.

It was not until a century after Ignatius that the process of episcopal appointment was described for the first time, in the *Apostolic Tradition*. This work is commonly ascribed to Hippolytus, the bishop of a schismatic community in Rome who died in exile, probably in 236. The *Apostolic Tradition*,

---

20. *POxy* 1066.

21. W. M. Ramsay, *The Cities and Bishoprics of Phrygia* (Oxford, 1895), 1: 130–35 and inscriptions 41–53. See also the inscription set up by a woman as a *hypodeigma* (example) to others, after her initial refusal to become a priestess had been punished by the god: M. Rice, "*CIG* 4142—A Forgotten Confession-Inscription from North-West Phrygia," *Epigraphica Anatolica* 29 (1997): 35–43.

22. John Chrysostom, *In ramos palmarum* 1, *PG* 59, col. 705. The sermon is sometimes ascribed to Methodius of Patara: *PG* 18, col. 388A.

23. *Quaestiones ad Thalassium, PG* 90, col. 769A; *Diversa capita, PG* 90, col. 1341C.

24. *Letter to the Philadelphians* 1.1–2.

25. *Letter to the Magnesians* 2.1–3.1.

which has to be pieced together from quotations in other works, is the earliest document for the liturgical practices in Rome. It declares that the bishop is elected by all the people and then consecrated in the presence of the laity, the presbyterate, and an unspecified number of other bishops, who all offer him the kiss of peace after the ordination. The involvement of these different groups of people affirms that the appointment of the bishop is based on a consensus of all. The actual ordination occurs through the imposition of hands by one or several bishops. The prayer accompanying this gesture contains, in a nutshell, an interpretation of the spiritual and practical aspects of the episcopal office. It calls down upon the new bishop the Holy Ghost whom God has delivered to Christ, who in turn passed it on to the apostles, thus asserting the continuity of the ecclesiastical tradition. In his new role as pastor of his flock and as archpriest, the bishop must minister to his community, and he must represent them to God through his prayers. He holds the same authority as the apostles to forgive sins. And he ought to lead a life pleasing to God, excelling in meekness and purity of heart. After the ordination, the new bishop receives the kiss of peace from all who are present and then celebrates the eucharist.[26]

In paying close attention to the process of ordination, the *Apostolic Tradition* gives voice to an idea that will become a powerful undercurrent to all later reflections on the episcopate: the bishop is a successor of the apostles and partakes of the same Spirit as they had. It is the apostolic succession of the bishop that bestows on him the Holy Spirit. As a consequence, spiritual authority can reside not just in the *person* of the bishop, but also in the episcopal *office* per se. According to the *Apostolic Tradition,* the Spirit is conferred on the bishop-elect by other bishops through the imposition of hands and the prayer of ordination. The apostolic succession is an *external* source of the Holy Spirit that is attached to the episcopal office. The institutional spiritual authority inherent in the episcopate is distinct from the personal spiritual authority held by the bishop and displayed in his conduct. Ideally, the former is bestowed as a confirmation of the latter. The relation of personal spiritual authority to spiritual authority acquired ex officio would remain a major concern, especially as the bishops grew in number and gained greater importance in civic life.

The *Didascalia,* a detailed church order that was composed in northern Syria, also dates from the first half of the third century. It was originally written in Greek but now survives only in a complete Syriac translation and in Latin fragments. The *Didascalia* purports to contain the teaching of the twelve apostles on the organization of Christian churches. It furnishes

---

26. *The Treatise on the Apostolic Tradition of St. Hippolytus of Rome,* ed. and trans. G. Dix, rev. H. Chadwick (London and Ridgefield, Conn., 1992), 2–3, pp. 2–6.

ample information on the preconditions for appointment to episcopal office, the duties of a bishop, and the personal traits required of a bishop to fulfill his role.[27] The *Didascalia* reflects a new stage in the structural development of the Christian communities, competently mapped out in a recent book by Georg Schöllgen.[28] By the time of the *Didascalia*, what had started as voluntary and spontaneous donations by the congregation to the communal chest had evolved into regular and fixed contributions, which were used in part to provide the clergy with salaries according to their rank. This development had several important consequences: it set the clergy apart from the laity, it transformed the members of the clergy from volunteering servants into salaried officials, and it created the economic conditions for treating ecclesiastical ministry as a career like any other. It is perhaps for this reason that the *Didascalia* takes great care to remind the lay members of the congregation of the spiritual and ascetic authority of the bishop, from which all other positive aspects of his administration will flow.

In appointing a bishop, the *Didascalia* notes, it is important to choose a candidate who enjoys a good reputation and who has no physical handicaps. The minimum age requirement is set at fifty years, although more important than the criterion of age is the candidate's moral qualification. His character must correspond to the description given in Paul's First Letter to Timothy, and special emphasis is placed on his ability to maintain his own household in order. Even if he is illiterate, he ought to be able to give religious instruction to his flock. The constitutive act that turns the candidate who has the support and consensus of all into a bishop is the imposition of hands, presumably in a manner comparable to that described in the *Apostolic Tradition* of Hippolytus.[29]

The desirable traits of character of a bishop are set out in the *Didascalia* in conjunction with his tasks and duties. The bishop should prepare for his task as interpreter of scripture through constant reading.[30] As the administrator of ecclesiastical charity to widows and orphans, to the poor and to strangers, the bishop should be charitable and generous. He should also be able to use his own good judgment in determining each individual's needs, so as to avoid favoritism and jealousy.[31]

The most prominent role ascribed to the bishop in the *Didascalia*, next to the administration of charity, is his authority to impose penance by excluding unworthy members from the community until their sincere repentance

27. R. H. Connolly, ed., *Didascalia Apostolorum: The Syriac Version Translated and Accompanied by the Verona Latin Fragments* (Oxford, 1929).
28. G. Schöllgen, *Die Anfänge der Professionalisierung des Klerus und das kirchliche Amt in der syrischen Didaskalie,* JAC Ergänzungsband 26 (Münster, 1988).
29. *Didascalia*, ed. Connolly, p. 32.
30. Ibid., p. 34.
31. Ibid., pp. 32–33, 98–101.

has made them worthy of readmission. The act of readmission consists in the imposition of hands by the bishop while the whole congregation prays over the penitent.[32] In order to fulfill this responsibility of administering the different degrees of penance, the bishop must be immune to bribery, impartial in his judgment even of rich or influential people,[33] and merciful and compassionate toward the sincerely penitent.[34] Ideally, though, the bishop should exercise constant admonition and care for his flock so that they will abstain from sin and he will have to exercise his penitential authority only in exceptional circumstances.[35] He can be effective in his admonition only if he himself leads an impeccable life. He should be restrained in his diet and shun all other luxuries as well.[36] He should, in sum, be the embodiment of all virtues: "And whatever of good there be that is found in men, let the same be in the bishop."[37] He should model himself after Christ and through his own example invite his congregation to imitate him.[38] Such impeccable conduct of the bishop brings many benefits: his admonition will be convincing, and his judgment will be accepted by all; moreover, the congregation will have no excuse for slackening in their own lives.[39] In short, the *Didascalia* regards the exemplary conduct of the bishop as indispensable for all the duties with which his office is charged: the distribution of charity, the admonition of sinners, and preaching.

The *Didascalia* sees the relation between the bishop and his congregation as reciprocal. The bishop's paternal love is like that of a bird who "keeps them warm with loving care, as eggs from which young birds are to come; or broods over them and cherishes them as young birds, for the rearing up of winged fowl."[40] In turn, it is the duty of the congregation to honor the bishop with the same respect that is due to a father.[41] The congregation is explicitly instructed about the role of their bishop:

> He is minister of the word and mediator; but to you a teacher, and your father after God, who begot you through the water [of baptism]. This is your chief and your leader, and he is your mighty king. He rules in the place of the Almighty: but let him be honoured by you as God, for the bishop sits for you in the place of God Almighty.[42]

32. Ibid., pp. 56, 104.
33. Ibid., pp. 34–35, 38, 44, 109–19 passim.
34. Ibid., pp. 42–43.
35. Ibid., p. 52.
36. Ibid., p. 34.
37. Ibid., pp. 35–36.
38. Ibid., pp. 36, 76.
39. Ibid., p. 40.
40. Ibid., pp. 60–62.
41. Ibid., p. 60.
42. Ibid., pp. 86–88; cf. pp. 92–94.

The *Didascalia* is the earliest church order to address the penitential authority of the bishop. The bishop not only represents Christ to his community; he also personally represents his community, including their sins, before God. Since he received his office from God, he is also personally accountable to God for their moral and spiritual welfare:[43] "For a layman has the care of himself alone, but thou carriest the burden of all."[44] In this regard too the bishop should imitate Christ and bear the sins of the people entrusted to him.[45] The *Didascalia* is insistent on the nexus between the bishop's personal conduct and his authority to bind and loose: "As therefore thou hast authority to loose, know thyself and thy manners and thy conversation in this life, that they be worthy of thy place."[46] With its inclusion of the power to bind and loose and of the ability to bear the burdens of others among the bishop's prerogatives, the *Didascalia* points to a connection between penitential authority and personal holiness that will concern us again later.

The last and most comprehensive church order is the *Apostolic Constitutions*. By the time this work was composed in the region of Antioch, around the year 380, the Christian church had enjoyed almost seven decades of peace and prosperity since the reign of Constantine. Within a few years, its triumph would be complete through the anti-pagan legislation of the emperor Theodosius. The *Apostolic Constitutions* is a compilation that draws heavily on earlier church orders. It may therefore be considered a repository of information that was considered of value at the time, rather than an accurate reflection of the internal conditions in late fourth-century communities in Syria. The passages in book 2 on the character and duties of a bishop derive from the *Didascalia,* and those on the election and appointment of bishops in book 8, chapters 4–5, are adapted from the *Apostolic Tradition* of Hippolytus; therefore neither need concern us any further.

## 1 TIMOTHY 3 AND ITS INTERPRETATIONS

The only passage in the New Testament that treats the episcopal ministry in any detail is found in Paul's First Letter to Timothy (1 Tim. 3:1–7). Although modern scholars have called Paul's authorship of this epistle into question, it is generally agreed to be a work of the first century or of the first decade of the second century. The patristic authors who later referred to it certainly took for granted that it was genuine. The passage follows:

43. Ibid., pp. 37, 78.
44. Ibid., pp. 56, 80–81.
45. Ibid., p. 81.
46. Ibid., p. 55.

The saying is sure: whoever aspires to the office of bishop *(episkopēn)* desires a noble task. Now a bishop must be above reproach, married only once, temperate, sensible, respectable, hospitable, an apt teacher, not a drunkard, not violent but gentle, not quarrelsome, and not a lover of money. He must manage his own household well, keeping his children submissive and respectful in every way—for if someone does not know how to manage his own household, how can he take care of God's church? He must not be a recent convert, or he may be puffed up with conceit and fall into the condemnation of the devil. Moreover, he must be well thought of by outsiders, so that he may not fall into disgrace and the snare of the devil.

This passage provides the baseline for all later reflection on the nature and character of the ideal bishop. In order to gain a closer understanding of the interpretation of these sentences in the patristic literature, I have traced the quotations of these verses by later authors.[47] After an overview of the use of citations from 1 Timothy 3:1–7 among the church fathers, I turn to the exegetical homilies that make this epistle their subject.

Late antique reflection on the ideal bishop developed in step with the historical development of the episcopate. In the first centuries, while there were several *episkopoi* whose duties were largely administrative, all that was expected of them was that they be respected and upright members of the community. Beginning in the fourth century, the enhanced visibility of the representatives of the church and the increased array of their responsibilities in a largely pagan world were not without consequence: on the one hand, they triggered new reflections on the relative worth of the public activities of the bishop versus the private pursuit of asceticism, and on the other, they made it more imperative than ever that the bishop lead an exemplary life. If that was the case, it was anticipated that his congregation would readily accept his teaching, while the pagans would recognize in him a worthy paragon of the new religion.

*Quotations from 1 Timothy 3 in the Church Orders and in Patristic Works*

The pattern of citations from 1 Timothy 3:1–7 is surprisingly uneven. Paul's advice is reiterated in the early church orders in the context of the identification of a suitable candidate for the episcopal ministry, his election, and

---

47. This was done by following up on the references to patristic writings on 1 Timothy 3 listed in J. Allenbach et al., eds., *Biblia patristica: Index des citations et allusions bibliques dans la littérature patristique*, 6 vols. (Paris, 1975–87). I am immensely grateful to Julia Verkholantsev for her patient and persistent assistance with this portion of my research. The following observations highlight the most prominent trends, without claiming to provide a complete documentation. For convenient access to selected patristic commentaries on these passages, see also P. Gorday, ed., *Ancient Christian Commentary on Scripture: New Testament*, vol. 9, *Colossians, 1–2 Thessalonians, 1–2 Timothy, Titus, Philemon* (Downers Grove, Ill., 2000), 168–73.

his ordination. The *Apostolic Tradition* of Hippolytus contains only the briefest allusion to 1 Timothy 3, when it demands that the bishop be "without reproach."[48] The most extensive treatment of the selection of a bishop, his qualities, and his duties is found at various points in the *Didascalia*, which makes ample use of 1 Timothy 3, augmented by other quotations from scripture. Beyond the usual advice to adhere to a virtuous lifestyle that holds up to all scrutiny, this work is particularly concerned with the financial and judicial aspects of the episcopal office. To discharge these duties properly, the *Didascalia* notes, the bishop must be impartial, immune to bribery, and capable of discernment.[49]

The use of citations from the First Letter to Timothy outside the church orders undergoes a significant change after the third century. Authors of the earlier period tend to treat individually each of the positive characteristics that, according to the epistle, recommend a man for the office of *episkopos*. Snippets of this passage are usually taken out of context, broken up into smaller segments, and reapplied wherever the author sees fit. This is in contrast to later authors, beginning in the late third century, who usually regard 1 Timothy 3:1–7 and the sequence of virtues it contains as an established and immutable list that has to be quoted in its entirety. Moreover, when the earlier writers extract smaller quotations from the original context, they do so to bring home the point that these character traits are expected not just of the *episkopos* but of every member of the congregation. Later authors continue to postulate the general applicability of these virtues, but they now also relate them specifically to bishops. Over time, the expectations of virtuous conduct of all Christians thus become focused on the person of the bishop as a model of Christian virtues.

In the earlier period, 1 Timothy 3:1–7 is rarely cited anywhere, except the church orders. The tendency at this time to take shorter segments out of context and to apply them in a general sense can be seen in Tertullian's use of Paul's demand that the bishop be married only once. Tertullian repeated this injunction of single marriage in his *Exhortation to Chastity*[50] and *On Monogamy*.[51] In both instances, he explains that the apostle's advocacy of a single marriage for the priesthood was intended to apply to *all* the faithful, since all Christians partake of the royal priesthood. Similarly, Tertullian in his *On the Soul* cites Paul's introductory phrase "whoever aspires to the office of bishop *(episkopēn)* desires a noble task," but he does so in a general discussion of concupiscence or desire.[52] Tertullian's Eastern contemporary,

48. *Apostolic Tradition* 2.1.
49. *Didascalia* 2.1–25.
50. Tertullian, *Exhortation to Chastity* 7.2.
51. Tertullian, *On Monogamy* 12.4.
52. Tertullian, *On the Soul* 16.6.

Clement of Alexandria, made equally generalized use of Paul's recommendation that the bishop not be avaricious or litigious. In his *On Virginity*, he included these words in a general exhortation to virtuous living.[53] These authors understand Paul's words as applying to all Christians, regardless of their rank and status within the community. The *episkopos* is not singled out, neither because of his exceptional virtues nor by his function nor through his ordination.

Origen, in the late third century, oscillates between the generalizing application of Paul's passage that had been typical of the earlier period and the assumption that certain men, because they possess the virtues catalogued by Paul, are identified as *episkopoi* before God. Origen addresses this issue in two passages in his *Commentary on Matthew*. In the first passage, he explains that those who conform to the virtues set out by Paul for bishops rightfully exercise the power to bind and loose.[54] In other words, the possession of virtues precedes and indeed is the precondition for the exercise of penitential authority that is largely the prerogative of bishops. In the second passage, Origen says that Jewish rabbis receive recognition in the eyes of the people because of the external markers of their position, such as the most prominent seat at banquets or in the synagogue. Bishops, by contrast, are recognized in the eyes of God because of their virtues: "For he who has in him the virtues that Paul lists about the bishop, even if he is not a bishop among men, is a bishop before God, even if the [episcopal] rank has not been bestowed on him through the ordination by men."[55] To illustrate his point, Origen invokes the example of the physician and the pilot of a ship. These men retain their skill and ability, even if they lack the opportunity to exercise them. The physician remains a physician even if he has no patients, and the pilot remains a pilot even if he has no ship to navigate. Taken to its logical conclusion, Origen's reasoning allows that there may be many more "bishops before God" than there are bishops among men. Moreover, it opens the door to the possibility that men who do not qualify as "bishops before God" are nonetheless ordained to the episcopate. This is in tune with Origen's general tendency to expose the worldliness of the church as an institution. Criticism of this nature would become even more pronounced in the post-Constantinian era.

Origen also seems to be the first author to apply Paul's catalog of virtues to bishops specifically, although not exclusively. Paul's advice that the *episkopos* should enjoy a good reputation, for example, is reiterated by Origen in order to drive home the point that the bishop should be recognized by all as outstanding in every way and that he should thus be a worthy represen-

53. Clement of Alexandria, *On Virginity* 1.13.5.
54. Origen, *Commentary on Matthew* 16.19.
55. Ibid., 23.12.

tative of the whole community.[56] In his *Commentary on the Letter to the Romans,* Origen explains that the different ministries of the church must observe the scriptural precepts that apply to them. The bishop will fulfill his ministry, Origen says, by practicing the virtues listed in 1 Timothy 3.[57] Origen puts forward a similar view in his *Commentary on Matthew* where he castigates those who seek the episcopate out of pride and vainglory. Their negative motivation will render them unable to practice the virtues expected of a bishop according to Paul.[58] Origen thus seems to regard the possession of virtues listed in Paul's passage as a touchstone for identifying those who are bishops in the eyes of God.

The Christian literature of the late fourth century and beyond shows a renewed interest in the episcopate. The expansion of the church and Christianity's new status as *religio licita* brought with them a more acute awareness of the public image of representatives of the church. Many more authors now demand, as Ignatius had already done two centuries previously, that the bishop be a worthy spokesman of Christianity, and that he act as an exemplar for his communities. These authors support their claims by reference to Paul's famous passage.[59]

In his treatise *On the Priesthood,* which will be discussed in more detail below, John Chrysostom refers to our Pauline passage only twice, first to point out that the bishop should be held in good repute by others, and second to discuss the desire for office.[60] Ambrose, himself a prominent bishop in the imperial capital of Milan, insists that priests and bishops should stand out in the community because of their virtuous conduct. In his *Letters,* he highlights the importance of hospitality and of the single marriage of the higher clergy. The former, he says, is significant because Paul specifically demanded it of bishops,[61] the latter because it lends credence to the bishops' exhortations to widows to avoid remarriage.[62]

Basil of Caesarea turns to to 1 Timothy 3 in his efforts to maintain a high quality of clergy. He was troubled by the doings of the *chorepiskopoi* under his

---

56. Origen, *Homily on Leviticus* 6.3. Origen uses a similar argument, again with reference to Paul's Letter to Timothy, to rebut Celsus's accusation that Christians attract uneducated and silly people: Origen, *Against Celsus* 3.48.

57. Origen, *Commentary on the Letter to the Romans* 8.10.

58. Origen, *Commentary on Matthew* 15.21–28.

59. In the debate about the celibacy of the clergy that begins in the fourth century, theologians frequently quote Paul's words that the bishop should be married only once. Since this debate concerns priests as well as bishops, and since it touches primarily on issues of sexual renunciation and only tangentially affects definitions and approaches to the episcopate, it will be largely omitted here.

60. John Chrysostom, *On the Priesthood* 2.5.60–61 and 3.10.57–58.

61. Ambrose, *On Abraham* 1.5.32 (I 294 C).

62. Ambrose, *Epistulae extra collectionem, Ep.* 5 (11).5; *Ep.* 14 (63).61–64.

jurisdiction, the rampant practice of simony, and the appointment of unworthy candidates. In a stern letter of admonition, he reminds the country bishops that "according to the ancient custom observed in the Churches of God" a detailed examination of the life and conduct used to be undertaken, following the criteria listed in 1 Timothy 3. Basil insists that this kind of scrutiny be applied to all candidates for the clergy, which in this context means priests and deacons.[63]

Bishops and other clergy, however, were not the only Christian leaders to whom the words of 1 Timothy 3: 1–7 were thought to apply. The same moral qualifications and exemplary conduct were also expected from heads of monastic communities. One of Basil's *Ascetical Discourses* stresses that "the one chosen as guide in this state of life [i.e., the monastic community] be such that his life may serve as a model of every virtue to those who look to him, and, as the Apostle says, that he be 'sober, prudent, of good behaviour, a teacher.'" Basil adds that a potential future abbot should be examined with regard to his spiritual and moral maturity, to make sure that "everything said and done by him may represent a law and a standard for the community."[64] This is elaborated further in a passage in Basil's *Long Rules* that also establishes a direct nexus between personal conduct and authority within a Christian community, again turning to short pieces of Paul's injunctions.[65] Basil's repeated use of the catalog of virtues from 1 Timothy 3 shows that Paul's advice was in a more general sense considered to apply to anyone who held a position of leadership among Christians, whether abbot or bishop.

### Commentaries on the Pauline Epistles

Paul's recommendations in his First Letter to Timothy regarding the *episkopoi* were, as we have just seen, mined by late antique authors for short snippets or for whole sentences to quote. A more comprehensive treatment might be expected from patristic commentaries on the epistle as a whole, but those are few in number. Jerome's series of commentaries on the Pauline epistles includes one on the Letter to Titus, but not on the First Letter to Timothy. However, his remarks on the passage in Titus 1:5–9 that deals with the moral character of priests draw heavily on the relevant verses of 1 Timothy 3. The catalog of episcopal virtues in both these epistles is eagerly repeated by Jerome, who seizes this opportunity to make pointed jabs against unworthy clergy who indulge in gluttony and excessive drinking, who are given to filthy lucre, who show favoritism in their appointments

---

63. Basil of Caesarea, *Ep.* 54.
64. Basil of Caesarea, *An Ascetical Discourse, PG* 35, col. 876B–C.
65. Basil of Caesarea, *Long Rules*, question 43.

to the priesthood, and who do not manage to keep their own household in order. The ideal, Jerome insists, is the bishop who embodies all the virtues. The reasoning he gives for the importance of episcopal virtues is not so much, as in the other authors we have encountered, the preaching and teaching authority of the bishop, but rather his penitential and judicial authority, where personal detachment and impartiality are paramount.

Jerome revisits the issue of ascetic virtues among the clergy in his spirited response to Jovinian. Against the latter's suggestion that the clergy need not excel in their conduct and that chastity is not required of them, Jerome upholds a strict ascetic ideal. He does so by quoting the entire passage of 1 Timothy 3:1–7, implying that it is addressed specifically to bishops who ought to take Paul's admonition as an incentive to improve themselves: "By being placed in the higher order an opportunity is afforded him [the bishop], if he chose to avail himself of it, for the practice of virtue."[66] Jerome is keenly aware that the ascetic authority of the virtuous man and the pragmatic authority of the ecclesiastical officeholder are two distinct qualities. Only those men whose virtues correspond to their rank in the clergy deserve praise and admiration: "You see then that the blessedness of a bishop, priest or deacon, does not lie in the fact that they are bishops, priests, or deacons, but in their having the virtues which their names and offices imply."[67] Jerome here proves to be an adherent of the idea, first given voice by Clement and Origen, of the "true" bishop in contradistinction to the bishop by ordination. He sums this up elsewhere in the terse statement "Not all bishops are bishops."[68]

Jerome's older contemporary John Chrysostom includes among his exegetical sermons one on 1 Timothy 3. This sermon is remarkable because it combines two unconnected and potentially conflicting strands of thought that we have already identified, without visible concern about inherent contradiction. One the one hand, John Chrysostom emphasizes the need for the bishop, because of his exalted and exposed position, to be a model and an inspiration not only to the Christian community, but also to the pagans, in the hope that this will bring them to conversion. On the other hand, he notes that the virtues required by Paul of bishops, such as hospitality or moderation in wine consumption, are neither particularly demanding nor particularly scarce among Christians. He tackles the issue head-on:

> Why said he not that he should be an angel, not subject to human passions? Where are those great qualities of which Christ speaks, which even those under their rule ought to possess? To be crucified to the world, to be always

66. Jerome, *Against Jovinian* 34.
67. Ibid., 35.
68. Jerome, *Epistle* 14.9 (to Heliodorus).

ready to lay down their lives . . . Why are not these things required by Paul? Plainly because few could be found of such character, and there was need for many bishops, that one might preside in every city. But because the churches were to be exposed to attacks, he requires not that superior and highly exalted virtue, but a moderate degree of it; for to be sober, of good behavior, and temperate, were qualities common to many.[69]

John here couches his acknowledgment of the general applicability of these virtues in the context of the historical narrative of the spread and expansion of the Christian church, a story in which bishops played an instrumental role. He also notes that the episcopate is not an honor, but a function, with reference to the etymology of *episkopein*, "to be an overseer."[70] This concession to the realities of ecclesiastical leadership is offset by John's other writings, most notably his *On the Priesthood*, discussed below, where he sketches a more lofty picture of the ideal bishop as a high priest.

A very similar approach was taken by Theodore of Mopsuestia, John Chrysostom's friend from the time they spent together in Libanius's classroom and later in a monastery near Antioch. His theological position on the two natures of Christ came under scrutiny during the Three Chapters controversy, with the result that his works were banned as heretical in 553. Like John Chrysostom, Theodore also wrote a treatise titled *On the Priesthood*, but the text does not survive. However, his exegetical commentary on the Pauline epistles, which includes a treatment of the First Letter to Timothy, invites a comparison of the views of these two friends. Theodore concedes, just like John, that the historical origin of the episcopate lies in a range of practical administrative tasks, as indicated in the leading sentence of Paul's remarks (1 Tim. 3:1): "Whoever aspires to the office of bishop desires a noble task." Theodore's commentary on this passage survives only in Latin, where the Greek *ergon* (translated in the NRSV as "task") is rendered with its exact Latin equivalent *opus:* "He does well to call it 'work' and not honor, for the discharge of ecclesiastical duties is not an honor, but work."[71] Theodore also agrees with John Chrysostom that the virtues required by Paul of an *episkopos* are not very demanding. John had explained this with reference to historical exigency that created the need for a large number of bishops of whom, it is implied, one ought not to expect too much. Theodore, by contrast, demands that the bishop should strive to match his elevated status within the church by intensifying his efforts to adhere to the code of conduct laid down by Paul.

The only extant detailed discussion in Latin of the First Letter to

---

69. John Chrysostom, *Homily on 1 Timothy 3* 10.2.
70. Ibid.
71. Theodore of Mopsuestia, *Commentary on the First Letter to Timothy* 3.1.

Timothy was composed as part of a series of commentaries on the Pauline epistles by Ambrosiaster, the elusive fourth-century author who passed himself off as Ambrose. He is mainly concerned with the selection of a suitable candidate and the moral conduct of the bishop. Ambrosiaster is aware that some seek the episcopal office out of ambition or greed, and that recent converts are prone to pride and boastfulness if they are appointed to the episcopate too soon. Such pitfalls can be avoided, Ambrosiaster recommends, if the potential bishop possesses the moral characteristics outlined by Paul, "for they are the markers of the episcopal dignity." Only if he practices what he preaches will the bishop avoid the devil's snare, and only then will his teaching be accepted as true.[72] Like Ambrose and his other contemporaries, Ambrosiaster seems well acquainted with the phenomenon of unworthy bishops, the dissolution they can generate within their communities, and the discredit they can bring upon the Christian church. Another fourth-century author, Pseudo-Augustine, interprets the Christian ministry in much the same vein. The value of the Christian church is measured by the morality of its representatives, just as the silliness of the traditional religion is exposed by the heinous practices of the pagan priests.[73]

The tendency of fourth-century authors to regard Paul's First Letter to Timothy as a catalog of specifically episcopal virtues is evident also in the more personal remarks of church fathers who were themselves bishops. At times, they hold up these criteria to praise their colleagues in office. Gregory of Nazianzus bestows high praise on Athanasius of Alexandria as a staunch adherent of Nicene orthodoxy and in this context finds it expedient to depict him as the perfect bishop whose life is in complete conformity with Paul's precepts.[74] At other times, these men of the church express their own fear of falling short of this yardstick. Gregory of Nazianzus explains that he absconded immediately after his father, Gregory the Elder, had ordained him to the priesthood, in part because he was afraid of his inability to meet the demands of his office. He finds it impossible for anyone to conform to the demands set out by Paul in his First Letter to Timothy, let alone those made by Christ.[75] Basil pours his heart out in a letter to a "pious man," in which he communicates his worry of failing to perform the duties imposed on him as a bishop. This is a heartfelt plea, not mere rhetoric or fishing for

72. Ambrosiaster, *Commentary on the First Letter to Timothy* 3.1–3.7.
73. Ambrosiaster, *Questions on the Old and New Testament* 114.11.
74. Gregory of Nazianzus, *Homily* 21.9–10. See also J.-R. Pouchet, "Athanase d'Alexandrie, modèle de l'évêque, selon Grégoire de Nazianze, Discours 21," in *Vescovi e pastori in epoca teodosiana*, 2 (Rome, 1997).
75. Gregory of Nazianzus, *Or.* 2 *(On His Flight)* 69.

compliments. Basil beseeches his friend to pray for him so that he may be able to continue to lead a "chaste," that is, God-fearing, life and that he may discharge his office in a manner that pleases God.[76]

Common to all these texts of the post-Constantinian era is the strong nexus they establish between the personal virtues of a bishop, the acceptance by others—including pagans—of his position of leadership, and the effectiveness of his pastoral care. These authors are finely attuned to the dialectical nature of leadership. The congregation, they point out, will accept a bishop's guidance in spiritual and moral issues only if he shows himself to be of outstanding moral integrity. A bishop must practice what he preaches. Jerome puts this succinctly in his *Commentary on the Epistle to Titus:* "The future leader of the church should possess eloquence that is intimately linked with integrity of conduct, so that his actions are not silenced by his preaching, or his words are an embarrassment because his deeds are deficient."[77] This is what I call the dialectic of episcopal leadership, meaning that the bishop has to earn the recognition of his authority through his exemplary conduct. At the same time, it was the bishop's possession of these virtues that first singled him out and recommended him for office. His role as bishop required that he act as a model who instilled in his community the desire to emulate and imitate him. In this regard, the ideal bishop of the fourth century fulfills a role comparable to that of the holy man.

### TREATISES ON ECCLESIASTICAL LEADERSHIP

So far we have examined scattered references in a variety of texts—church orders, biblical commentaries, letters—to assemble a spectrum of approaches to the episcopal role in late antiquity. These references allow only a glimpse of each author's approach, but their quantity and their distribution over time lends them significance as indicators of general attitudes and their development through the centuries.

In addition, there is a sizeable number of treatises devoted specifically to the nature of ecclesiastical leadership, to which I now turn. None of them were composed before the fourth century—a further indication that the newly gained public prominence of the Christian religion challenged the men of the church to give shape and definition to their position in an increasingly Christian society. Among modern scholars, these works are often referred to as treatises on pastoral care, which makes them sound like

---

76. Basil of Caesarea, *Ep.* 213.1.
77. Jerome, *Commentary on the Letter to Titus* 1.

practical manuals for spiritual shepherds on how to tend their flock. In reality, they are much more than that. The works discussed below all address the nature of spiritual leadership, the conflict between the active and the contemplative life, and the personal qualifications of the Christian minister. It is this last aspect in particular that is of interest here.

The chronological range of these treatises extends from the late fourth to the late sixth century, beginning with Gregory of Nazianzus's *In Defense of His Flight* and ending with Gregory the Great's *Pastoral Care*. The earlier texts in particular employ a very vague terminology with regard to the ecclesiastical ministry. It is by no means clear whether they speak of priests or bishops when they use the Latin *sacerdos* or the Greek *hiereus*. This distinction is a modern concern that imposes itself from hindsight.[78] The authors well into the fifth century were content with the fact that they were discussing clergy who had been ordained through the imposition of hands, who could claim to be the successors of the apostles, and whose tasks revolved around preaching, the celebration of the eucharist, and ecclesiastical administration, especially of charity.

Gregory of Nazianzus gave voice to his views of the priesthood at a highly charged moment in his life. His father, Gregory the Elder, had ordained him to the priesthood at Christmas 361, thereby designating his son as his successor. This, Gregory claims not very convincingly, took him by surprise, and in his initial panic he hastened to return to the tranquility of the monastic retreat of his friend Basil in Pontus. But by Easter of the following year, he was back in Nazianzus. His *Second Oration*, entitled *In Defense of His Flight*, purports to be a sermon he delivered before the congregation in order to explain himself.[79] The length and literary craftsmanship of this work, however, seem to indicate that it was intended for a reading public, at least in its present form. As the first coherent treatment of the nature of the priesthood in literature (as opposed to the church orders, which are rule books), Gregory's *Second Oration* would exert great influence on later such works, especially those by John Chrysostom and Gregory the Great. [80]

78. For the use of *sacerdos* in the Theodosian Code, see A. di Bernardino, "L'immagine del vescovo attraverso i suoi titoli nel codice teodosiano," in *L'évêque dans la cité du IV^e au V^e siècle: Image et autorité*, ed. E. Rebillard and C. Sotinel, Collection de l'École Française de Rome 248 (Rome, 1998).

79. A. Louth, 'St. Gregory Nazianzen on Bishops and the Episcopate," in *Vescovi e pastori in epoca teodosiana*, 2 (Rome, 1997), draws attention to Gregory's emphasis on *philosophia* as the essential precondition for the ideal bishop.

80. For a summary treatment, see M. Lochbrunner, *Über das Priestertum: Historische und systematische Untersuchung zum Priesterbild des Johannes Chrysostomus* (Bonn, 1993), 39–66. On Gregory's calculated efforts to create an "image" of himself as a holy man, in *Oratio* 2 and in his other autobiographical works, see N. McLynn, "A Self-Made Holy Man: The Case of Gregory Nazianzen," *JECS* 6 (1998): 463–83.

Having first rejected, and then accepted the priesthood, Gregory is in a position to argue for the awesome nature of the priestly office and the unattainable requirements made on the person of the priest, on the one hand, and the practical need to fill such appointments with reasonably suitable, if imperfect, candidates, on the other. His practical side comes through when he speaks of the church as one body, where each member must perform the task that is assigned to him, and when he mentions that in every organization there are those who rule and those who are ruled.[81] He admits that he was moved to return also by his personal attachment to his elderly parents, by obedience to his father, and by his desire to reciprocate the affection that the congregation had shown him.[82] An additional reason that prompted Gregory to accept the priesthood was his desire to do his share to counterbalance the large numbers of unworthy and unprepared clergy who had recently flooded the church to satisfy their ambition or their greed:

> They push and thrust around the holy table, as if they thought this order to be a means of livelihood, instead of a pattern of virtue, or an absolute authority, instead of a ministry of which we must give account. . . . For at no time, either now or in former days, amid the rise and fall of various developments, has there ever been such an abundance as now exists among Christians, of disgrace and abuses of this kind.[83]

As his speech winds down to a close, Gregory does not fail to mention that he has, in fact, been prepared for this moment from his earliest youth. Not only had he grown up in a pious household, but he had also surrendered himself to a life of renunciation and ascetic self-fashioning:

> There was moreover the moderation of anger, the curbing of the tongue, the restraint of the eyes, the discipline of the belly, and the trampling under foot of the glory which clings to the earth. I speak foolishly, but it shall be said, in these pursuits I was perhaps not inferior to many.[84]

Weighing all these considerations, Gregory admits that he realized that his initial urge to seek the tranquility and solitude of monastic retreat would have been a selfish undertaking.[85]

Framed by these personal remarks are Gregory's views on the nature of the priesthood and the character of the ideal priest. He brings up the awesomeness of the priest's liturgical function in consecrating the eucharist,[86]

---

81. Gregory of Nazianzus, *Or.* 2 *(On His Flight)* 3–5.
82. Ibid., 1, 102–3, 112.
83. Ibid., 8.
84. Ibid., 77.
85. Ibid., 6–7.
86. Ibid., 95.

a theme that would later be resumed by John Chrysostom and Ambrose, among others. In contrast to later authors on the subject, Gregory does not dwell on the nuisance of the administrative duties of the priesthood. He does, however, go into great detail in comparing the priest to a physician who is responsible for healing and strengthening the souls entrusted to his care.[87] This requires both the ability for accurate diagnosis as well as the prescription of the right medicine suited to the disposition of the patient. Gregory insists on the importance of the priest's ability to address each individual according to his or her personal needs, in his admonition and in his preaching. In essence, the qualities that Gregory requires here in the context of the pastoral care of priests are nothing else but the gift of discernment that, as we shall see below, gave a special quality of immediacy to the teaching of the *pneumatophoroi* and the desert fathers.

Most important in Gregory's view is that the priest himself be a model of what he preaches:

> A man must himself be cleansed, before cleansing others; himself become wise, that he may make others wise; become light, and then give light; draw near to God, and so bring others near; be hallowed, then hallow them; be possessed of hands to lead others by the hand, of wisdom to give advice.[88]

According to Gregory, the effectiveness of a priest's instruction, and indeed the quality of the priesthood as a whole, depend entirely on the priest's own striving for personal holiness. This holiness, however, was not guardedly preserved in monastic isolation, but shared in ministry to others.

John Chrysostom probably wrote his treatise *On the Priesthood* during the years that he was in Antioch, probably in the late 380s.[89] It must have been something of an instant success, for Jerome records in 392, in his *Lives of Illustrious Men,* that he has read it.[90] The premise of the work is John's defense against any accusations of wrongdoing for his clever manipulation of the ordination of his friend and monastic companion Basil (not identical with the famous bishop of Caesarea), while managing to escape the same fate himself. This gives him occasion to dwell on the enormity of the responsibility of the priestly ministry, and to describe in detail the different functions that a priest must fulfill. The word he uses throughout, *hierosynē,* refers

---

87. Ibid., 18ff.
88. Ibid., 71.
89. On the relation of this treatise to Gregory's *Oratio 2,* see H. Dörries, "Erneuerung des kirchlichen Amts im vierten Jahrhundert: Die Schrift *De sacerdotio* des Johannes Chrysostomus und ihre Vorlage, die *Oratio de fuga sua* des Gregor von Nazianz," in *Bleibendes im Wandel der Kirchengeschichte,* ed. B. Moeller and G. Ruhbach (Tübingen, 1973).
90. Jerome, *Lives of Illustrious Men* 129.

to the priesthood in general, without distinguishing between the offices of presbyter and bishop.[91]

While Gregory of Nazianzus had taken his own experience—initial rejection of office, followed by eventual acceptance—as an opportunity to explain the relative merits of ecclesiastical office versus monastic retreat as exemplified in the internal conflict of one person, John Chrysostom assigns each side in this conflict to a different character. He casts Basil in the role of the former monk who agrees to become a cleric, and himself in the role of the monk who shuns ecclesiastical office.[92] Considering that the author was at this time a deacon on his way up in the ecclesiastical hierarchy, this rhetorical role-play alone casts serious suspicions on the autobiographical value of the entire treatise. Nonetheless, *On the Priesthood* is an important statement about the nature of the priesthood. It was appreciated by posterity as a veritable "mirror of bishops." Isidore of Pelusium, an Egyptian scholar-turned-monk who is known to us mainly through his extensive correspondence, sent a copy of Chrysostom's treatise to a certain Eustathius in around 440, recommending it for its inspirational nature:

> I have sent the book you asked for, and I expect that you will derive profit from it, as everybody usually does. For there is nobody, no single heart that has not been moved to divine love by reading this book. It shows how venerable and difficult to attain the priesthood is, and teaches to exercise it without reproach. For John, the wise announcer of the secrets of God, the eye of the church of Byzantium and of the whole [church], has elaborated it so finely and with such great diligence that all will discover therein their virtues or their reproach, both those who exercise their office in a manner pleasing to God and those who administer it with negligence.[93]

In order to justify his decision to avoid ordination, John in this work compares his personal failings and shortcomings[94] with the impeccable and virtuous conduct of his friend Basil, who had demonstrated his love of humankind in a selfless act of intervention for a friend.[95] It is essential that the bishop possess such qualities for the exercise of his office. John devotes less space than Gregory to the bishop's pastoral duties, although he, too,

---

91. *On the Priesthood*, ed. Malingrey, 72 n. 1. On the ideal of the episcopate in John's panegyrical sermons, see J.-N. Guinot, "L'apport des panégyriques de Jean Chrysostome à une définition de l'évêque modèle," in *Vescovi e pastori in epoca teodosiana*, 2 (Rome, 1997).

92. This was noted by L. Meyer, "Perfection chrétienne et vie solitaire dans la pensée de S. Jean Chrysostome," *Revue d'ascetique et de mystique* 14 (1933): 245ff.

93. Isidore of Pelusium, *Ep. liber* 1.156, *PG* 78, col. 288B (my translation).

94. John Chrysostom, *On the Priesthood* 2.5.11ff., 3.10.94ff.

95. Ibid., 2.6.31ff.

invokes the image of the bishop as the physician of souls.[96] Instead, he approaches the episcopal office from two complementary angles, the spiritual and the administrative.

John pays particular attention to the spiritual power inherent in the bishop's liturgical functions. He dwells on the bishop's role in consecrating the eucharist even more than Gregory had done. It is a task that requires complete ritual purity:

> For when thou seest the Lord sacrificed, and laid upon the altar, and the priest standing and praying over the victim, and all the worshippers empurpled with that precious blood, canst thou then think that thou art still amongst men, and standing upon the earth? Art thou not, on the contrary, straightaway translated to Heaven? . . . By their agency [i.e., that of the priests] these rites are celebrated, and others nowise inferior to these both in respect of our dignity and our salvation. For they who inhabit the earth and make their abode there are entrusted with the administration of things which are in Heaven, and have received an authority which God has not given to angels or archangels.[97]

This attention to the awesomeness of the transformation of the eucharistic sacrifice into the body and blood of Christ and the participation of the priest in this transformation seems to be a common concern of Greek theologians at the end of the fourth century, especially those in the intellectual orbit of Antioch. As Johannes Quasten has suggested, it was probably formulated in an attempt to counter Arianism by emphasizing the distance between the divine and the human realm.[98]

The other sacral function of the bishop that is of great importance in Chrysostom's work is his power to bind and loose through the imposition of penance, and the related function of performing baptisms.[99] Both bring a complete regeneration of the individual in the Spirit; and in both, the bishop acts in the role of a father who gives new life. In order to help sinners, the bishop should also shoulder the burdens of others.[100] He is, in fact, personally responsible before God for any sins in his congregation. John Chrysostom will repeat this thought later in the sermons he delivers in

96. Ibid., 2.3.41.
97. Ibid., 3.4.18–5.11.
98. J. Quasten, "Mysterium tremendum: Eucharistische Frömmigkeitsauffassungen des vierten Jahrhunderts," in *Vom christlichen Mysterium: Gesammelte Arbeiten zum Gedächtnis von Odo Casel OSB*, ed. A. Mayer, J. Quasten, and B. Neunheuser, 66–75 (Düsseldorf, 1951). See also Lochbrunner, 151–56; A. M. Ritter, *Charisma im Verständnis des Joannes Chrysostomos und seiner Zeit: Ein Beitrag zur Erforschung der griechisch-orientalischen Ekklesiologie in der Frühzeit der Reichskirche* (Göttingen, 1972), 98–108.
99. John Chrysostom, *On the Priesthood* 3.5–6.
100. Ibid., 6.6.31–36.

Constantinople.[101] He thus ascribes to the bishop ex officio the same role that the *pneumatophoros* and some of the holy men we will encounter later chose to take upon themselves on behalf of their intimate associates.

John seems to be the earliest theoretician on the episcopate who draws attention to the manifold mundane tasks that are likely to distract the bishop from his spiritual resolve. All too easily the bishop may get drawn into a whirl of emotions that disturb the calm of his soul: "wrath, despondency, envy, strife, slanders, accusations, falsehood, hypocrisy, intrigues, anger," and the list goes on.[102] He mentions the care of widows and virgins in the community, the bishop's judicial authority, and the daily round of visits expected of him.[103] In order to ensure impartiality and immunity to pressure or bribery in all his administrative work, it is important, John notes, that the bishop does not accede to his position through favoritism of any kind, which would later leave him open to pressure or blackmail. He has harsh words to say about the fierce competition that often surrounded episcopal elections in his day.[104] These indignities and distractions that affect the episcopate have to be counteracted by the appointment of worthy candidates who possess the proper preparation in faith, disposition, and virtue. For this reason, *On the Priesthood* has often been identified as a call for internal improvement and reform.[105]

The bulk of the work consists of considerations on the ideal qualities of the priesthood. John insists that the bishop should possess virtues in a perfect balance: "He ought to be dignified yet free from arrogance, formidable yet kind, apt to command yet sociable, impartial yet courteous, humble yet not servile, strong yet gentle."[106] One further essential qualification for a good bishop is introduced, namely, his rhetorical skill and his familiarity with scripture and theology.[107] John's insight into the importance of rhetoric, of course, betrays his own schooling in the classroom of Libanius of Antioch. But the urgency of his concern for the bishop's teaching and preaching springs from his desire to counteract heresy from the pulpit and through Bible study. Suitable candidates for the priesthood may be found among experienced monks, John acknowledges, although the mere practice of fasting, vigils, and other deprivations alone is no guarantee of the possession of virtues. John himself, despite his earlier monastic training, was convinced of his own lack of suitability for ecclesiastical leadership.

---

101. John Chrysostom, *In acta apost. hom.* 3.4–5, *PG* 60, cols. 39–40; *Hom.* 11, 2 *in 1 Thess.*, *PG* 62, cols. 463f. Cf. Lochbrunner, 255–57.

102. *On the Priesthood* 3.9.13—14.

103. Ibid., 3.12–14.

104. Ibid., 3.11.

105. Lochbrunner, 89.

106. *On the Priesthood* 3.11.145–48.

107. Ibid., 4.4–5.3.

In Chrysostom's view, the proper exercise of the priesthood is a much greater accomplishment than the pursuit of the ascetic life can ever be, for there are many men and women who can perform feats of asceticism, but only very few who are qualified to become shepherds of their flock.[108] Moreover, it is much more difficult to uphold a life of Christian virtues under the scrutiny of one's congregation and in the face of daily administrative and personal challenges than it is to live a life of austerity in the seclusion of a hermitage.[109] The priesthood, and not the ascetic life of the monk, is in John's eyes the pinnacle of Christian perfection. Spiritual and ascetic authority may be valuable in themselves, but for those who have been elected to office, they are merely qualifications that assist them in their calling: "It behooves one who undertakes this care to have much understanding, and, before understanding, great grace from God, and uprightness of conduct, and purity of life and superhuman virtue."[110]

John Chrysostom's work draws attention to the necessity for priests and bishops to be exemplars of the holy life. The ideal candidates for the priesthood are therefore those who had already removed themselves from the congregation in order to take up the monastic life. John is well aware that his exalted view of the responsibilities of the priesthood results in expanding the divide between it and the laity: "Let the distinction between the pastor and his charge be as great as that between rational man and irrational creatures, not to say even greater, inasmuch as the risk is concerned with things of far greater importance."[111] John's recognition of the vital importance of the manifold duties with which the priesthood is charged for the salvation of others will eventually lead him to disassociate the office of the bishop from the person who holds that office. This idea is still absent in *On the Priesthood* but is expressed in no uncertain terms in a later sermon: "We are God's ambassadors to the people. If this claim seems harsh to you, consider that this concerns not us as individuals, but the episcopal office itself; it does not concern one or the other person, but the bishop. Nobody should hear me [as a person], but the dignity [of the office]."[112]

Within a few years of John Chrysostom's composition of *On the Priesthood*, Ambrose of Milan wrote his *On the Duties of the Clergy* in 388 or 389, one and a half decades into his own episcopate. Its explicit intention was to provide the clergy with a guideline of the character traits and practical skills that are advantageous in gaining and maintaining the confidence of their congre-

108. Ibid., 2.2.1–7, 6.5–7.
109. Ibid., 3.10, 176–268; 6.5–6.
110. Ibid., 3.8.11–15.
111. Ibid., 2.2.12–15.
112. *Hom.* 3, 5 *in Col.*, *PG* 62, col. 324. Cf. Lochbrunner, 258–61.

gation.[113] The work is inspired in form and content by Cicero's *De officiis*. The first book deals with that which is virtuous, the second with that which is useful, and the third with a combination of both. Ambrose does not delineate the tasks and functions of the clergy in a systematic way, although he often refers to them. His focus is rather on providing ethical guidance on the acquisition and practice of those virtues that are particularly befitting to the clergy. He illustrates these virtues with extensive reference to biblical examples and, whenever he can, also to examples from classical literature. His concluding words emphasize that this method was the intention of his work:

> These things I have left with you, my children, that you may guard them in your minds—you yourselves will prove whether they will be of any advantage. Meanwhile they offer you a large number of examples, for almost all the examples drawn from our forefathers, and also many a word of theirs, are included within these three books; so that, although the language may not be graceful, yet a succession of old-time examples set down in such small compass may offer much instruction.[114]

In his outline of the ideal character of priests and bishops, Ambrose borrows heavily from Paul's catalog of episcopal virtues in 1 Timothy 3. Bishops ought to be hospitable, kind, just, without desire for the belongings of others, and they ought to avoid litigation at all costs, even to the point of suffering injustice.[115] Earlier in the same treatise, he adds a further argument for the importance of sacerdotal virtues. Priests and bishops must be publicly perceived to be adorned with virtue so that those who observe them in the performance of their ministry at the altar will worship God who adorned them in this way and whose glory is reflected in his servants.[116] Ambrose recognizes the bishop's sacerdotal function and insists that it receives its justification from the bishop's personal conduct. But where Chrysostom had called attention to the priest's celebration of the eucharist to emphasize the importance of a pure life of the celebrant as its minister and mediator, Ambrose takes a step away from the altar, as it were, and acknowledges that the bishop has stepped into the public limelight. No longer an internal officer of an exclusive religious group, the bishop now performs his many tasks on behalf of an expanding Christian community under the scrutiny of pagan neighbors. He has become distinct from the community and is distinguishable to outsiders. The virtues that some theologians two centuries

---

113. N. B. McLynn, *Ambrose of Milan: Church and Court in a Christian Capital* (Berkeley and Los Angeles, 1994), 255–56.

114. Ambrose, *On the Duties of the Clergy* 3.22.138.

115. Ibid., 2.21.106.

116. Ibid., 1.50.256.

previously demanded of all Christians are now expected primarily of the bishop. He is perceived by insiders and outsiders alike as the representative of Christianity. It depends on his conduct whether the church is credited or discredited. Indeed, he may attract converts through his example. Augustine's well-known story of his conversion under the impression of Ambrose's preaching is testimony to the crucial role that individual bishops could play in this regard.

Next in chronological sequence comes Julianus Pomerius's treatise *On the Contemplative Life*. The author was a well-respected professor of rhetoric in late fifth-century Gaul. The only other details known about his life are that he hailed from the province of Mauretania in North Africa, that in 497 he was the teacher of Caesarius of Arles, and that he maintained a friendly correspondence with Ennodius of Pavia and Ruricius of Limoges. He was known to have written three further works, all dealing with the practice of Christian virtues: *On the Soul and Its Quality, On the Formation of Dedicated Virgins,* and *On Contempt for the World and for the Things That Will Perish.*[117] Pomerius composed *On the Contemplative Life* at the behest of a certain Julianus whom he respectfully addresses throughout the volume. This Julianus is perhaps identical with the bishop of Carpentras, near Arles, of the same name. Pomerius explains the origin of his work in the preface: "You bid me, then, to discuss in a few words the nature of the contemplative life and to explain as briefly as I can the difference between it and the active life; whether one charged with ruling a church can become a sharer in the contemplative virtue."[118] The book may be characterized as a call to internal reform, as it combines outspoken criticism of clerical indignities with a systematic treatment of virtues and vices that borrows as much from ancient philosophy as it does from Augustine.

Pomerius begins by reminiscing about how Julianus had toyed with the idea of abandoning his episcopal see and retreating to solitude, "from despair of fulfilling your charge."[119] Julianus, as Pomerius recalls, was "deeply moved and grieved" because "you could neither discharge your office with any zeal nor abandon it without sin."[120] Pomerius wrote his treatise roughly a century after John Chrysostom's work, at a time when the church had established its presence in all the major cities throughout the empire, and his approach is more pragmatic than Chrysostom's. Where John invoked the awesome dignity of the ecclesiastical ministry and the great demands it places on the spiritual abilities of its bearer to the extent of being too

117. A. Solignac, "Julien Pomère," *DSp* 8 (1974): cols. 1594–1600; on the interpretation of his work, see J. C. Plumpe, "Pomeriana," *Vig Christ* 1 (1947): 227–39.
118. Julianus Pomerius, *The Contemplative Life* 1 Prol. 3.
119. Ibid., 1.16.
120. Ibid., 1.17.

overwhelming for some (including himself), Pomerius simply takes it for granted that men of good upbringing and suitable social class will be ordained to the clergy. His concern is how they can discharge their office for the benefit of the church. How can they resist the temptation of enriching themselves, of basking in the respect that their office commands, or of relishing the applause for their carefully crafted sermons?

Instead of weighing priesthood against monasticism, Pomerius shifts the terms and distinguishes between active virtue and contemplative virtue. He considers the latter superior: "The active life is the journeying; the contemplative is the summit. The former makes a man holy; the latter makes him perfect."[121] Nevertheless, it is possible for a priest to partake of the contemplative virtue, if he discharges his office properly and according to "the apostolic teaching":

> Therefore, if holy priests—not such as the divine threat declares are to be sentenced and condemned, but such as the apostolic teaching commends—convert many to God by their holy living and preaching; if they display no imperiousness, but do everything humbly and show themselves through love of holy charity affable to those over whom they have been placed; if they in some cases cure the weaknesses of their carnally living brethren by the medicine of healing words and in others bear patiently with those whom they judge to be incurable; if in the lives they live and in their preaching they seek not their own glory but Christ's; if they do not woefully waste either their words or their deeds as the price of courting favor, but always ascribe to God whatever honor is paid them as they live and teach in a priestly manner; if the dutiful greetings of those they meet do not make them proud but weigh them down; if they consider themselves not honored but burdened by the praises of those who compliment them; if they console the afflicted, feed the needy, clothe the naked, redeem the captives, harbor strangers; if they show wanderers the way of salvation and promise hope to those who despair of gaining pardon; if they spur on those who make progress, and arouse those who are delaying, and are constantly occupied with whatever pertains to their office: who will be such a stranger to faith as to doubt that such men are sharers in the contemplative virtue, by whose words as well as example many become coheirs of the kingdom of heaven?[122]

This passage stands at the conclusion of book 1, which deals with the contemplative life. A large part of the discussion in this book revolves around the limitations of teaching by example. Pomerius is less confident than earlier authors about the impact of a priest's upright conduct. He maintains that it is unlikely that a priest merely by his exemplary lifestyle can bring

121. Ibid., 1.12.
122. Ibid., 1.25.

obstinate sinners to mend their ways. He must also admonish them through his preaching.[123] Also, certain truths of the Christian faith, such as the life of Christ or the nature of the Trinity, cannot be imparted through the exemplary living of the priest, but have to be taught by preaching.[124] In this regard, Pomerius agrees with John Chrysostom on the importance of preaching and instruction for combating heresy.

Book 2 is devoted to a detailed and concrete discussion of the active life. Pomerius begins by expressing his apprehension that many clerics who read this will bristle at the implicit criticism of their unworthy behavior.[125] In a long, poetic passage that is reminiscent of Origen's definition of priests "before God," Pomerius describes the qualities of "the true priests who are the heads of churches," and who are priests "by divine approbation":

> They especially have received the charge of caring for souls. Ably bearing the responsibility for the people entrusted to them, they untiringly supplicate God for the sins of all as for their own; and, like an Aaron, offering the sacrifice of a contrite heart and a humble spirit, which appeases God, they turn the wrath of future punishment from their people. By the grace of God they become indicators of the divine will, founders of the churches of Christ after the Apostles, leaders of the faithful, champions of truth, enemies of perverse teaching, amiable to all the good, terrifying even in appearance of those of evil conscience, avengers of the oppressed, fathers of those regenerated in the Catholic faith, preachers of the things of heaven, shock troops in battles unseen, patterns of good works, examples of virtues, and models for the faithful. . . . These are they who have merited the priesthood not by courting favor but by living spiritually; who, elevated not by the support of human patronage but by divine approbation, do not applaud themselves because of the excellence of their high office.[126]

These "true priests" represent the ideal of the priesthood that the clergy should strive to attain. Pomerius does not go into further detail about them, nor does he explain in what relation they stand to the ordained clergy of his day. He also does not associate the "true priests" in any way with the monastic life, or with men who are recognized as holy men or saints.

The subsequent chapters in Pomerius's work contain concrete advice to priests on a wide range of issues: the admonition, rebuke, and, if necessary, excommunication of sinners; the administration of church finances not as if it were personal property, but for the benefit of the poor and needy; and the avoidance of concupiscence for money, food, and wine through "spiri-

123. Ibid., 1.20.
124. Ibid., 1.18–19.
125. Ibid., 2 Prol.
126. Ibid., 2.2.1–2.

tual abstinence," which allows for the use of these goods, provided it is undertaken in an attitude of complete indifference. Pomerius is too much of a pragmatist to demand radical lifestyle changes of the priests. He does not believe that sinners can be brought to contrition merely by observing the exemplary lifestyle of their priests. All he asks for in the priesthood is a reform in outlook, a sense of responsibility for the spiritual and material well-being of their flock, and moderation in their desire for the comforts of life.

The third book turns to a philosophical discussion of virtues and vices. Pomerius highlights the importance of four virtues in particular for the active life of priests: justice, temperance, fortitude, and prudence. Justice is described as "something of a social virtue" because it increases in the measure in which it is applied.[127] The priest who helps others to grow in their faith himself experiences an augmentation of virtue as a result:

> They act contrary to justice who, when they have been chosen because of the merit of their way of life or their learning, give preference to leisurely study over the fruitful good of ruling the common folk and who, though they could help the church in its labors, shun the work of a burdensome administration for the sake of enjoying repose.[128]

The contemplative life in pursuit of learning and the active life of administration are equally valuable before God. The scholar and the priest should follow the path laid out for them, in the confidence that "they travel towards one homeland and arrive at one kingdom, doing service in different capacities as Christ, the King of all, calls them."[129] This is Pomerius's answer to the dilemma of his friend Julianus, which prompted the composition of this work. The priesthood is neither a burden nor a distraction from man's supreme purpose to perfect himself in solitude, but it is a calling by God to reach personal sanctification through the active life.

Gregory the Great's *Pastoral Care* had its origin in the months after his accession to the episcopal see in Rome in 590. He had already spent the previous eleven years in the service of the church, first as a deacon, then as papal legate to Constantinople. Prior to his ecclesiastic career, Gregory had acquired ample experience in civil administration, since his privileged senatorial background and his extensive studies in grammar, rhetoric, and law had led to his appointment as city prefect in Rome in 572/573. His *Pastoral*

---

127. Ibid., 3.28.1.
128. Ibid., 2.28.1. This is one of the very few passages where Pomerius acknowledges that personal conduct can count as one of the qualifications for the priesthood, the other being education.
129. Julianus Pomerius, *The Contemplative Life* 2.28.2.

*Care* reveals the concern of an experienced administrator for the practical aspects in the exercise of ecclesiastical office.[130] It also addresses the tension between the contemplative and the active life to which Christian office-holders are exposed.[131] Like John Chrysostom's treatise, Gregory's *Pastoral Care* begins as an apology to a close friend for his own desire to hide in order to avoid the responsibility of office. The work enjoyed instant popularity. The author himself sent copies to several bishops and priests of his acquaintance. It also reached the court of the emperor Maurice in Constantinople and was translated there into Greek.[132] It was widely circulated in the Latin Middle Ages, when it was even read as a "mirror of princes": religiously sanctioned ecclesiastical leadership and religiously sanctioned royal leadership were obviously thought to have a great deal in common. With *Pastoral Care*, finally, we have a proper and complete manual for priests, a how-to guide for the discharge of the priestly office that is concrete testimony to Gregory's manifold efforts to breathe new life into the ecclesiastical administration of Italy. This was not an easy task. In his personal letters, Gregory admits that he was often overwhelmed by the challenge of maintaining a religious outlook in the midst of administrative work: "Under the pretext of the episcopate, I am reduced to the concerns of the world."[133]

Gregory's *Pastoral Care* proceeds in systematic and logical fashion, arranged in four books:

> The nature of the case requires that one should carefully consider the way in which the position of supreme rule ought to be approached, and when it is duly reached, how life should be spent in it; how, in a life of rectitude, one should teach others; and, in the proper performance of his teaching office, with vigilance one should realise each day one's weakness. All this must be ensured lest humility be wanting when office is assumed, the way of life be at variance with the office accepted, teaching divest life of rectitude, and presumption overrate teaching.[134]

Writing two centuries after John Chrysostom, Gregory senses the need to remind the priests in his charge not to take their ordination into the

130. J. Richards, *Consul of God: The Life and Times of Gregory the Great* (London and Boston, 1980). For a detailed analysis of Gregory's view of the practical aspects of the episcopal office, see A. Guillou, "L'évêque dans la société méditerranéenne des VI$^e$–VII$^e$ siècles: Un modèle," *Bibliothèque de l'École des Chartes* 131 (1973): 5–19, repr. in his *Culture et société en Italie Byzantine (VI$^e$–XI$^e$ s.)* (London, 1978).

131. R. A. Markus, *Gregory the Great and His World* (Cambridge, 1997), 16–33.

132. For the dissemination of the work, see Guillou, 17–18.

133. Gregory the Great, *Registrum* 1.5. See also G. Arnaldi, "Gregorio magno e la giustizia," in *La giustizia nell'alto medioevo (secoli V–VIII)*, 2 vols., Settimane di Studio del Centro Italiano di Studi sull'Alto Medioevo 42 (Spoleto, 1995).

134. Gregory the Great, *Pastoral Care*, prologue.

Christian ministry lightly nor to neglect the duties of their office. He follows Chrysostom in declaring ordination to be the final confirmation of personal virtues, a responsibility for service to others that those in possession of the requisite virtues cannot reject. He places particular emphasis on the congruity of personal lifestyle and teaching. Only if the priest himself is perceived as practicing what he preaches will his words be heeded and he will become an exemplar to others. All of book 3 is dedicated to the issue of preaching. After dealing with teaching by example, Gregory gives detailed and practical advice on how to address an audience that consists of men and women of different social backgrounds who have different life experiences and spiritual needs. Gregory here reaches an unprecedented level of reflection on preaching, which was only barely hinted at in Chrysostom's treatise. He places a high prize on the priest's role as interpreter of the Word of God and on his interaction with his congregation through his sermons. The possession of personal virtues validates and lends authority to the priest's words of textual interpretation and moral admonition from the pulpit. In other words, the bishop's ascetic authority lends credence to his claim to possess spiritual authority.

# CHAPTER THREE

# Spiritual Authority

Spiritual authority is the authority that comes from the possession of the Holy Spirit. In its purest form, it is received as a divine gift, without any participation or preparation on the side of the recipient. The active involvement of the individual to prepare himself for the receipt of this gift, or to enhance the gift that has already been received, falls under the purview of what I call ascetic authority and will be discussed in the next chapter. The present chapter begins with an investigation of the conception of spiritual authority among the Greek church fathers. The distinction they made between bearers of the Spirit *(pneumatophoroi)* as passive recipients of the Spirit and bearers of Christ *(christophoroi)* as conscious collaborators of the Spirit shows how ascetic authority—with its emphasis on an individual's active contribution—could be placed at the service of spiritual authority. The Spirit is, by its very nature, expansive and communicates itself, through the *pneumatophoros,* to others. One of its effects on the individual is to open up and maintain unclogged his channels of communication with the divine, which he can then impart to his surroundings. In this way, the Spirit-bearer becomes a holy man in communication with others. The second part of this chapter therefore examines how individual holy men were appreciated by their contemporaries for their ability to work intercessory prayer. The third and last part of the chapter studies a specific kind of intercessory prayer, namely, that for the remission of sins as it was offered by martyrs, holy men, and bishops. It is in this context that the nexus to ascetic authority is most pronounced, because the efficacy of intercessory prayer is thought to correlate directly with an individual's personal conduct.

The critical modern reader may find it strange or unnecessary to treat spiritual authority in isolation, given that it is in reality often coupled with ascetic authority. But there are exceptions where spiritual authority is operative by itself—for example, in the holy fools who employed every trick in the book to disguise their holiness from their contemporaries. Moreover, since the Christian authors themselves deal with spiritual authority as a separate category, we must take them at their word. Finally, a clear (perhaps artificially so) definition of spiritual authority can serve as an important diagnostic tool in identifying the commonalities among holy men who practice different lifestyles.

## CARRIERS OF THE GIFTS OF THE SPIRIT

### Pneumatophoros *and* Christophoros

In the growing Christian communities of the first centuries, certain individuals were singled out by their spiritual authority—the presence of the Holy Spirit or a special connection with Christ made manifest in special gifts or qualities. When Jesus was gathering his disciples, they became his "brothers" and "sisters." As children of the same "father" in heaven, they formed one large spiritual family, whose members had been touched, transformed, and elevated by their personal encounter with God. These men and women had associated themselves with Jesus before his death, had been in the presence of the resurrected Christ, or had received the grace of the descent of the Holy Ghost. The apostles' personal experience with God lent a special force to their preaching, and those who followed their beliefs looked to them as leaders and teachers. Some of the men and women who had joined the Christian community after the events of Pentecost were privileged as recipients of the Holy Spirit, even though they had not known the living or the resurrected Christ. In the Jerusalem church described in the Acts of the Apostles and the communities to whom Paul addressed his epistles, some members had the gift of the Spirit to exorcise, speak in tongues, and utter prophecies. These people were recognized as bearers of the Spirit *(pneumatophoroi;* sing., *pneumatophoros)* or bearers of Christ *(christophoroi;* sing., *christophoros).*

The idea that certain individuals are invested with the gifts of the Spirit did not come to an end with the apostolic age. In subsequent centuries, the application of the designation "bearer of the Spirit" or "bearer of Christ," which had originally been reserved for the prophets and teachers, was enlarged to include martyrs, monks, holy men, priests, and bishops. They were recognized as such because the Spirit was manifest in a myriad of different ways. As Pseudo-Macarius put it in the late fourth century: "And even though there are thousands of *pneumatophoroi,* [God's] grace is manifest in them in this way or that, in many parts and in many ways."[1] The concept of

---

1. Pseudo-Macarius, *Homily* 5.2.1.

Spirit-bearers is central to the writing of the theologians Clement of Alexandria (ca. 150–ca. 220) and Origen (185–253). It plays an important role in the monastic spirituality of the fourth century, especially among authors of a mystical bent, such as Pseudo-Macarius and Didymus the Blind. To bear the Spirit becomes such a distinctive feature in the monastic pursuit of holiness that many authors of the fourth century and later invoked this concept if they wanted to bestow especially high praise on certain holy men. The emphasis these authors placed on the possibility of the Spirit to make itself manifest in individuals in their own day and age enabled them to link the present with the past in way that transcended time and history.

The most prominent gift of the Spirit that a *pneumatophoros* communicates for the benefit of others is that of teaching and preaching. Anyone whose teaching was believed to be invested with divine authority was considered a *pneumatophoros*. The divinely inspired gift of teaching was given first and foremost to the apostles, the evangelists, and the prophets, as well as to Moses.[2] The fourth-century biblical commentator Didymus the Blind remarked that the first verse of Psalm 20 was said "either by the man who was a bearer of the Spirit, or by the Holy Spirit himself who was in him."[3] Elsewhere, he compared the *pneumatophoros* to a flutist, playing on the double meaning of the Greek word *pneuma* as "breath" and "spirit": "In the same way as the flute-player produces the sound through the breath (*ek pneumatos*), so also the Spirit-bearing men (*pneumatophoroi*) are praiseworthy flutists."[4] In other words, the Spirit flows through the *pneumatophoros* and inspires his words in the same way as the flute-player uses his breath to produce a tune, an idea that was revisited by Didymus's contemporary Macarius of Alexandria.[5] The same connection between the Spirit and inspired preaching was made by Epiphanius of Salamis in the late fourth century in his rebuttal of the teachings of Paul of Samosata: "Whom shall I believe? With whom shall I agree? From whom shall I receive life in their teaching? From the holy evangelists and Spirit-bearers, who speak the Word that has been sent by the Father, or from these followers of Paul the Samosatian?"[6]

In addition to preaching and teaching, the *pneumatophoros* has the gift of discernment. He is able to recognize the true character of people he encounters. According to Pseudo-Macarius, "The inner man, who is called soul and mind, precious vessel, can be recognized and known only by God and by those who are perfect and Spirit-bearers."[7] It was thus high praise

---

2. Didymus the Blind, *Commentary on Zacharias* 1.307.
3. Didymus the Blind, *Commentary on the Psalms* 20–21, 7.20–21.
4. Didymus the Blind, *Commentary on Ecclesiastes* 3–4.12.
5. Pseudo-Macarius, *Homily* 47.14.
6. Epiphanius, *Panarion* 65.5.8 (my translation).
7. Pseudo-Macarius, *Homily* 18.7.2.

when Palladius referred to his teacher Evagrius Ponticus, the great theorist of monasticism in the fourth century, as "the blessed Evagrius, a man who was a Spirit-bearer and who had discernment *(anēr pneumatophoros kai diakritikos)*."[8] Discernment further enabled the bearer of the Spirit to recognize demons even of the most deceitful kind. The mere presence of a *pneumatophoros* could force demons who had long been concealed to identify themselves and to reveal truths about others. As Pseudo-Macarius put it: "The spirits of evil [are] burnt up when they come near to a Spirit-bearing soul."[9] Countless hagiographical narratives tell such stories. One incident involves Macarius himself, who came across a skull by the roadside. The skull first introduced himself as belonging to a pagan priest and then identified his interlocutor: "But you are Macarius the Spirit-bearer."[10] Of particular relevance to the present study is the ability of *pneumatophoroi* to pray on behalf of others, which will be explained in greater detail below.

It was crucial to distinguish the true bearers of the Spirit from charlatans and pretenders. How was this done? In the early second century, Hermas suggested: "Evaluate the person who says that he is a bearer of the Spirit, on the basis of his works and his life."[11] The "works" that confirmed the legitimacy of a *pneumatophoros* were usually miracles as the result of intercessory prayer. The "life" of a *pneumatophoros* that lent credence to his spiritual abilities had to show his observance of the scriptures at the very least, and intense ascetic practices at best. The frequent application of *pneumatophoros* to holy men, monastic leaders, and bishops thus begs the question of the interrelation of divine grace and spiritual authority, on the one hand, with personal conduct and ecclesiastical office, on the other.

The bearer of Christ *(christophoros)* is a related concept. While this designation does not apply to the prophets of the Old Testament, who came before Christ, it is frequently used with reference to the apostles and, more generally, all those who are followers of Christ. A spurious letter by Ignatius of Antioch employs both terms in its address: "To Hero, the deacon of Christ, and the servant of God, a man honoured by God, and most dearly loved as well as esteemed, who carries Christ and the Spirit within him *(christophoros kai pneumatophoros)*, and who is mine own in faith and love."[12] In the same, over-arching sense, Athanasius referred to his fellow orthodox Christians as "lovers of Christ and bearers of Christ."[13] More specifically,

8. Palladius, *HL* 11.5 (my translation).
9. Pseudo-Macarius, *Homily* 18.4.7.
10. *Sayings of Macarius the Egyptian* 3.38, *PG* 34, col. 257.
11. *The Shepherd of Hermas*, Mand. 11.16. The noun used is that for "human being," "individual" *(anthrōpos)*, not "man" *(anēr)*, suggesting the possibility that women could also be recognized as Spirit-bearers.
12. Ignatius of Antioch, *Letter to Hero*, address.
13. Athanasius, *Against the Arians* 3.45.

though, the designation "Christ-bearer" was applied to martyrs and holy men whose lives, conduct, and deaths bore witness to their imitation of Christ. "After Christ [came] the Christ-bearers," declared Gregory of Nyssa in his *Encomium on Saint Stephen*.[14] Likewise, the martyrs of the Great Persecution were "Christ-bearers" who were "striving for the greater gifts," according to Phileas of Thmuis.[15] Women, too, could earn this epithet. In a letter attributed to Ignatius of Antioch, the author conveyed greetings "to Mary, my daughter, most faithful, worthy of God, and bearing Christ,"[16] while Gregory Nazianzen used this epithet to praise his mother, Nonna.[17]

While there is some overlap in the meaning and application of "bearers of the Spirit" and "bearers of Christ," it is important to keep in mind what distinguishes these concepts. Spirit-bearers are most prominently, although not exclusively, recognizable because of their teaching and preaching, which is inspired by the Holy Ghost. They can thus be equated with holders of spiritual authority. Christ-bearers are identified as such because they have followed the example of Christ, either in the course of their life, as is the case with ascetics and monks, or through their manner of death, as is the case with martyrs. They thus represent what we have termed ascetic authority. The essential difference between Spirit-bearers and Christ-bearers is that the former exist in a definite state of grace upon which they have no influence, while the latter exist in a tentative state of spiritual distinction that allows for and indeed requires augmentation in the lifelong effort to imitate Christ. To some degree, this conscious and sustained effort of the individual to mold himself or herself after Christ should be the goal of every Christian. John Chrysostom spoke of those "who walk on the Christ-bearing road"[18] and encouraged spiritual leaders to help others in this process: "Let us strive to become fathers of genuine [i.e., spiritual] children, let us be builders of Christ-bearing temples, let us be caretakers of heavenly athletes."[19]

## Gnōstikos *and* Pneumatikos

The need for divinely inspired instruction was especially relevant in the context of the quest for spiritual perfection. Long before the establishment of monastic communities with their well-regulated daily routines, small circles of disciples gathered around their teachers in much the same way as philosophical schools had grown around Plato, Aristotle, and the Neoplatonic

---

14. Gregory of Nyssa, *Encomium on Saint Stephen* 2.
15. Eusebius, *HE* 8.10.3.
16. Ignatius, *Letter to Mary at Neapolis,* address.
17. *Greek Anthology* 8.29.
18. John Chrysostom, *De non iudicando proximo, PG* 60, col. 763.
19. John Chrysostom, *Against the Enemies of the Monastic Life* 3.21.

philosopher Plotinus.[20] The followers of a Christian teacher sought not merely knowledge in matters of faith, but true insight into the divine mysteries, a kind of revelatory participation in the eternal truth. More than that, they desired to transform their lives after the model of Christ. The role of the teacher in this process was paramount. In order to guide others, he first had to have attained perfection himself, often by following his own teacher. The gift of discernment enabled such a teacher to dole out the right portion of insight or to impose the proper amount of practical exercise that fostered the spiritual growth of each disciple according to his abilities and needs. This kind of instruction became extremely popular in Egypt from the late third century. The desert fathers attracted to Egypt individuals from all over the Roman Empire who came to emulate their lifestyle and receive instruction from them. Anthony is the most prominent, but by no means the first, hermit who withdrew to the solitude of the desert and there attracted disciples. Side by side with eremitic monasticism emerged the more formal arrangement of coenobitic, or communal, monasticism, which was pioneered by Pachomius in the 320s. Some of the greatest hermit-teachers lived in the fourth century. Macarius the Egyptian and Didymus the Blind have already been mentioned. To their number should be added Evagrius Ponticus, who will concern us below.

There is a discernible lineage in the thinking about spiritual guidance that begins with Clement of Alexandria in the late second–early third century, moves on to Origen (d. ca. 253), and from him to Evagrius Ponticus (d. 399). They all discuss the qualities of the ideal teacher in some detail. To Clement, the person in a position to provide spiritual instruction is the *gnōstikos*. The word comes from the same root as *gnōsis*, true knowledge of the divine. Knowledge of the divine is coupled with love of divine wisdom. Hence the *gnōstikos* is also the true philosopher (the literal meaning of *philosophia* being "love of wisdom"). Here is Clement's definition of the *gnōstikos* in a nutshell: "Our philosopher holds firmly to these three things: first, contemplation; second, fulfilling the commandments; third, the formation of people of virtue. When these come together they make the Gnostic Christian *[gnōstikos]*."[21] All aspects of the individual are thus involved in being a *gnōstikos:* the soul and the mental capacities in order to attain knowledge of God, the body and the will that governs it in order to observe the teachings of Christ, and a man's social ability to communicate in order to instruct others. Insight, practice, and teaching are intimately linked. The *gnōstikos's* highest goal is to emulate Christ: "It is the Christian Gnostic *[gnōstikos]* who is 'in the image and like-

20. For this trajectory, see R. Reitzenstein, *Historia Monachorum und Historia Lausiaca: Eine Studie zur Geschichte des Mönchtums und der frühchristlichen Begriffe Gnostiker und Pneumatiker* (Göttingen, 1916), 77–124.
21. Clement of Alexandria, *Stromata* 2.10, 46.1. Cf. 7.1, 4.2.

ness,' who imitates God so far as possible, leaving out none of the things which lead to the possible likeness, displaying continence, patience, righteous living, sovereignty over the passions, sharing his possessions so far as he can, doing good in word and deed."[22] According to Clement, every Christian should strive to become a *gnōstikos,* to observe the Christian teachings at all times and in every aspect of his existence.[23]

Yet Clement implicitly acknowledges a gradation in the attainment of *gnōsis* when he discusses those *gnōstikoi* who become teachers of others. It is unthinkable to Clement that the man who has been privileged with divine *gnōsis* would *not* pass his knowledge on to others: "Human beings learn to share as a result of justice; they pass on to others some of what they have received from God out of a natural attitude of kindliness and obedience to the commandments."[24] Just as the *gnōstikos* strives to become "like unto" God, the disciple desires to emulate his teacher. This involves a succession of several steps: faith, knowledge *(gnōsis),* love, and the "heavenly inheritance."[25] The kind of spiritual love that Clement has in mind is a formative process in which the lover's desire for the beloved makes him become like the beloved: "An ignorant man has sought, and having sought, he finds the teacher; and finding has believed, and believing has hoped; and henceforward having loved, is assimilated to what was loved—endeavouring to be what he first loved."[26]

Clement's definition implies not only that the *gnōstikos* is, by his very nature, a teacher, but also that he is, in the truest sense, a priest: "For it is possible even now for those who practice the Lord's commandments, and who live perfectly according to the Gospels and who are *gnōstikoi,* to be registered in the list of the apostles. Such a man is truly a priest of the Church and a veritable servant *(diakonos)* of God's will, when he practices and teaches the things of the Lord; and he is not ordained with the imposition of human hands, neither is he believed to be just, because he is a priest, but rather, he is enlisted in the priesthood because he is just."[27]

Clement here draws a critical distinction between true priests and priests by ordination, a distinction that will continue to trouble the church through the ages. It allows for the possibility that true priests do not receive ordination, while those who are ordained to the priesthood may fall short of the mark for true priests. Both scenarios bear great danger, the former because people with spiritual gifts may operate outside the

22. Ibid., 2.19, 97.1.
23. Ibid., 7.7, 35.1–3.
24. Ibid., 2.16, 73.4.
25. Ibid., 7.10, 55.6.
26. Ibid., 5.3, 17.1.
27. Ibid., 6.12, 106.1 (my translation).

ecclesiastical hierarchy, the latter because the ranks of the clergy may be filled with unworthy men.

Origen, Clement's disciple and later successor as instructor at the catechetical school in Alexandria, was the first Christian theologian to produce commentaries on most of the books of the holy scriptures. In Origen's writings, the perfected Christian is usually called *pneumatikos*, although Origen sometimes also uses Clement's designation *gnōstikos*. As the Greek word *pneuma* means "Holy Spirit," the word *pneumatikos* has its exact correspondence in the English word "spiritual." Origen follows Clement in recognizing the *pneumatikos* as the true Christian.[28] The *pneumatikos* perfects himself through constant study of the scriptures; he practices asceticism in order to increase his spiritual and mental abilities in the same measure as he minimizes attention to the needs of his body; and he demonstrates his state of perfection through his actions. In other words, Origen identifies ascetic living and its visible effects as both the preparation for and the manifestation of spiritual authority. As the *pneumatikos* shares in the divine Spirit and continually lives in its presence, he is a true successor of the apostles; he is equal to the apostles; he is like an angel—indeed, he is a divine man *(theios anēr)* and a friend of God. These laudatory designations will later become a staple of hagiographical literature, applied in the praise of martyrs and saints.

Like Clement before him, Origen distinguishes between clergy by ordination and the "true priests" who, as partakers of the spirit, are imbued with divine authority to fulfill the priestly functions of preaching and teaching, and who can act as physicians of souls. But Origen exhibits greater boldness than his teacher in following this thought to its logical consequence. He proclaims that not only those who are seen to belong to the college of priests, but even more so those who comport themselves in a priestly manner are the true priests of God.[29] He also insists that the man who conforms to the Pauline injunctions about the ideal bishop (presumably those in the First Letter to Timothy) is a bishop not before men, but before God, having attained this rank without the need for ordination by human hands.[30] Such proclamations could easily become the seed of conflict and competition between "true priests" and "priests by ordination." One arena in which this conflict would flare up again and again is that of the formulation of Christian doctrine, when those who claimed to speak with divine authority were confronted by those who claimed to represent the ecclesiastical tradition. The complicated process by which heresy became heresy and ortho-

28. The following is heavily indebted to W. Völker, *Das Vollkommenheitsideal des Origenes: Eine Untersuchung zur Geschichte der Frömmigkeit und zu den Anfängen christlicher Mystik* (Tübingen, 1931), 168–92.
29. Origen, *Homily on Josiah* 9.5.
30. Origen, *Commentary on Matthew* 23.1–12 (comm. series 12).

doxy became orthodoxy need not concern us here. Of greater interest to the present inquiry are Origen's and Clement's "true priests," the *gnōstikoi* and the *pneumatikoi*. They were the holy men of late antiquity. They were the martyrs and the desert fathers who were endowed with special spiritual gifts of teaching, prayer, and miracle working.

There is one further area in which Origen stakes out potentially dangerous ground for conflict, and does so with greater clarity than Clement, and this regards the guidance of souls. One of the paramount tasks of the *pneumatikos*, as a follower of Christ, is to bring sinners to repentance through his love and compassion. This is accomplished not only through teaching and exemplary living, but also in no small degree through admonition. The *pneumatikos* weeps with sinners over their sins, shares the burdens of their misdeeds, prays on their behalf, and assures them of divine forgiveness for their sins. In other words, he exercises in concrete terms the power to bind and loose that Jesus granted to Peter (Matt. 16:18–19). Because the *pneumatikos* is imbued with the same spirit as Peter, he has a claim to the same authority. This, of course, places the *pneumatikos* in direct competition with the bishop, whose penitential authority is based both on the continuity of the institution that he represents and on the moment of ordination when the Spirit was passed on to him. The complex issue of penitential authority will be explored in the following section.

The most influential theorist of spiritual instruction during the flourishing of Egyptian monasticism in the fourth century was Evagrius Ponticus. He composed an entire treatise entitled *Gnōstikos*. Evagrius himself had chosen the life of a hermit in the Egyptian desert in a sudden and radical departure from the world. The son of a *chorepiscopus* from the Pontus region south of the Black Sea, Evagrius had been ordained as a lector by Basil of Caesarea, and as a deacon by Gregory of Nazianzus, whom he accompanied to Constantinople. His reputation and popularity in the capital received a harsh blow when he developed a strong and insuppressible affection for a married woman of the nobility. Guilt-ridden and encouraged by a dream vision, Evagrius made a hasty departure for Egypt. He lived there as a hermit for sixteen years, first in Nitria and then in Kellia, until his death in 399. Evagrius was equally famous for his ascetic practices as for his teaching. One of his disciples was Palladius of Helenopolis, who devoted a whole chapter of his *Lausiac History* to him. Evagrius's thought was greatly influenced by Origen, and thus indirectly also by Clement.

Two centuries after Clement had declared that every Christian should strive to be a *gnōstikos*, Evagrius addressed the limited and self-selected circle of monks who made the attainment of *gnōsis* their life's goal. Evagrius's writing gives a concrete locus to the quest for *gnōsis:* it now becomes firmly anchored in the monastic environment. His lasting influence on monastic philosophy can hardly be overestimated. His ideas also laid the foundation for a potential competition between monks and clergy over the possession and administration of the Spirit. If, as Evagrius intends, the monk strives to be a *gnōstikos*, and if, as Clement and Origen have argued, the *gnōstikos* is also a true priest, this opens the door for the monastic rejection of the institutional clergy and the services it has to offer, especially the eucharistic liturgy. Some instances of this attitude and the attempts to contain it will be discussed below.

To offset these theoretical treatments by Clement, Origen, and Evagrius, it is useful to look briefly at a concrete description of a *pneumatikos*. The spiritual teacher in question is none other than Origen. The work in his praise was composed by his disciple Gregory the Wonder-worker. The *Address of Thanksgiving to Origen* is Gregory's farewell speech to his beloved teacher, delivered in Caesarea in Palestine at the end of his studies in the presence of other students and Origen himself. It depicts Origen as the true *pneumatikos* who has the power to transform the lives of those who become his followers. Gregory had experienced this in person. True to the social standing of his family as part of the local nobility in Cappadocian Pontus, he had received an extensive education in the traditional vein, and was on his way to acquire further qualifications in jurisprudence in Berytus, when he met Origen in a chance encounter in Caesarea, where the latter was teaching at the time. Gregory immediately fell under the spell of Origen's eloquent teaching and profound erudition, gave up all prospects for the career in the civil service for which he had been so carefully groomed, and dedicated himself to a life of Christian study. After five years in the classroom of Origen, he returned to Neocaesarea, where he led a monastic existence together with a few like-minded friends. It did not take long until the local community and the neighboring bishops recognized Gregory's talents and he was made bishop of his city, a position he held for at least two decades until his death, which occurred sometime between 270 and 275. Gregory's career follows a pattern that would become typical in the fourth century: a son of the provincial upper crust who is groomed for a position of civic leadership then adopts the monastic life, only to be recruited into a leadership role within the church. His *Address of Thanksgiving* presents Origen as a larger-than-life figure, whose sanctity radiated to all those around him, including Gregory himself, who probably found this speech a convenient literary vehicle to stake his own claim to holiness by association with his revered teacher.

According to Gregory, Origen "looks and seems like a human being but, to those in a position to observe the finest flower of his disposition, has already completed most of the preparation for the re-ascent to the divine world."[31] In their first encounter, Origen displayed the gift of discernment in teaching for which the desert fathers would become famous: "We were

31. Gregory the Wonder-worker, *Address of Thanksgiving to Origen* 2 (10).

pierced as by a dart by his discourse even from the first."[32] His teaching was carefully tailored to suit the needs of his disciples, as Gregory explains by invoking the metaphor of his own soul as a rocky and overgrown field that first needed to be tilled to ensure that the seeds of Origen's wisdom fell on prepared soil.[33] Being with Origen afforded his disciples a foretaste of paradise.[34] To them, Origen's personal example was as eloquent a lesson as his words, for he refused to lecture on anything that he did not himself strive to put into practice.[35] Origen had attained such a level of intellectual acuity and purity that he could communicate matters of the Spirit directly and unsullied by the sluggishness of his own mind. Gregory expresses his boundless admiration:

> He [Origen] is the only living person whom I have either met myself or heard others tell about who could do this, who had trained himself to receive the purity and brightness of the sayings into his own soul, and to teach others, because the Leader [i.e., Jesus, or the divine *Logos*] of them all, who speaks within God's friends the prophets, and prompts every prophecy and mystical, divine discourse, so honored him as a friend as to establish him as his spokesman.[36]

As his oration winds down to a tearful close, and Gregory professes to be bracing himself for his return to the cares of the world, he asks one last thing of his teacher: "But you, our beloved head, arise and send us off now with prayer. As you saved us by your holy instruction during our stay, save us also by your prayers as we depart."[37] A true *pneumatikos* in the eyes of his devoted disciple, Origen passed on the divine Spirit through word and deed and inspired others to follow his example. In addition to his instruction, his prayers are also valued and sought after. This ability to pray connects the figure of the *pneumatikos,* who is prominent in the theological literature of the second and third centuries, with the holy men of the fourth century and beyond, who are known to us through documentary and hagiographical sources. These men will concern us next.

### SPIRITUAL LEADERSHIP AND PRAYER

In their strict asceticism and inspired teaching, the desert fathers of the fourth century claimed their place as heirs of the *pneumatophoroi* of early

32. Ibid., 6 (78).
33. Ibid., 7 (93)–7 (99).
34. Ibid., 15 (183).
35. Ibid., 11 (135).
36. Ibid., 15 (175–76).
37. Ibid., 19 (204).

Christianity.[38] The true *pneumatophoros* in whom the Spirit overflows is always also a teacher. His teaching, however, is different from that of the preacher who regularly addresses a large gathering of people in his homilies. The *pneumatophoros* instructs his disciples individually or in small groups, both by giving them words to contemplate and live by and by his example. Spiritual guidance is the foundation of monastic spirituality as it first took shape in Egypt and then spread to Palestine and beyond.[39] The desert fathers who had left civilization behind in order to concentrate on a life of meditation and prayer soon attracted visitors who wanted to partake of their wisdom. Groups of disciples clustered around the "Old Men," some staying for a few months before moving on to be inspired by another Old Man or returning to the world, others remaining for a lifetime. The sharing of the Spirit thus generated the nucleus of monastic communities joined in the common pursuit of personal perfection. The Spirit that was channeled through an Old Man could radiate even beyond his inner circle of disciples to the laypeople who simply wanted to reap the benefits of being loosely associated with him, but without making a dramatic change in their lives.

The activity that gives purpose and cohesion to these followers of a holy man—both the inner circle of monastic disciples and the outer circle of laypeople—is prayer. The ability to intercede for others before God is one of the distinctive marks of the spiritual individual, as will become clear in the following. The Greek term for this ability is *parrhēsia*, which literally means "the freedom to say everything" and is best translated "boldness of speech." *Parrhēsia* is the common ground where the spiritual abilities of the *pneumatophoros* and the miraculous powers of the holy man overlap. For what else are miracles if not the result of successful intercessory prayer? This function of the holy man has not been sufficiently appreciated until recently and therefore deserves to be treated in some detail here.

Intercessory prayer is of vital importance in joining a spiritual father to his followers and vice versa. It is, as it were, the daily bread of their interaction. Spectacular miracles may sometimes be the result, but those are more like the icing on the cake. Essentially sensationalist in their approach, the hagiographers of late antiquity tend to overemphasize miracles. Their accounts are carefully crafted literary productions with the purpose of lionizing a particular holy man. Closer to the original setting of this interaction through personal conversation are the actual letters exchanged between a

---

38. Reitzenstein, *Historia Monachorum und Historia Lausiaca;* P. Nagel, *Die Motivierung der Askese in der alten Kirche und der Ursprung des Mönchtums* (Berlin, 1966), 69–75.

39. For general background, see D. H. Chitty, *The Desert a City: An Introduction to the Study of Egyptian and Palestinian Monasticism under the Christian Empire* (Oxford, 1966); for a concise introduction, see M. Dunn, *The Emergence of Monasticism: From the Desert Fathers to the Early Middle Ages* (Oxford, 2000), 1–81.

holy man and his followers. In some instances, the actual papyri or ostraca bearing such letters have survived; in other cases, we depend on the later compilation by an editor of the correspondence of a holy man. This kind of documentary evidence provides a useful corrective to hagiographical writing because it is largely unadulterated by literary embellishments. It gives us actual snapshots of a spiritual leader at work. What emerges from these texts with great clarity is the existence of prayer communities, centered around one or several holy men, which are conceptualized in kinship terms as a family of "brothers," "sons," and "fathers." In view of the frequent emphasis, in the sources and in modern scholarship alike, on the towering importance of the holy man within his community, it is perhaps surprising to note that these people offer prayers on behalf of each other. It is not only the holy man who prays for his followers, but his correspondents also offer up prayers for him. Still, they readily acknowledge and anticipate that the holy man's prayers are more efficacious than theirs in bringing forth miraculous relief of all kinds of ills and ailments. In their view, there is a direct connection between the personal conduct, possession of virtues, and ascetic lifestyle of their "father" and the efficacy of his intercession, echoing the connection made by Clement, Origen, and others between spiritual gifts and ascetic living.

There are four clusters of such correspondence of living holy men from late antique Egypt, and an additional one from sixth-century Palestine.[40] The Egyptian letters are documentary in character in that they are autographs, written by the authors on papyrus or pottery shards; the correspondence from Palestine has been subject to minimal editorial revision and was circulated in manuscript form. The earliest holy man to have engaged in such correspondence was Paphnutius, who lived in the mid-fourth century. Eight letters addressed to him survive. Most of his correspondents asked for Paphnutius's prayers, sometimes offering their own prayers on his behalf, [41] always using the standard formulae that are the staple of late antique epistolography.[42] Some asked with a specific intention, hoping to obtain divine favor in illness or other tribulation through Paphnutius's intercession.[43] The

---

40. For a more detailed treatment of these texts, see C. Rapp, "'For Next to God, You Are My Salvation': Reflections on the Rise of the Holy Man in Late Antiquity," in *The Cult of Saints in Late Antiquity and the Middle Ages: Essays on the Contribution of Peter Brown*, ed. J. Howard-Johnston and P. A. Hayward (Oxford, 1999).

41. *Jews and Christians in Egypt: The Jewish Troubles in Alexandria and the Athanasian Controversy*, ed. and trans. H. I. Bell (London, 1924), pp. 100–120; nos. 1923, 1924, 1925, 1926, 1928, 1929 [= PJews].

42. PJews 1924, 1925, 1927, 1929. On requests for or assurances of prayer as epistolographic conventions, see H. Koskenniemi, *Studien zur Geschichte und Phraseologie des griechischen Briefes bis 400 n. Chr.* (Helsinki, 1956), 134–37 and 147–48.

43. Letter by Athanasius: PJews 1929. See also PJews 1926, 1928.

establishment of personal relations and the exchange of prayers are to be expected in the context of spiritual guidance in the monastic milieu. Paphnutius's correspondents, however, were not monastic apprentices, but pious people who lived in the world, such as the woman Valeria, the prefect of Augustamnica Ausonius, and perhaps even the patriarch of Alexandria.[44] Equally surprising is that some of the prayer requests asked for Paphnutius's intercession not for a particularly concrete benefit, but on behalf of the sins of his correspondents. Ammonius, for instance, wrote: "I always know that by your holy prayers I shall be saved from every temptation of the Devil and from every contrivance of men, and now I beg you to remember me in your holy prayers; for after God you are my salvation."[45]

The boundless confidence of Paphnutius's correspondents in the efficacy of his prayers was expressed by a certain Athanasius, who may be identical with the patriarch of Alexandria of the same name: "For the prayers which you offer are taken on high owing to your holy love, and according as you ask in your holy prayers so will our state prosper."[46] This mention of Paphnutius's "holy love" indicates that, in the perception of his correspondents, the efficacy of his prayers was directly linked to his spiritual state. In the words of Justinus, another of Paphnutius's correspondents: "For we believe that your citizenship is in heaven, and therefore we regard you as our master and common patron."[47] Valeria declared: "I trust by your prayers to obtain healing, for by ascetics and devotees revelations are manifested."[48] She addressed Paphnutius as *christophoros,* Christ-bearer, a designation that—as has been noted above—was often used for ascetics and holy men who through their life and conduct had acquired certain gifts of the Spirit. Another correspondent was confident that he could depend upon Paphnutius "by reason of your most glorious and most revered way of life, since you renounced the boasting of the world and abhorred the arrogance of the vainglorious . . . because God in abundant measure, it seems, granted you favour to find a fitting and salutary renunciation accordant with the times."[49] The letters addressed to Paphnutius thus show us with a concreteness and immediacy that is often lacking in the polished literary products of this

---

44. PJews 1923–29. To this group should perhaps be added the letter by Justinus to Paphnutius, *PHeid* 1 (1905) 6 = *Die Septuaginta-Papyri und andere altchristliche Texte der Heidelberger Payrus-Sammlung,* ed. A. Deissmann (Heidelberg, 1905); also reproduced in M. Naldini, *Il Cristianesimo in Egitto: Lettere private nei papiri dei secoli II–IV* (Florence, 1968), no. 41. Valeria: PJews 1926; Ausonius: PJews 1924, with Bell, 100; Athanasius: PJews 1929, with Bell, 115–18.

45. PJews 1923. Similarly, PJews 1925 and *PHeid* 1 (1905) 6 = Naldini 41.

46. PJews 1929. See also PJews 1926 and 1928.

47. *PHeid* 1 (1905) 6 = Naldini 41 (my translation). The text is uncertain.

48. PJews 1926.

49. PJews 1927.

period that there was a shared conviction about the dependence of efficacious intercessory prayer on personal conduct. Paphnutius's correspondents confirm from a grass-roots perspective what the theologians discussed in the previous section had formulated in the abstract: that an elevated spiritual state is both a gift from God and a reward for ascetic efforts.

This nexus between intercessory abilities and asceticism is also evident in the letters addressed to other holy men: Nepheros, a holy man who lived in the mid-fourth century in the Herakleopolite nome of Egypt,[50] received a letter from one of his numerous correspondents saying that because Nepheros was "just," his prayers would be heard by God.[51] More telling is the correspondence of the hermit John in the region of Hermopolis. [52] One of the three letters addressed to him is a request for prayers on behalf of the author and his whole household. The author called John a "man of God" and expressed his hope that just as John's prayers had relieved him in the past of a great "burden," they would continue to do so in the future.[53] It has been suggested that the "burden" may have been an onerous labor or an illness, [54] but it may also, in my view, refer to the burden of sins that weighed on the conscience of John's correspondent. Those who had spiritual authority were often expected to intercede specifically for sinners, as the next chapter will show.

The most ample documentation for the concrete worries and prayer needs of a large group of followers is offered by the several hundred papyri and ostraca of limestone and pottery, dating from the turn of the seventh century, which were found at the monastery of Epiphanius at Thebes. Epiphanius was only one of several holy men to whom letters and prayer requests were addressed, albeit the most prominent one. Often, the letter writers specified their concerns. They either asked the "fathers" for help from the torment of their sins[55] or they hoped to obtain more concrete benefits, such as the restoration of health in sickness.[56] The men and wo-

50. B. Kramer, J. C. Shelton, and G. M. Browne, *Das Archiv des Nepheros und verwandte Texte* (Mainz, 1987), 3. For a fine-tuning of the dating of the archive, to around 352, see R. S. Bagnall, "Fourth-Century Prices: New Evidence and Further Thoughts," *ZPE* 76 (1989): 74–75.

51. *Ep.* 1.

52. *PHerm* Rees 7–10 = *Papyri from Hermopolis*, ed. with translations and notes by B. R. Rees (London, 1964), pp. 12–20; reproduced in Naldini 82–85.

53. *PHerm* Rees 8 = Naldini 83.

54. See *Nepheros Archiv*, 22 n. 1.

55. *The Monastery of Epiphanius at Thebes*, pt. 2, *Coptic Ostraka and Papyri*, by W. E. Crum, and *Greek Ostraka and Papyri*, by H. G. Evelyn White (New York, 1926; repr., 1973), e.g., letters 129, 199, 279. For the historical context of this monastic institution, see pt. 1, *The Archaeological Material*, by H. E. Winlock (New York, 1926; repr., 1973).

56. Letters 144, 246, 250, 329, 359.

men who approached Epiphanius and his fellow ascetics were emphatic and explicit in their belief that these men were holy and possessed the power of intercession. They were convinced that the exemplary ascetic lifestyle of these holy men assured their prayers being heard by God. Acknowledging these men's privileged connection to the divine, they often praised them for having perfected all virtues[57] and addressed them as *christophoroi*.[58] It was only through the mediation and intercession of these holy men that the letter writers hoped for access to God. The extent to which the supplicants depended on the holy men is expressed in terms such as these: "I have set my heart upon thy fatherhood next after God" or "I have no helper beside God and thee."[59]

The Egyptian papyri and ostraca support three important points. First, living holy men of the fourth century were considered "bearers of Christ," thus continuing to make manifest in a tangible way the tradition regarding *christophoroi* and *pneumatophoroi* that Clement and Origen had expounded in the preceding centuries in more abstract terms. Second, in the eyes of the petitioners who address the holy men there is a direct dependence between personal conduct, specifically an ascetic lifestyle, and the efficaciousness of intercessory prayer. Third, the prayers of these holy men are sought for spiritual tribulations, especially the burden of sins, in addition to physical ailments and similar such concerns.

The need for spiritual assurance continues to be a concern even as we move on in time. It is also very pronounced in the correspondence of Barsanuphius and John, two holy men who lived near Gaza on the coast of Palestine, during the first two decades of the sixth century. The corpus of their correspondence consists of 850 letters that they dictated in response to the queries and requests addressed to them.[60] These letters were subjected to some editorial touch-ups before being circulated in manuscript form. They thus lack the direct immediacy of the papyri and ostraca from Egypt, but their documentary character is still significantly greater than that of the literary hagiographical production of the same period. The correspondents of Barsanuphius and John represented a cross section of society: pious laypeople, philosophy professors, and military leaders, as well as priests, bishops, and monks. Besides concrete concerns such as how best to deal with an infestation of grasshoppers[61] or whether it is appropriate to

---

57. *Ep.* 130, 164, 184, 319, 359, 473, 483.
58. *Ep.* 133, 142, 144, 180, 261, 306, 315, 474, 515.
59. *Ep.* 192 and 271.
60. Barsanuphe et Jean de Gaza, *Correspondance*, ed. F. Neyt and P. De Angelis-Noah, SCh 426, 427, 450, 451, 468 (Paris, 1977–2002). For a detailed treatment of this rich body of material, see the forthcoming book by Jennifer Hevelone-Harper.
61. *Ep.* 684.

share one's winepress with a Jewish neighbor,[62] many of the correspondents asked for guidance in spiritual matters. The *Letters of Barsanuphius and John* highlight how spiritual guidance is connected with personal holiness, and they clarify a further aspect that is of great importance for the present investigation: the holy men's ability to "bear the burden" of others.

The forty-nine letters that Barsanuphius wrote to his disciple John of Beersheba show his full awareness of his personal responsibilities as a spiritual adviser.[63] Especially striking is his willingness to lend support to his disciples and fellow monks by shouldering part of the share that has fallen to them. Barsanuphius spoke about himself with a confidence bordering on boastfulness that is otherwise present only when hagiographers write about others. He instructed John to regard him as a role model and to follow in his footsteps, held by his hand.[64] In his last letter in the sequence to John, Barsanuphius looked back on their correspondence, asserting that he had given John a complete course of instruction, from the novitiate to perfection. John should meditate on his words as a means to his personal salvation, for they contain the Old and the New Testament.[65] Barsanuphius knew and let it be known that he was the channel through which the divine *logos* was communicated to John.

Barsanuphius also maintained relationships with other fellow monks.[66] One of them, Euthymius, confidently expected to be buried in the same tomb as Barsanuphius. He was certain that, on the Day of Judgment, the Old Man's abundant good deeds would also be counted in his own favor.[67] In other words, Barsanuphius's ample stock of virtues was expected to compensate for any deficiencies on the part of Euthymius.

A further fifty-one letters of correspondence between Andrew and Barsanuphius and John the Prophet, the holy man's closest associate and author of some of the letters in the collection, highlight Barsanuphius's ability to convey the certainty of God's forgiveness of sins and his willingness to shoulder part of his brothers' sins.[68] Andrew was a complainer. Plagued by a chronic illness and irritated by the "brother" who lived with him, he was anxious about his inability to fast, troubled by his unkind thoughts toward his cell mate, and concerned about these impediments to his spiritual progress. Barsanuphius sent him numerous letters of assurance, promising

---

62. *Ep.* 686.
63. He cannot be identical with John the Prophet, the author of many letters in the collection, since both are mentioned in *Ep.* 3 and 9.
64. *Ep.* 22, 31.
65. *Ep.* 49.
66. *Ep.* 59–71.
67. *Ep.* 60; cf. 69.
68. *Ep.* 72–123.

to pray for him, invoking their spiritual unity, and expressing his desire to take Andrew to heaven with him.[69] Like Euthymius, who in his request for his burial arrangement hoped on the Day of Judgment to benefit from the abundance of Barsanuphius's good deeds, Andrew was assured that he could depend on the Old Man's pledge to carry half of his burdens.[70] But Andrew was not to remain passive. He was expected to bear the full weight of the remaining half. Barsanuphius not only asserted that his prayers would sustain Andrew in times of tribulation;[71] he even had the confidence to announce that, through him, Christ assured Andrew of the complete remission of all his sins from the time of his birth to the present.[72] Barsanuphius's and John's entire correspondence with their fellow monks is permeated by the idea that a fraternal relationship based on mutual prayer and the bearing of each other's burdens provides a safeguard against the dangers on the path to perfection and a remedy against the punishment that follows sin. Barsanuphius often encouraged his associates by quoting Galatians 6:2 ("Bear one another's burdens, and in this way you will fulfill the law of Christ") and Proverbs 18:19 ("A brother who is assisted by a brother is like a strong and fortified city").[73]

The *Letters of Barsanuphius and John* forcefully underscore the crucial importance of prayer in shaping the interaction between a holy man and his followers. More specifically, the prayers that were most valued were those for the lightening of the burden of one's sins. The efficacy of Barsanuphius's prayer was directly linked to the intensity of the asceticism he practiced. His virtues had reached such a level that he could share their benefits with others, making up for their deficiencies as if from a well-stocked bank account of good deeds. This confluence of asceticism, intercessory prayer, and the ability to alleviate the burden of the sins of others distinguished the holy men and monastic leaders who were *pneumatophoroi* from other Christians, and which attracted admirers, followers, and disciples. Assistance to sinners, however, was not given by these outstanding individuals alone. It was also one of the main tasks of the bishop.

### CARRYING THE BURDENS OF OTHERS' SINS

The complex ways in which spiritual authority, ascetic authority, and pragmatic authority at times intersect, at other times overlap, and at yet other times are in competition are brought into focus through consideration of

69. Esp. *Ep.* 93, 96, 105, 113, 118.
70. *Ep.* 73.
71. *Ep.* 105, 107.
72. *Ep.* 115.
73. My translation of the Septuagint text.

the alleviation of one man's sin by another. We need not be concerned here with the difficult collateral issues of man's ability to sin, the nature of sin itself, and the distinctions between capital and other sins, nor will we deal with the development of penitential discipline in the church. The question is this: What exactly are the personal qualities of the man who has the ability to assure others that their sins are forgiven and who can alleviate others of the burden of their sins?[74]

### The Role of Monks and Hermits

The cleansing of all sins was provided through the Christian initiation ritual of baptism. The full-body immersion into the baptismal waters brought complete purification and signaled a new birth in the Spirit. The adults who sought baptism thereby indicated their willingness to undergo a complete transformation of their spiritual state and to adjust their lifestyle in accordance with the teaching of the church.[75] An analogous decision to lead an even more intensified Christian life was entry into the monastic state. Any sins committed in this state weigh that much more heavily. This view of monasticism was not formulated until monastic life was institutionalized and the ritual of monastic initiation was regularized. Pseudo-Dionysius the Areopagite, the elusive author of the early sixth century who posed as the disciple of Paul known from Acts 17:34, was the first to attribute sacramental character to monastic consecration by a priest when he called it a *mysterion*.[76] He also gave voice to the concept of entry into the monastic life as a second baptism, which became popular in the religious literature of Byzantium.[77] The analogy with baptism is enforced by the fact that the newly initiated monk received a new name and that he had a spon-

---

74. The following owes much to the studies of J. Hörmann (*Untersuchungen zur griechischen Laienbeicht: Ein Beitrag zur allgemeinen Bussgeschichte* [Donauwörth, 1913]) and K. Holl (*Enthusiasmus und Bussgewalt beim griechischen Mönchtum: Eine Studie zu Symeon dem Neuen Theologen* [Leipzig, 1898; repr., Hildesheim, 1969]). For an excellent introduction to the complex issues associated with penance and intercessory prayer, including art historical evidence, see E. Dassmann, *Sündenvergebung durch Taufe, Busse und Martyrerfürbitte in den Zeugnissen frühchristlicher Frömmigkeit und Kunst* (Münster, 1973), esp. 103–82.

75. Infant baptism did not become the norm until Christianity had gained a firm foothold in late Roman society, beginning in the late fourth/early fifth century.

76. Ps.-Dionysius Areopagita, *Ecclesiastical Hierarchy* 6.2.

77. P. Oppenheim, "Mönchsweihe und Taufritus: Ein Kommentar zur Auslegung bei Dionysius dem Areopagiten," in *Miscellanea liturgica in honorem L. Cuniberti Mohlberg*, vol. 1 (Rome, 1948). See also G. Constable, "The Ceremonies and Symbolism of Entering Religious Life and Taking the Monastic Habit, from the Fourth to the Twelfth Century," in *Segni e riti nella chiesa altomedievale occidentale*, XXXIII Settimane di Studio del Centro Italiano di Studi sull'Alto Medioevo (Spoleto, 1987). Holl, 205ff. Jerome notes that when the recently deceased Blesilla had taken her vow of perpetual virginity, this was tantamount to a second baptism: *Ep.* 39.3–4.

sor *(anadochos)* who fulfilled the same ritual role as the godfather at baptism, vouching with his own good reputation for the postulant.[78] The seventh-century *Life of Symeon the Fool* gives vivid expression to this idea. On the eve of their admission into the monastic life, Symeon and his companion John were told by their future brethren: "Blessed are you, for tomorrow you will be reborn and become pure from all sin, as when you were born, as if on the day you were baptized."[79] In the true manner of fools, the postulants take this comment literally and begin to fret at the prospect of receiving baptism a second time, re-baptism being strictly prohibited by the church.

### *The Spiritual Guide and the Penitent Monk*

The monastic state is usually presented as a state of real or intended absence of sin in thought and in deed. As I shall argue below, monasticism can also be conceived as a state of extended penance to obliterate existing sin. The early hermits and monks made every effort through their *askēsis* to attain physical and mental purity. They adopted a regimen of limited food intake, reduced sleep, extended periods of prayer and meditation, combined with manual labor to provide for their upkeep. The physical exertions of hermits and monks were not a goal in themselves but were meant to increase their spiritual abilities. Asceticism was a tool to achieve spiritual growth. Hermits and monks subjected their bodies to a lifetime of ever more demanding physical rigors. The duration of their ascetic efforts set them in contrast to the martyrs whose bodily suffering was compressed into the short period of time prior to their execution. In this way, those who lived the monastic life, whether in solitude or in a community, became the successors of the martyrs, once the Edict of Milan (312) had declared an end to the persecutions and thereby removed the opportunities for dramatic singular acts of martyrdom.[80] Saint Anthony set the example for this when he translated his disappointment at being passed over for martyrdom in the Great Persecution into the resolve to subject himself to a "daily martyrdom" in his conscience.[81] Parallel to Anthony's "daily martyrdom" as a solitary in the desert was the "continual martyrdom" of Pachomius, who pioneered monastic life in a communal setting. His disciple and successor Theodore affirmed that Pachomius had after his death joined the saints, apostles, prophets, and

---

78. *Life of Stephen the Younger* 21. For further references to later authors, see Holl, 206–9.
79. Leontius of Neapolis, *Life of Symeon the Fool*, p. 65.
80. E. Malone, *The Monk and the Martyr: The Monk as Successor of the Martyr*, Catholic University of America, Studies in Christian Antiquity 12 (Washington, D.C., 1950).
81. *Life of Anthony* 47.1. The concept of "daily martyrdom" had already been formulated, however, by Tertullian and Clement before him.

martyrs in heaven, "because he was at all times a martyr, through hunger, thirst, and vigils."[82]

The control of the body through ascetic practices was intended to create the conditions for mental and spiritual growth. Striving for perfection was a continuous process. More advanced monks were therefore in a position to provide guidance as spiritual fathers for younger, less experienced apprentices. Their role was analogous to that of the philosopher who acted as a teacher and guide for his disciples, as Pierre Hadot has so beautifully shown.[83] The spiritual guide acted like the *pneumatophoroi* who were discussed earlier. He was able to offer guidance to others because he had attained certain spiritual qualities: the discernment between good and evil thoughts in himself and in others, the gift of immediate recognition of the causes of a troubled soul, and the ability to gauge accurately the degree to which a young disciple needed to be challenged to stimulate his growth, without the risk of breaking him.[84] In the context of eremitic monasticism, the spiritual father was the person to whom the disciple bared his soul and made full confession of his sins and of the thoughts that troubled him, in order to receive words of encouragement and concrete advice on the most effective way to ameliorate his current tribulation. The ultimate aim of the intervention of the spiritual father was to facilitate the reconciliation of the disciple with God, so that the the disciple could attain a state of spiritual tranquility. It was often the prayers of the spiritual father that assisted the disciple in this process. Barsanuphius, who, as we have seen, was willing to shoulder the burdens of his disciples, acted in such a way through his promises to his disciples.

In the communal monastic setting of the *coenobia* the reconciliation of the younger monk who had strayed from the path to perfection and had committed a sin was directed not only toward God, but also toward the community. The individual who had separated himself from the community through his impious actions and his impure thoughts was assisted by his

---

82. Theodore, *Laudatio on the Deceased Pachomius*, ed. E. Amélineau, in *Monuments pour servir à l'histoire de l'Égypte chrétienne au IV siècle: Histoire de saint Pakhôme et de ses communautés*, Annales du Musée Guimet 17/2 (Paris, 1889), 650.

83. P. Hadot, "The Spiritual Guide," in *Classical Mediterranean Spirituality*, ed. A. H. Armstrong (New York, 1986).

84. There is an extensive literature on spiritual guidance and "fatherhood." Especially relevant are I. Hausherr, *Spiritual Direction in the Early Christian East* (Kalamazoo, 1990; first published in French, 1955); A. Louf, "Spiritual Fatherhood in the Literature of the Desert," in *Abba: Guides to Wholeness and Holiness East and West*, ed. J. R. Sommerfeldt, Cistercian Studies Series 38 (Kalamazoo, 1982); K. T. Ware, "The Spiritual Father in St. John Climacus and St. Symeon the New Theologian," in *Studia Patristica* XVIII/2, *Papers of the 1983 Oxford Patristics Conference*, ed. E. A. Livingstone (Kalamazoo and Louvain, 1989); and J. Chryssavgis, *Soul Mending: The Art of Spiritual Direction* (Brookline, 2000), 49–58.

spiritual father in the monastery in making amends for his misdeeds, often by undergoing some kind of punishment. This kind of discipline was commonly practiced already in the Pachomian monasteries and was also advocated by Basil of Caesarea for his monastic foundation. The Byzantine monastic tradition has continued to value such spiritual guidance and kept it separate from administrative responsibility. The former was entrusted to one or several Old Men or spiritual fathers; the latter was the task of the abbot. The spiritual father performed in the monastic context, whether eremitic or coenobitic, the same function as the priest or bishop in his congregation: he heard confession, prayed for the sinner, and imposed penance. In this manner, he facilitated the renewed access of the individual to God, and brokered his readmission into the community of his brothers.

## Monasticism as a State of Penance

Penance and prayer were essential components of the monastic life. These aspects of the monastic life have not been sufficiently explored in scholarship, obscured as they have been by an emphasis on the Christian continuation of pagan and Jewish asceticism that is perhaps most obvious in the voluntary abstinence from food, sex, and sleep.[85] But a closer look at the penitential practices of the Christian church in the first centuries shows remarkable similarities with what are usually thought of as ascetic practices of the monks. In his treatise *On Penance*, written in 203/204, about seven years after his baptism, Tertullian explained the meaning of the Greek word *exomologēsis*, which encompasses aspects of confession, public declarations of regret and repentance, and propitiation of the community and the clergy, all in the hope of attracting the mercy of God's forgiveness:

> And thus *exomologesis* is a discipline for man's prostration and humiliation, enjoining a demeanor calculated to move mercy. With regard also to the very dress and food, it commands (the penitent) to lie in sackcloth and ashes, to cover his body in mourning, to lay his spirit low in sorrows, to exchange for severe treatment the sins which he has committed; moreover, to know no food and drink but such as is plain, not for the stomach's sake, to wit, but the soul's; for the most part, however, to feed prayers on fastings, to groan, to weep and make outcries unto the Lord your God; to bow before the feet of the presbyters, and kneel to God's dear ones; to enjoin on all the brethren to be ambassadors to bear his deprecatory supplication (before God).[86]

85. Nagel, 62 and passim, refers to the "asketische Bussleistung" of the early monks but does not develop this thought any further; it is also implicit in Oppenheim.
86. Tertullian, *On Penitence* 9.3–4.

Tertullian was the first author to lay out in such detail the actions expected of the penitent. For the purposes of this study, it is irrelevant whether each and every one of the practices he described were particular to the church of Carthage or whether they were more widespread. The most prominent acts he enumerates continue to be mentioned in the context of penance throughout our period and beyond: fasting, the wearing of sackcloth, weeping, and confession. In addition to the practices that literally reshaped the outward appearance of the penitent sinner, it was often also advised that he or she engage in the giving of alms, an activity that contributed to the wellbeing of the symbolical "body of Christ" as represented by his church. Origen indicates seven different ways that are open to Christians for the remission of sins. In descending order, these are baptism, martyrdom, almsgiving, forgiveness of the sins of one's neighbor, assisting a sinner in mending his ways, abundance of charity, and finally penance through the shedding of abundant tears and confession to a priest.[87] These penitential practices were recommended for the sinners in the churches of the cities and towns of the Roman Empire. But is it important to note that they were also part of the daily routine of the monks who lived in the seclusion of a monastery and especially of those who had withdrawn to the solitude of the desert. Penitential asceticism was a spiritual necessity for the individual who felt the burden of his sinfulness, but its effects could radiate beyond its practitioner. The Bohairic *Life of Pachomius,* which celebrates the foundation of communal monasticism by Pachomius and his disciples, made this point very eloquently, showing that the founder's penitential practices of fasting and prayer, even if they were performed behind monastery walls, were directed toward the benefit of others: Hearing reports of a famine and an epidemic, Pachomius fasted and prayed for the duration of the crisis, and then took the additional preventive measure of praying for the swelling of the Nile to assure an ample harvest. This passage is followed by a very extensive description of how "when he [Pachomius] prayed he would pray for the whole world in kind," asking God for the needs of monks, married people, sinners, pagans and heretics, rulers, and the clergy.[88] We will have occasion further below to observe such all-embracing generosity in prayer for the whole world on the part of other holy men and also of martyrs.

The practice of Christian asceticism in our period is loaded with admissions of sinfulness and the need for repentance. In the words of one of the desert fathers, Abba Matoes, "The nearer a man draws to God, the more he sees himself a sinner."[89] This is not limited to the prominent practitioners of

87. Origen, *Homily on Leviticus* 2.4.
88. *Life of Pachomius* (Bohairic) 100–101.
89. *Sayings of the Desert Fathers,* Matoes 2.

the holy life with their spectacular feats of physical endurance. The penitential intention behind ascetic practices was evident in communal as much
as in eremitic monasticism. By the mid-fourth century, repentance *(metanoia)* had been integrated into the annual liturgical cycle of monastic communities in Middle Egypt, where, as Tim Vivian has recently shown, the
monks gathered every year for a day of ritual prostrations and prayer. [90] At
the end of the fourth century, the newly founded Pachomian monastery at
Canopus near Alexandria was given the name Metanoia. The name was
intended to invoke the association of purification with repentance, for the
monastery was built directly above a former pagan site.[91] Still in the early seventh century, John Climacus noted the existence of a monastery on the
Sinai especially for the penitent. These were not necessarily men with a
heavy conscience or even a criminal record, such as Moses the Robber, one
of the more colorful figures in the *Sayings of the Desert Fathers,* but monks who
had made repentance for their sinful state their personal vocation.[92] Farther
away, in the Tur Abdin area of Mesopotamia during the fifth and sixth centuries, "the mourners" developed their own kind of asceticism with an
emphasis on personal penitence.

The outward appearance of the desert hermits as the result of their
asceticism—the parched and emaciated body, the long and matted hair, the
ragged cloak, the piercing eyes—was the externally visible affirmation of
their internal self-consciousness as penitent sinners. In addition to fasting,
vigils, meditation, and prayer, it was the gift of tears, the ability to weep over
the sins of oneself and of others, that was especially valued. A fantastic story
was told about Irene of Chrysobalanton, an aristocratic nun in tenth-century
Constantinople: her flow of tears reached such torrential proportions that
a basin had to be installed next to her seat in the church to collect the precious liquid.[93] Irene's story serves to underline the continued importance of
compunction *(penthos)* in the spiritual life of the Greek East from late antiquity through the Byzantine Empire, a topic that has been explored and documented in a magisterial study by Irénée Hausherr.[94] Back in the fourth century, Abba Macarius, who himself had been a disciple of Anthony, gave this
advice to another desert dweller: "Flee from men, stay in your cell, weep for
your sins, do not take pleasure in the conversation of men, and you will be

---

90. T. Vivian, "Monks, Middle Egypt, and Metanoia: The Life of Phib by Papohe the Steward
(Translation and Introduction)," *JECS* 7 (1999): 547–71.

91. A. de Vogüé, Foreword to *Pachomian Koinonia,* vol. 1 (Kalamazoo, 1980), XXII. See also J.
Gascou's detailed article "Metanoia," *Coptic Encyclopedia* 5 (1991): 1608–11.

92. John Climacus, *Ladder of Divine Ascent, PG* 88, col. 704A–B.

93. *Life of Irene of Chrysobalanton* 14.

94. I. Hausherr, *Penthos: The Doctrine of Compunction in the Christian East* (Kalamazoo, 1982; first
published in French, 1944).

saved."[95] Heartfelt penance, the monks knew well, could blot out sin. The flow of tears could have the same cleansing effect as the baptismal font. Nilus of Ancyra advises on the solitary life: "Consider fasting a weapon, prayer a wall, and tears a wash basin."[96] In a sermon on the theme of the baptism of Christ, delivered on the Feast of Epiphany in the year 381, Gregory of Nazianzus reminded his congregation that penance constitutes a form of baptism:

> I know of a fifth [kind of baptism] also, which is that of tears, and is much more laborious, received by him who washes his bed every night and his couch with tears; whose bruises stink through his wickedness; and who goeth mourning and of a sad countenance; who imitates the repentance of Manasseh and the humiliation of the Ninerites upon which God had mercy; who utters the words of the Publican in the Temple, and is justified rather than the stiff-necked Pharisee; who like the Canaanite woman bends down and asks for mercy and crumbs, the food of a dog that is very hungry.[97]

Anastasius Sinaites expressed the same idea, but in fewer words: "Tears are the true bath of the Christian."[98] His *Questions and Answers* provide us with a rare glimpse of Egyptian monastic spirituality in the late seventh century, long after the heyday of the monastic settlements in Kellia and Nitria. Elsewhere, he illustrated this point with the story of the tear-soaked handkerchief of a robber that blotted out his heinous deeds.[99] Such tears of repentance over concrete actions could move God's forgiveness. Tears were also shed out of a general sense of humility and the recognition of one's sinful nature. This is the advice of Evagrius Ponticus, the great theologian of Egyptian monastic spirituality in the fourth century:

> When you are of the mind that you do not stand in need of tears for your sins along with your prayer, then give some thought to the distance that separates you from God, whereas you ought to be in him constantly. Then you will shed more abundant tears than ever.[100]

Evagrius knew that the shedding of tears was a very special gift. It was

---

95. *Sayings of the Desert Fathers,* Macarius 41.
96. *Gli scritti siriaci di Nilo il Solitario,* ed. and trans. into Italian B. Bettiolo, Publications de l'Institut Orientaliste de Louvain 30 (Louvain, 1993), no. 87, p. 36: "Considera che il digiuno è un'arma e la preghiera un muro e lavacro le lacrime." This saying is absent from the Greek in *PG* 79.
97. Gregory of Nazianzus, *Or.* 39.17.
98. Anastasius Sinaites, *Questions and Answers, PG* 89, col. 752.
99. Anastasius Sinaites, *Homily in Psalm* 6, *PG* 89, cols. 1112–16.
100. Evagrius Ponticus, *On Prayer* 78.

prized so highly that he even had to warn those who were able to weep copiously against becoming boastful of their ability.[101]

*Intercessory Prayer by Holy Men*

Weeping and prayer were intimately connected. Weeping was the outward gesture that accompanied fervent prayer for the remission of sins. In Evagrius's words: "Pray with tears and your request will find a hearing. Nothing so gratifies the Lord as supplication offered in the midst of tears."[102] Those who had, through long experience, reached a certain degree of perfection were capable of praying (and weeping) not only for themselves, but also for others. An inscription at the monastic site of Saqqara in Egypt records: "This is the spot on which our lord and father Apa Jeremias bowed himself, until he removed the sins of the people of the whole world. May his (?) holy blessing descend upon us. Amen Amen, so be it, Amen (?)."[103]

The ability of holy men to pray for others was highly valued by their contemporaries and certainly contributed to their popularity.[104] Holy men and *pneumatophoroi* were expected to pray on behalf of those in need of assistance.[105] The spiritual fathers whom we encountered in the documentary evidence discussed above may have performed fewer miracles than the sensationalistic hagiographical record of late antiquity would lead us to expect from holy men, but they did offer up prayers for their correspondents. In some instances, they even gave assurance for the forgiveness of sins or promised their help to alleviate the burden of the sins of their followers. The life of retreat in prayer was very different from that of asceticism and almsgiving, and an *apa* who decided to embark exclusively on this path could meet with the consternation of his monastic colleagues. This is what happened to Apa Banes, according to an apophthegma preserved in the Coptic collection. The monks were so irritated at Banes' rejection of the

101. Ibid., 7. The "gift of tears" is greatly valued in the Syriac monastic tradition, especially in the writings of Isaac of Nineveh. For an introduction to this issue, see S. Brock, *The Syriac Fathers on Prayer and the Spiritual Life* (Kalamazoo, 1987). I am grateful to Cynthia Villagomez for her help on this point.
102. Evagrius Ponticus, *On Prayer* 6.
103. H. Thompson, "The Coptic Inscriptions," in *Excavations at Saqqara (1908–9, 1909–10)*, ed. J. E. Quibell (Cairo 1912), 4: 55, no. 188. The inscription is not dated, but the site was active from the late fifth to the ninth century.
104. C. Pietri "L'évolution du culte des saints aux premiers siècles chrétiens: Du témoin à l'intercesseur," in *Les fonctions des saints dans le monde occidental (III^e-XIII^e siècle)*, Collection de l'École Française de Rome 149 (Rome, 1991), sees the rise of the saints in connection with the struggle against Arianism. As the anti-Arian reaction emphasized the remoteness of Christ, the Christians depended to a greater degree than before on the saints as intercessors.
105. Eusebius, *Commentary on Psalms* 103, *PG* 23, col. 1292A.

lifestyle they held dear that they needed the reassurance of the local prophet Abraham:

> Why do you trouble yourselves? In fact, during the time when Apa Banes distributed alms, did he nourish a village, a town, a county? Now, Banes is able to raise both hands [in prayer] to make sure that barley comes to the whole world in abundance. He is also able to ask God to forgive the sins of this entire generation.[106]

The ability of holy men to pray for others is a recurring theme in the monastic literature of late antiquity, where it usually serves the dual purpose of underlining their compassion for others, which motivates their prayer, and of emphasizing their advanced state of holiness, which guarantees its success. Miracles were often, but not always the result.

In hagiography, the holy man's intercession on behalf of sinners is usually couched in colorful stories that culminate in a miracle.[107] Typically, a sinner who had suffered divine punishment for a misdeed—in the form of paralysis, sudden voice loss, or some other ominous occurrence—approached the holy man with the request to be "loosed" by him. This is exemplified in the story of the prominent Ishmaelite who broke his vow to God to abstain from meat, and then found that the bird he had shot and was about to eat had turned into stone. In his shock and distress, he appealed to Symeon the Stylite, who had been instrumental in his conversion, and asked "that through his all-powerful prayers he [Symeon] might free him from the bonds of sin."[108]

The necessity to remain in communication with God through prayer was so much taken for granted that there is little theoretical reflection on the nature of prayer itself. An exception is John Cassian, who had spent many years with the fathers in Egypt. Not long after his return to the West in 404, he founded a men's and a women's monastery in Marseilles where he composed his *Institutes* and *Conferences* to communicate his experience to a

---

106. *Les sentences des pères du désert: Nouveau recueil* (Solesmes, 1977), chap. 249.

107. For an attempt at classifying and comparing different kinds of prayer as reported in the *Vitae* of Martin of Tours and of Augustine, see S. Dagemark, "Prayer as Hagiographic Motif in *Vita Martini* and *Vita Augustini*," in *La preghiera nel tardo antico dalle origini ad Agostino, XXVII Incontro di Studiosi dell'Antichità Cristiana, Roma, 7–9 maggio 1998* (Rome, 1999). See also P. van Deun, "Euchē distingué de proseuchē: Un essay de précision terminologique chez les pères grecs et les écrivains byzantins," in *The Impact of Scripture in Early Christianity*, ed. J. den Boeft and M. L. van Poll-van de Lisdonk, Supplements to Vigiliae Christianae 44 (Leiden, 1999), 202–22.

108. Theodoret of Cyrrhus, *HR* 26.18. Compare *HR* 1.3, where Theodoret explains that the ascetic practices of James of Nisibis purified his soul to such an extent that he was able to work miracles: "And so his familiar access to God increased every day, and his requests for what he needed to ask from God were granted immediately."

Latin readership, becoming the first to translate the monastic ideal to the West. Cassian made a distinction between four different kinds of prayer— supplication, prayer, pleading, and thanksgiving. He lists them in ascending order, each correlated with the spiritual state of the individual:

> These, then, are the four rich sources of prayer. Out of contrition for sin is supplication born. Prayer comes of the fidelity to promises and the fulfillment of what we have undertaken for the sake of a pure conscience. Pleading comes forth from the warmth of our love. Thanksgiving is generated by the contemplation of God's goodness and greatness and faithfulness. [ . . . ] The first type seems especially appropriate for beginners, for they are still goaded by the stings and by the memory of past sin. The second type is appropriate for those who are making progress in the acquisition of virtue and in the exaltedness of their souls. The third is suitable for those who live as they have promised to do, who see the frailty of others and who speak out for them because of the charity that moves them. The fourth suits those who have pulled the painful thorn of penitence out of their hearts and who in the quiet of their purified spirit contemplate the kindness and mercy that the Lord has shown them in the past, that He gives them now and that He makes ready for them in the future. Aflame with all this their hearts are rapt in the burning prayer which human words can neither grasp nor utter. Sometimes the soul which has come to be rooted in this state of real purity takes on all the forms of prayer at the same time. It flies from one to the other, like an uncontrollable grasping fire. It becomes an outpouring of living pure prayer which the Holy Spirit, without our knowing it, lifts up to God in unspeakable groanings. . . . In no way can our spirit attain those more exalted modes of prayer of which I have been speaking except by the step-by-step journey upward through all those pleas we pour forth.[109]

Cassian derived this four-part scheme of supplications, prayers, intercessions, and thanksgivings from Paul's First Letter to Timothy (1 Tim. 2:1). Origen had already commented on this passage in his *On Prayer.* He noted that prayer on behalf of others or for specific things *(enteuxis)* was incumbent upon those who had greater *parrhēsia,* access to God.[110] However, the hierarchical arrangement of all four kinds of prayer and the correspondence of each of them to a particular degree of personal perfection was Cassian's own contribution. According to him, intercessory prayer on behalf of others is the highest form of prayer, as it requires a self that is completely devoid of its own needs, combined with immense compassion for humankind.

109. John Cassian, *Conferences* 9.15–16. Cassian later explains how one can be certain that one's prayers reach God: *Conferences* 9.32–34. Cf. *Conferences* 10.6: "Each soul in prayer is stirred and shaped in accordance with the measure of its purity."
110. Origen, *On Prayer* 14, esp. 14.2.

The precondition for a holy man's spiritual authority, including his ability to approach God in prayer, was thus spiritual perfection, achieved with the help of ascetic efforts that turned his soul into the fertile ground where *parrhēsia* could take root and grow. The purpose of his intercessory prayer was often to propitiate God to remove the sin of others. Here, however, the holy man did often not remain passive but assisted in the process of bringing down divine forgiveness by offering to shoulder half the burden of the sin of others. This process of vicarious penance has been aptly termed "Bussübernahme" by Joseph Hörmann.[111] The stories of accomplished *abbas* carrying the burden of others are so frequent that they might almost be considered an integral part of the process of spiritual guidance. We have already encountered the example of Barsanuphius, who offered to help his disciple Andrew by carrying half of his burdens. Other holy men offered to take the entire weight of the sin of others upon themselves. Four centuries before Barsanuphius, Clement of Alexandria in his *What Rich Man Will Be Saved* related what he called "a great example of sincere repentance and a great token of regeneration, a trophy of a resurrection that can be seen." On a visit to an unidentified city, the apostle John "noticed a strongly built youth of refined appearance and ardent spirit" and entrusted him to the local bishop for upbringing and education. Not long after his baptism, the young man fell into bad company and eventually became the leader of a band of robbers. The bishop gave him up for dead. Not so John. As soon as he found out about the fate of the young man, he went to the robbers' lair to seek him out in person. The young man reacted first with fear, then with shame and compunction when he heard John's assuring words: "I myself will give account to Christ for you. If need be, I will willingly undergo your penalty of death, as the Lord did for us. I will give my own life in payment for yours." The young robber was moved to tears, threw away his weapons, embraced John, and was "baptized a second time through his tears." John assisted his renewed conversion with his prayers and through continual fasting, as well as with soothing words of counsel.[112] The penitential fasting of John, combined with his willingness to shoulder the burden of the sins of the young man under his tutelage, here has the effect of bringing about a second baptism through tears of compunction. The final embrace of John and the repentant robber points to a special ritual gesture that in later centuries was sometimes said to accompany the reconciliation of sinners with

---

111. Hörmann, 205–11, with examples. The "confession inscriptions" from second- and third-century Lydia are an intriguing pagan parallel. In one of them, a brother makes restitution for the transgression of his sister and sets up a stele on her behalf to propitiate the goddess Anaitis: F. S. Steinleitner, *Die Beicht im Zusammenhange mit der sakralen Rechtspflege in der Antike* (Munich, 1913), no. 17, p. 45; cf. p. 94.

112. Clement of Alexandria, *The Rich Man's Salvation* 42.1–15.

their spiritual fathers: the holy man took the hands of the penitent and guided them to his own neck, then embraced the neck of the penitent in his turn.[113] In the early seventh century, John Klimax told a similar story of a monk who had been so afflicted by the sin of pride that he wrote his confession down and gave it to his spiritual father, while lying prostrate on the ground. The father then asked the monk to put his hand on his neck and explained: "This sin shall be on my neck, brother."[114]

An equally touching story was told of Mary, who had been brought up in seclusion by her uncle Abraham of Qidun, a Syrian ascetic who lived in the fifth century. She yielded to temptation once, then ran away and became a prostitute. Abraham, assuming the disguise of a soldier, went to seek her out at the tavern she now called home. He played along in his role until they were alone in her bedroom. Then, removing his disguise, he pleaded with her to return with him: 'Won't you speak to me, my daughter? . . . Wasn't it for your sake that I have come here? The sin shall be upon me, and I will answer on your behalf to God on the day of judgment. I will be the one who does penance for this sin." Mary finally relented, softened by Abraham's compassion. She declared her complete dependence on him as a negotiator with God on her behalf: "If you are certain that I *can* repent, and that God will receive me, then I come and fall at your feet, supplicating your venerable person; I kiss your holy feet because your compassion stirred you to come after me in order to raise me up from this foul abyss of mine."[115] For a murderer like the robber in Clement's story, or for an adulteress like Mary, it took the promises of a holy man to pay the debt for their sin, coupled with a dramatic gesture of compassion, to convince them that God's forgiveness was available to the penitent.

The vicarious penance and the prayers performed by the holy men, whose ascetic authority enhanced and solidified their spiritual authority, had the effect of reconciling sinners with God and their neighbors. Martyrs were able to accomplish the same by virtue of their spiritual authority alone, as we shall see next.

### *The Role of the Martyrs*

Christian martyrdom was often conceived of as a second baptism, a "baptism of blood" that washes away sins.[116] This concept would later also be applied

---

113. Hörmann, 207–8.
114. John Climacus, *Ladder of Divine Ascent*, step 23, *PG* 88, col. 980A–B.
115. *Life of Abraham of Qidun*, in *Holy Women of the Syrian Orient*, intr. and trans. S. P. Brock and S. Ashbrook Harvey, 34–35 (Berkeley, 1987).
116. This is a dominant theme in the writings of Cyprian, including his letters to imprisoned Christians. See E. L. Hummel, *The Concept of Martyrdom According to St. Cyprian of Carthage*, The

to monastic tonsure, as has been noted above. Martyrdom was also a form of participation in the history of salvation, in that the martyr imitated and relived in his or her own body the sacrificial death of Christ on the cross. The spiritual benefits that were generated by this experience were myriad. During the period prior to their execution, when the future Christian martyrs were undergoing judicial trials, tortures, and imprisonment, they became the center of attention of their fellow Christians. Members of the community and the clergy paid them frequent visits, attended to their needs, and joined with them in the celebration of the liturgy or in prayer. The imprisoned martyrs were surrounded by an almost palpable aura of holiness. They were rendered oblivious to the pain that was inflicted on their bodies, and received premonitory visions of their imminent ascent to paradise—expressions of divine pleasure and assurance of divine assistance with their ordeal. The true focus of the martyrdom stories, however, was on the benefits that the future martyrs could bestow on their fellow Christians. It was especially the martyrs' ability to pray effectively on behalf of others that was highlighted. Their intercessory powers appeared to increase in the measure of their anticipated suffering. Once the martyrdom was consummated in death, the martyrs were regarded as powerful intercessors in heaven, and their tombs became the locus of a cult. Even the *confessores (homologetai)* who had been preparing themselves for a martyr's death, but whose lives were spared, were held in special regard. Several confessors of the Great Persecution of Diocletian, for example, became bishops and later attended the Council of Nicaea. One of them was Paphnutius from Egypt (not identical with the spiritual father mentioned earlier), who had lost an eye in the persecution. The emperor Constantine demonstrated his reverence for Paphnutius's ordeal by kissing the scar on his face.[117]

### Martyrs and Prayer

The idea of martyrdom as bestowing a special ability for intercessory prayer was particularly prevalent in the Christian communities in Gaul, North Africa, and Egypt in the second and third centuries.[118] The imprisoned martyrs assumed an active role in dispensing their prayers liberally for the benefit of others. *The Letter from the Church at Vienne and Lyon,* preserved in Eusebius's *Church History,* reports the local martyrdom of Christian men and

---

Catholic University of America, Studies in Christian Antiquity 9 (Washington, D.C., 1946), 108–28.

117. Socrates, *HE* 1.11.2; confessors turned bishops in the early fourth century: Sozomen, *HE* 1.10.

118. B. Kötting, "Die Stellung des Konfessors in der Alten Kirche," *JAC* 19 (1976): 7–23.

women in the year 177, during the reign of Marcus Aurelius. The *Letter* devotes much space to the praise of the imprisoned martyrs for their self-lessness and brotherly love, noting especially their readiness to forgive even their torturers, and their prayers on behalf of others: "They defended all and accused none; they loosed all and bound none; they prayed for those who treated them so cruelly, as did Stephen, the fulfilled martyr."[119] The prayers of these Gallic martyrs were general and generous; they included "all," even their adversaries, and refrained from specifying an intention.

The prayers of the imprisoned martyrs in third-century North Africa, by contrast, were explicit in their intent and direction. In 203, in the amphi-theater of Carthage, there took place the public execution of Perpetua, a young nursing mother, and her servant Felicity, who had given birth to a daughter in prison. Perpetua's imprisonment, trial, and execution must have caused quite a stir in Carthage, for her father was a prominent man. Not only that, he and most of her relatives were pagans. Perpetua recorded her experiences in a diary, which was completed after her death by another author and now constitutes one of the most interesting and touching doc-uments of the self-fashioning of martyrs in the Roman Empire. As is perhaps not surprising, Perpetua was very alert to her own spiritual growth during the period leading up to her martyrdom. She describes how she experi-enced the work of the Spirit as it directed her thoughts, moved her tongue, and inspired her dreams with visions. The passage is worth quoting in full:

A few days after, while we were all praying, suddenly in the midst of the prayer I uttered a word and named Dinocrates [Perpetua's younger brother, now deceased]; and I was amazed because he had never come into my mind save then; and I sorrowed, remembering his fate. And straightway I knew that I was worthy, and that I ought to ask for him. And I began to pray for him long, and to groan unto the Lord. Immediately the same night, this was shown me.

I beheld Dinocrates coming forth from a dark place, where were many oth-ers also; being both hot and thirsty, his raiment foul, his color pale; and the wound on his face which he had when he died. This Dinocrates had been my brother in the flesh, seven years old, who being diseased with ulcers of the face had come to a horrible death, so that his death was abominated of all men. For him therefore I had made my prayer; and between him and me was a great gulf, so that either might not go to the other. There was moreover, in the same place where Dinocrates was, a font full of water, having its edge higher than was the boy's stature; and Dinocrates stretched up as though to drink. I was sorry that the font had water in it, and yet for the height of the edge he might not drink.

And I awoke, and I knew that my brother was in travail. Yet I was confident I should ease his travail; and I prayed for him every day till we passed over into

119. Eusebius, *HE* 5.2.5.

the camp prison. (For it was in the camp games that we were to fight; and the time was the feast of the Emperor Geta's birthday.) And I prayed for him day and night with groans and tears, that he might be given me.

On the day when we abode in the stocks, this was shown me.

I saw that place which I had before seen, and Dinocrates clean of body, finely clothed, in comfort; and the font I had seen before, the edge of it being drawn to the boy's navel; and he drew water thence which flowed without ceasing. And on the edge was a golden cup full of water; and Dinocrates came up and began to drink therefrom; which cup failed not. And being satisfied he departed away from the water and began to play as children will, joyfully.

And I awoke. Then I understood that he was translated from his pains.[120]

Perpetua's anticipated martyrdom enabled her to work a vicarious baptism for her brother, who had been raised, like herself, in a pagan household and had died at too young an age to seek Christian baptism for himself. Her visions are permeated with baptismal imagery: the fountain of water is evocative of the baptismal fountain, and Dinocrates' transformation from the ragged appearance of severe illness to a picture of health and purity is reminiscent of the white garments that neophytes wear after their baptism and alludes to the notion of baptism as a ritual of healing and restoration. Perpetua's confidence in her own ability to bring on this transformation through her prayers, only barely mitigated by her insistence that she was moved to do so by the Spirit, may seem exaggerated to the modern reader. But it was not an isolated phenomenon.

Several decades later, during the persecution that the emperor Decius (249–251) unleashed with his empire-wide order to perform sacrifices, the martyrs in Carthage were yet more specific in the purpose of their intercession. They prayed for those in the community who had committed sins, and especially for those who had, under pressure from the Roman authorities, taken part in pagan sacrifice. More than that, they issued written confirmation of their prayers in the form of *libelli pacis*. Apostasy from Christianity was considered one of the capital sins—a perpetration so monstrous, as most ecclesiastical authorities at the time agreed, that no penance could ever be sufficient to expiate it. Baptism removed all pre-baptismal sins, and after baptism a graduated system of penance existed for the atonement of lighter offenses, but the ecclesiastical mediation of divine forgiveness was powerless when it came to the capital sins of apostasy, murder, and adultery. The perpetrators of capital sins could only hope for God's mercy on the Day of Judgment, and perhaps for reconciliation with the church on their deathbed. The willingness of the Carthaginian martyrs to pray for those who had lapsed was a stunning demonstration of confidence in their powers of

---

120. *Passio of Perpetua and Felicity* 7–8.

intercession, both on the side of the imprisoned martyrs and on the side of those who sought their assistance. It was a bold declaration of spiritual authority, born out of the need of a Christian community to make a new beginning after it had been traumatized by the order to sacrifice and humiliated by the compliance of some of its members.

The consequences of Perpetua's prayers for her dead brother were known only to herself. But the lapsed Christians of Carthage were very much alive, and those who had been assured of the intercession of the martyrs expected to be reintegrated into the congregation. The value of the prayer of those who were on the threshold of martyrdom was accepted by all. But the belief of some that the prayers of Carthaginian martyrs could effect a renewal of the baptismal purification from sin and blot out even the gravest sin of apostasy placed Bishop Cyprian (248/249–258) in an awkward position, between the need to uphold his penitential authority as a bishop and his desire to recognize the prayers of the martyrs. At the core of the conflict was the question of who could claim possession of spiritual authority, in this instance hinged on the power of conciliatory prayer. Was it the future martyr, who was assured through his suffering for the sake of Christ of a special proximity to God? Or was it the bishop, who had in his ordination been placed in the succession of the first *pneumatophoroi,* the apostles, and whose pastoral responsibilities elevated him above the rest in practical terms?

The confessors of the Decian persecution in Alexandria engaged in similar acts of compassion toward the lapsed, causing Bishop Dionysius no small amount of consternation, which he shared in a letter to Bishop Fabius of Antioch, preserved by Eusebius:

> Thus even the divine martyrs among us, who now sit by Christ's side as partners in His kingdom, share His authority, and are His fellow-judges, opened their arms to their fallen brethren who faced the charge of sacrificing. Seeing their conversion and repentance, they were sure that it would be acceptable to Him who does not in the least desire the death of a sinner, but rather his repentance; so they received them, admitted them to the congregation as "bystanders," and allowed them to take part in services and feasts. What then, brothers, is your advice to us in this matter? What must we do? Shall we take our stand in full agreement with them, uphold their merciful decision, and deal gently with those they pitied? Or shall we condemn their decision as improper, and set ourselves up as judges of their attitude, wound their gentleness, and turn their practice upside down?[121]

We don't know how Dionysius of Alexandria solved this dilemma, but we are well informed about Cyprian's response. Cyprian had come to the epis-

121. Eusebius, *HE* 6.42.5–6.

copal throne of Carthage without much prior experience in the church, let alone the clergy. Converted as an adult, he chose a life of celibacy, disposed of most of his estate, and then, in short succession, was made presbyter and bishop in 248/249. His appointment was welcomed by the Christian congregation, which valued his prior training as a rhetorician and his network of connections. But as a newcomer to the clergy, he was met with less enthusiasm by a number of priests. Within a year or two after his election, the Decian persecution broke out. Cyprian himself went into hiding, convinced that he would serve his flock better by counseling them through his letters than by attracting the attention of the persecutors. His thought on the *libelli* developed over the course of the persecution, in response not only to the letters of the confessors in prison, but also with a view to preserving peace and unity within his church,[122] for during Cyprian's absence, some priests had honored the martyrs' *libelli* and readmitted penitent apostates to the eucharist. Their decision could not easily be revoked.

Cyprian's solution was to defuse the conflict by redefining the contested ground. The martyrs, he affirmed, had intercessory power with God with regard to admission to the kingdom in heaven. The bishop's prayer could do the same, but, in addition, the bishop was responsible for the welfare of the kingdom of heaven as it exists, however imperfectly and insufficiently, in the here and now in the church. While the martyrs could issue recommendations, it was only the bishop's prerogative to readmit sinners into the community. In essence, Cyprian was carving out a sphere of competence that was exclusively the bishop's. And it belonged to the bishop because of the authority invested in his office. The question of the possession of spiritual authority in the individual was thus diverted and became a question over the area in which this authority was operative and effective. The persecutions resumed a few years later under Valerian. This time, Cyprian remained with his congregation. He suffered a brief period of exile, and then was martyred in Carthage in 258.

### Martyrdom and Ecclesiastical Rank

The suffering that the confessors had endured during their trials translated into a special status within their communities after their return. Many confessors were made part of the clergy by their congregation, which wished to give recognition to their spiritual achievement and hoped to benefit from their spiritual gifts. According to the *Apostolic Tradition*, a confessor who had suffered judicial trial, imprisonment, or any other form of punishment,

---

122. For an outline of the development of Cyprian's thought, see O. D. Watkins, *A History of Penance* (London, 1920; New York, 1961), 176–99.

including binding in chains, was considered to hold the same honor *(timē)* as a deacon or priest: "But if a confessor has been in chains in prison for the Name [of Christ], hands are not laid on him for the diaconate or the presbyter's office. For he has the honor *(timē)* of the presbyterate by his confession. But if he be appointed bishop, hands shall be laid on him."[123] Likewise the *Testament of Our Lord,* a fifth-century church order from Syria that is heavily indebted to the *Apostolic Tradition:* "For he [the confessor] has the honor of the clergy having been sheltered by the hand of God by his confessorship."[124]

These statements regarding the confessors bring into focus the complex character of the episcopate. First of all, they make an implicit distinction between dignity and office. The confessors are automatically entitled to the former but achieve the latter only through proper initiation. Such niceties may well have been lost on the congregations, and the two were easily conflated. It was in order to avoid such misunderstandings that the *Apostolic Constitutions,* a compilation of the late fourth century, unambiguously declared that confessors ought not to usurp the dignity *(axiōma)* of the clergy.[125] Further, these guidelines take for granted that the superior spiritual qualities of the confessors translate into the corresponding ecclesiastical rank of deacons and priests with the privilege to stand at the altar. Implicit in this ruling is the acknowledgement that the episcopate does not carry any increment in honor above the presbyterate but was rather an administrative position of elevated rank. It was for this reason, as we shall see momentarily, that Cyprian wanted to groom the confessors he had admitted into the clergy for their future tasks before promoting them to the episcopate. These statements seem to indicate that the higher dignity that the bishop enjoyed as the head of his clergy was the result of the spiritual nature inherent in his office, which placed him in the succession of the apostles, and which was conferred on him at the moment of his ordination. The spiritual authority that an individual acquired through his efforts in martyrdom—or asceticism for that matter—had its exact correspondence in the dignity of the priesthood or, in the case of young men or neophytes, of the deaconate.

Cyprian's practice during the Decian persecution in Carthage shows how this question of dignity versus office could be resolved in practical terms. He appointed two young confessors, Aurelius and Celerinus, as readers. In this way, he noted, they could continue to give witness to their faith and be an inspiration and example to the congregation while they were per-

123. *Apostolic Tradition* 10.1–2 (my translation).
124. *Testamentum Domini,* trans. A. Vööbus, in *The Synodicon in the West Syrian Tradition,* CSCO, Scriptores Syri, 162 (Louvain, 1975), 43.
125. *Apostolic Constitutions* 8.23.

forming their task of reading from the scripture during the liturgy. They were held in the same honor as priests through the allocation of a regular stipend and could expect eventually to be ordained to the priesthood and later the episcopate as the need arose. A third confessor, Numidicus, was made a priest immediately, again with the prospect of later elevation to the episcopate.[126] He was more advanced in age and had endured greater physical suffering than the other two, which may explain his direct appointment to a higher rank in the clergy. Cyprian thus combined recognition of the special status of the confessors with integration into the ecclesiastical hierarchy at the appropriate level, sealed by a proper ordination rite. For many Christian believers, such distinctions between clergy and otherwise holy men were immaterial when their own salvation and well-being were at stake. A Syriac letter addressed by the presbyter Cosmas on behalf of his community to Symeon the Stylite contains the solemn promise to obey all his teachings lest they be cursed by him, and proclaims Symeon "the anointed priest given to us by God who effected reconciliation between God and his creation."[127]

### The Clergy and the Penitent

Holy men and martyrs offered intercessory prayer and vicarious penance on behalf of sinners, but their penitential abilities were limited to post-baptismal sins. The initial cleansing from sin and acceptance into the church through baptism was the exclusive purview of priests or bishops. They were also the ministers of penance for post-baptismal sins within the context of the church.

The purification from sin was no trivial issue in the first Christian centuries, a time when conversion to Christianity was an extended process that involved a long period of preparation that culminated in baptism, conferred by the bishop usually just before Easter. During this preparatory period, the catechumens were expected to prove themselves worthy by adjusting their life in accordance with Christian teaching. They were assisted and observed in this process by a sponsor who would stand surety for them and vouch for their seriousness of intent at the time of baptism—the predecessor of the godparent in infant baptism, which became increasingly the norm, begin-

---

126. Aurelius: Cyprian, *Ep.* 38; Celerinus: Cyprian, *Ep.* 39; Numidicus: Cyprian, *Ep.* 40, with commentary on Cyprian's reference to him as a presbyter, possibly from another city, who is now integrated into the clergy at Carthage; Hummel, 147–52. See also V. Saxer, "Institution et charisme dans les textes canonico-liturgiques et autres du III$^e$ siècle," in *Miscellanea historiae ecclesiasticae VIII*, ed. B. Vogler, Bibliothèque de la Revue d'Histoire Ecclésiastique 72 (Brussels and Louvain, 1987), 41–65, esp. 60–65.
127. *Syriac Life of Symeon the Stylite*, p. 195.

ning in the late fourth century. The ritual of baptism itself, with the full-body immersion in the font followed by the sealing of the body with blessed oil, was conceived as a cleansing from all sin, a complete and total rebirth in the Spirit. From that moment on, any sins, big or small, weighed heavier because they had been committed after the receipt of God's grace. Not only did they alienate the individual from the community of Christians; they estranged him or her from God, incurring his wrath and the threat of his punishment on the Day of Judgment.

The process of atoning for one's sins within the church took place in stages: confession by the sinner either to an individual or to the community; pronouncement by the priest or bishop of the required penance; performance of whatever penance had been imposed; and finally readmission into the community in a solemn ritual that symbolized both the reintegration into the community and the readmission into communion with God, made evident in the ritual laying on of hands by the bishop on the successful penitent.[128] The most extreme form of alienation from the community was excommunication, imposed by the priest or bishop along with certain penances to prepare the sinner for readmission to the congregation. Other, lighter forms of penance could also be applied, commensurate in intensity and duration with the severity of the sin. These penitential practices, as has been noted before, included prayer, fasting, and almsgiving, as well as lamentations and wearing ashes and sackcloth.

The clergy administered penance by virtue of their succession and imitation of the apostle Peter, to whom Jesus had said:

> And I tell you, you are Peter, and on this rock I will build my church, and the gates of Hades will not prevail against it. I will give you the keys of the kingdom of heaven, and whatever you bind on earth will be bound in heaven, and whatever you loose on earth will be loosed in heaven. (Matt. 16:18–19)

In the Middle Ages, this power to bind and loose, especially in its most extreme form of excommunication, became one of the most potent weapons of the episcopate in exerting authority over their flock, over theological or political adversaries among their fellow bishops, and indeed over secular rulers. For the period of late antiquity, the sources often do not distinguish whether priests or bishops, or both, were involved in the penitential process. Moreover, there seems to be no uniformity of custom with

---

128. Watkins's *A History of Penance* contains a complete dossier of the Greek and Latin sources, with commentary, up to the year 450. A French equivalent is C. Vogel, *Le pécheur et la pénitence dans l'église ancienne* (Paris, 1966); for a similar German publication, see H. Karpp, *Die Busse: Quellen zur Entstehung des altkirchlichen Busswesens*, Traditio Christiana 1 (Zurich, 1969). B. Poschmann (*Paenitentia secunda: Die kirchliche Busse im ältesten Christentum bis Cyprian und Origenes*, Theophaneia 1 [Bonn, 1940; repr., 1960]) gives his own interpretive spin, emphasizing the importance of the involvement of the congregation as a whole, not just the bishop, in the reconciliation of sinners.

regard to the actual role of priests. The Greek East had the office of a penitential priest, who heard the confession of sinners in private—a custom that was apparently introduced in the mid-third century to protect the *lapsi* of the Decian persecution from the embarrassment of public confession. However, the penitential priest probably did not preside over the solemn readmission of the penitent into the church that culminated in the bishop's laying on of hands. In 391, Bishop Nectarius of Constantinople abolished the office amidst a sex scandal involving the penitential priest, a woman of the aristocracy who had been doing penance in a church, and a deacon who had taken advantage of her on that occasion.[129]

The earliest explicit statement that specifically mentions the bishop in the reconciliation of sinners is made by Tertullian in his *On Modesty*, composed in 210 after he had adopted the rigorist stand of the Montanists that no penance could be sufficient for the three capital sins of apostasy, adultery, and murder.[130] Only a few years later, the consecration prayer for the ordination of a bishop preserved in the *Apostolic Tradition* calls down the Holy Spirit upon the new bishop so that he may discharge his ministry properly, including the power to bind and loose that had been granted to the apostles.[131] A few decades after that, the *Didascalia* announced that the administration of penance is the exclusive domain of bishops, who had inherited the power to bind and loose,[132] a point that is reiterated, like most of the *Didascalia*, in the *Apostolic Constitutions* of the late fourth century.[133] By that time, John Chrysostom proclaimed that there is no greater *exousia* (power, authority) than that of binding and loosing sin.[134] Whether performed by priests and bishops at first or—since the third century—by bishops only, the liturgical act of confirming the penitent sinner's readmission into the community of the church was exclusively the responsibility of the clergy, while their ability to broker reconciliation with God was shared by martyrs, holy men, and monks.

The penitential prerogative of priests and bishops is not rooted in their spiritual gifts or their ascetic distinction. It would be impractical to make such demands on the large numbers of priests and bishops throughout the empire. Rather, it derives from the definition of their office as standing in the succession of the apostles and from the process of their ordination, which, like monastic tonsure and martyrdom, could be regarded as a second baptism that washed away previous sins. This idea took root in certain

---

129. Socrates, *HE* 5.19.1–9; Sozomen, *HE* 7.16.8–9.
130. Tertullian, *De pudicitia* 18, with commentary by Watkins, 125f.
131. *Apostolic Tradition* 3.5.
132. Relevant passages in Watkins, 224–33.
133. *Apostolic Constitutions* 2.1–25.
134. John Chrysostom, *On the Priesthood* 3.5.

circles at a relatively early date and was referred to in the early fourth century, at the Council of Neocaesarea.[135] It is mentioned again shortly after 381, but again in the form of reference to an opinion held by others. Gregory of Nazianzus, in his tirade against the unworthy bishops whom he blamed for the premature end of this episcopate of Constantinople, anticipated that his adversaries would claim that the imposition of hands at their ordination had had the same purifying effect as baptism.[136] Not much later, Gregory's successor Nectarius is reported to have engaged in a conversation with Martyrius, his long-standing friend and physician, who reminded the former *praetor urbanus* of the spiritual renewal worked by baptism and ordination:

> But you, O blessed one, . . . were cleansed by baptism, and were then accounted worthy of the priesthood. Both these ordinances are appointed by the Divine law for purification from sin, and it seems to me that you now differ in no respect from a new-born infant.[137]

Accordingly, the priesthood could be understood as a state of purity and of absence of sin. In this regard, it acquired through ordination what the monastic life strove to attain through asceticism. Ordination also transferred onto the bishop the same Spirit that Christ had given to the apostles. The administration of penance and the readmission of the penitent fell within the purview of the bishop's pragmatic authority inasmuch as it was a procedure that involved a prescribed sequence of actions. But inasmuch as the bishop passed on the Spirit to the reconciled penitent through the imposition of hands, the administration of penance became part of the spiritual authority inherent in his office. In Cyprian's view, this penitential power enables both bishops and martyrs to work before God for the remission of the sins of the penitent. In the concluding paragraph of *On the Lapsed*, he uses the image of the penitent sinner as a debtor for whom the martyrs intercede and on whose behalf the bishops intervene: "He [God] can mercifully pardon the penitent, the toiler, the supplicant. He can carry to his credit *(in acceptum referre)* whatsoever the martyrs have sought, and the bishops *(sacerdotes)* wrought for such as these."[138] In short, the bishop (or priest; the Latin is ambiguous) can also carry the burden of the sins of others, but his ability to do so is a result of his position in the clergy.

Finally, since the effective discharge of this duty depended on the

---

135. Neocaesarea, can. 9, H-L I/1, p. 331. But note the careful phrasing, explaining that "most" say that all other sins, except that against the flesh, are taken away through the imposition of hands.
136. Gregory of Nazianzus, *Carmen* 2.1.12, vv. 503–22.
137. Sozomen, *HE* 7.10.3.
138. Cyprian, *On the Lapsed* 36; trans. Watkins, 209.

bishop's personal and moral integrity, his ascetic authority became a pastoral necessity. In this aspect of the bishop's pastoral care the dialectic of episcopal leadership comes into play, as was noted in the previous chapter. The principle is expressed very clearly already in the *Didascalia,* which — true to its nature as a book of advice for laity and clergy in the congregations—devotes a great deal of book 2 to the bishop's task of admonishing sinners and readmitting the penitent. His character, it is noted, should be such that he can serve as an example to his congregation and thus prevent them from sinning. If they have fallen, he should be gentle in his admonition and firm in his rebuke.[139] In other words, the bishop's personal conduct should be the moral yardstick for the congregation. If he then has to hit them with the penalty of penance, his punishment will not be suspected as coming from a hypocrite, but it will be gladly accepted.

This is brought to the fore in the literary portrayal of bishops, when they are depicted as acting like spiritual fathers or *pneumatophoroi* while exercising the power to bind and loose that was part of their office. Novatian, the schismatic bishop of Rome who advocated a rigorist position toward post-baptismal sin, was attacked in an anonymous treatise written sometime between 235 and 257. But even this hostile author has to admit that "as long as Novatian was in the Church of Christ, he wept over the sins of his neighbors as if they were his own, bore the burdens of his brethren, as the Apostle exhorts, and strengthened with his exhortations those who were weak in the divine faith."[140] Similar praise was bestowed on Ambrose of Milan, the bishop of another imperial capital, by his hagiographer Paulinus: his readiness to weep with the penitent often moved the latter to tears, while his discretion in hearing confessions of serious crimes was "leaving a good example to future bishops that they should be intercessors before God rather than accusers before men."[141] In this instance, the spiritual authority of the individual bishop assisted him in the discharge of the spiritual authority inherent in his office.

A more radical view was taken by certain rigorists within the church. They insisted that the bishop's exemplary conduct and ascetic lifestyle were not merely an advantage, but an absolute spiritual necessity, without which a bishop forfeited his prerogative to bind and loose. Origen, who reserved the designation of "true priests" only for the bearers of the Spirit, did not mince his words on this issue. He railed against bishops who claimed to have inherited the power to bind and loose from Peter, but failed to imitate his way of life:

---

139. *Didascalia* (Latin) 2.1–25.
140. *Ad Novatianum* 13.8.
141. Paulinus, *Life of Ambrose* 9 (39).

We must say that they speak wholesomely if they have the way of life on account of which it was said to that Peter: "Thou art Peter;" and if they are such that upon them the church is built by Christ, and to them with good reason this could be referred; and the gates of Hades ought not to prevail against him when he wishes to bind and loose. But if he is tightly bound with the cords of his sins, to no purpose does he bind and loose.[142]

According to the rigorist position, the bishop's administration of penance and other sacramental, liturgical, and pastoral aspects of his ministry had to be supported and guaranteed through his personal spiritual authority and ascetic comportment. The aim was to emphasize the importance of the spiritual aspect of the episcopal office, but without challenging the existence of the hierarchy of the clergy as such. Such rigorist tendencies generated several schisms. While the confessors struggled with Cyprian over who should hold spiritual authority in the matter of penitence, whether the martyrs or the bishop, the rigorists and the mainstream were at loggerheads over the definition of the nature of episcopal leadership and the relative importance of spiritual, ascetic, and pragmatic authority in this context.

First was the Novatian schism.[143] It began in 250, when Novatian, a very able and promising priest, had himself appointed—through dishonest means and by only a small number of clergy, as his detractors would later say—to the episcopal see of Rome despite the fact that Cornelius had received that office with the support of the clergy. The argument Novatian brought forward to discredit his competitor was Cornelius's lack of ascetic and spiritual credentials. Instead of becoming a martyr, Cornelius had cheated in the Decian persecution and obtained a *libellus* certifying that he had sacrificed. Novatian also tried to stem the tide of inflationary penitential lenience toward the lapsed who had sacrificed under duress, and acted himself in the manner of the holy men who practiced vicarious penance for the benefit of others: he prayed for them and offered to carry part of their burdens, as even his enemies admitted. Novatian upheld a strict position on the severity of the three cardinal sins: those who were guilty of murder, adultery, or apostasy should be admitted by the church only to do penance, but they could not expect forgiveness here on earth. Their only hope was to be granted forgiveness in heaven. Novatian's position gained many followers throughout the empire, from Spain to Pontus. The fifth-century church historian Sozomen reports that still in his day the Novatians had their own church and clergy in Constantinople.[144] Their last traces peter out in the seventh century.

142. Origen, *Commentary on Matthew* 12.14, *Patrologia graeco-latina* 10, col. 650B.
143. H. J. Vogt, *Coetus sanctorum: Der Kirchenbegriff des Novatian und die Geschichte seiner Sonderkirche* (Bonn, 1968); Watkins, 197–221.
144. Sozomen, *HE* 8.1.8–15.

Similar circumstances led to the Donatist Schism that troubled North Africa from the time of the Great Persecution of Diocletian until the Vandal conquest and beyond, and whose clergy caused Augustine great headaches throughout his episcopate.[145] Here it was the appointment of Caecilian as bishop of Carthage in 311 that was vehemently opposed by Donatus, bishop of Casae Nigrae, and his followers. A few years previously, while still an archdeacon, Caecilian had become a *traditor*, a traitor to the faith, when he handed over the scriptures to the Roman persecutors. In Donatus's eyes, this rendered him unworthy of promotion to the episcopate. What is more, it also rendered invalid all ordinations and other sacraments that Caecilian had performed. Donatus's rejection of Caecilian and other lapsed clergy, as well as the clergy they ordained, led him to establish a separate church. Donatus's rigorist position with regard to apostasy was also evident in his insistence that lapsed clergy could obliterate their sin only in a renewed baptism.

In both these schisms, the mainstream that defined and enforced "orthodoxy" and the rigorists were on common ground with regard to the appreciation of ascetic authority and moral integrity as an asset in the clergy's discharge of its pastoral and administrative duties. They also agreed on the importance of spiritual authority in validating the clergy's liturgical actions, such as baptisms and ordinations to the clergy. Their fundamental disagreement concerned the source of this spiritual authority. The rigorists insisted that it be present in the individual priest or bishop, as result of his personal exemplary lifestyle, in other words, of his ascetic authority. The mainstream, however, allowed that spiritual authority was also inherent in the office itself, as the Spirit was passed on in the ordination through the apostolic tradition. This grace was irrevocable, even if the conduct of the individual cleric might prove be objectionable.

Spiritual authority conferred through ordination is what ultimately sets bishops apart from martyrs and holy men. This additional distinction of the bishop is evident also in the ritual gesture that completes the reconciliation of the sinner. In the case of a holy man, as has been noted, it consisted of some kind of embrace—a meeting of fellow sinners. The bishop, by contrast, readmits sinners through the imposition of hands, thus communicating the Holy Spirit that he himself had received in like manner. This act is called *anadechesthai*, the same word that is used for the baptismal sponsor as he receives the newly baptized from the font—further affirmation of the similarity between baptism and penance. That the apostolic succession of bishops should be such an important component in the spiritual authority

---

145. W. H. C. Frend, *The Donatist Church: A Movement of Protest in Roman North Africa* (Oxford, 1952; repr., 1985), 141ff.

required for the exercise of their penitential duties is not surprising. After all, the administration of penance is the one function that is attested as the exclusive domain of bishops since the end of the second century (in contrast to the celebration of the eucharist, for example, which priests are also qualified to do) and that was directly commissioned by Jesus to the apostle Peter. The exercise of his penitential prerogative allows the bishop to place himself in a long and unbroken chain of tradition and enables him to remind his congregation of who is really in charge.

CHAPTER FOUR

# Ascetic Authority

We have defined spiritual authority as the gift of the Spirit, and its holders, following the terminology of Clement and Origen, as *pneumatophoroi* or *gnostikoi*. One of the ways in which this gift could be shared with others was through intercessory prayer. Especially valued was prayer on behalf of sinners. Such prayers were offered up by holy men, martyrs, and bishops, all of whom had a claim to spiritual authority. This gave rise to conflict and competition between martyrs and bishops at the time of Cyprian. The analysis of this and similar conflicts enabled us to identify two ways in which the presence of spiritual authority was made evident: the physical suffering of the martyrs and the imposition of hands at the ordination of the bishops. A third way was through the daily "martyrdom" of asceticism, the topic of this chapter.

Once the persecutions had come to an end, it was the hermits and monks who carried on the heritage of the martyrs as "bearers of the Spirit." In fact, the origins of Egyptian monasticism[1] reach back to the last decades of the third century, a generation in fact before Anthony's celebrated withdrawal from his village. Men (and women) were inspired to retreat to the desert in order to attain intimate knowledge and intuitive understanding of the divine mysteries. They spent their days reading and meditating on the scriptures, reciting biblical verses, and chanting psalms. Even while they en-

1. I concentrate here on Egyptian monasticism because it was the most influential in shaping the monastic tradition both in Byzantium and in the Latin West. Syrian monasticism arose independently. Its demarcation from lay Christians is less pronounced than in the Egyptian tradition. This results in a very different relation between monks and bishops. The best comprehensive introduction is still A. Vööbus, *A History of Asceticism in the Syrian Orient: A Contribution to the History of Culture in the Near East*, CSCO Subsidia 14, 17, 81 (Louvain, 1958–88).

gaged in manual labor to support themselves, their activity was accompanied by the continuous murmur of biblical recital. Most important for the present inquiry is the fact that they subjected themselves to a daily routine of physical *askēsis*. In the manner of penitents, they strove to expiate their own sins, and perhaps even to build up "credit" for the sins of others. In distinction to martyrdom, which was brought on by external circumstances—the church fathers insisted that martyrdom should not be sought, but neither should it be refused—the monastic way of life was open to anyone who felt the "call" from God and followed it.

The chicken-and-egg question of which came first, asceticism or spiritual authority, is impossible to resolve. On the one hand, the very ability to practice asceticism, especially in its more extreme forms, was considered a special gift of God.[2] On the other hand, asceticism was the only way in which individuals could, through their own efforts, hope to acquire the gifts of the Spirit, most prominently the ability to give instruction and to pray on behalf of others. This was equally true for those who led a regulated life of moderate ascetic practices inside a monastery as for those who lived by themselves and performed spectacular feats of physical endurance. The general attainability of virtues through ascetic living was one of the distinctive advantages of the monastic profession. John Chrysostom pointed this out to concerned parents whose sons wanted to be monks rather than to study rhetoric with a view to a later public career: the limited ability of the student, the ignorance of the teacher, the lack of funding, and the meanness of fellow students could all conspire to prevent the student from completing his course. Even the few who were able to surmount these obstacles could see their promising career cut short by the displeasure of the ruler, the envy of colleagues, the difficulty of the times, the absence of friends, and poverty. "However," John Chrysostom concluded, "this is not the case with monks. But there, only one thing is required, genuine desire and noble purpose. For if that is the case, there is nothing to prevent one from reaching the perfection of virtue."[3]

Asceticism was a path to personal perfection open to all. It was also highly visible. Those who embarked on it adopted a distinct physical appearance that signaled their profession. At the very least, they showed the trappings of voluntary poverty in clothing and living quarters. They wore brown or black cloaks made of coarse fabric, and their cells were small, unadorned, and devoid of personal possessions, except perhaps a book or two and the tools they needed for their handiwork. The more advanced ones also dis-

2. P. Nagel, *Die Motivierung der Askese in der alten Kirche und der Ursprung des Mönchtums* (Berlin, 1966), esp. 74.
3. John Chrysostom, *Against the Enemies of the Monastic Life* 3.13 (my translation).

played the signs of deprivation of food and sleep in their frail bodies and piercing glance. The neglect of their body was made visible in their long, matted hair and beard and in the characteristic smell that came from the rejection of bathing. Even those who adopted a more moderate lifestyle in small, regulated communities were expected to display their inner state of detachment from the world and control over their emotions in their sub-dued demeanor—their controlled movements as they walked and gesticulated, the tone of voice when they spoke, and the direction of their glance when they looked around. Basil of Caesarea confirms our earlier observations about the connection between penitential practices and asceticism in a letter written shortly after his own retreat to Annisi in 358. He begins his detailed recommendations for the outward appearance of ascetics with the remark "From the humble and submissive spirit comes an eye sorrowful and downcast, appearance neglected, hair rough, dress dirty; so that the appearance which mourners take pains to present may appear our natural condition."[4] In this manner, ascetic efforts were made evident to visitors and disciples. Monastic literature broadcast the physical appearance of ascetics to the rest of the world and to posterity as incontrovertible evidence of their elevated spiritual status. The ascetic "look" was both outward manifestation and advertisement of personal holiness. Late antique authors, following the ancient tradition of physiognomy, placed a high prize on the proper appearance as revealing the inner qualities of the true ascetic, while discrediting as charlatans those who merely put on the show of external markers of holiness, but without having acquired them through legitimate means.[5]

Individual physical effort and its public recognition are two of the characteristics of ascetic authority. A third is its affirmation through the possession of spiritual abilities, especially the ability to instruct others. Herein lies the seed for potential conflict with priests and bishops whose duties entailed teaching and preaching. The ascetics of the Egyptian desert were held in high regard as teachers in the spiritual life. Disciples apprenticed themselves as "sons" to their spiritual "fathers," some for a short period of time, weeks or months, until they moved on to be instructed by the next *abba*, others remaining with their spiritual father for the duration of his life, assisting him in his old age. Palladius of Helenopolis is an example of a migrating ascetic in search of instruction. After seven years as a disciple of several spiritual fathers, including Evagrius, he returned to his place of origin and became bishop of Helenopolis in Bithynia. He later gave a vivid description of his encounters with the holy men and women of Egypt, Palestine, and Syria

---

4. Basil of Caesarea, *Ep.* 2.6.
5. This has been highlighted in T. Shaw, "Askesis and the Appearance of Holiness," *JECS* 6 (1998): 485–99, and D. Caner, "Nilus of Ancyra and the Promotion of a Monastic Elite," *Arethusa*, 2000, 401–10.

in his *Lausiac History.* By an ironic turn of literary fate, the monks who permanently attached themselves to a desert father were, by contrast, often nameless figures in the monastic literature of late antiquity. This is true, for instance, of the two disciples of Anthony who tended to his needs in his old age, who witnessed his death, and who buried him, according to his wishes, in a secret place.

The monastic movement in Egypt generated an enormous amount of literature from the pens of disciples and admirers. The words of wisdom that came from the lips of the "Old Men," as they were often affectionately called, were collected in the *Sayings of the Desert Fathers.* Others committed to writing the experiences of their pilgrimage from one father to another, combining anecdotes of these men's extraordinary ascetic feats with memorable quotations from their teaching. This is the origin of the pilgrimage account by the fourth-century noblewoman Egeria, as well as the *Historia Lausiaca* by Palladius of Helenopolis, the anonymous *History of the Monks in Egypt,* and John Cassian's *Conferences.* Full-length biographies were another kind of hagiographical writing, spanning the entire course of a person's life from birth to death. The pioneering work in this vein is Athanasius of Alexandria's *Life of Anthony.* It incited Jerome to compose three *Vitae,* which were the first hagiographies in Latin: the *Life of Paul the Hermit,* who was active in Egypt prior to Anthony; the *Life of Hilarion,* who propagated the monastic ideal in Palestine; and the *Life of Malchus the Prisoner,* an adventuresome tale of a cave-dwelling monk. By the fifth century, not only hermits and monks were the subject of hagiographical writing, but also bishops. The praise of asceticism was now applied to men who were active in the world. The resulting adjustment in the literary presentation of episcopal saints is discussed in the epilogue.

The literary products of early monasticism give the impression of an uneasy relation between the desert fathers and the clergy that was continually renegotiated, depending on historical circumstance and on the players involved. Potential for conflict arose from the competing claims of both sides for spiritual authority. Although some scholars, such as Karl Heussi,[6] suggest that the origins of this conflict must be sought earlier, there is at the moment insufficient evidence to support or to disprove this idea.

Both monks and clergy claimed to teach with spiritual authority, but they were at variance with regard to the origin of that authority and the content, method, and medium of their teaching. The monks had prepared themselves through a lifetime of asceticism and deprivation to become vessels of the Holy Spirit. The wisdom and insight they imparted to others was thus the product of divine inspiration. The lessons they shared consisted mostly

6. K. Heussi, *Der Ursprung des Mönchtums* (Tübingen, 1936; repr., Aalen, 1981).

of practical advice on how to achieve personal spiritual progress. They acted as masters, as it were, sharing the skills of their trade with their apprentices. Their teaching method was tied to their quality as "bearers of the Spirit," who possessed the gift of discernment. Like good physicians, they were able to dole out the exact amount of insight that was required at just that moment—not too little so as to encourage growth through challenge, and not too much so as to avoid discouragement. It lies in the nature of the teaching of these masters of spiritual perfection that it had to be dispensed in a personal encounter with the disciple, through the act of oral communication. The lesson itself was ephemeral; what counted was its implementation by the disciple, who would strive to render its essence visible through his life. Countless tales describe how aspiring monks traveled to seek out a spiritual master, in order to ask him: "Father, give me a word." In response, they were granted a short aphorism that seemed to address their particular situation and needs at that moment. These aphorisms were treasured by their recipients. Eventually, these stories were shared with others, and before long, they were written down so that many could enjoy them. Scholars now agree that the roots of the written version of *The Sayings of the Desert Fathers* must be sought in the fourth century.[7] This confinement of oral teaching to the written word on the page subverts the original purpose of spiritual instruction and results in reducing the spiritual teaching of the desert fathers to a mechanically reproducible medium, namely, the book, which combines the advantage of greater accessibility and dissemination with the disadvantage of depersonalizing the process of discipleship.

In contrast to the desert fathers, the priests and bishops derived their authority and their mission to teach from their ordination. Two aspects of the ordination ritual are crucial in that respect: the prayer over the ordinand when the divine Spirit is called down upon him and the imposition of hands, which places him in the continuation of a tradition that reached back to the apostles who had known Christ and had received his Spirit. Although it was often demanded that only truly spiritual men should become clerics, in practice the candidates for the clergy were, more often than not, recruited from among the well-respected and prominent members of the local community, a point that will be expanded later. Such men recommended themselves for office because they were well educated, of prosperous background, and enjoyed the respect of their fellow citizens. They possessed the rhetorical skills that were useful for their administrative work and that made their teaching and preaching agreeable to their listeners. In contrast to the intimate personal encounter in the monastic setting between master and apprentice, the setting of instruction provided in the parish re-

7. C. Faraggiana di Sarzana, "Il *Paterikon Vat. Gr.* 2592, già di Mezzoiuso, e il suo rapporto testuale con lo *Hieros. S. Sepulchri gr.* 113," *Bollettino della Badia Greca di Grottaferrata* 47 (1993): 79.

sembled more that of a large lecture room. The priest or bishop offered instruction in the lessons of the Christian faith. Rather than tailoring his teaching to the needs of one individual, he addressed a large audience that included certified members of the community as well as catechumens and interested nonbelievers. Rather than sharing with a select few the wisdom that came from his own experience, the priest explicated the scriptures to the whole congregation on the basis of his learning and addressed moral admonitions to them as he saw fit. His teaching was not that of the spiritual guide, designed to encourage his audience to imitate his example and to change their lives in dramatic ways on the narrow path to personal perfection. Rather, the priest acted like a shepherd who was called to prevent his sheep from going astray, who ensured that they all moved in the same direction, and who kept them on the broad road of Christian morality.

The practice of asceticism, the monastic tradition, and their literary representation in late antiquity have generated a rich corpus of scholarship since the beginning of the last century and continuing to the present day. The main lines of development have been clearly mapped out,[8] and areas of particular interest—whether literary, social, or religious—have been signposted and filled in with meticulous detail.[9] Rather than going over this well-charted ground, I wish in the following to contribute two new ideas to our understanding of the purpose of the monastic enterprise, namely, the relevance of the Egyptian desert as a location and as an abstract ideal, and the importance of the figure of Moses as a biblical model of leadership. These investigations will pave the way for the discussion of the ambivalent monastic attitude toward ecclesiastical office in the following section.

## THE IMPORTANCE OF THE DESERT

The desert is of crucial importance to the development of the monastic experience. Much more than a concrete geographical setting, it was regarded as a historical stage on which the history of salvation was played out, beginning with the Old Testament, continuing through the story of Jesus, and reenacted by the early Egyptian monks. It was also associated with the highly desirable state of mind of complete detachment from the cares of the

---

8. See S. Schiwietz, *Das morgenländische Mönchtum*, 2 vols. (Mainz, 1904–13); Heussi; D. H. Chitty, *The Desert a City: An Introduction to the Study of Egyptian and Palestinian Monasticism under the Christian Empire* (Oxford, 1966); P. Rousseau, *Ascetics, Authority, and the Church in the Age of Jerome and Cassian* (Oxford, 1978).

9. G. Gould, *The Desert Fathers on Monastic Community* (Oxford and New York, 1993); D. Burton-Christie, *The Word in the Desert: Scripture and the Quest for Holiness in Early Christian Monasticism* (New York, 1993); J. E. Goehring, *Ascetics, Society, and the Desert: Studies in Early Egyptian Monasticism* (Harrisburg, 1999); S. Elm, *Virgins of God: The Making of Asceticism in Late Antiquity* (Oxford and New York, 1994).

world. Finally, it provided the literary imprint, as it were, for the writing of later monastic authors.

One of the fundamental differences between paganism and the Judeo-Christian tradition lies in the favored abode of their divinities. Unlike the God of Moses and of Jesus, no pagan deity would ever have chosen to appear to mortals in the desert. The gods of classical antiquity preferred to amuse themselves or to encounter humans in lush landscapes, flowering meadows, shaded groves, near gently gurgling springs, or perhaps in the sea or on mountaintops.[10] The wealthy and educated elite of the Greco-Roman world imitated their divinities and sought respite from the cares and troubles of the city by escaping to their country estates. Stoic and Epicurean philosophers enjoyed retreats to the countryside with their like-minded friends, where they could engage in unhindered discussion. This carried over into literature. Cicero's *Tusculan Conversations*, for example, are set in the green hills near Rome. Learned upper-class Christians continued this tradition.[11]

In the history of the Judeo-Christian God with his people, the desert has always played a special role, beginning with the story of Moses in the Exodus and continuing with Jesus' temptation and his several, shorter retreats to the desert. From the late third century, the desert again became the locus of intense spiritual experience. This time, it was the hermits and monks of Egypt who sought a new encounter with God. Their efforts, I will argue in the following, were closely tied to their geographical surroundings. It was their intention and desire to actively imitate the experience of Moses and Israel. The sudden and plentiful burst of literary production that was generated by the admirers and practitioners of Egyptian monasticism had the effect of establishing this way of life, in its desert locale, as canonical. It provided the imprint for all later monastic endeavors and necessitated the adaptation of ideals first formulated in the specific environment of Egypt to other locations.[12]

The dominance of the desert discourse that was generated in Egypt was accepted but at the same time subtly adapted to suit other circumstances by the monastic pioneers of Cappadocia, especially Basil of Caesarea. A more nuanced understanding of the difference between the Egyptian and the Cappadocian attitudes toward monastic withdrawal in the desert will lay the

10. R. Buxton, *Imaginary Greece: The Contexts of Mythology* (Cambridge, 1994), 80–113.

11. J. Fontaine, "Valeurs antiques et valeurs chrétiennes dans la spiritualité des grands propriétaires terriens à la fin du IV^e siècle occidental," in *Epektasis: Mélanges patristiques offert au Cardinal Daniélou*, ed. J. Fontaine and C. Kannengiesser, 571–95 (Paris, 1972).

12. J. E. Goehring, "The Encroaching Desert: Literary Production and Ascetic Space in Early Christian Egypt," *JECS* 1 (1933): 281–96, repr. in his *Ascetics, Society, and the Desert: Studies in Early Egyptian Monasticism* (Harrisburg, 1999).

groundwork for the subsequent exploration of different attitudes toward ecclesiastical office with all the involvement in mundane matters that this entails.

### The Desert in the Old Testament

In the Judeo-Christian tradition, the desert occupies a place of central importance. In the succinct words of G. H. Williams, it encompasses four distinct concepts:

> (a) the wilderness as a moral waste but a potential paradise, (b) the wilderness as a place of testing or even punishment, (c) the wilderness as the experience or occasion of nuptial (covenantal) bliss, and (d) the wilderness as a place of refuge (protection) or contemplation (renewal).[13]

In the story of Exodus, the desert functions mostly as a place of encounter with God, who made his presence known through revelation, chastisement, nourishment, and protection. After spending forty years of his youth at the court of the pharaoh, and another forty years as a shepherd in the desert of Madiam, Moses received God's call and spent the last forty years of his life leading his people through the desert until they finally reached the promised land.[14] Moses's first encounter with God occurred in the desert, near Mount Horeb, "the mountain of God." He noticed the burning bush, and when he drew closer heard the voice of God telling him to lead the Israelites out of Egypt.[15] It is this experience of the direct call by God heeded by human obedience, which the monks wished to replicate. God later communicated his commandments to Moses in the desert of Mount Sinai.[16] As he gave Moses the stone tablets on which they were inscribed, God allowed himself to be seen at a distance not only by Moses, but also by Aaron, Nadab, Abihu, and the seventy elders of Israel: "And they saw the God of Israel. Under his feet there was something like a pavement of sapphire stone, like the very heaven for clearness."[17] The image evokes the smooth surface of a cool and clear pool of water, in stark contrast to the arid and rugged mountain terrain of the Sinai. Later, Moses was summoned to the mountain on his own. He entered into the cloud and remained there, communicating with God for forty days.[18] God showed his power in the desert not only through revelation,

13. G. H. Williams, *Wilderness and Paradise in Christian Thought: The Biblical Experience in the History of Christianity and the Paradise Theme in the Theological Idea of the University* (New York, 1962), 18.
14. Acts 13:18.
15. Exod. 3:1ff.
16. Exod. 19ff.
17. Exod. 24:1–11.
18. Exod. 24:15–18.

but also by providing sustenance to his people in need by sending manna down from heaven for six consecutive days: "It was like coriander seed, white, and the taste of it was like wafers made with honey."[19] The desert was also the location of a further miracle that the Christians later imbued with new significance. At one point on their march, the Israelites were decimated by the bites of poisonous snakes. At God's command, Moses fashioned a snake of bronze and affixed it to a pole, so that everyone who looked at it was preserved from any ill effects of the snakebites.[20]

Once the people of God had reached the promised land, it was no longer the physical landscape and the hardships of the desert of Egypt and the Sinai Peninsula that occupied their religious imagination, but God's fearful ability to either transform any region into a desert or, inversely, to render a desert into populated and fertile land. The book of Ezekiel, the book of Daniel, and some psalms speak not of God's power as residing within a preexisting desert, but of his ability to render any place deserted and desolate as he chooses. He could make cities devoid *(erēmos)* of people, and he could lay to waste whole stretches of land, turning them into desert: "When I make the land of Egypt desolate and when the land is stripped of all that fills it, when I strike down all who live in it, then they shall know that I am the Lord."[21] The book of Daniel prophesied the desecration of the Temple in Jerusalem at the hands of Antiochus II Epiphanes in 167 B.C. by coining the new and chillingly evocative phrase the "abomination of desolation."[22] But God not only showed his power by creating a wasteland. He could also turn desolated land into a garden of luxury and build up cities: "And they will say: 'This land that was desolate has become like the Garden of Eden; and the waste and desolate and ruined towns are now inhabited and fortified.'"[23] These promises of God's power in the desert exerted great influence on the early monastic imagination, as the monks who settled in the uninhabitable parts of Egypt were engaged in a communal effort of fulfilling God's promise.

## The Desert in the New Testament

The desert continued to play an important role in the New Testament. Just like the desert of Egypt, that of Judaea was a liminal space where God made himself known, beginning with John the Baptist, the "voice in the desert"

---

19. Exod. 16:1ff., esp. Exod. 16:31.
20. Num. 21:4–9.
21. Ezek. 32:15; cf. also Ezek. 30:7–8, 33:29, 35:3–4.
22. Dan. 9:27, 11:31, 12:11 (the NRSV translates: "the abomination that desolates"); cf. Matt. 24:15; Mark 13:14; Luke 21:20.
23. Ezek. 36:35. Cf. also Ezek. 34:25–31.

who announced the coming of Christ, in accordance with the prophecy of Isaiah.[24] The desert was not only a space where one could encounter God, it was also a space where the forces of evil might be present. The demon had driven a possessed man to the desert many times before Jesus healed him.[25] And Jesus himself was transported by a demon, and tempted by him, for forty days in the desert.[26] Only once Jesus had proven himself through this test—just as the people of Israel had to undergo tribulations on their forty-year journey to the promised land—could he begin his active life of preaching and healing. The desert in the New Testament was also a concrete landscape, at a distance from the towns, where solitude could be found. Jesus often retreated to the desert to pray on his own.[27] He also went there to escape the crowds—usually without success, as the people followed him anyway.[28] At a great distance from sources of food, Jesus provided for his followers through the multiplication of loaves and fishes.[29] The Gospel of John explores the parallels between Christ and the story of Moses: while Moses through his prayer obtained manna from heaven, Christ himself is the bread of life.[30] Further, just as the bronze snake was lifted up by Moses on the pole to provide healing from snakebites for all, so will Christ be lifted up on the cross to bring salvation to humankind.[31]

## The Monastic Experience of the Desert

The image of the desert as a place of encounter with God, which is unique to the Jewish tradition and is reinforced by the experiences of John the Baptist and Jesus, had a strong attraction for the Christians of the late third century and beyond. They cherished the image of a desolate landscape, devoid of distractions, not even allowing the possibility of engaging in agricultural labor, where the individual was stripped naked of all worldly paraphernalia. This is the place where God called his people to go so that he could encounter them. Many people followed the "call." The most memorable story of such a radical departure from the world and its cares is that of Anthony.[32] This story itself, told masterfully by Athanasius in his *Life of*

---

24. Matt. 3:3; cf. Isa. 40:3.
25. Luke 8:29.
26. Matt. 4:1–11; Mark 1:12–13; Luke 4:1–13.
27. Mark 1:35; Luke 5:16.
28. Mark 1:45; Luke 4:42.
29. Matt. 14:13–21; cf. Matt. 15:32–39; Mark 6:30–44; cf. Luke 9:12–17.
30. John 6:31 and 49.
31. John 3:14–15.
32. For a concise overview of the concrete relevance of the desert of Upper Egypt in Coptic monasticism, see T. Vivian, *Histories of the Monks of Upper Egypt and the Life of Onnophrius by Paphnutius* (Kalamazoo, 1993), 18–26.

*Anthony,* would later be instrumental in calling Augustine and many others to the monastic life. Although Augustine ended up practicing a moderate form of ascetic retreat, he admits that he did at one point feel the attraction of the desert: "Terrified by my sins and the dead weight of my misery, I had turned my problems over in my mind and was half determined to seek refuge in the desert *(in solitudinem).*"[33]

A large and complex range of associations is connected with the concept of the desert in Christian monasticism. Three aspects in particular deserve to be highlighted: first, the desert of Egypt as a specific geographical setting; second, the desert as a state of mind; and third, the desert as a typological landscape.

### *The Desert of Egypt as a Specific Geographical Setting*

The story of Exodus shaped the perception of the Egyptian desert as a historical setting and as a place of encounter with God. The monastic experience of the desert was, in addition, influenced by the indigenous Egyptian view of the desert, which has its roots deep in the pre-Christian era. In the traditional, Egyptian understanding, the desert was a threatening space—a view that must have resonated especially among the native Egyptians who joined the monastic movement.[34] Egyptian religion distinguished between the "black land" of the fertile Nile Valley, which was associated with the god Osiris and his son Horus, and the "red land" of the desert and mountainous terrain beyond it, which was the domain of the trickster god Seth.[35] The desert was also the location of the tombs of the dead and thus of religious pollution. Finally, it was the place where, after the triumph of Christianity, the pagan deities were thought to have withdrawn and whence they to continued to emerge and pester people in the form of demons. Anthony's progressive withdrawal into the desert amounted to nothing less than a territorial battle with the demons, who protested vociferously against his advance and attempted to stop it with all their might. When Anthony had himself walled into a tomb—a tremendous act of bravery, considering the associations with death and religious impurity—his satanic adversary immediately feared that this initial encroachment on his territory would pave the way for further inroads, and therefore descended on him with an army of demons.[36]

33. Augustine, *Confessions* 10.43.70.
34. A. Guillaumont, "La conception du désert chez les moines d'Égypte," *Revue de l'Histoire des Religions* 188 (1975): 3–21, repr. in his *Aux origines du monachisme chrétien: Pour une phénoménologie du monachisme,* Spiritualité Orientale 30 (Begrolles-en-Mauges, 1979), pp. 11–14 (77–80).
35. E. Hornung, "Seth: Geschichte und Bedeutung eines ägyptischen Gottes," *Symbolon* n.s. 2 (1974): 43–63.
36. Athanasius, *Life of Anthony* 8.

For the next step in his retreat, Anthony took up residence farther away, in an abandoned fortress. Here, too, the demons immediately protested: "Get away from what is ours! What do you have to do with the desert?"[37] Finally, Satan himself came to Anthony's cell to admit his defeat: "I no longer have a place—no weapon, no city. There are Christians everywhere, and even the desert has filled with monks."[38]

In the Christian imagination, these traditional, indigenous associations of the Egyptian desert with demons, death, and pollution were combined with the idea of the desert of Egypt and the Sinai as a landscape of concrete historical and spiritual significance, where the first act of God's history with his people had been played out. It was the location of the Exodus, the Passage of the Red Sea, and the location of God's first covenant with Israel. The Christians who retreated to the desert followed quite literally in the footsteps of God's chosen people, the Israelites of old. They modeled themselves after the prophets, especially Elijah and Elisha, and after John the Baptist. The monks and hermits who took up residence in the desert participated in the common project of bringing this experience to life again, thus imbuing the concrete geographical setting of their ascetic life with new significance. This historicizing dimension of the monastic enterprise was not confined to the actual itinerary of Moses and Israel during the Exodus but in an extended sense applied to all desert settings. Moreover, it was in the barren and arid wastelands where the monks could fulfill, for all to see, God's promise of old to transform the wasted land into a city, and to render the desert into a garden, a foretaste of paradise.[39]

### The Desert as a City

The transformation of the desert into a city is a powerful concept, especially in the ancient world of the eastern Mediterranean, which was noted for its city culture. The cities were the center of all social, economic, political, and cultural life. In an abstract sense, the *polis* was also an important tool for conceptualizing human social relations, ever since Aristotle proclaimed that man was a *zōon politikon*, a political or social being. The fifth-century bishop Theodoret of Cyrrhus still distinguished between the life of the desert and the life of the city *(erēmitikos bios* and *bios politikos).*[40] The opposite of the city, both in a topographical and a demographical sense, was the desert. The desert was a wide open space with no clear delineation of its

---

37. Ibid., 13.
38. Ibid., 41.
39. F. Heim, "L'expérience mystique des pélerins occidentaux en Terre Sainte aux alentours de 400," *Ktema* 10 (1985): 193–208, esp. 205–8.
40. Theodoret, *HR* 25.

boundaries. The city, by contrast, was a well-defined area, often surrounded and protected by a wall. The desert was marked by a scarcity of supplies; the city was a place of commerce, entertainment, and all kind of distractions and pleasures. The desert was also a place of loneliness, while the city was characterized by the presence of crowds. To fuse the two, to speak of the transformation of the desert into a city, populated by men and women in pursuit of the solitary life, was thus a powerful image.[41]

Through the effort of the Egyptian monks who were assuming the role of the new people of God, the desert was transformed into its urban opposite. The key passage that illustrates this process comes from the *Life of Anthony:* "He persuaded many to take up the solitary life. And so, from then on, there were monasteries in the mountains and the desert was made a city by monks, who left their own people and registered themselves for the citizenship in the heavens."[42] The Christian tradition built upon and added to the ancient cultural tradition of the appreciation of the *polis* by imagining heaven as a city, the Heavenly Jerusalem.[43] In the *Apocalypse of Paul,* which probably dates from the fourth century, for example, heaven was described as a gated city with strictly regulated access. Only those who have completed a lifelong quest of renunciation had a chance to enter.[44] Only by becoming strangers to the world could the Christian ascetics acquire citizenship in heaven.[45] The construction of a "new city" stood as a strong countercultural symbol that made manifest the power of God through his servants. Ever since Athanasius coined the phrase in the *Life of Anthony,* the transformation of the desert into a city through a communal monastic endeavor became a hagiographical commonplace and was applied to other desert landscapes. Two examples from Palestine may suffice to illustrate this point. Cyril of Scythopolis, who chronicled the growth of monasticism in sixth-century Palestine, explained that Sabas had founded one of his many monastic establishments in the vicinity of Jerusalem because he wanted "to make the desert into a city."[46] The *Life of Mary of Egypt,* which was most likely composed in the seventh century but whose narrative seems to take place at an earlier point in time, describes how Zosimas and his fellow monks every year departed from their monastery to spend Lent in solitude: "As soon as they crossed the Jordan, they separated and moved far away from each other and

---

41. Palladius, *HL* 48.2: Elpidius attracts so many disciples that the mountain where he lives becomes a *polis.*
42. Athanasius, *Life of Anthony* 14.
43. On the importance of the concept of the city in the writings of the church fathers, see also B. E. Daley, "Building a New City: The Cappadocian Fathers and the Rhetoric of Philanthropy," *JECS* 7 (1999): 431–61.
44. *Apocalypse of Paul* 24.
45. Basil of Caesarea, *Ep.* 223.
46. Cyril of Scythopolis, *Life of Sabas* 37.

made the desert their city."[47] There, in the most remote and most inaccessible location, Zosimas would encounter Mary, who was doing penance for her earlier life as a prostitute.

Asceticism and monasticism were one way to transform a wasteland into a civilized urban environment. Charity was another. It is in this sense that Gregory of Nazianzus praised Basil for his foundation of a charitable institution, comprising a multitude of buildings for different purposes, as a "new city" named after its founder "Basileias."[48] Other family members did the same: during a famine Peter, the youngest brother of Basil and Gregory, provided food to the needy who had flocked to the region of the family's ascetic retreat, with the effect that "because of the crowds of visitors, the desert seemed to have become a city."[49]

Those who inhabited the desert were called (using a Greek neologism)[50] "citizens of the desert" *(erēmopolitai)*.[51] The apostle Paul had noted that "our citizenship is in heaven" (Phil. 3:20). Now the desert became the place, populated by those who lived the life of angels, where heaven on earth could be glimpsed. The Latin fathers do not seem to use the term "citizen of the desert,"[52] although they sometimes describe the desert as a *civitas*.[53] In Greek Christian writing, the prototype of the *erēmopolitēs* was John the Baptist, who was frequently called a "citizen of the desert."[54] The term could also be applied generally to all who practiced ascetic virtues in a monastic setting. Basil of Caesarea explained that, in addition to apostles and prophets, the desert was home to the monks as "citizens of the desert."[55] In the early fifth century, Nilus of Ancyra set out the advantages of the monastic life whose practitioner, the *erēmopolitēs*, would be remem-

47. *Life of St. Mary of Egypt*, trans. Kouli, pp. 74–75.

48. Gregory of Nazianzus, *Oratio* 43 *On Saint Basil the Great* 63.

49. Gregory of Nyssa, *Life of Macrina* 12.34 (my translation).

50. Before the *Life of Anthony*, there is only one attestation of a cognate of the word, *erēmopolis*, in Euripides' tragedy *The Trojan Women*, where it is used as the adjective with which Hecuba refers to herself as a mother bereft of her city and her children: Euripides, *Troades*, ed. W. Biehl (Leipzig, 1970), line 603.

51. For further references, see G. J. M. Bartelink, "Les oxymores *desertum civitas* and *desertum floribus vernans*," *Studia Monastica* 15 (1973): 7–15.

52. Bartelink, 12 n. 17.

53. Eucherius of Lyons, *In Praise of the Desert*, PL 50, col. 709C; Jerome, *Ep.* 2. The Greek word for citizenship, *politeuma*, used by Paul in Philippians 3:20, is translated in the Vulgate as *conversatio*, while non-Vulgate translations render it as *municipatus*. Cf. G. B. Ladner, *The Idea of Reform: Its Impact on Christian Thought and Action in the Age of the Fathers* (Cambridge, Mass., 1959), 346 n. 18.

54. The monastic *schēma* imitates the "citizen of the desert" John the Baptist, according to the commentary on the liturgy ascribed to Basil of Caesarea: F. E. Brightman, "The *Historia Mystagogica* and Other Greek Commentaries on the Byzantine Liturgy," *JThS* n.s. 9 (1907–8): 262.

55. Basil of Caesarea, *Ep.* 42.

bered long after his death, when the wealthy in this world will already have been forgotten.[56] The transformation of the desert or wilderness into a city was always an occasion for a great rhetorical display of marvel. Jerome described the desert as a "city more pleasant than all others" *(omni amoeniorem ciuitatem).*[57] The paradox of the desert as city, the creation of a new society, a new *politeia* of seekers of God, was given lively expression in a metrical homily *(memre)* in Syriac, entitled *On Hermits and Desert Dwellers,* which is, probably falsely, ascribed to Ephrem. The Syrian ascetic tradition arose quite independently of other developments elsewhere and originally allowed for the intensified practice of Christian virtues and celibacy within the local Christian communities. From the mid-fourth century, however, the Egyptian model with its emphasis on the solitary life in radical withdrawal from the world began to influence Syriac monasticism. This homily is evidence of the adaptation of these ideas, deriving its structure from the contrast between the hermit and the person in the world. The passages that play on the paradox of the transformation of the desert into a *politeia* of God are worth quoting in full, for they also speak to the powerful notion of prayer of holy men for the whole world, which was discussed earlier:

> The desert, frightful in its desolation, became a city of deliverance for them [the hermits],
> where their harps resound, and where they are preserved from harm.
> Desolation fled from the desert, for sons of the kingdom dwell there;
> it became like a great city with the sound of psalmody from their mouths.
> They saw that Elijah never suffered any misfortune from the wilderness;
> but the moment he entered civilization, mad Jezebel pursued him.
> As long as John was in the desert, the crowds went out to greet him.
> But he no sooner entered civilization, and Herod cut off his head.
> This is why they forsook and left a world full of danger,
> and made the wilderness their dwelling until they receive their rewards.
> They found two advantages in that desolate place they went out to:
> they were preserved from transgressions, and from the insults of men. . . .
> The wilderness that everyone fears has become a great place of refuge for them,
> where assistance flows from their bones to all creation.
> Civilization, where lawlessness prevails, is sustained by their prayers.
> And the world, buried in sin, is preserved by their prayers.[58]

56. Nilus of Ancyra, *Liber de monastica exercitatione* 21, *PG,* col. 79B.
57. Jerome, *Ep.* 2.
58. J. P. Amar, "On Hermits and Desert Dwellers," in *Ascetic Behavior in Greco-Roman Antiquity: A Sourcebook,* ed. V. L. Wimbush (Minneapolis, 1990), pp. 66–80, esp. vv. 157–64, 429–44, 497–504.

## The Desert of Egypt as a Garden and Paradise

The monks who made the Egyptian desert their home bore testimony to the transformative power that God continued to exercise even in their own day. The transformation of desert into city is one powerful image that could be invoked to underscore this. Another, no less evocative image is that of the transformation of the desert into a garden. The prophet Isaiah had said: "For the Lord will comfort Zion; he will comfort all her waste places, and will make her wilderness like Eden, her desert like the garden of the Lord."[59] In the monastic literature of Egypt, the garden or paradisiacal setting was expressed in a variety of ways.[60] First of all, in a very concrete and tangible way, Anthony and many other hermits like him cultivated the land where they lived to provide for themselves and their visitors. They often chose to settle near sources of water or—if they happened to be in an arid spot—produced the miraculous appearance of a spring, in imitation of Moses striking the rock with his staff. Their gardens became harbingers of paradise where all creatures lived in harmony. Wild beasts miraculously desisted from attacking their crops, often in response to a stern admonition by the monastic cultivator.[61] There are other stories of monks living in perfect harmony with nature: a crocodile offered its service to ferry Abba Helle across the Nile;[62] snakes guarded the cell of Amoun against robbers;[63] an antelope allowed Makarios to drink her milk, and a hyena sought his help to restore the eyesight of her blind cub;[64] and a lion was tamed and became a faithful servant of its monastic master Gerasimos after the *abba* had removed a thorn from its paw. This took place, the author of the *Spiritual Meadow* explains, "to show how the beasts were in subjection to Adam before he disobeyed the commandment and fell from the comfort of paradise."[65]

The wonderfully transformed landscape was inhabited by men and women who had themselves been wonderfully transformed. Fasting and sex-

---

59. Isa. 51:3. Cf. also Isa. 35:1–2: "The wilderness and the dry land shall be glad, the desert shall rejoice and blossom; like crocus it shall blossom abundantly, and rejoice with joy and singing." Isa. 41:19–20: "I will put in the wilderness the cedar, the acacia, the myrtle, and the olive; I will set in the desert the cypress, the plane and the pine together, so that all may see and know, all may consider and understand, that the hand of the Lord has done this, the Holy One of Israel has created it."

60. For a detailed documentation, see K. S. Frank, *Aggelikos Bios: Begriffsanalytische und begriffsgeschichtliche Untersuchung zum "engelgleichen Leben" im frühen Mönchtum*, Beiträge zur Geschichte des alten Mönchtums und des Benediktinerordens 26 (Münster, 1964).

61. Athanasius, *Life of Anthony* 50.

62. *HM* 11.9.10–13 Schulz-Flügel (12.6–9 Ward).

63. *HM* 8.2–6 Schulz-Flügel (9.5–6 Ward).

64. Palladius, *HL* 18.9 and 27–28.

65. John Moschos, *Spiritual Meadow* 107.

ual abstinence restored their physical existence to the original state of purity before the Fall of Adam. No longer attached to the world nor troubled by care for their body, they were regarded as leading the "life of angels" in anticipation of the paradise to come.[66] The specific setting of the monastic project in Egypt, it seems to me, carried with it all these associations of the desire to actualize in the present day the history of salvation, which had begun with God's first covenant, and to prove that the Christians were the legitimate successors of Israel and carried on its inheritance.

### The Desert as a Place of Spiritual Growth

The continued struggle for spiritual progress by all Christians after their baptism is, according to Augustine, analogous to the wanderings of the Israelites through the desert after the crossing of the Red Sea. His affirmation that "the world is this desert [of Egypt]" already contains in a nutshell the idea that would later become influential in Western, especially Irish monasticism, that the Christian existence is that of the *peregrinus*, a stranger in this world embarked on a lifelong pilgrimage to a better place.[67] The hermits and monks in late antique Egypt applied this notion in a concrete way. To them, the *erēmos* was much more than the physical landscape where one could follow the example of Moses, John the Baptist, or Christ, and where they could participate in and contribute to the history of salvation. Their aim in withdrawing from society was also to reap spiritual benefits for themselves—not dissimilar from the countryside retreat of wealthy and learned pagans. In the monastic literature, *erēmos* was often coupled with *hēsychia*. When Origen was overwhelmed with the frustrations of his task as teacher, for example, he admitted to feeling the pull toward "the desert and tranquility *(epi tēn erēmian kai hēsychian)*."[68] The physical distance from the city and the absence of its distractions were accompanied by tranquility, which prepared the soul for union with God. In imitation of Jesus, who escaped to the desert to pray in solitude, John Chrysostom explained, Christians, too, must escape the noise and distractions of the cities and retreat to the desert, if they want to communicate with God. This "desert," he adds, does not need to be a remote mountain, but it may also be a small place of retreat from the turmoil of the world.[69] In the desert, the individ-

---

66. Frank; Nagel, 34–62.
67. "Saeculum autem hoc eremus est," Augustine, *Sermo* 4.9.9 (Classis prima: Sermones de scripturis), *PL* 38, 37. See also Augustine, *Enarratio in Ps.* 72.5, *PL* 36, col. 917.
68. Origen, *Homilies on Jeremiah* 20.8.
69. John Chrysostom, *Against the Anhomoeans* 10. 2. See also Eucherius of Lyons, *In Praise of the Desert*, *PL* 50, col. 707A–B: "The desert may rightly be called a place of prayer, for God himself has approved it and taught by his example that it is appropriate for prayer. Humble prayer will

ual was stripped naked of all the markers of identity that had mattered in his previous social context and was forced to throw himself at the mercy of God. The elimination of external stimuli was the first and easiest step on this quest, since it consisted of a one-time act of physical withdrawal from the world. Much more difficult was the concentration of the mind and soul on the divine, because it required a continuous effort.[70] John Cassian advised that the monk should sit in his cell in contemplation and solitude so that

> like a splendid fisherman . . . he may eagerly and without moving catch the swarms of thoughts swimming in the calm depth of his heart, and surveying with curious eye the depths as from a high rock, may sagaciously and cunningly decide what he ought to lure to himself by his saving hook, and what he can neglect and reject as bad and nasty fishes.[71]

Desert life also harbored its own perils. The elimination of all external distractions helped to focus the soul on contemplation of the divine, but it also threw the mind back on itself and magnified one's inner thoughts and doubts. Old ingrained concerns, desires of the world, and memories of the pleasures of one's previous life continuously threatened to invade the mind and disturb its equilibrium. In the stillness of the desert, the human soul became like the surface of a pool of water that reflects, as in a mirror, all internal faults.[72] John Cassian explained: "For whatever faults we bring with us uncured into the desert, we shall find to remain concealed in us and not to be got rid of."[73] He then added a vignette from his own experience: during his withdrawal to the desert, even though he lived in solitude, he still managed to experience anger—not at a neighbor, but at the few objects in his cell, his pen, his knife, his flint for making fire.[74] John Cassian here experienced concretely what Evagrius Ponticus had formulated in the abstract:

> Against people of the world, the demons fight primarily through things, against monks, they fight mostly through thoughts. For they are deprived of things because of the desert. And in the same measure as it is easier to sin internally than in actuality, in the same degree is the internal war more

---

more easily penetrate the clouds if it rises from the desert because that solitary place gives it increased merit."

70. For an instructive modern example of desert spirituality, see the personal statement of a present-day hermit: R. Wild, "I Am in the Desert," *Studies in Formative Spirituality* 1/2 (1980): 207–16.

71. John Cassian, *Conferences* 24.3

72. *Sayings of the Desert Fathers*, Systematic Collection 2, Ward p. 1.

73. John Cassian, *Institutes* 8.18.

74. Ibid., 8.19.

difficult than that about things. For the intellect is a thing that is easily set in motion and badly equipped to hold in check prohibited imaginations.[75]

Another internal danger for the desert dweller were thoughts of vainglory. Those who had mastered the hardships of life in the desert could easily become inflated with pride over their ascetic achievements and the specific virtues for which they were recognized by others.[76] This could result in disdain of communal monastic settings or indeed in the vehement rejection of all that the institutional church represented, a topic to which I will return below.

### Beyond Egypt and the Desert Landscape

The concrete location of the Egyptian desert, with its historical connotations, could be replaced by desert landscapes in Palestine or Syria, but without losing the connection to the typological significance of the retreat to a barren landscape conducive to spiritual growth. During his retreat to the desert of Chalkis near Antioch, Jerome extolled his abode with great flourish in his Letter 14 to his friend Heliodorus, whom he tried—in vain—to cajole into joining him. Jerome played on the contrast between the barrenness of the desert and the flowering of spiritual benefits that only life in the desert could bring. The person who exposed his body to the harshness and deprivation of the desert could, he said, stroll through paradise in his mind.[77] Basil of Caesarea's extended praise of the monastic life in his Letter 42 referred to the desert of Palestine, without even mentioning the desert of Egypt and its connection to the Israelites. The desert, to him, was the place where Christ himself, "the friend of the desert," had lived, where the Oak of Mamre stood, where Jacob had had a vision of angels, where Elias had stood on Mount Carmel, where Esdras had been a prophet, where John the Baptist had lived, and where Jesus had prayed on the Mount of Olives.[78] The landscape of Syria could not claim such concrete biblical associations, but it nonetheless offered the spiritual benefits of the desert setting. The hermit Julian, who lived in the region of Osrhoene, near the Euphrates, in the early fifth century, was said to be in the habit of walking a great distance, "separating himself from all human company and turning into himself [so as to] enjoy solitary intercourse with God and gaze as if in a mirror upon that divine and inexpressible beauty." Then he returned to his eremitic dis-

---

75. Evagrius Ponticus, *Praktikos* 48.
76. John Cassian, *Institutes* 11.6ff. See also *HM* 1.4.1ff. (Schulz-Flügel).
77. Jerome, *Ep.* 14.10.
78. Basil of Caesarea, *Ep.* 42.5.

ciples "like some Moses."[79] Later he traveled to Mount Sinai, "making passable the impassable desert," and remained there for a period of time, "thinking the deserted character of the place and tranquility of soul supreme delight."[80]

## The Desert as a State of Mind

While the desert is highly conducive to cultivating inner tranquility and facilitating communication with God, the attainment of this "desert state of mind" is not necessarily tied to a specific kind of landscape or location. Although John Chrysostom was well aware of the advantages of a physical retreat to the desert, he was able to disassociate the desert state of mind from the desert as a landscape: "Let us seek after the desert, not only that of the place, but also that of disposition."[81] The association of desert and mental rest, and the idea that the "desert" state of mind could be attained regardless of location, appeared in the literature of the Judeo-Christian tradition long before the first hermits began to populate the desert of Egypt. The first to mention it was Philo of Alexandria in the first half of the first century.[82] Philo saw the desert not only as a desirable place far removed from the moral corruption of the town, but also as a location of ideal climatic conditions where the air was light and pure and which was therefore more conducive to *askēsis*.[83] Clement followed Philo in establishing a connection between the desert and tranquility.[84] To him, however, the physical setting of the desert was only relevant insofar as it generated the proper mental disposition. The desert landscape itself was not indispensable. Accordingly, he insisted that the true *gnōstikos* could live in the city as if he were in the desert.[85] For Origen, finally, the desert was synonymous with *hēsychia,* a state of detachment from irrelevant worldly cares that allowed a total concentra-

---

79. Theodoret, *HR* 2.4.

80. Ibid., 2.13.

81. John Chrysostom, *De compunctione ad Stelechium* 2.3.

82. The material and most observations in the following are largely derived from Guillaumont. See also B. McGinn, "Ocean and Desert as Symbols of Mystical Absorption in the Christian Tradition," *Journal of Religion* 74 (1994): 155–81. K. Bosl, "*Erēmos-Eremus:* Begriffsgeschichtliche Bemerkungen zum historischen Problem der Entfremdung und Vereinsamung des Menschen," *ByzForsch* 2 (1967): 73–90 ( = *Polychordia: Festschrift Franz Dölger,* ed. P. Wirth, vol. 2).

83. Philo of Alexandria, *De vita contemplativa* 22–23. See also his explanation of why God chose to give the Law to Moses in the desert: *De decalogo* 2. Philo, however, is not the first to make this point, according to Guillaumont, 6 (72) n. 1.

84. Clement of Alexandria, *Paedagogus* 2.10 (112.2). He uses the word *galēnē.*

85. Clement of Alexandria, *Stromata* 7.12 (77.3).

tion on the inner self, an ideal that had already appealed to the Stoic philosophers.[86] The desert abode in and of itself was no guarantee of spiritual advancement.

Spiritual perfection and the desert state of mind could be attained in other surroundings as well. Even the great Anthony is reported to have been humbled by a revelation that showed him his equal, who lived, of all places, in the city. He was a physician who was generous in his charity and steadfast in his prayer.[87] One of the few desert mothers, Amma Syncletica, seems to echo Cassian's predicament mentioned above with her remark "It is possible to be a solitary in one's mind while living in a crowd, and it is possible for one who is solitary to live in the crowd of his own thoughts."[88] For all his appreciation of the physical desert experience, Jerome was also able to distinguish between the desert as a geographical space and the desert as a metaphor for complete solitude of the individual with God, which is equal to paradise: "As long as you are at home, make your cell your paradise, gather there the varied fruits of Scripture, let this be your favourite companion, and take its precepts to your heart. . . . But to me a town is a prison and a solitude, paradise. Why do we long for the bustle of cities, we whose name *(monachus)* speaks of loneliness?"[89] Jerome here and elsewhere insisted that the spiritual effects of the exposure to the harshness of desert life could also be achieved within the confinement of the monastic cell.[90] In the mid-fifth century, and not in Egypt, but in Syria, Theodoret of Cyrrhus insisted that perfection can be attained in any kind of setting: "But lest anyone should suppose that virtue is circumscribed in place and that only the desert is suitable for the production of such a yield, let us now in our account pass to inhabited land, and show that it does not offer the least hindrance to the attainment of virtue."[91]

The Cappadocian fathers were especially eloquent advocates of the internalized "desert." They insisted that any landscape that offered tranquility at a distance from the city, even the lush countryside, could serve as a "functional desert." Even more radically, they allowed that the exercise of monasticism was not tied to any particular location at all. Basil of Caesarea explained in a letter to his friend Gregory of Nazianzus that monastic withdrawal *(anachōrēsis)* with the goal of tranquility *(hēsychia)* consists in the ef-

---

86. Origen, *Homilies on Jeremiah* 20.8. For the terminology, see also P. Miquel, *Lexique du désert: Étude de quelques mot-clés du vocabulaire monastique grec ancien,* Spiritualité Orientale 44 (Bégrolles-en-Mauges, 1986), 145–80.
87. *Sayings of the Desert Fathers,* Anthony 24.
88. Ibid., Syncletica 19.
89. Jerome, *Ep.* 125.
90. Compare also Jerome, *Ep.* 24.3 and 4 to Marcella, describing the virtuous life of the virgin Asella, who had lived in a narrow cell on her parents' property from a very young age.
91. Theodoret, *HR* 4.1.

fort to liberate the soul from attachment to things of the world, but that it does not necessarily require a physical retreat.[92] Gregory of Nazianzus concurred. In his *Autobiography*[93] and in his *Oration in Praise of Athanasius*[94] he remarked that monasticism is an internal disposition, independent of one's location. Basil's brother Gregory of Nyssa carried this notion to an extreme when he attempted to justify his pilgrimage to Jerusalem by explaining how his carriage was transformed into a veritable monastery on wheels: "The chariot served for us as a church and a monastery, for the psalmody in common and the fasting unto the Lord during the entire journey."[95]

### The Desert as a Typological Landscape

The formative imprint of the Egyptian desert as a model extended not only to the sought-after spiritual formation of the individual, but also to the conventions of literary representation of any kind or place of retreat. James Goehring has shown the pervasive and lasting imprint of the Egyptian monastic experience on later writing on related subjects. In the earliest monastic literature of Egypt, the desert came to play an important role as a metaphorical space that signaled the extent of the inner distance of the monk from the cares of the world.[96] In actual fact, the practitioners of asceticism in Egypt lived in a variety of settings, in cities, towns, villages, agriculturally active areas, in addition to remote desert locations. The desert-dominated rhetorical model was given literary expression in the second half of the fourth century in the *Life of Anthony*, the *History of the Monks in Egypt*, and in the *Sayings of the Desert Fathers*. From then on, it shaped and dominated the actions of individuals, the way they thought about themselves, and the way in which others wrote about them, even in regions of the empire where monasticism had its own, distinct roots and even when the individuals in question had not personally shared the lifestyle of the desert fathers. The Egyptian monastic discourse thus acts like a glaze that gives a distinct tint and appearance to monastic writing.

This explains how "the desert" became a loaded expression among Christian authors that evoked associations of retreat and spiritual growth, regardless of the actual nature of the location. Several authors of the late fourth and early fifth century described lush, prosperous settings as a mo-

---

92. Basil of Caesarea, *Ep.* 2.
93. Gregory of Nazianzus, *Autobiography* 329–30.
94. Gregory of Nazianzus, *Homily* 21 *On Athanasius* 20.
95. Gregory of Nyssa, *Ep.* 2.
96. J. E. Goehring, "The Encroaching Desert: Literary Production and Ascetic Space in Early Christian Egypt," *JECS* 1 (1993): 281–96, repr. in his *Ascetics, Society, and the Desert: Studies in Early Egyptian Monasticism* (Harrisburg, 1999).

nastic "desert." Jerome's *Life of Paul the Hermit* shows all the marks of a carefully crafted literary artifact and does not lack in charming descriptions of
the ideal outdoor setting: Paul's cave, although located in a barren landscape far removed from civilization, was itself like an oasis, with shaded trees
and a gentle gurgling spring. Yet Paul was cast in the role of the desert hermit par excellence, competing for that status with Anthony in Athanasius's
description.

Basil of Caesarea gushed about his retreat near Annisi in the Pontus
region as if it provided him the same spiritual benefits as the Egyptian
desert. But according to the description that follows, his actual physical environment resembled a pleasant country abode more than the forbidding
wilderness of Egypt:

> I departed into Pontus in quest of a place to live in. There God has opened to
> me a spot exactly answering to my taste, so that I actually see before my eyes
> what I have often pictured to my mind in idle fancy. There is a lofty mountain
> covered with thick woods, watered towards the north with cool and transpar
> ent streams. A plain lies beneath, enriched by the waters which are ever drain
> ing off from it; and skirted by a spontaneous profusion of trees almost thick
> enough to be a fence; so as even to surpass Calypso's island, which Homer
> seems to have considered the most beautiful spot on the earth . . . the chief
> praise of the place is, that being happily disposed for produce of every kind
> [for food], it nurtures what to me is the sweetest produce of all, quietness.[97]

Basil's brother Naucratius had embraced this way of life some time
before his famous brother. The pleasant setting of this hermitage, which
even provided hunting grounds, is described by Gregory of Nyssa in his *Life
of Macrina:*

> So Naucratius went off to live by himself, having found a remote point on the
> Iris River. The Iris flows through the middle of Pontus, has its source in
> Armenia, makes its way through our regions and empties into the Black Sea.
> Here, the young man found a spot bristling with deep forest and hidden in a
> hollow with a rocky cliff overhead, far from the noises of the city, military activ
> ities and the business of rhetoric in the lawcourts.[98]

Here again, tranquility and the practice of Christian virtues could be
achieved in an idyllic location, as long as it was removed from the city.
Jerome, Basil, and Gregory of Nyssa were educated men of their times. In
their description of the ideal monastic setting, they combined the classical
literary device of the description of the *locus amoenus,* so typical of bucolic

97. Basil of Caesarea, *Ep.* 14.
98. Gregory of Nyssa, *Life of Saint Macrina* 9.

literature, with a nod to the Christian, and especially monastic, predilection for the ideal of the desert. The same literary craftsmanship is evident in Eucherius of Lyon's work *In Praise of the Desert,* composed in 426.[99] Eucherius was no stranger to the monastic tradition. Born into a senatorial family in southern Gaul, he soon joined the monastic circle of the island of Lérins and eventually became bishop of Lyon. John Cassian dedicated the second part of his *Conferences* to him.[100] Eucherius's work extolled the island of Lérins off the coast of southern Gaul as the ideal place of monastic retreat in the Egyptian desert tradition and celebrated the return of Hilarius to the island from his episcopal duties in Arles as an imitation of Moses's entry into the desert after crossing the Red Sea. However, in actual appearance, as Eucherius himself noted, the island resembled a paradisiacal garden with brooks, meadows, and flowers, rather than a wilderness. Yet, as a metaphorical desert, Lérins has now become the location of monks who represent the true Israel:

> You [Hilary] are now the true Israel who gazes upon God in his heart, who has just been freed from the dark Egypt of the world, who has crossed the saving waters in which the enemy drowned, who follows the burning light of faith in the desert, who experiences things formerly bitter now made sweet by the wood of the cross, who draws from Christ a drink of water springing up into eternal life, who feeds his spirit with the bread from on high, and who receives the word of God in the gospel as if from Sinai. Because you keep company with Israel in the desert, you will certainly enter the promised land with Jesus.[101]

### The Desert Experience as a Time of Transition and Preparation

What part did the life of solitude associated with the concept of the desert, whether in Egypt or elsewhere, play in an individual's life? Here the monastic authors disagree. Most regarded it as the pinnacle of a lifelong quest, but there were others who saw it as an intermediary period of preparation for communal living or service in the church. John Cassian was an advocate of the former view. He recommended that life in solitude should be preceded by an extended stay in a monastic community, where withdrawal from the

99. Eucherius of Lyons, *In Praise of the Desert.* See also I. Opelt, "Zur literarischen Eigenart von Eucherius' Schrift *De laude eremi,*" *VC* 22 (1968): 198–208. This poem exerted great influence on the German mystics in the Middle Ages. See H. Bayer, "*Vita in deserto:* Kassians Askese der Einöde und die mittelalterliche Frauenmystik," *ZKG* 98 (1987): 1–27. The *Life of Hilarius of Arles,* composed by Honoratus of Marseilles at the end of the fifth century, also speaks of Lerins as a "paradise on earth" *(terrestrem . . . Lirinensis insulae paradisum,* 7.1,)* where Hilarius dedicates himself to penitential ascetic practices.
100. L. Cristiani, "Eucher (saint), évêque de Lyon," *DSp* 4 (1961): cols. 1653–60.
101. Eucherius of Lyons, *In Praise of the Desert* 44.

world was combined with the practice of virtues within the community, supported by the regular rituals of liturgical celebration.[102] Even those who were
experienced monks were not always able to endure the hardships of desert
life. This is the moral of the story told of Abba Gelasius, the abbot of a
monastery in Nilopolis, who cured himself of his recurring desire to retreat
to the desert by subjecting himself for a brief trial period to the physical dis-
comforts of eating raw vegetables and sleeping outdoors.[103] According to this
view, the radical retreat to the desert was the ultimate challenge, the culmination of monastic life that had to be mastered first within a community.

This was not, however, the only possible approach. At the same time,
there was an opposing trend that regarded the communal life as more demanding than the solitary existence. Abba Matoes explained this to a monk
who was troubled by his propensity to gossip: "It is not through virtue that I
live in solitude, but through weakness; those who live in the midst of men
are the strong ones."[104] Spiritual progress did not depend on the austerity of
the setting, but on the sincerity of the soul, helped along by proper guidance. In the words of an Old Man: "He who lives in obedience to a spiritual
father finds more profit in it than one who withdraws to the desert."[105] It is
important to bear in mind that it was not uncommon in late antiquity for
individuals to experiment with eremitic or communal living at different
phases in their lives.

In fact, not all *erēmopolitai* became permanent citizens of the desert of
Egypt. Many stayed only for a brief time to expose themselves to the concrete
desert experience. They traveled to Egypt or the Holy Land to seek instruction from the spiritual fathers and then returned home, either to found
monastic establishments of their own, as did John Cassian in Italy, or to
become members of the clergy, as did Palladius of Helenopolis in Bithynia.
In the first case, monastic living continued to be a lifelong vocation; in the
second, a transitory stage in a life dedicated to the Christian church.

The transitional stage of complete withdrawal as a time of preparation
for great heroic deeds after reentry into society—in a transformed state and
with greater powers than before—is, of course, a common motif in legends
and fairy tales, including Christian hagiography.[106] The *Life of Anthony*, for

102. John Cassian, *Institutes* 8.18.
103. *Sayings of the Desert Fathers*, Gelasius 6. Another story tells of cenobitic monks who are mis-
led by a hermit's hospitality to believe that the desert life is more luxurious than that in their
monastery: *Sayings of the Desert Fathers*, Systematic Collection 97.
104. *Sayings of the Desert Fathers*, Matoes 13. See also the hermit who wants to abandon the
desert in the hopes of making greater spiritual progress inside a monastery: *Sayings of the Desert
Fathers*, Paphnutius 5.
105. *Sayings of the Desert Fathers*, Systematic Collection 163.
106. A. Goddart-Eliott, *Roads to Paradise: Reading the Lives of the Early Saints* (Hanover, N.H.,
1987).

example, dramatically plays out the moment when Anthony emerged after twenty years of being walled up in an abandoned fortress: he was radiant, showed no signs of aging, and was from then on capable of working miracles. Numerous other hagiographical texts followed this pattern. As will be explained in the next section, the specific tripartite scheme of secular education, monasticism, and ministry is most commonly applied in the lauda- ✓ tory description of bishops, modeled on the biblical exemplar of Moses.

### MOSES AS THE BIBLICAL MODEL OF LEADERSHIP

The desert of Egypt is of great importance as the backdrop for the beginnings of the monastic movement. It established the concrete context for all subsequent monastic enterprises and provided the notional framework for all later reflection on the nature of monastic living. The monks in Egypt, it has been noted, saw themselves as the true Israel that carried God's history with his people into the present. It is now time to turn to the figure of Moses and its significance for the conceptualization of authority in late antiquity. Moses was considered the biblical model par excellence for bishops, especially among Greek authors. This is not surprising, since he was believed to hold all the aspects of authority of our tripartite scheme. His spiritual authority is evident in the fact that God revealed himself to him in the burning bush and again in the cloud on Mount Sinai, and then heeded Moses's prayers on behalf of the people. Moses's ascetic authority is manifest in his many virtues, especially meekness *(praotēs)*, for which he became proverbial. Most prominent is his pragmatic authority: as a general, he led his people out of Egypt; as a lawgiver, he brought them the Ten Commandments; as a benefactor and provider, he took care of their physical needs during the long exodus.

In late antiquity, Moses was held in high regard by Jews, pagans, and Christians alike.[107] The Jews maintained that he was greater than Jesus,[108] pagans admired his contributions to the progress of civilization, and Christians saw him as an earlier version either of Christ[109] or of the apostles, especially of Peter.[110] Moses was celebrated as a larger-than-life figure, worthy of

---

107. The following is based, in large part, on C. Rapp, "Comparison, Paradigm, and the Case of Moses in Panegyric and Hagiography," in *The Propaganda of Power,* ed. Mary Whitby (Leiden, 1998).

108. Anastasius of Sinai, *Viae dux* 14.1.

109. See, for example, Orosius, *Against the Pagans* 7.27.3. Cf. J. E. Bruns, "The 'Agreement of Moses and Jesus' in the 'Demonstratio Evangelica' of Eusebius," *Vigiliae Christianae* 31 (1977): 117–25; M. J. Hollerich, "Religion and Politics in the Writings of Eusebius: Reassessing the First 'Court Theologian,'" *Church History* 59 (1990): 309–25.

110. Tertullian, *Against Marcion* 4.24. For further literary and artistic evidence, see also C. A. Kneller, "Moses und Petrus," *Stimmen aus Maria-Laach* 60 (1901): 237–57.

imitation by everyone, and especially by those in a position of responsibility, such as rulers, lawgivers, and generals.[111] In the late fourth century, Gregory of Nyssa composed his *Life of Moses* at the request of a young man who had asked him for a precept for the perfect life.[112] In his encomium on his brother Basil of Caesarea, Gregory noted that "the great Moses is set forth as a common example for all who those who look to virtue."[113] The powerful effect of the story of the life of Moses as a common and universal model was also underlined by Basil of Caesarea when he said that the moment we hear it "we are immediately captured by yearning for the virtue of the man."[114]

If Moses was the model for any perfect and virtuous man, then this especially applied to holy men. And indeed, the hagiographical literature abounds with comparisons between holy men and Moses. These take three different forms. First, a specific action of the holy man is compared to a specific aspect of, or event in, the life of Moses.[115] The martyr Mamas, for instance, is said to follow the example of Moses, since he, too, had the occupation of a shepherd.[116] Second, Moses may be included in an enumeration of *exempla* from the Old Testament—augmented, on occasion, with figures of the New Testament, especially John the Baptist and the apostles—which a holy man is said to emulate and often to surpass. The ancients distinguished between the rhetorical devices of *exemplum* and *comparatio*. *Exemplum* is a brief reference that sets an individual in relation to a great model of the past. In classical literature, this is a figure from history or mythology; in Christian writing it is usually a figure from the Old or the New Testament. *Comparatio* is a detailed, point-by-point comparison of isolated characteristics of an individual with those of a great figure from the past. Frequently used in panegyric and hagiography, it serves to demonstrate that the individual in question lags in no way behind, and perhaps even surpasses, the hero of the past.

Gregory of Nazianzus's *Oration on Athanasius of Alexandria* skillfully com-

111. Philo of Alexandria, *Life of Moses* 1.158, and 2.1.1–3. On Philo's treatment of Moses, see also L. Bieler, *THEIOS ANĒR: Das Bild des göttlichen Menschen in Spätantike und Frühchristentum* (Darmstadt, 1967; first published in two vols., Vienna, 1935–36). Clement of Alexandria, *Stromata* 1 (22) 150.5–(29) 182.3.

112. Gregory of Nyssa, *Life of Moses* 1.

113. Gregory of Nyssa, *Funerary Oration on Saint Basil* 20.

114. Basil of Caesarea, *On the Martyr Gordius, PG* 31, col. 492A.

115. Basil of Caesarea is brought up in the educational system of his surroundings, just like Moses: Gregory of Nyssa, *Funerary Oration on Saint Basil* 1. Basil is also applauded for this in Gregory's *Life of Moses* 2. Paul's apostolic activities are compared to those of Moses by John Chrysostom, *Panegyrics on Saint Paul* 7.4, p. 302. Moses is invoked as precedent for the transferal of the relics of Saint Babylas by the Caesar Gallus: John Chrysostom, *Homily on Saint Babylas, PG* 50, cols. 531f. Meletius's arrival as the new bishop of Antioch, upon which he immediately proceeds to expel the heretics, is compared to Moses's arrival in Egypt: John Chrysostom, *Homily on Meletius, PG* 50, col. 516.

116. Basil of Caesarea, *On the Martyr Mamas, PG* 31, col. 593B.

bines *exemplum* and *comparatio*. First comes a long list of names: Enoch, Noah, Abraham, Isaac, Jacob, the Twelve Patriarchs, Moses, Aaron, Joshua, the Judges, Samuel, David, Solomon, Elias, Elisha, the prophets, John the Baptist, the disciples of Christ, those who were ennobled by their miracles, and those who suffered a violent death for their faith. Athanasius is then set in relation to these luminaries: "Athanasius took up the competition against some of these, he lagged a little behind others, but there are yet others whom he surpassed, if that is not too bold a statement." What is more, Athanasius embodied the totality of all different virtues represented by each of these men, thus outdoing them all.[117] Third and last, a saint may be set in relation to Moses through detailed *comparatio* at a specific and isolated place in the narrative. The eulogy by Gregory of Nyssa on his deceased brother Basil of Caesarea, for instance, concludes with the detailed demonstration of the many parallels between the life of Basil and that of Moses.[118] Gregory of Nazianzus displays a predilection for comparisons with Moses in his funerary orations: his father, Basil the Elder, is a second Aaron or Moses[119] and imitates Moses in praying to God on behalf of his people;[120] Gregory's friend Basil is said to have the philanthropy typical of a Moses or an Elias[121] and follows the example of Aaron and Moses in admonishing those who have gone astray.[122]

This example shows that laudatory comparisons with Moses are applied particularly to men who are not only distinguished by their exemplary lives of piety, but who also occupy positions of responsibility, Basil the Elder being a rhetor and Basil holding the episcopate of Caesarea. In fact, Moses seems to be adduced as the model of preference in the literary representa-

---

117. Gregory of Nazianzus, *Homily* 21 *On Athanasius*, PG 35, col. 1085. See also Gregory of Nyssa, *On Bishop Meletius*, PG 46, col. 857C; Gregory of Nazianzus, *Oratio* 43 *On Saint Basil*, PG 36, cols. 589–97; John Chrysostom, *Panegyrics on Saint Paul* 1.1; John of Damascus, *Encomium on Saint John Chrysostom*, PG 96, col. 777C–D. Along with Elias and John the Baptist, Moses is a model for those who are fasting: Basil of Caesarea, *Constitutiones asceticae*, PG 31, cols. 1357C–60A. Similarly, but with the exclusion of John the Baptist: Theodoret, *HR* 26.7 (Symeon).

118. Gregory of Nyssa, *Funerary Oration on Saint Basil* 20–23. Preceding the *comparatio* with Moses are similar, but shorter comparisons with Paul, John the Baptist, Elias, and Samuel. See also the detailed discussion by M. Harl, "Moise figure de l'évêque dans l'éloge de Basile de Grégoire de Nysse (381)," in *The Biographical Works of Gregory of Nyssa: Proceedings of the Fifth International Colloquium on Gregory of Nyssa (Mainz, 6–10 September 1982)*, ed. A. Spira (Cambridge, Mass., 1984). On Gregory's interpretation of Moses in general, see the detailed work by J. Daniélou, "Moses bei Gregor von Nyssa: Vorbild und Gestalt," in *Moses in Schrift und Überlieferung* (Düsseldorf, 1963; first published in French, 1954).

119. Gregory of Nazianzus, *Oratio* 7 *On His Brother Caesarius*, PG 35, col. 757C.

120. Gregory of Nazianzus, *On His Father*, PG 35, col. 1021A.

121. Gregory of Nazianzus, *Oratio* 43 *On Saint Basil the Great*, PG 36, col. 544B.

122. Ibid., col. 593B–C.

tion of bishops.[123] Many bishops themselves invoked Moses as precedent for their own actions, sometimes with an apologetic intention. When John Chrysostom returned to Constantinople after a long absence in Asia Minor, for example, he found himself in a situation that contrasted favorably with that which Moses faced after spending forty days in the desert. He ended his sermon in a long *comparatio* with Moses, concluding: "This we experienced, I and Moses."[124] Similarly, Athanasius justified his flight from Arian persecution by pointing to biblical precedent, including Moses's flight from the anger of the pharaoh.[125] Finally, Theophilus of Alexandria is reported to have called himself "another Moses" in an attempt to silence his critics, who had attacked him because of his unprecedented move in ordaining a bishop without assigning him an episcopal see.[126]

One author who systematically applied the model of Moses in order to expound the honor of a saintly bishop is Palladius, in his *Dialogue on the Life of John Chrysostom.* This work was composed after John had been sent into exile by a coalition of ecclesiastical, aristocratic, and court circles in Constantinople, supported by the bishops of Asia Minor and the patriarch of Alexandria. On three occasions, Palladius placed John's suffering in relation to events in the life of Moses: John was placed under house arrest by the emperor Arcadius and thus resembles Moses against whom the pharaoh's heart had hardened;[127] John had to bear the consequences of his resistance to secular authority, just like Moses;[128] and John had to retreat from the world, just as Moses had to depart from the palace of the pharaoh.[129]

The most emphatic literary device for setting an individual in relation to a great figure from the past was complete identification. Thus it was the highest form of praise to call an individual a "new Moses" or "our Moses." It is important to note that in this particular form, and with one notable exception that will be discussed below, this laudatory identification is in the

123. See also A. Sterk, "On Basil, Moses, and the Model Bishop: The Cappadocian Legacy of Leadership," *Church History* 67 (1998): 227–53; A. Wilson, "Biographical Models: The Constantinian Period and Beyond," in *Constantine: History, Historiography, and Legend,* ed. S. N. C. Lieu and D. Montserrat (London and New York, 1998).

124. John Chrysostom, *On His Return* 5.

125. Athanasius, *Defence of His Flight,* PG 25, col. 657A.

126. Palladius, *Dialogue on the Life of St. John Chrysostom* 7.15. Compare John Chrysostom, *On Diodorus of Tarsus,* PG 52, col. 761: Bishop Diodorus used to call John, then still a deacon, "the staff of Moses," thus claiming for himself, as a bishop, the role of Moses. Another example of self-comparison with Moses by a bishop is Theodoret of Cyrrhus. At the outset of the composition of his *Historia religiosa,* Theodoret invokes divine assistance for his task, the same assistance that also came to the succour of Moses when he wrote the Pentateuch: Theodoret of Cyrrhus, *HR* 1.1.

127. Palladius, *Dialogue on the Life of St. John Chrysostom* 9.138.

128. Ibid., 18.225.

129. Ibid., 19.133.

fourth and fifth centuries reserved almost exclusively for bishops. Here are a few examples. The Gothic bishop Ulfilas, according to the Arian church historian Philostorgius, was held in such esteem by the emperor Constantine that Constantine called him "a Moses of our times."[130] Gregory the Wonder-worker, bishop of Neocaesarea, is also praised as "a Moses in our times" by Gregory of Nyssa.[131] Jacob, the later bishop of Nisibis, is called "a new Moses" by Theodoret of Cyrrhus.[132] Also in the mid-fifth century, Pope Sixtus was addressed as "new Moses" in a letter by two eastern bishops.[133] Monastic leaders were on rare occasions also touted as "new Moses." This was the case with Sabas, who in the sixth century was an active promoter of monasticism in Palestine. Cyril of Scythopolis compares the two Isaurian brothers who were instrumental in erecting a whole array of new buildings in Sabas's largest monastery to the architects of the Tabernacle, Bezabel and Oholiab. He then extends this comparison by calling Sabas a "new Moses."[134] These juxtapositions of saintly men with Moses reveal a pronounced preference among Greek authors of the fourth and fifth centuries to regard Moses as the prototype of the Christian leader and especially of the bishop.

There is one important exception to this predilection of Greek authors to apply the Moses identification to holy men and especially bishops, and that is Eusebius of Caesarea's *Life of Constantine.*[135] Eusebius was a learned theologian who had seen for himself the demoralizing effects of the Great Persecution. Constantine's official recognition of Christianity was therefore a cause of great jubilation for him. Eusebius composed his *Church History* and the *Life of Constantine,* among many other works, to advertise and immortalize the many benefactions that Constantine had bestowed on the church.[136] The *Life of Constantine,* composed after the emperor died in 337, is constructed around the idea that Constantine is another Moses. This is brought out in bold brushstrokes in the description of the battle of the Milvian Bridge, where Constantine's defeat of Maxentius, who then drowns

130. Philostorgius, *HE* 2.5.
131. Gregory of Nyssa, *Life of Gregory the Wonder-worker, PG* 46, col. 908C; also col. 949A: Gregory resembles Moses in prayer.
132. Theodoret, *HR* 1.5.
133. *Xysti III papae epistolae et decreta, Ep.* 4, *PL* 50, col. 595A.
134. Cyril of Scythopolis, *Life of Sabas* 32.
135. For a more detailed treatment of the argument that follows, see C. Rapp, "Imperial Ideology in the Making: Eusebius of Caesarea on Constantine as 'Bishop,'" *JThS* n.s. 49 (1998): 686–95. M. Hollerich, "The Comparison of Moses and Constantine in Eusebius of Caesarea's *Life of Constantine,*" *Studia Patristica* 19 (1989): 80–95, elaborates on the Moses comparison, but without noting the implications for the designation of Constantine as *episkopos.*
136. On Eusebius in general, see T. D. Barnes, *Constantine and Eusebius* (Cambridge, Mass., and London, 1981).

in the Tiber, is compared to Moses's role in the parting of the Red Sea.[137] More subtle reminiscences are Constantine's flight from the court of Diocletian when the formation of the second tetrarchy was announced, which resembled Moses's departure from the court of the pharaoh;[138] and Constantine's portable church that he intended to take on his planned campaign against Persia, which had the shape of the Tabernacle.[139]

Throughout the work, Eusebius highlights especially Constantine's activities in support of Christianity, his legislation on behalf of Christians, his generous donations to Christian causes, and his care for the doctrinal unity of the church. In this manner, he speaks to Constantine's pragmatic authority. But Eusebius does not limit himself to describing Constantine as a benefactor of the church. He also draws attention to the spiritual aspect of Constantine's life. He does this by attributing to the intervention of the supreme Christian deity Constantine's success in eliminating all adversaries and gaining the throne of Rome and then of Constantinople. Constantine's imperial rule was a gift of God, received without any significant participation on the part of the beneficiary, in the way that defines spiritual authority. Ascetic authority is also given its due place, in references to Constantine's earnest prayers, to his study of the scriptures, and to his penchant for preaching to his court.

Once the Moses comparison has been recognized as the leitmotif in Eusebius's *Life of Constantine*, the two passages in Eusebius's work that refer to Constantine as an *episkopos* are no longer puzzling. They are merely an extension of the equation of Constantine and Moses. In the first passage, Eusebius remarks that Constantine convened synods to settle divergences of opinion throughout the empire, "like some general bishop constituted by God."[140] Later in the work, in the context of expounding Constantine's personal piety, Eusebius notes that the emperor was fully justified to address a group of bishops he was entertaining with these words: "You are bishops whose jurisdiction is within the church. I also am a bishop, ordained by God to oversee whatever is external to the church."[141] And indeed, Eusebius continues, Constantine acted as an overseer *(epeskopei)* for all his subjects as he encouraged them to lead a pious life.

Much ink has been spilt over these passages, which represent the first conceptualization of a specifically Christian imperial ideology.[142] It may

137. Eusebius, *VC* 1.38.2–5. Eusebius exploits the comparison with Moses leading the Israelites through the Red Sea already in the description of this battle in his *Church History: HE* 9.5–8.
138. *VC* 1.20.2.
139. *VC* 4.56; cf. the table of contents at the beginning of the work.
140. *VC* 1.44.1.
141. *VC* 4.24.
142. For references to the earlier literature, see D. de Decker and G. Dupuis-Masay, "L' 'épiscopat' de l'empereur Constantin," *Byzantion* 50 (1980): 118–57, and J.-M. Sansterre, "Eusèbe

suffice to note that Eusebius does not appear to claim that Constantine occupied the ecclesiastical office of a bishop, nor that he had been ordained to the episcopate, but rather that his actions were those appropriate for an "overseer" of ecclesiastical affairs. The designations of Constantine as *episkopos* are carefully set in the context of the emperor's concrete measures fostering the cause of the church, as befits the religious leader of his people. It would be too facile to interpret Eusebius's references as caesaropapism in the making. I would submit instead that there is a significant and intrinsic connection between Eusebius's predilection for setting Constantine in relation to Moses and the passages referring to Constantine's function as *episkopos* of the church. After all, Moses was the prototypical religious leader, entrusted with concrete power, but exercising it in the service of his God. The *Apostolic Constitutions* explain that "Aaron was called a prophet, but Moses, because he was king *(basileus)* and archpriest *(archiereus)*, was called god of Pharao."[143]

Eusebius's designation of Constantine as *episkopos* serves as a reminder of the complexity of conceptions of leadership in late antiquity. In the literature of the time, whether it relates to emperors or to bishops, pragmatic authority never seems to exist on its own but is embedded in a larger context where spiritual and ascetic authority also play their part.    ✓

### Moses and Aaron

The Christian literature of the East regarded Moses as the embodiment of ecclesiastical leadership, while Aaron was seen in the position of an assistant. The *Didascalia* states unequivocally: "Aaron is the deacon, and Moses is the bishop."[144] Gregory of Nazianzus evokes the same imagery when he discusses in his *Autobiography* how he came to act as his father's auxiliary in administering the see of Nazianzus. His father, to whom he implicitly assigns the role of Moses, begged him "to set yourself beside Aaron and Samuel as a worthy minister of God."[145]

Among Latin authors the prototype of the bishop was not Moses, but Aaron. In contrast to Moses, who had a special relation to God while hold-

de Césarée et la naissance de la théorie 'césaropapiste,'" *Byzantion* 42 (1972): 131–95. See also G. Dagron, *Empereur et prêtre: Étude sur le "césaropapisme" byzantin* (Paris, 1996) 145–47.

142. For references to the earlier literature, see D. de Decker and G. Dupuis-Masay, "L' 'épiscopat' de l'empereur Constantin," *Byzantion* 50 (1980): 118–57, and J.-M. Sansterre, "Eusèbe de Césarée et la naissance de la théorie 'césaropapiste,'" *Byzantion* 42 (1972): 131–95. See also G. Dagron, *Empereur et prêtre: Étude sur le "césaropapisme" byzantin* (Paris, 1996) 145–47.

143. *Apostolic Constitutions* 29.

144. *Didascalia apostolorum* 30.

145. Gregory of Nazianzus, *Autobiography* 507–8.

ing pragmatic authority in the form of political leadership, Aaron was known purely as a priest. In a letter of 396, addressed to the church at Vercelli where the episcopal see had fallen vacant, Ambrose advised the congregation there on the qualities they ought to look for in their future bishop. In this context, he emphasized that Aaron was the biblical prototype of the bishop as high priest. However, in his *De officiis ministrorum*, which sets down general guidelines for Christian conduct as it behooves especially the clergy, Ambrose does not especially single out Aaron or Moses as Old Testament prototypes for bishops. Two centuries later, Isidore of Seville was inspired to write his own *De ecclesiasticis officiis* (composed between 598 and 615). Often touted as the capstone of the patristic age, Isidore's prolific literary output shows the vantage point of someone who can look back and take stock of a long tradition of Christian thought and ecclesiastical growth. Accordingly, he gave a brief biblical background for each of the offices of the clergy. The prefiguration of the bishop, Isidore observed, was Aaron, while Moses was the prefiguration of Christ.[146]

This emphasis on Aaron as the prototypical bishop points to a very different understanding of the episcopate between Greek East and Latin West that became evident already in the fourth century. In the Greek tradition, the secular and ecclesiastical spheres were fused, and ecclesiastical leadership always carried overtones of secular leadership. The Latin fathers had a different view: to them, the church existed in radical opposition to the world, and leadership within one was assumed to the exclusion of the other. This fundamental difference in attitudes to the *saeculum* would become even more pronounced in the centuries to come.

### Moses and the Three Stages of Life: Education, Contemplation, Ministry

The Greek predilection for Moses as the prototype of the bishop was in large part connected with the nature of his leadership. An additional reason why he made a suitable model for bishops was the evolution of his life in three stages, each exactly forty years in length. Moses's life was a progression from forty years at the court of the pharaoh, followed by forty years in the desert of Madiam, and finally forty years of leading the Israelites. In other words, it represented a sequence of education, contemplation, and ministry. The importance of this pattern was noted over thirty years ago by Marguerite Harl.[147] The idea of three periods in the life of Moses goes back to Philo of Alexandria and finds its fullest expression in the works of Basil of Caesarea

---

146. Isidore of Seville, *De ecclesiasticis officiis* 2.5.1–4.

147. M. Harl, "Les trois quarantaines de la vie de Moise, schéma idéal de la vie du moine-évêque chez les Pères Cappadociens," *Rev. ét. gr.* 80 (1967): 407–12.

and Gregory of Nyssa. In his *Life of Moses,* Philo showed that Moses was reared in the secular learning of the Egyptians until he ruptured his ties to Egyptian civilization and retreated to the desert of Mariam where his religious contemplation was eventually rewarded by a direct encounter with God in the burning bush. From this moment on, Moses returned to society and became the leader of the people of Israel. Basil of Caesarea gave further contours to this pattern by explaining that each of these stages in Moses's life lasted for exactly forty years.[148] In his first *Homily on the Hexahemeron,* Basil explains that when Moses was eighty years of age, his forty years in the desert culminated in his vision of God "in the way in which it is possible for a human being to see him, or rather, in the way in which it was impossible for anyone else [to see God]."[149] Gregory of Nyssa also showed familiarity with this tripartite scheme. It was given poetic expression by Jerome: "To fit him for leadership of the Jewish people Moses was trained for forty years in the wilderness and it was not till after these that the shepherd of sheep became the shepherd of men."[150]

The three phases in Moses's life—education, contemplation, and ministry—provide a biographical pattern with which many bishops of the fourth and fifth centuries could identify. For these men, the monastic experience was an important transitory stage in their life. First came the secular education, then the spiritual formation in the desert or another monastic setting, followed by a return to service in society, by holding ecclesiastical office or by composing religious treatises. The personal desert experience—whether it took place in an actual or a typological desert—appears to have been an essential part of their spiritual formation. It is as if they needed to build up their credentials so that they could then engage in theological writing, or embark upon ecclesiastical careers with greater authority, having themselves tasted of the harshness of asceticism and the sweetness of its divine rewards.

The men who fit this pattern follow an almost generic biography: they commanded an impressive education, which would later contribute to their pragmatic authority. Yet they opted to forgo the prospects of a career for which they had been trained and instead chose to withdraw from the world and to dedicate themselves to the monastic life. Eventually, they were ordained to the priesthood, thus making them viable future candidates for the episcopate should a see fall vacant. The timing of their ordination at this advanced stage in their lives shows that it was conferred not only in the hope

148. Basil of Caesarea, *Comm. on Isaiah, PG* 30, cols. 117–668, quoted in Harl, "Les trois quarantaines de la vie de Moise," 409 n. 8. This is a text of contested authenticity.
149. Basil of Caesarea, *Homilies on the Hexaemeron* 1.2.
150. Jerome, *Ep.* 125.

of securing their talent, but in large part as a confirmation of the ascetic authority they had acquired through their monastic experience.[151]

A few examples from East and West may suffice to illustrate this biographical trajectory. Others could easily be found.[152] The first bishop who fits this pattern is Basil of Caesarea. After completing his studies at Athens, Basil went on a pilgrimage to the monastic sites in Egypt, Syria, and Mesopotamia and then established his own monastic retreat near Annesi. Four years later, he was ordained to the priesthood (362) and, after another eight years, was called to the episcopate of Caesarea (370).

Gregory, Basil's friend from their student days in Athens, had to be persuaded by the latter to experience the monastic life for himself. After several months at Basil's monastic establishment, Gregory returned to the fold of his family in Nazianzus. He was ordained to the priesthood by his father in the same year as Basil. Ten years after that (372), Gregory was appointed by Basil, who had by then become a bishop himself and wished to surround himself with allies, to the episcopal see of a minor town. Less than a decade later, Gregory became bishop of Constantinople, but within a few years, appalled by internal corruption and vociferous doctrinal disputes, he resigned.

John Chrysostom equally did not embark upon a secular career after the completion of his studies. He sought baptism instead, spent a short time in the *askētērion* of Diodore of Tarsus, and then was ordained lector in Antioch. John's ordination to the deaconate came in 380/381, after he had returned from six years of eremitic life near Antioch (372–378). Ordination to the presbyterate followed after another six years (386). Twelve years later, he was called to the episcopal throne in Constantinople.

John Cassian stayed with the monks of Palestine and Egypt for twelve years after the completion of his studies. Then, on a visit to Constantinople in 399, he was ordained to the deaconate by John Chrysostom. About five years later, he was made priest. He never became bishop but spent the rest of his life at his own monastic foundation in Marseille.

John Chrysostom and John Cassian are the only individuals in this

---

151. The necessity of ascetic retreat for the future bishop, interpreted as a time of intense occupation with scriptural exegesis in preparation for his duty as physician of souls and defender of the doctrinal purity of the body of the church, is highlighted by S. Elm, "The Diagnostic Gaze: Gregory of Nazianzus' Theory of Orthodox Priesthood in His Orations 6 *De pace* and 2 *Apologia de fuga sua*," in *Orthodoxie, Christianisme, Histoire/Orthodoxy, Christianity, History*, ed. S. Elm, E. Rebillard, and A. Romano, Collection de l'École Française de Rome 270 (Rome, 2000).

152. For further examples from northern Italy, including Filastrius and Gaudentius of Breschia, see C. Pietri, "Une aristocratie provinciale et la mission chrétienne: L'exemple de la *Venetia*," 89–137, repr. in his *Christiana respublica: Éléments d'une enquête sur le christianisme antique*, vol. 2 (Rome, 1997).

group who were ordained to the lower orders of the clergy, the lectorate and the deaconate, respectively. All others were directly appointed to the priesthood, without transversing the *cursus honorum* of the ecclesiastical hierarchy. It was not uncommon that the priesthood was conferred directly on individuals to confirm their qualifications—whether ascetic, spiritual, or scholarly—that would later make them potentially attractive candidates for office in the church, but without actually calling them to serve at the time of their ordination. In other words, ordination to the priesthood was always an honor but did not always entail a task. The virtual ordination of Daniel the Stylite in the mid-fifth century mentioned at the beginning of this book fits this pattern of ecclesiastical recognition of special qualities, in this case of spiritual and ascetic authority.

The same pattern can be observed among some Latin church fathers. Jerome had received an excellent education in Rome. He then was baptized and devoted himself to a life of asceticism and study, first in Aquileia, then in the desert near Antioch. During this period (375–378) he was ordained to the priesthood by Paulinus of Antioch, who probably wished to secure his talents, both scholarly and monastic, for the church. Then followed a period of travel and several years of service as secretary to Bishop Damasus in Rome (382–385). After Jerome's ambitions to become Damasus's successor came to naught, he eventually founded a monastery in Bethlehem where he continued his life of scholarship until his death in 419.

Rufinus of Aquileia had befriended Jerome during their years of study in Rome. With Jerome, he retreated to a monastery near Aquileia instead of pursuing a career in the civil service. After a seven-year pilgrimage to the monks in Egypt, Rufinus founded a monastery on the Mount of Olives in Jerusalem. During his sixteen years in the Holy Land (381–397), he was ordained to the priesthood. He also found himself at variance with his erstwhile friend Jerome because of his interest in Origen's theology. Even though they were priests, neither Jerome nor Rufinus was ever asked to exercise this function by serving in a parish.

Whereas external circumstances did not permit Jerome and Rufinus to complete all three stages patterned on the biography of Moses, the case is different with Augustine and Paulinus of Nola. Augustine's educational ambitions had taken him from North Africa to Rome and then to Milan, where he experienced his final conversion to Christianity. A short period of learned retreat was followed by his baptism at the hands of Ambrose in 387. He then returned to his hometown of Thagaste and founded a monastery there. After a few years, in 391, he was ordained to the priesthood in Hippo by the elderly bishop Valerius and charged with the preaching duties in that community. Four years later, he succeeded Valerius as bishop of Hippo (395).

Paulinus came from a senatorial family, was educated at Bordeaux, and embarked on a splendid public career culminating in the governorship of

Campania. He retired to devote himself to religious study, received baptism, and in 394 accepted ordination to the priesthood in Barcelona under the condition that he would not be tied to that church. Paulinus then went to Nola in Campania and established a monastic community there in the vicinity of the shrine of Saint Felix, whom he regarded as his patron saint. A few years later, after the death of his wife, he became bishop of Nola.

All of these highly educated men were prolific authors of theological works and of letters. For this reason, they are often thought of as scholars turned clerics. But as these sketches of their lives reveal, it was only after a considerable interval of time spent in pursuit of the ascetic ideal that they were co-opted into the institutional church. Only after their immersion in the tradition of spiritual and ascetic leadership pioneered by the Egyptian fathers were these men called to assume a position of pragmatic leadership in ecclesiastical office.[153] They followed the pattern of the life of Moses, whom the Cappadocian fathers especially had adopted as a model for the episcopate. If they were afraid of losing the benefits of their spiritual formation, this did not prevent them from assuming the episcopal ministry. In this matter, they subscribed to the idea of the desert as a state of mind, which was independent of one's geographical location or station in life.

This excursus into the desert mentality of early Christian monasticism has been necessary in order to diffuse two traditional assumptions that have become commonplace but stand in need of revision. First is the assumption that desert and city are diametrically opposed, resulting in a strong rejection of the city—and by extension, of the episcopate, which has the city as its stage—by ascetics and monks. In fact, as we have seen, the notion of the desert became a literary topos and the value of the desert retreat was reconceptualized as a state of mind of internal detachment. The second assumption is that the monastic experience of withdrawal and retreat is a one-way street from which there is no return. In fact, many prominent men of the church followed the model established by Moses of education, contemplation in withdrawal, and service in the world. Eroding these long-held oppositions of desert versus city and monasticism versus worldly engagement allows for a clearer view of the possibility of an interrelation between the holy life and ecclesiastical office. Far from being incompatible, the former was often seen as the precondition of the latter, as the next chapter will show.

---

153. It is conceivable that they were influenced in their positive view of the third, community-oriented stage by the tradition of Syrian monasticism. When it emerged in the third century, Syrian asceticism had its own local roots, which were only in the course of the second half of the fourth century exposed to the influence of the Egyptian practice. In Syria, ascetic groups of men and women existed within and alongside the Christian communities centered on a particular church and its clergy. Instead of an abrupt and violent break with the world, the Syrian ascetics carved out their own place within it.

## MONKS AS BISHOPS AND BISHOPS AS MONKS

"Monks should flee bishops"—this adage by John Cassian is often quoted to illustrate what is perceived as the fundamental incompatibility of the monastic life with the episcopate, or indeed any clerical office.[154] This line of thought is heavily indebted to the work of German Protestant scholars of the early twentieth century like Karl Heussi and Hans von Campenhausen whose unspoken premise was a sharp delineation of the spiritual and the secular sphere, the former being represented by monks, the latter by the clergy. Accordingly, they detected a pervasive dualist struggle between monasticism and ecclesiastical hierarchy, not dissimilar from the dichotomy between charisma and institution postulated by Max Weber. The evidence usually adduced in support of this view are the numerous accounts of monastic repudiation of ecclesiastical office. But, as I will argue, these passages are often taken out of context and cited without consideration of the motivation of these actions by humility, whether real or pretended.

Scholars have also noted the appropriation of monastic charisma by the institutional church. (Powerful bishops recruited monks )into their clergy either in order to gain highly respected allies in doctrinal conflicts or in order to combat the corruption of the clergy that became a problem beginning in the late fourth century. In recent years, however, scholars like Henry Chadwick, Philip Rousseau, and Conrad Leyser[155] have drawn attention to the large number of men with a monastic formation who had no objection to joining the clergy. It has been noted above how the most prominent church fathers of the fourth century made their personal transition from study to the episcopate through the intermediary stage of a monastic formation. To equate ascetic authority exclusively with monks and pragmatic authority exclusively with the priesthood and then to pit the two against one another would thus be an oversimplification. In this section, I will explore the interaction between monastic lifestyle and office in the clergy in order to deemphasize the difference between the two.

154. John Cassian, *Institutes* 11.18. The entire passage reads: "Wherefore this is an old maxim of the Fathers that is still current,—though I cannot produce it without shame on my own part, since I could not avoid my own sister, nor escape the hands of the bishop [who ordained me],—viz., that a monk ought by all means to fly from women and bishops. For neither of them will allow him who has once been joined in close intercourse any longer to care for the quiet of his cell, or to continue with pure eyes in divine contemplation through his insight into holy things."

155. H. Chadwick, "Bishops and Monks," *Studia Patristica* 24 (1993): 45–61; Rousseau, *Ascetics, Authority, and the Church*, chap. 4 ("Ascetics in the Church"), 56–67; id., "The Spiritual Authority of the 'Monk-Bishop': Eastern Elements in Some Western Hagiography of the Fourth and Fifth Century," *JThS* n.s. 22 (1971): 380–419; C. Leyser, *Authority and Asceticism from Augustine to Gregory the Great* (Oxford, 2000).

### Ordination as Confirmation of Virtue

The relation of monasticism and ministry is, in fact, not a stark, black-and-white contrast, but rather a tapestry of mutating shades of gray, as becomes immediately clear when the context of the remark that "monks should flee bishops" is taken into account. Cassian places the remark at the end of his treatment of vainglory as one of the spiritual challenges to the monk. Even in the solitude of the desert, he says, the hermit can become puffed up with pride over the magnitude of his sacrifice in renouncing family, career, and riches or become overly proud in his ascetic habits and emaciated appearance. It is this overconfidence of the monk in his attainment of virtue, Cassian continues, that can also lead to

> a desire for the priesthood or diaconate. And it represents that if a man has even against his will received this office, he will fulfil it with such sanctity and strictness that he will be able to set an example of saintliness even to other priests; and that he will win over many people, not only by his manner of life, but also by his teaching and preaching.[156]

Cassian here as elsewhere shows the influence of his teacher Evagrius Ponticus. A large part of Evagrius's *Praktikos* is taken up by a discussion of the eight evil thoughts that can obstruct one's spiritual progress. Later authors will develop his scheme into the "seven deadly sins." Vainglory is one of them, and Evagrius defines it as the monk's desire to receive public recognition for his efforts. This desire is a demon that can lead to fantasies of performing miracles in front of admiring crowds or of being selected for ecclesiastical office, even if the monk makes a show of resisting this honor: "This demon predicts . . . that they will attain to the priesthood. It has men knocking at the door, seeking audience with them. If the monk does not willingly yield to their request, he is bound and led away [for ordination]."[157]

These warnings are well taken. It was not unheard of that one or the other solitary in the desert was carried away by boastfulness to the point where he either claimed to be a priest or rejected the liturgical community of the church and the eucharist. One monk in Scetis was overheard in his cell as he delivered a rousing sermon to an imaginary congregation.[158] Another monk was so deluded by his visions of Christ and the angels that he came to church and announced to his fellow monks: "I have no need for the Eucharist. For I have seen Christ today." It took one year of confinement,

---

156. John Cassian, *Insitutes* 11.14. Elsewhere, Cassian observes that the monk who suffers from accidie or boredom may be attracted by the prospect of taking up "some dutiful and religious offices": *Institutes* 10.2.
157. Evagrius Ponticus, *Praktikos* 13.
158. Cassian, *Institutes* 11.16.

prayer, and a more relaxed lifestyle to cure him from such delusions of grandeur.[159] Evagrius, Cassian, and these illustrative anecdotes all address the desire for ordination in the context of boastfulness and vainglory. Their remarks only make sense on the assumption that ordination to the priesthood is a great honor for the monk. It is, in fact, regarded as a confirmation of his personal virtues.

This view is evident already in the early church orders and in the comments on the "mirror of bishops" in 1 Timothy 3 discussed above. It could also apply to exceptional individuals who had no monastic background. Gregory of Nazianzus's panegyric on Athanasius, whose anti-Arian position he greatly admired, explores this theme to the fullest, depicting the Alexandrian as the model of what a bishop should be: "Nor can I say whether he received the priesthood as the reward of virtue, or to be the fountain and life of the Church."[160] He later claims that Athanasius conforms to "the model for future bishops" set down in Paul's First Letter to Timothy.[161] And he concludes by declaring that "his life and habits form the ideal of an episcopate."[162] In other words, ordination to the priesthood gave official sanction to the spiritual authority of the recipient as a *pneumatophoros*.

It also was believed to confer a blessing on the bishop who performed the ordination. This is at least how the bishop of Rhaithou on the Sinai Peninsula excused himself for having ordained Abba Matoes to the priesthood against his will: "Forgive me, abba; I know you did not want it but it was in order that I might be blessed by you that I dared to do it." Matoes's concrete concern that he would now have to be separated from his brother in the eremitic life was addressed by ordaining the latter also. His more abstract concern about his own unworthiness could only be resolved by his complete avoidance of consecrating the eucharist: "Both of them died without having approached the sanctuary to make the offering. The old man [Matoes] used to say, 'I have confidence in God that I shall not suffer great condemnation through the laying on of hands since I do not make the offering. For the laying on of hands [during the ordination] is for those who are without reproach.'"[163]

The papyrological evidence from late antique Egypt recently examined by Ewa Wipszycka shows that a remarkable number of monks had received ordination to the priesthood. A sizeable proportion of them did not celebrate the eucharist or exercise any other priestly function, so that it must be assumed that ordination was conferred upon them in recognition of their

---

159. Palladius, *HL* 25.4–5.
160. Gregory of Nazianzus, *Homily* 21 *On Athanasius* 7.
161. Ibid., 10.
162. Ibid., 37.
163. *Sayings of the Desert Fathers,* Matoes 9.

virtuous conduct.[164] Perhaps the three bishops who are mentioned in papyri of the sixth and seventh centuries not in conjunction with a particular city but as "bishop of God" belong in the same category.[165]

The same practice of honorific ordination to the priesthood is attested for the holy men of Syria. There, Barses, Eulogius, and Lazarus were in the second half of the fourth century "ordained bishops, but not of any city, for the title was merely an honorary one, conferred on them as a compensation for their excellent conduct," according to Sozomen's *Church History*.[166] Theodoret of Cyrrhus gives three examples: Macedonius the Barley-eater, he recounts, possessed such *sancta simplicitas* that he was not even aware of being ordained by Bishop Flavian of Antioch during the liturgy. Contrary to his fears, this did not prevent him from returning to his ascetic routine on a nearby mountaintop.[167] The hermit Acepsimas, Theodoret notes, did not resist priestly ordination simply because he knew that he had only a few days to live.[168] Salamanes, finally, who had walled himself up in a windowless hut, is said to have remained impassive throughout the process of his ordination, which the bishop conferred after digging a hole through the holy man's abode.[169] Clearly, mountain dwellers, men on the brink of death, and those who wall themselves up were not ideal candidates for active ministry in the church. Their ordination served merely as a confirmation of their monastic virtue and allowed for their symbolic integration into the institutional church.[170] It seems that Jerome's ordination to the priesthood at the hands of Paulinus of Antioch occurred for similar reasons, for Jerome consented to it only under the condition that he would not have to give up his monastic life.[171] The ordination of monks with a reputation for personal sanctity restored the ideal of the priesthood that Origen had declared imperiled when he distinguished between "true priests" and "priests by ordination", and gave official sanction to the spiritual authority of the *pneumatophoros* and the *christophoros*.

There are hardly any comments on monks who covet ordination out of

---

164. E. Wipszycka, "Les clercs dans les communautés monastiques d'Égypte," *The Journal of Juristic Papyrology* 26 (1996): 135–66. See also L. S. B. McCoull, "Paul of Tamma and the Monastic Priesthood," *Vig. Christ.* 54 (1999): 316–20.

165. R. L. B. Morris, "Bishops in the Papyri," in *Proceedings of the 20th International Congress of Papyrologists, Copenhagen, 23–29 August, 1992* (Copenhagen, 1994), 587.

166. Sozomen, *HE* 6.34.1.

167. Theodoret, *HR* 13.4–5.

168. Ibid., 15.4.

169. Ibid., 19.2.

170. In "Eccentrics and Coenobites in the Late Roman East," *Byz Forsch* 24 (1997): 35–50, P. Rousseau discusses this process of what he calls "enfolding" of holy men and ascetics into the church, especially in Syria.

171. Jerome, *Against John of Jerusalem* 41.

personal ambition in the sense of a desire for the power and influence that high office in the church entails. Saint Sabas, the leader of Palestinian monasticism in the early sixth century, made a display of his lack of ambition when he postponed his appointment by remarking that "the desire to be made a cleric is the origin and root of thoughts of love of power."[172] John Chrysostom insisted that those who desire office are automatically disqualified from it because the ambitious nature of such men will later leave them open to flattery and bribery and eager for further promotion.[173]

Eventually, attempts were made to eliminate the conferral of this kind of honorary priesthood without concrete duties. At the Council of Chalcedon in 451, it was decreed that any such existing ordinations carried no weight, and that henceforth all clergy should be ordained to serve at a specific location, whether church, chapel, or monastery.[174] This regulation may have restricted the performance of actual ordinations to those who were willing and able to exercise their clerical duties, but it did not result in a complete abandonment of an idealized view of the priesthood.

## The Conferral of Ordination

Many protagonists of hagiographical texts and other narratives are reported to have received ordination. The hagiographers tend to emphasize the worthiness of the recipients by insisting that this was done against their will, or even without their prior knowledge. The ordination of monks and holy men could thus be regarded as an act of divine approval, expressed through human agency. The archbishop who eventually succeeded in ordaining the initially resistant Sabas to the priesthood explains: "For by laying on of hands I have simply confirmed the divine election."[175]

The hagiographers of exceptionally holy men insist that the ordination of these paragons of virtue did not add anything to their authority and was merely an external gesture of confirmation and approbation. In some instances, this was underscored by having the ordination take place not through the actual imposition of hands, but at a distance, in a vision or in a dream. A good example of such a virtual ordination is Daniel the Stylite, mentioned in chapter 1. The patriarch of Constantinople stood at the bottom of the pillar when he ordained him to the priesthood, without the requisite imposition of hands.[176] Even more dramatic was the ordination of Gregory

172. Cyril of Scythopolis, *Life of Sabas* 18.
173. John Chrysostom, *On the Priesthood* 3.10.36ff.
174. Chalcedon, can. 6, H-L II/2, pp. 787–89. Bishops are not specifically mentioned but must be implied in the blanket prohibition of such ordinations.
175. Cyril of Scythopolis, *Life of Sabas* 19.
176. *Life of Daniel the Stylite* 43.

the Wonder-worker, described with palpable pleasure by Gregory of Nyssa. In order to avoid ordination, Gregory Thaumaturgus went from one place of hiding to another. As a last resort, the exasperated bishop Phaidimos of Amaseia, "disregarding the intervening distance by which he was separated from Gregory (he was three days' journey away), but looking to God and saying that both of them were equally present to the sight of God, laid on Gregory his word in place of his hand, consecrating to God one who was not present bodily."[177] In addition to virtual and long-distance ordination through the performance of the appropriate prayers, there was the quasi ordination of some holy men who received notice of their ordination directly from God in the form of dreams or visions.[178] Symeon the Stylite (the Elder) was honored with a vision, according to his Syriac *Vita*, in which he was standing at the altar of a martyr's chapel while a hand from above gave him a golden scepter with the words "With this you will lead the flock of the Church of Christ."[179] His imitator, Symeon the Younger, also had a divine vision according to which he was enlisted in the ranks of the priests of the Old Testament, but in his case this was followed by the formal ordination through Bishop Dionysius of Seleuceia.[180]

The divine sanction conferred through ordination of a holy man could not be removed, although it was sometimes possible to shed the concrete functions of the ecclesiastical ministry. Theodore of Sykeon in the early seventh century had only reluctantly accepted the episcopate and eventually wished to resign in order to resume his monastic discipline. His metropolitan refused to honor his request because "he could not let a man of such virtue resign." The matter was eventually referred to the authorities in Constantinople. The patriarch, in accordance with an imperial directive, accepted Theodore's resignation but insisted that the former bishop be given the *ōmophorion*, the bishop's stole, "so that he would retain his rank, because he was a holy man."[181]

### The Perils of the Priesthood

Many monks expressed their fear of losing their spiritual gifts or slackening in their ascetic discipline if they assumed the concrete responsibilities of ecclesiastical office. They did not want to suffer the fate of Theodore of

---

177. Gregory of Nyssa, *Life of Gregory the Wonder-worker* 3.
178. On virtual ordination among holy men in Syria, see P. Escolan, *Monachisme et église: Le monachisme syrien du IVᵉ au VIIᵉ siècle, un ministère charismatique*, Théologie Historique 109 (Paris, 1999), 274–76.
179. *Life of Symeon the Stylite* (Syriac), trans. Doran, p. 107.
180. *Life of Symeon the Younger* 2, pp. 148–51.
181. *Life of Theodore of Sykeon* 79.

Sykeon and refused to even entertain the idea of receiving ordination. They were convinced, as Athanasius thinks Dracontius was, that "the bishop's office is an occasion for sin" and "from it comes opportunity for sinning."[182] The first and foremost concern of the monk was to maintain his state of mental tranquility and detachment. John Chrysostom noted with exasperation: "If you ask a monk to take over any task, he will first ask if this would disturb his *anapausis*."[183] Exchanging the safety and seclusion of the monastic abode for the company of men of the world could mean a slow, but sure spiritual death. For this reason, Anthony politely refused the invitation of a military commander to extend his visit, since he knew full well that he would quickly suffocate in such unaccustomed surroundings:

> Just as fish perish when they lie exposed for a while on dry land, so also the monks relax their discipline when they linger and pass time with you. Therefore, we must rush back to the mountain, like the fish to the sea—so that we might not, by remaining among you, forget the things within us.[184]

For similar reasons, Anthony also declined an invitation from the emperor Constantius to visit him in Constantinople, after his disciple Paul had reminded him: "If you go, you will be called Anthony, but if you stay here, you will be called Abba Anthony."[185] Former monks who had joined the clergy experienced difficulties in maintaining their ascetic habits. Apa Apphy found it impossible after he had become bishop of Oxyrhynchus to maintain his customary ascetic practices. He asked God: "Has your grace left me because of my episcopate?" The answer was "No, but when you were in solitude and there was no one else it was God who was your helper. Now that you are in the world, it is man."[186] One way to combat the negative effects of exposure to the world was to intensify one's asceticism. Netras subjected himself to much greater austerities after he had become bishop of Pharan in the fifth century. He explained to his disciple: "I do this in order not to destroy the monk in me."[187]

### Rejection of Ordination

Just as vainglory leads to coveting the episcopate, it is humility that leads to indifference to the prospect of ordination and, when it is offered, to its rejec-

---

182. Athanasius, *Letter to Dracontius* 9. Cf. the discussion of this letter by D. Brakke, *Athanasius and the Politics of Asceticism* (Oxford, 1995), 100–110.

183. John Chrysostom, *De compunctione ad Demetrium* 1.6, PG 47, col. 403.

184. *Life of Anthony* 85.

185. *Sayings of the Desert Fathers*, Anthony 31.

186. Ibid., Apphy 1.

187. Ibid., Netras 1.

tion. Jerome confidently announced that he harbored the proper attitude in his retreat in the Holy Land; by this time, he seems to put behind him his earlier yearnings for the see of Rome: "For we who lie hid in our cells do not covet the bishop's office. We are not like some, who, despising all humility, are eager to buy the episcopate with gold."[188] Some were indeed successful in resisting ordination,[189] sometimes through dramatic gestures. Ammonius cut off his ear and threatened to cut off his tongue next, in order to render himself incapable of becoming a priest and preacher.[190] Nilammon, a highly regarded hermit outside the city of Gera in Egypt who was elected to be its bishop, managed to will his own death while Patriarch Theophilus and the people were assembled outside his cell in prayer. Sozomen, who reports this story, adds: "Thus died Nilammon . . . rather than accept a bishopric of which, with extraordinary modesty, he considered himself unworthy."[191] Less dramatic, but no less effective was Pachomius's effort to escape ordination at the hands of Athanasius of Alexandria simply by hiding.[192]

In a paradoxical inversion, the humility that prompts the rejection of ordination actually demonstrates a candidate's supreme qualification for ecclesiastical office. This idea and its application were not new, nor were they exclusive to the church. In the realm of imperial politics, demonstrative *cunctatio* (hesitation) traditionally preceded the appointment of a new emperor.[193] Jean Béranger has brilliantly analyzed the implications of this "almost ritual gesture" of refusal of power by the *princeps* of the Roman Empire. It creates the appearance that power is not assumed by the emperor, but conferred by the people who urge him to accept. The consensus of the people can then be taken as a manifestation of divine providence. And the refusal itself demonstrates the humility and philanthropy of the future ruler who agrees to his new responsibility selflessly and in spite of himself.[194] Analogous sentiments prevailed in the ecclesiastical context. The *Letter by Pseudo-Clement of Rome to James*, a text of the fourth century, purports to narrate how the apostle Jacob designated Clement as his successor and made him a bishop. Clement's vehement protestations of his own unwor-

---

188. Jerome, *Apology (Against Rufinus)* 1.32.
189. For example, the former military man who had lived as an ascetic for twenty years and managed to resist ordination to the priesthood: Palladius, *HL* 68.
190. Palladius, *HL* 11.1–3.
191. Sozomen, *HE* 8.19.4.
192. *Life of Pachomius* (Bohairic) 28.
193. E. Hermann, *Ecclesia in Re Publica: Die Entwicklung der Kirche von pseudostaatlicher zu staatlich-inkoroprierter Existenz* (Frankfurt am Main, 1980), 45–46; L. Wickert, "Princeps," *RE* 22/2, cols. 2258–64.
194. J. Béranger, "Le refus du pouvoir," in his *Principatus: Études de notions et d'histoire politiques dans l'antiquité gréco-romaine*, ed. with the collaboration of F. Paschoud and P. Ducrey (Geneva, 1973).

thiness only confirmed for Jacob that he had made the right choice.[195] According to the Council of Valencia in 374, it was considered one of the *signa sanctitatis* if men made false statements about themselves in order to avoid ordination.[196] Ambrose made an attempt to sway public opinion against himself in the interval between his election by popular demand and his ordination. He ordered the execution of criminals and publicly invited a troupe of female entertainers to his house.[197] But these actions failed to have the desired effect, and he was ordained in 374. Palladius, who spent several years as a monk in Egypt and later became bishop of Helenopolis in Bithynia, includes in his *Historia Lausiaca* a cameo appearance, casting himself in the role of the humble monk who is entirely indifferent to the prospect of episcopal ordination. Palladius reports how John of Lycopolis, one of his spiritual fathers, teasingly asked him:

> "Do you want to become a bishop *[episkopos]*?" I said to him: "I am one." He said to me: "Where?" I said: "(I am bishop) over the kitchens, the shops, the tables and the pots. I am their bishop [*episkopō auta*, i.e., I am their overseer], and if there is any sharp wine, I excommunicate it, but I drink the good. . . ." He said to me with a smile: "Stop your jokes. You have to be ordained bishop, and toil much and be afflicted. If then you would escape afflictions, depart not from the desert. For in the desert no man can ordain you bishop."[198]

Behind this amusing pun on the original meaning of the word *episkopos* as describing the function of overseer stands the reality that the monastic life of the desert does not require the administrative services of a bishop.

Forced ordination was usually the result.[199] This is amply attested in the sources, to the extent that it becomes a commonplace in episcopal hagiography. It is impossible for us to decide whether the protests of the bishop-elect were genuine or whether they were merely a gesture to further cement his candidacy, nor can we be certain whether the reports of such protestations are based on fact or pious fabrication. What we do know is that forced ordination was generally considered a safeguard against ambition and simony in episcopal appointments. A law of 469 of the emperor Leo makes this connection clear:

195. (Ps.-)Clement, *Letter to James* 3.1–3.
196. *Conciles gaulois du IVᵉ siècle*, ed. C. Munier and trans. and annot. J. Gaudemet, SCh 241 (Paris, 1977), 110
197. *Life of Ambrose* 3.7.
198. Palladius, *HL* 35, 10–11. See R. T. Meyer, "Holy Orders in the Eastern Church in the Early Fifth Century as Seen in Palladius," in *Studia Patristica* 16/2, TU 129 (Berlin, 1985), 38–49.
199. For further examples of forced ordination among the monks of Egypt, see R. Cherubini, "Ammonas di Sketis (+ 375 circa): Un esempio di influsso monastico in un vescovo egiziano del IV sec.," in *Vescovi e pastori in epoca teodosiana*, 2: 334–42 (Rome, 1997).

An archbishop is ordained not with money but with prayers, and he should also be so destitute of ambition as to be compelled to take the office tendered him, and, having been requested, he should decline, and having been invited, he should flee; he is unworthy of the priesthood unless he is ordained against his consent.[200]

It seems that the avoidance of ordination, or at least its appearance, was a widespread phenomenon, as Basil's response to Amphilochius in his first *Canonical Letter* indicates: "Those who swear that they will not receive ordination, declining orders upon oath, must not be driven to perjure themselves, although there does seem to be a canon making concessions to such persons. Yet I have found by experience that perjurers never turn out well."[201] If the rejection of ordination was expressed in sufficiently forceful terms, and supported by an oath, according to Basil, it was obviously respected, and the candidate was not pressed further. On the other hand, initial refusal of ordination, protestations of one's unworthiness, even making moves to run away seem to have become ritualized gestures that followed the election, confirmed it, and preceded ordination. This is the impression given in John Chrysostom's description of the attempted appointment of himself and his friend Basil in his younger years. John deliberated, he says, "whether I attempted flight or *submitted* to be captured" (emphasis mine). He opted for flight, since "looking to myself I found nothing worthy of such an honor," but not without ensuring that Basil was tricked into ordination—an act of dissembling that imposed a great strain on their friendship.[202] Later in his life, John was ready, even without being "captured," to become a priest in Antioch and, eventually, bishop of Constantinople. Gregory of Nazianzus, in his autobiographical poem, also makes a display of his initial alarm at the ordination to the priesthood that was forced upon him by his ailing father.[203] A remnant of this attitude of ⟨ritualized protestation⟩ is the custom, reportedly still observed in the Coptic Church at the beginning of the twentieth century, that the newly elected patriarch of Alexandria is brought to Cairo in chains.[204] Rituals of this kind as well as the pretended gestures of refusal only confirm the ⟨weighty importance that was attributed to humility⟩ among other monastic virtues, as a precondition for ecclesiastical office. It must be admitted, though, that some monks who had taken up active priestly service were sufficiently miserable to make a dramatic escape. Such was the case of Apa

200. CJ 1.3.30.3–4.
201. Basil of Caesarea, *Ep.* 188.10.
202. John Chrysostom, *On the Priesthood* 1.3.10–16.
203. Gregory of Nazianzus, *Autobiography* 340ff.
204. W. R. W. Stephens, trans. John Chrysostom, *On the Priesthood*, NPNF, 35 n. 2. citing Stanley, *Eastern Church*, VII, p. 226.

Pinufius in fourth-century Egypt. He became the presbyter of a large coeno-bium, but then suddenly departed and sought admission as a novice into another monastery in order to regain his peace.[205]

## Monks Joining the Clergy

The recruitment of monks into active service in the priesthood and, in some cases, the episcopate seems to have become a common phenomenon around the mid-fourth century. Their preparation through ascetic living constituted a further asset when lifelong celibacy became a requirement for ecclesiastical office: for the higher clergy in the West since the fifth century, and for the episcopate in the East since 692. The earliest cases of monks serving as bishops come from Egypt. In 345, Pachomius was summoned before the Synod of Latopolis to explain himself because of his gift of clair-voyance. He had to remind two of his interrogators, Bishops Philo and Mouei, that they had previously been monks in his monastery, where they had had ample opportunity to witness his engagement with demons.[206] In 354, Athanasius of Alexandria sent a letter to Dracontius to plead with him to come out of hiding and accept ordination to the see of Hermopolis Parva to which he had been elected. He attempted to sway Dracontius by men-tioning that a total of seven former monks had also acceded to leading posi-tions in the church.[207] Athanasius was the first ecclesiastical leader to exploit the pool of monastic talent in a systematic way. He made it his policy to appoint monks to vacant bishoprics, knowing that he could depend on their loyalty in his struggle with Arians and Melitians.[208] Theophilus of Alexandria (385–412) is reported to have continued this tradition by appointing seven or eight bishops from among the disciples of Isaac, who was himself a disci-ple of Macarius of Egypt, who in turn had been a disciple of Saint Anthony.[209] Palladius of Helenopolis mentions a few monks-turned-priests in his *Lausiac History:* Macarius of Alexandria, Moses the Egyptian, and Dorotheus the cave dweller.[210] On her pilgrimage to Egypt and the Holy Land Egeria also encountered monks who had become bishops or priests.[211]

205. John Cassian, *Institutes* 4.30. 2.

206. *Vita prima of Pachomius* 112.

207. Athanasius, *Letter to Dracontius* 7. Brakke(100) seems to think that the Paul of Latopolis mentioned here is identical with the Philo mentioned in the *Vita prima of Pachomius*, and that the Muitus from the Upper Thebaid of Athanasius's passage is identical with the Mouei in the *Vita prima.*

208. See the useful and detailed discussion in Brakke, 99–110.

209. Palladius, *Dialogue on the Life of St. John Chrysostom* 17.

210. Palladius, *HL* 19, 22, 47.

211. Egerie, *Journal de voyage,* ed. P. Maraval, SCh 296 (Paris, 1997) 8.4, 9.1, 19.5, 23.1 (bish-ops); 14.2 (priest).

In inscriptions, individuals were formally identified as "cleric and monk"[212]— further proof that priesthood and monasticism were far from being mutually exclusive but could comfortably coexist.

In Palestine and Syria, the appointment of monks to actual service in the priesthood seems to set in a few decades later than in Egypt, with the fifth century.[213] Here as in Egypt, bishops were eager to position monks in the priesthood because of their moral excellence. The monks who resisted this trend did so, like their Egyptian counterparts, out of concern for a loss of their spiritual tranquility. Another reason for their rejection has its roots in the Syrian monastic tradition, which had always put a high prize on the charismatic gifts of the individual, whether monk or layman, celibate or married. The monks of Syria therefore objected not to the office as such, but to the receipt of ordination, for they knew that their charisma had no need of further confirmation by the institution.[214] Philipe Escolan notes in this regard that "the monastic priesthood [in Syria] is more symbolic than it is functional."[215] Still, Theodoret of Cyrrhus in his *History of the Monks in Syria* mentions five accomplished ascetics who actually held episcopal office, but often late in life and after long years spent in charge of monastic communities.[216] He is at pains to point out that their ascetic resolve did not slacken, that they lived "with the labors of a monk and the cares of a bishop."[217] Aphthonius, for example,

> received the episcopal see, but without changing either his rough ascetic cloak or his tunic made from goat's hair; and he ate the same food as before his epis-copate. Despite taking on this charge he did not tend that flock any less, but spent most of his days there, now resolving the strife of those quarreling, now exercising care of those wronged by anyone, at other times addressing exhor-tation to his disciples; and he performed each of these tasks while, in between, stitching the rags of his companions or cleaning lentils or washing grain or doing something else of the kind.[218]

Unlike Athanasius and Theophilus in Egypt, powerful bishops elsewhere in the empire in the late fourth or early fifth century did not go out of their

---

212. S. J. Saller, *The Memorial of Moses on Mount Nebo* (Jerusalem, 1941), 1: 258–60: a frag-mentary inscription from the late fourth century.

213. For more details, see H. Bacht, "Die Rolle des orientalischen Mönchtums in den kirchen-politischen Auseinandersetzungen um Chalkedon (431–519)," in *Das Konzil von Chalkedon*, ed. A. Grillmeier and H. Bacht, 2: 299–307 (Würzburg, 1953).

214. Escolan, 267–311.

215. Ibid., 298.

216. Theodoret, *HR* 1.7 (James of Nisibis); 2.9 (Acacius of Beroea); 10.9 (Helladius of Tarsus).

217. Theodoret, *HR* 17.1 (Abraham of Carrhae).

218. Theodoret, *HR* 5.8.

way to appoint monks to positions in the clergy. John Chrysostom was fully aware that a monastic formation, desirable as it was, did not provide sufficient training for the ministry. This was a task that required administrative and rhetorical skills, too.[219] Basil of Caesarea likewise did not make it his policy to appoint monks to the clergy in greater numbers than his predecessors or contemporaries. He viewed the church as one body, whose well-being is guaranteed as long as each member fulfills the part that he was allotted. Rejuvenation of the whole had to come from the intensified efforts of each member in his own place. What counted was not the appointment of monks to the priesthood, but the adoption of monastic values by the priesthood.[220]

## Bishops Living as Monks

Many bishops indeed made sincere efforts to justify their appointment and lend greater credibility to their activities by embracing a simple and modest lifestyle. In this way, they sought ascetic authority in order to bolster their pragmatic authority. As patriarch of Constantinople, John Chrysostom was known to have enjoyed frugal repasts by himself, to have shunned invitations to the mansions of local aristocrats, and to have avoided entertaining at his residence.[221] Basil of Caesarea also continued to practice a lifestyle of moderate asceticism. In his new role as bishop, Ambrose, the former provincial governor, transformed himself into a man "of much abstinence, and many vigils and toils, whose body was wasted by daily fasts."[222] Bishops not only adjusted the external circumstances of their life to suit their new position; they also followed a different, more charitable code of behavior toward others. Sidonius Apollinaris, himself a bishop in late fifth-century Gaul, describes the transformation of his acquaintance Maximus, a former Palatine officer, after the latter had joined the priesthood. The formerly affable, attractive, and self-confident man had become shy and reticent, his pallor and his speech signaling his newly adopted Christian life, along with the short hair and long beard. The repast he served his old friend on a moderately bedecked table was not at all lavish, offering more legumes than

219. A. M. Ritter, *Charisma im Verständnis des Joannes Chrysostomos und seiner Zeit: Ein Beitrag zur Erforschung der griechisch-orientalischen Ekklesiologie in der Frühzeit der Reichskirche* (Göttingen, 1972), 90–98; M. Lochbrunner, *Über das Priestertum: Historische und systematische Untersuchung zum Priesterbild des Johannes Chrysostomus* (Bonn, 1993), 87–97.

220. K. Koschorke, *Spuren der alten Liebe: Studien zum Kirchenbegriff des Basilius von Caesarea*, Paradosis 32 (Freiburg, Switzerland, 1991), 230–33.

221. Palladius, *Dialogue on the Life of St. John Chrysostom* 12.7–29; cf. Photius, *Bibliotheca*, cod. 59.91–92.

222. *Life of Ambrose* 38.1; cf. N. B. McLynn, *Ambrose of Milan: Church and Court in a Christian Capital* (Berkeley and Los Angeles, 1994), 254.

meat. Most important, at Sidonius's request on behalf of his friend Turpio, Maximus remitted the interest on a rather large loan that he had made prior to this clerical appointment, and even extended the loan period for a further year. He did so, he explained, because he was now a cleric.[223]

Bishops also found ways to surround themselves with their unmarried clergy, thus turning the bishop's residence into a quasi-monastic community. The earliest such establishment was most likely the clergy around Bishop Valerian of Aquileia, a circle that counted among its members the newly baptized Rufinus of Aquileia. Jerome describes it in his *Chronicle* for the year 374 as resembling "a choir of angels."[224] However, it is Eusebius of Vercelli who is generally credited with pioneering the fusion of monastic living with service in the clergy in the West. He probably founded his *monasterium* after 363, when he returned from exile to the East, where he had visited Scythopolis, Cappadocia, and the Thebaid. The evidence for this foundation is scant and not quite contemporary: two references by Ambrose of Milan and eight anonymous sermons delivered in Vercelli before the year 400.[225] Ambrose's *Letter to the Church in Vercelli*, composed in 396, advises the Christians of that city on how to select a new bishop. In this context, he highlights the fact that Vercelli's tradition of combining monasticism with clerical office is unusual and therefore ought to be preserved:

> Eusebius of holy memory was the first in Western lands to bring together these differing matters, both while living in the city observing the rules of the monks, and ruling the Church with fasting and temperance. For the grace of the priesthood is much increased if the bishop constrain young men to the practice of abstinence, and to the rule of purity; and forbid them though living in the city, the manners and mode of life of the city.[226]

Eusebius's practice, Ambrose notes elsewhere, assured that the clergy in its pious devotion resembled the order of angels.[227] The sermons that can be attributed to Eusebius complete this picture with further details, such as communal living quarters, sexual continence, manual labor, edifying reading, and frequent prayer, all leading up to the idealized impression that this "college of fellow-priests" was "a gathering not so much of men but of virtues."[228]

223. Sidonius Apollinaris, *Ep.* 4. 24.6.
224. Jerome, *Chronicle* 374.
225. J. T. Lienhard, "Patristic Sermons on Eusebius of Vercelli and Their Relation to His Monasticism," *Revue Bénédictine* 87 (1977): 164–72.
226. Ambrose, *Ep.* 1.63.66.
227. Ambrose, *Sermo* 56, *PL* 17, cols. 743–45.
228. "Ut . . . illud non iam diuersorum congregatio clericorum, sed consacerdotum collegium uideretur," [Maximus of Turin], *Sermo* 22, *PL* 57, 891A; "in diuersorio illo non tam hominum esset congregatio quam uirtutum," [Maximus of Turin], *Sermo* 23, *PL* 57, 892C.

After Eusebius's successful experiment of combining monastic life and ministry, it was Augustine who installed a *domus episcopi* or *monasterium clericorum*, as he liked to call it, in North Africa.[229] The deacons and priests who had received their formation in this institution would later be appointed by Augustine to key episcopal positions throughout Numidia.[230] Augustine's "monastery of the clergy" was, in effect, a continuation of the monastic group that he had gathered around himself after his return to Africa.[231] One of its younger members was Augustine's biographer Possidius. The emphasis was on the abandonment of private property and the absence of ostentatious luxury, except for the duty of extending hospitality to visitors and travelers. They derived their livelihood exclusively from church funds. Augustine's slogan "I don't want hypocrites" explains his motivation, which stemmed from an acute sense of the importance of the exemplary personal life of the clergy for the well-being of the community.[232]

Other former monks who had been coerced into the episcopate did the same. Martin of Tours preferred to live as a monk in a community just outside Tours rather than in the city itself. His biographer, Sulpicius Severus, applauds the constancy of his monastic dedication, which remained entirely unaffected by his ordination to the episcopate: "There was the same humility in his heart, and the same holiness in his garments. Full alike of dignity and courtesy, he kept up the position of a bishop properly, yet in such a way as not to lay aside the objects and virtues of a monk." Many among Martin's eighty fellow monks later became highly desirable candidates for episcopal appointments. "For what city or church would there be that would not desire to have its priests from among those in the monastery of Martin?" [233]

The practice of clergy living as monks seems to have been more common in the West, where the celibacy of priests was also more widespread, than in the East. The few Eastern examples are all connected to individuals who had received their monastic formation in Palestine. As a newly appointed bishop in Cyprus, Epiphanius of Salamis, a former monk and founder of a monastery not far from Jerusalem, surrounded himself with disciples in his *episkopeion*, including the two authors of his biography. Some of these "brothers" were later appointed to the clergy. Epiphanius's disciple Polybius eventually became bishop of Rhinocorura in southern Palestine,[234] where

---

229. Augustine, *Sermo* 355.2.
230. P. Brown, *Augustine of Hippo: A Biography* (London, 1967; rev. ed., Berkeley, 2000), 143. See also P. Stockmeier, "Aspekte zur Ausbildung des Klerus in der Spätantike," *Münchener Theologische Zeitschrift* 27 (1976): 217–32.
231. Augustine himself describes this setup in *Sermo* 355.
232. Augustine, *Sermo* 355.6.
233. Sulpicius Severus, *Life of Martin* 10.
234. Polybius and John, *Life of Epiphanius, PG* 41, col. 112; cf. also col. 72 (a communal meal of the clergy); col. 93 (Sabinus, a deacon in the *episkopeion*).

the clergy attached to the episcopal see shared living quarters, meals, and "all other things." Sozomen reports that this practice had been introduced in the mid-fourth century and was still observed in his day, a century later.[235] On a much smaller scale, Porphyry of Gaza, who had been an ascetic in Jerusalem, continued to practice his asceticism in the company of two disciples even after he was appointed to the see of Gaza.[236]

The hagiographical and theological literature of late antiquity that has been the basis of our investigation until now establishes the ideal of the priesthood. In these texts, ordination as priest or bishop is regarded as a confirmation of personal virtue. For this reason, monks and holy men were prime candidates for ecclesiastical office. This was also the reason for the reluctance of monks and holy men to accept ordination out of humility. Those monks and holy men who were indeed co-opted into the hierarchy of the church always entered at the level of priests and were often quickly promoted to the episcopate. This is an important point, for it sets the promotion of monks and holy men apart from the regular ecclesiastical career path, where future priests spend a significant period of time as lectors and deacons in preparation for their later tasks. The qualification that monks and holy men brought to the episcopate was their ascetic authority as a visible sign of their spiritual gifts. Underlying this siphoning-off of monks into office was the spiritually exalted view of the episcopal office that began to be formulated from the second century onward. According to this view, the bishop was a spiritual leader who mediated between the people and God. And who better but a monk or holy man to fill this position?

235. Sozomen, *HE* 6.31.6–11.
236. Mark the Deacon, *Life of Porphyry of Gaza*, passim.

# PART TWO

# CHAPTER FIVE

# Bishops in Action

Moving on from theory to practice and from the religious to the secular, we now take pragmatic authority as our focus and explore the bishop's role in his city. To achieve a better understanding of the nature of the bishop's concrete role in society, the following chapters aim to bring into focus the similarities and differences between public episcopal activities and those of holy men, on the one hand, and prominent citizens, on the other. Imperial and canon law as well as inscriptions provide the evidentiary basis for study and are supplemented by anecdotal evidence from literary works of the period, church histories, and saints' *Lives*.

At this juncture, it is useful to turn to the categories introduced by Peter Brown to describe the role of holy men in late antique society. In an article in 1983, Brown drew attention to the role of the holy man as "exemplar," representing a model of ideal behavior that others are encouraged to imitate.[1] What we have discussed so far is the analogous role of the bishop as exemplar. This aspect of the bishop's role came to the fore in the treatises on the priesthood and, albeit to a lesser degree, in the comments on Paul's injunction of the ideal behavior of the bishop in 1 Timothy 3. These texts emphasize the absolute necessity of the exemplarity of the bishop for his exercise of pastoral care, for his mission to outsiders, and for his liturgical duties.

In his city, the bishop was expected to perform manifold tasks and activities for the physical well-being of his congregation, activities that only indirectly contributed to its spiritual nourishment. Here, the concept of the holy man as *patronus* becomes relevant. This idea was introduced by Peter

---

1. P. Brown, "The Saint as Exemplar in Late Antiquity," *Representations* 1 (1983): 1–25.

Brown in 1971 to help explain the concrete role of holy men in the Syrian countryside.[2] Brown pointed out that Syrian holy men—and the phenomenon is discernible in other regions as well—acted as advocates, protectors, and intercessors with authorities on behalf of the rural population. The holy man was able to act in this way because his asceticism had placed him at a distance from the world and hence rendered his authority unassailable. A letter to Paphnutius, one of the holy men mentioned earlier at the center of a prayer community in fourth-century Egypt, confirms the importance of this notion of patronage. His correspondent declared: "We regard you as our master and common patron."[3]

The following pages will show that the bishop's role in practical matters was analogous to that of the *patronus* or public benefactor, whether he was a holy man or a prominent citizen. Bishops provided food in times of famine, helped Christians in distress, and pleaded with authorities for tax remission and other favors. In contrast to the activities of holy men, episcopal activities covered a wider range of concerns, to a large extent because bishops had greater access to steady financial resources. Also, the means by which bishops intervened were different. Where holy men would intercede with God in prayer and occasionally produce a miracle, bishops worked with the power that was at their disposal: persuasion through rhetoric, influence through social networking, and the threat of excommunication. In this sense, the bishop's public activities overlapped not only with those of holy men, but also with those of civic leaders and public benefactors.

To set the tone, I begin with a juxtaposition of Synesius of Cyrene and Theodore of Sykeon, the former a leading citizen, the latter an accomplished ascetic, and both reluctant bishops. Then, resuming the earlier discussion of 1 Timothy 3, I consider the common late antique misconception that the episcopate was an honor, analogous to a civic magistracy. As the following chapters will show, it is not always easy to distinguish between a bishop's position of civic prominence and the role of Christian leadership he was expected to embody.

## SYNESIUS OF CYRENE AND THEODORE OF SYKEON

It is instructive to bear in mind the enormous diversity of social backgrounds, personal religious engagement, and career paths that brought individual men to the episcopate. The examples of Bishops Synesius of Cyrene and Theodore of Sykeon illustrate the two opposite ends of this spectrum.

Most of what we know of Synesius's life depends on the information he

2. P. Brown, "The Rise and Function of the Holy Man in Late Antiquity," *JRS* 61 (1971): 80–101.

3. *PHeid* 1 (1905) 6 = Naldini 41 (my translation).

provides in his own works, especially his collection of 156 letters. Synesius was born around 370 in Cyrene (North Africa) into a wealthy family that could proudly trace its ancestry back to the Dorian colonists who had founded the city in the seventh century B.C.[4] His family belonged to the landholding provincial aristocracy, which meant that Synesius inherited the rank of *curialis*. This entailed membership in the city council, the *curia* (Greek: *boulē*), along with the expectation that he would serve his city in various ways, not only by taking up administrative office but also making financial contributions to enhance its beauty and improve its infrastructure.[5] To prepare him for such a leading role in society and for the life of learned leisure that his social status demanded, Synesius received a good higher education in rhetoric and grammar. During his years of study in Alexandria he became an eager and devoted pupil of the woman philosopher Hypatia. A few years after the completion of his studies, he went on an embassy to the imperial court in Constantinople. The provincial council of Cyrenaica selected him for this honor to represent the concerns of his region before the emperor Arcadius. However, Synesius paid for all the expenses of the journey himself—a common form of public service, known as liturgy (Greek: *leitourgia*), among the wealthy at the time. The purpose of the embassy was to present to the emperor the *aurum coronarium* (a "gift" of golden wreaths presented to the emperor every five years by each province) and to plead for a remission of the taxes for which the province was still in arrears. Not only was this granted, Synesius also received a lifelong exemption from taxes himself. He stayed in the capital for three years (397–401). His famous treatise *On Kingship* takes the form of a speech delivered before the emperor Arcadius. Soon after his return to Cyrene, Synesius got married. The union was sealed by none other than Theophilus, the bishop of Alexandria, and soon brought forth three sons, the last two being twins. A man of devout religiosity, Synesius probably had received baptism not long before his marriage[6] but continued to be fascinated by

---

4. For a brief biography, see P. Maraval, "Synésius de Cyrène," *DSp* 14 (1990): cols. 1422–29; Synesius 1, *PLRE* 2: 1048–50; and S. Vollenweider, "Synesius von Cyrene," in *Lexikon der antiken christlichen Literatur*, 578–80 (Freiburg, 1998). More detailed studies are A. J. Bregman, *Synesius of Cyrene: Philosopher and Bishop* (Berkeley and Los Angeles, 1982), and D. Roques, *Synésius de Cyrène et la Cyrénaïque du Bas-Empire* (Paris, 1987).

5. For Synesius's activities as a "provincial aristocrat," see C. H. Coster, "Synesius, a *curialis* of the Time of the Emperor Arcadius," *Byzantion* 15 (1940–41): 10–38; J. H. W. G. Liebeschuetz, "Synesius and Municipal Politics of Cyrenaica in the 5th Century AD," *Byzantion* 55 (1985): 162.

6. The date of his baptism is uncertain, as are many other dates in Synesius's life. A convincing suggestion places it in 401, in fulfillment of a vow, just after his return from Constantinople: A. Cameron, J. Long, with L. Sherry, *Barbarians and Politics at the Court of Arcadius* (Berkeley, 1993), 28–34.

Neoplatonic philosophy until the end of his life. He liked to divide his time between his favorite pursuits of prayer, books, and hunting.[7] In addition to *On Kingship*, he composed hymns and philosophical treatises, as well as shorter works on hunting and dream analysis, and, of course, letters.

In the closing years of the fourth century, the region where Synesius's extensive properties were located suffered from invasions of the Ausurians. The military response of the provincial authorities against the ravages of the invaders was so ineffectual that Synesius became actively involved organizing a militia for the defense of the region. In 411, he was ordained bishop of Ptolemais, the metropolis of Cyrenaica. For the last two years of his life, he became an advocate for "his" new city and the region in general.[8] He took a decisive stand against a rapacious and cruel provincial governor, Andronicus, who was extorting payments from well-born citizens by brutal force and violating the right of the church to grant asylum. After his first warnings went unheeded, Synesius did not hesitate to wield the authority of his episcopal office and took the extreme measure of excommunicating Andronicus.[9] But once Andronicus had been relieved of his post after only a short time in office, it was Synesius who—motivated by Christian sentiments—intervened on his behalf to protect him from prosecution.[10]

On another occasion, Synesius traveled to the town of Palaebisca to bring order into the affairs of the local church, where the people at a time of doctrinal crisis and weak and distant leadership had appointed for themselves their own bishop, without observing proper ecclesiastical procedure.[11] Their choice had fallen on a certain Paul, a young and energetic man, who had just returned from imperial service[12] to take care of agricultural land that he had recently acquired. They appreciated the fact that he was a man who could "injure his enemies and be useful to his friends."[13] This, in a nutshell, is the definition of a late antique *patronus*. The people of Palaebisca chose Paul as the leader of their church because he could be a powerful advocate for them: He was from a well-known local family and thus enjoyed social clout among his peers. He was wealthy and thus would be less prone to corruption and could be expected to act as a financial benefactor. He must have received a decent education in the classical vein in order to have gained his position in the imperial bureaucracy, and this would enable him

---

7. Synesius, *Ep.* 57 (Garzya 41), p. 58.
8. On Synesius's activities as a bishop, see J. H. W. G. Liebeschuetz, "Why Did Synesius Become Bishop of Ptolemais?" *Byzantion* 56 (1986): 180–95.
9. Synesius, *Ep.* 57 (Garzya 41); 58 (Garzya 42); 72 (Garzya 72); 79 (Garzya 79).
10. Ibid., 90 (Garzya 90).
11. Ibid., 67 (Garzya 66).
12. Fitzgerald's translation, p. 151, of *strateia* as "military career" is too narrow.
13. Synesius, *Ep.* 67 (Garzya 66).

to give pleasing speeches and rousing sermons, or to approach secular authorities by letter. Moreover, he had acquired an extensive network of acquaintances at the imperial court that he could mobilize in order to gain imperial favors for the local church. Social status, wealth, education, and networking abilities were the highly desirable characteristics of anyone who held a position of leadership, whether in the city or in the church. This was true for Paul as much as for Synesius—both made a direct transition from a privileged social position to the episcopal office.

As a bishop, Synesius did his best to fulfill these expectations of civic leadership. He continued to be a vocal advocate for the resistance against the marauding Ausurians and even stood on night watch himself on the city walls of Ptolemais.[14] He also fulfilled his episcopal role as a shepherd of his flock in doctrinal matters, speaking out against the followers of the heresy of Eunomius.[15] Personal misfortunes, the death of his wife and of all his sons, affected him deeply. His plans for the foundation of a monastery for his retirement were cut short by his own death, in 413.

Throughout his life, Synesius acted as a civic leader and an advocate for his city and his region. To a certain extent, this was expected from a man of his station in society, but the intensity of his dedication to public matters must be ascribed to his personal choice. His proven record as an effective *patronus* must have prompted his election to the episcopate, despite the fact that he had not previously held any office in the church. Synesius himself hesitated for several months before accepting his election and later admitted that he would rather have died than become a bishop.[16] In the end, he only consented to his election under two conditions: first, that he did not have to separate from his wife (the celibate life of bishops was at that time increasingly encouraged), and, second, that he could not be expected in his preaching to abandon the philosophical views on the origin of the soul, the end of the world, and the resurrection of the body that he held dear.[17] He was acutely aware of his lack of what we have termed spiritual authority and the ability to offer up efficacious prayer: "The city ought thus to understand the imprudence it committed towards me in appointing one to the priesthood who had not sufficient confidence in his mission to enable him to go to God and pray on behalf of the whole people, but one who has need of the prayers of the people for his own salvation."[18] To Synesius, the ultimate goal of the priesthood was contemplation of the divine, something that he had striven for in the tranquil times of his earlier years. This kind of contem-

---

14. Liebeschuetz, "Bishop of Ptolemais," 191–93.
15. Synesius, *Ep.* 5 (Garzya 4).
16. Ibid., 57 (Garzya 41), p. 58.
17. Ibid., 105 (Garzya 105), pp. 187–89.
18. Ibid., 13 ( Garzya 13), p. 34.

plation was incompatible with the life of action that his new duties as a bishop demanded. The letters from this period show him greatly troubled by the incompatibility of the spiritual and the pragmatic aspects of the episcopal office, as he saw it.[19]

For the electorate of the church of Ptolemais, Synesius's ability to perform the public functions of the episcopate and, like Paul of Palaebisca, to "injure his enemies and be useful to his friends" in the way of a true *patronus* carried greater weight than his personal lifestyle or his beliefs. His accession to the episcopate did not change the nature of his public activities on behalf of others, but the means by which they could be achieved. Synesius continued to be concerned with intervention on behalf of the oppressed and with the protection of the area against bandits, but as a bishop he had at his disposal a new arsenal of ecclesiastical instruments of reprimand and punishment, including excommunication, which he used to great effect against Andronicus.

The development of Synesius's life can be seen as a progression from a focus on the spiritual element of a deeply religious soul to the pragmatic demands of the episcopal office.[20] These he was able to fulfill because, like Paul of Palaebisca, he had all the worldly qualifications for a role of public leadership in the manner of a *patronus*. What was missing, in the case of Synesius, was the ascetic element. The story of Theodore of Sykeon can serve as a counterpoint that throws into relief how asceticism can substitute for secular qualifications and still enable a man to act as a *patronus*.

While we know about Synesius from autobiographical remarks scattered throughout his many writings, especially his letters, Theodore did not leave any written record of his own. The only source of information at our disposal is the *Vita* that was composed after his death by his disciple George. It has all the peculiarities of a hagiographical text: it was written from hindsight, and with the declared intention to celebrate Theodore as a saint and to advertise his monastery in Galatia Prima, where the author now served as abbot. With Theodore, we move to central Anatolia and to the very end of the chronological spectrum of this study.[21]

Theodore was born under the emperor Justinian (527–565) and died under the emperor Heraclius, in 613. He spent most of his life in the town of Sykeon in western Galatia, where—the *Vita* tells us—an impressive complex of monastic buildings was set up to accommodate his growing number of followers. Current archaeological fieldwork has tentatively identified

19. Ibid., 57 (Garzya 41), p. 66.
20. On Synesius's spiritual side, see P. Graffigna, "Il vescovo tardoantico tra philosophia e prostasia: Sinesio di Cirene," in *Vescovi e pastori in epoca teodosiana*, 2 (Rome, 1997).
21. For a detailed historical commentary on Theodore's impact on the region, see S. Mitchell, *Anatolia: Land, Men, and Gods in Asia Minor,* vol. 2, *The Rise of the Church* (Oxford, 1993), 122–50.

Sykeon with a late Roman/early Byzantine site about eighty kilometers west of Ankara. The remains of two churches and the proximity of a river support that identification.[22] According to the hagiographic account, already Theodore's birth was surrounded by miracles. His mother, Mary, was an innkeeper who provided physical comfort of all kinds to travelers. The night she conceived Theodore—his father was a former circus performer traveling on imperial business—she saw a large shining star descending from heaven straight to her womb. As a child, Theodore frightened his mother with his insistence on strict fasting and his secret visits, in the dark of night, to the nearby chapel of Saint George. He sought the company of experienced holy men and, before he was fourteen years old, had played his part in bringing down rain during a drought in a joint prayer with his spiritual father Glycerius.[23] He received an elementary education between the ages of eight and fourteen but also made an effort—with divine assistance—to learn all the psalms by heart.[24] Soon thereafter, he left his family and for two years lived alone in a cave, until his relatives learned of his whereabouts from the deacon who secretly brought him whatever meager food he ate. They dragged him out "looking like a corpse," giving off a foul odor, with matted hair and worms eating away at his body.[25] Word of his ascetic achievement spread rapidly. The bishop of Anastasioupolis came to honor him and in quick succession ordained him lector, subdeacon, and priest. He was at that time only eighteen years old. This tale fits the pattern that we noted before of ordination as a confirmation of personal virtue and ascetic achievement.

The *Vita* then goes on to describe Theodore's pilgrimage to Jerusalem and the hermits and monasteries in the area—the first of three visits that he would pay to the Holy Land—where he received the monastic habit.[26] Upon his return to Galatia, he developed his own ascetic discipline, living at the oratory of Saint George. He spent the whole period of Lent in a small iron cage, weighed down with over fifty pounds of iron chains that the villagers had made especially for him by melting down their farming tools. In the summer, the intense sun would make him faint; in the winter, storms would make him rigid with cold, his bare feet frozen to the iron floor of his cage.[27]

God rewarded his efforts in many ways: Theodore could cast out demons,

---

22. J. Walker, "In Search of Saint Theodore in Central Anatolia: Archaeological Survey of Late Roman Galatia," in *Abstracts of Papers, Twenty-fourth Annual Byzantine Studies Conference,* Lexington, Kentucky, October 20–22, 1998. I am grateful to Joel Walker and Peter Brown for sharing the results of their survey with me.

23. *Life of Theodore of Sykeon* 14.

24. Ibid., 13.

25. Ibid., 20.

26. Ibid., 24.

27. Ibid., 27–31.

heal from illness, end infestations of locusts, and divert wild rivers.[28] He also had the gift of foreknowledge, which enabled him not only to foretell the beginning and the end of the reign of the emperor Maurice (in 582 and 602 respectively), the overthrow of the new emperor, Phocas (in 610), and the success of the military expedition of Domnitziolus, the nephew of Phocas, but also to identify the true source of the silver used in the chalice and paten his archdeacon had purchased in the capital—the chamber pot of a prostitute.[29]

The hagiographer recounts that Theodore attracted many admirers and followers in the surrounding countryside, especially among those who had benefited from his miracles, so that further buildings had to be added to the oratory of Saint George for the use of his disciples and for those who came to seek healing. To release Theodore from all administrative cares, an abbot was appointed to look after the day-to-day operation of the monastery.[30] Eventually, at the request of the clergy and the wealthy and influential citizens of Anastasioupolis, Theodore was ordained bishop of that city, by force and despite his protestations.[31] He now established his residence in the city but continued to travel to the surrounding villages whenever his presence and his miraculous powers were required. Despite his efforts to adhere to his accustomed way of life, he soon felt his ascetic standards slackening. Moreover, he was faced with great difficulties in performing a bishop's duties: an ambitious and greedy financial officer whose oppression caused a riot in a village, envious men who attempted to poison him, accusations of overgenerous spending for the poor, and constant interruptions of his private prayers with urgent matters of administration.[32]

Finally, after eleven years in the episcopate, Theodore announced his intention to withdraw from the episcopate and returned to his monastery. But his superior, the metropolitan Paul of Ancyra, was not prepared to "let a man of such virtue resign." The matter was therefore referred to the patriarch of Constantinople, who was willing to honor Theodore's request but at the same time ordered that he be given the *ōmophorion*, the bishop's stole, "so that he would retain his rank, because he was a holy man and it was through no fault of his that he was resigning from the bishopric."[33] The patriarch's words reported in the *Vita* show the continued vitality in the seventh century of the concept of ordination as a recognition of ascetic author-

28. Ibid., 26, 31, 35, 36, 45.
29. Ibid., 42, 54, 119, 120, 152.
30. Ibid., 40, 41.
31. Ibid., 58.
32. Ibid., 75–78.
33. Ibid., 79.

ity that could exist independent of the conferral of pragmatic authority within the church.

At the invitation of the emperor Maurice who wanted to profit from his prayers, the *Vita* continues, Theodore traveled to Constantinople. In the course of his stay, he gained privileges for his monastery, which was now placed under the direct jurisdiction of the patriarch, and performed many miracles, including the healing of the emperor's child.[34] Upon his return to Galatia, he resumed his usual activities for the benefit of the country population: exorcisms; miracles of healing; making rain; halting infestations of beetles, locusts, worms, or dormice; and providing grain during a famine.[35] Theodore also sent letters to the provincial governor to protect some villagers and managed to quell a violent uprising in a nearby village.[36]

Theodore had a special connection to Domnitziolus, the nephew of the new emperor, Phocas, who usurped the throne in 602. Their association began when Domnitziolus was leading a contingent of troops through Anatolia and visited Theodore, who assured him that he would remain unharmed. In gratitude, he sent to Theodore's monastery the generous gift of a golden cross, adorned with relics. Later, Theodore visited Domnitziolus's house in Constantinople and gave his blessing to the whole household, including the general's barren wife, who eventually gave birth to three sons, just as the saint had predicted. When, as a result of the overthrow of Phocas, Domnitziolus's life was in danger, Theodore intervened on his behalf in a letter to the new emperor, Heraclius.[37]

In a summary passage near the end of the *Vita*, the hagiographer records that Theodore encouraged sinners to do penance through fasting, prayers, and almsgiving; that he was at pains to reconcile men who had a grievance against one another; and that he admonished those who were engaged in lawsuits to give up their litigation and to adopt neighborly love instead. He also assisted those who brought before him their complaints against the oppression of officials and tax collectors.[38] In this summary record of Theodore's care for the spiritual and physical well-being of the people around him, the hagiographer shows no concern about whether Theodore performed these actions while he was holding the episcopal see of Anastasioupolis or not, whereas the modern reader would be tempted to identify the

---

34. Ibid., 82–97.
35. Ibid., 98–104, 115, 118, 145.
36. Ibid., 115–16.
37. Ibid., 120, 128, 140, 152. In the historical sources of the period, this general is called Komentiolos. Cf. W. E. Kaegi, Jr., "New Evidence on the Early Reign of Heraclius," *BZ* 66 (1973): 308–30, repr. in his *Army, Society, and Religion in Byzantium* (London, 1982).
38. *Life of Theodore of Sykeon* 147.

ministry of penance and the encouragement to reconciliation as specific to the episcopate.

The differences between the personal lives of Theodore and Synesius could not be more pronounced. Theodore was the son of a single mother who was working her way up in the world, and he had only an average education. He did not leave a single scrap of writing, nor did his hagiographer deem his sermons worth recording. He was a devout Christian from earliest youth and never wavered in his dedication to the monastic life. He was given to spectacular feats of asceticism and had the power to work miracles. The monastery he founded attracted an ever-increasing number of followers. Synesius, by contrast, was born into privilege and could enjoy a life of leisure. He received an extensive higher education and was an accomplished author. He lived at a time, in the late fourth/early fifth century, when conversion to Christianity was an active choice, and thus received baptism only as an adult. He was a family man, happily married, with three sons.

Yet when it came to their public roles, Theodore and Synesius are comparable on many levels. Both acted as advocates and benefactors of the people around them. Both had done so prior to their elevation to the episcopate. In fact, it was this very ability to "injure one's enemies and to be useful to one's friends" that made them desirable candidates for the episcopal office. Both made it their task to maintain social order and peace; both went to Constantinople and obtained favors from the emperor. In both instances, their accession to the episcopate added administrative duties to their daily schedule, and these proved sufficiently bothersome to Theodore to tender his resignation. But it was not these additional tasks that defined the leadership role of Synesius and Theodore, nor was it their rank within the ecclesiastical hierarchy.

Here it is helpful to draw on the three kinds of authority—spiritual, ascetic, and pragmatic—discussed in the previous chapter. Synesius's greatest advantage was his pragmatic authority, and this was the direct result of his social standing. As a prominent citizen, he was able to do great good for his native city of Cyrene, and as a bishop, he did the same for the city of Ptolemais. He knew that he had substantial influence among his contemporaries—but that did not come from his episcopal appointment. It came from the respect that his family, one of the oldest in the region, enjoyed; it came from his education, which had trained him in the use of rhetoric for networking and lobbying in public speeches and letters; it came from the fact that he cultivated his reputation as a man of leisure who was happiest when he was with his books in his study, his family at home, or his dogs on the hunt.

Although he was aware that the episcopate required certain virtues, Synesius seems to have made no particular effort to acquire or to display them. Quite to the contrary, he only accepted the appointment under two conditions: that he was not expected to lead a chaste life, and that he could not be asked to give up certain of his beliefs that were shaped by Neoplatonic philosophy rather than Christian theology. Ascetic authority, visible in a person's lifestyle, thus seems to have played a negligible role in Synesius's episcopate. More difficult to pin down is his spiritual authority. Throughout his life, Synesius sought to nurture his personal spirituality. He speaks of his habits of prayer and contemplation, although his conception of the supreme deity probably owed more to the philosophy he had absorbed in Hypatia's lecture room than to the theology taught in the church of Alexandria by Patriarch Theophilus, with whom Synesius was on friendly terms. The aim of Synesius's philosophy was the care of his own soul. We are not informed that he had any gifts of the spirit, let alone that he shared them with others. Synesius also seems to have made very little of his ordination as a potential source of the "spirit" of the apostles. The defining characteristics of Synesius's episcopate, then, were his pragmatic authority and, to a lesser degree, his spiritual authority as a deeply religious person—both of which he had acquired outside the institutional church, and both of which were not affected in scope or nature by his appointment as bishop.

Theodore, by contrast, had no social distinction to show for himself. His way of gaining the recognition of his contemporaries was through extreme asceticism, which he had practiced since childhood. His ascetic feats made evident his spiritual abilities to work miracles and to act as a spiritual guide to others who joined him at his monastery. It was the authority he had acquired in the eyes of the villagers of the surrounding countryside and on the part of the grateful general Domnitziolos that enabled him to pursue his social activism on behalf of his region. Theodore's tenure as bishop of Anastasioupolis had no effect on the nature of his activities. In the hagiographical narrative, Theodore's episcopal ordination merely serves as an official recognition and public validation of his personal sanctity.

This comparison allows us to fine-tune our earlier definition of pragmatic authority by questioning its sources and the means by which it can be put into action. Pragmatic authority in the sense of appointment to the episcopate as an *opus* or work can originate either in a man's privileged social position, as in the case of Synesius, or in a man's outstanding ascetic record, as in the case of Theodore. One might even go so far as to speculate that for men of low social status, the only way to attain the episcopate was by proving their spiritual qualifications through highly visible acts of asceticism.

Two points that arise from this comparison of Synesius and Theodore deserve to be highlighted. First, ordination to the episcopate did not necessarily disrupt or change the continuity of a man's activities, whether he was a prominent citizen or a well-known ascetic. Second, in the eyes of the electorate, the most desirable qualification of a candidate for the episcopate was his ability to "be useful to his friends." Episcopal ordination was thus pri-

marily a confirmation of preexisting qualifications, whether spiritual or social, and only in the second place the bestowal of a license to a greater scope
of activities and/or the conferral of additional spiritual powers.

### THE EPISCOPATE: WORK OR HONOR?

The singular position that the bishop occupied within his city as a public
benefactor and an administrator made the episcopate highly desirable.
Christian authors therefore found it necessary to issue frequent warnings
that the episcopate should not be sought. They did so by taking recourse to
the passage in 1 Timothy 3:1 where Paul sets down the ideal qualities of the
bishop: *ei tis episkopēs oregetai, kalou ergou epithymei.*The literal translation
would be "If someone desires the function of overseer, he wishes for a noble
task." The Greek word for "task" is *ergon,* the Latin *opus.* Both have their
most literal equivalent in the English "work." Greek and Latin commentators took this opportunity to observe that the episcopate is a task—we might
say a ministry—and not an honorific distinction. Where monks were supposed to avoid vainglory in seeking the episcopate, the advice to Christian
citizens was to avoid ambition.

The first Latin author to express this notion seems to have been Jerome in
his *Commentary on the Epistle to Titus,* composed in 386: "He [Paul] says 'work,'
not 'honor,' nor 'glory.'"[39] At around the same time, John Chrysostom admitted that to strive for the episcopate in the true sense of a task was a good thing,
but insisted that one ought to avoid yearning for it as a magistracy *(archē)* or a
source of authority *(authentia).*[40] A few decades later, Augustine picked up this
point in his *City of God.* Commenting on 1 Timothy 3:1, he remarked: "He
[Paul] wanted to explain what the 'episcopate' is, for the word designates a
work, not an honor."[41] Theodore of Mopsuestia reiterated this argument in
his *Commentary on the Epistle to Timothy.* Originally composed in Greek, in 428,
the work now survives only in a Latin translation.[42] At the close of the patristic age, the Spaniard Isidore of Seville resumed the words of Jerome and
Augustine in his *De ecclesiasticis officiis.*[43] By that time, the injunction that the
episcopate is a work, not an honor had acquired almost formulaic character.

39. Jerome, *Commentary on the Letter to Titus* 1, *PL* 26, col. 598B: "Opus inquit, non honorem,
non gloriam." Jerome here refers to 1 Tim. 3:1.
40. John Chrysostom, *Hom.* 10 *on 1 Tim. 3,* chap. 3, *PG* 62, col. 547; *Hom. 3 on Acts* 5, *PG* 60,
col. 40. The same idea is also expressed in his *On the Priesthood* 3.10.55–94.
41. Augustine, *City of God* 19.19: "Exponere uoluit quia sit episcopatus, quia nomen est operis,
non honoris."
42. Theodore of Mopsuestia, *In Ep. ad Tim. 1,* 3.1, pp. 97–98: "Bene *opus* dixit et non 'digni-
tatem,' nec enim dignitates sunt ecclesiasticae functiones, sed opus."
43. Isidore of Seville, *De ecclesiasticis officiis* 2.5.8, p. 59: "Episcopatus autem, ut quidam pru-
dentium ait, nomen est operis et non honoris."

Such emphasis on the priesthood or episcopate as an *opus* or "task" is reminiscent of the original functions of the *episkopoi* as overseers in the first two centuries.

By the late fourth century, when Jerome uttered his words of caution, the situation of the church had changed dramatically. Constantine's acceptance of Christianity as a legitimate religion in 313, and the subsequent adoption of this new religion by most of his successors, resulted in an ever-increasing number of conversions, and in Christianity's gradual permeation of the social hierarchy. By the end of the fourth century Christianity had reached not only the privileged class of the *curiales* in the many urban centers of the empire, but even the senatorial aristocracy. Christianity had become a visible force in society, and its highest representative in each city, the bishop, held a position of great influence and responsibility.

These comments are based on a sharp distinction between *opus* and *honor,* in Latin, or *ergon* and *timē,* in Greek. *Honor* and *timē* denote honor and distinction in the broadest sense.[44] The warning against seeking ordination as an *honor* instead of as an *opus* is aimed at those who wish to instrumentalize ecclesiastical office as an affirmation of their status in society.[45] At the level of the urban elite of the *curiales,* status usually translated into holding municipal office. To hold a magistracy was indeed considered a great honor and contributed to a man's recognition in the eyes of his contemporaries, even if he had to pay in order to receive his office and was expected to dispense large amounts of his private funds for the common good. Indeed, the words "honor" and "magistracy" could be used interchangeably.[46] The insistence of the patristic commentators that the episcopate is work and an occupation thus does much more than issue a warning against coveting the highest ecclesiastical ministry. It indicates the danger of conflating it with a civil magistracy.

A similar ambiguity is present in the expression used to describe concrete acts of public service. The ancient Greek word for public service, performed at personal expense, is "liturgy" *(leitourgia).* It could also mean service to pagan deities. Christian authors adopted the word for their own use and employed it to refer to their service of God, not just in the celebration by the congregation of ecclesiastical ritual that we now accordingly call "the liturgy," but also in the ecclesiastical ministry of an individual.[47] Isidore of Pelusium, the mid-fifth-century priest-turned-monk, made this very clear in a letter of complaint against a corrupt priest who had managed to purchase his office

44. See also "The Latin and Greek Lexicon of Honour" at the end of J. E. Lendon, *Empire of Honour: The Art of Government in the Roman World* (Oxford, 1977), 272–79.
45. Lendon, esp. 90–95.
46. Just. Dig. 50.4.14.
47. Shepherd of Hermas, Sim. 9. 27; Gregory of Nazianzus, *Or.* 12.5, *PG* 35.

for money: "He hunted after clerical office, which is in fact a ministry *(leitur-gia)*, but [to him] seemed like a public magistracy *(archē)*."[48] Isidore's conservative interpretation of "liturgy" would have been lost on most of his contemporaries, for whom the giving of expensive public liturgies was a source of personal civic pride, in the same way as was officeholding.

Even to Christians, it will not always have been obvious that the episcopal office should not be regarded as an honor analogous to public office. Indeed, the church fathers encouraged them to look to the church as the venue for discharging their public duties and releasing their social ambitions, instead of seeking public office. Already in the second century, Tertullian reminded Christians: "But your orders, and your magistracies, and your very place of meeting, the church, are Christ's."[49] In the same spirit, Origen had responded to the reproach by the pagan Celsus that Christians were loath to participate in the political life of the empire by pointing out that they had their own offices to fill, namely, in the church.[50] Jerome observed: "We in the church also have our senate, namely the assembly of presbyters."[51] Personal ambition, civic pride, and the desire for recognition could thus find an outlet within the institution of the church as much as within the *civitas*. These notions were reinforced by the conceptualization of the afterlife in heaven as the equivalent of an exclusive corporation of members who had distinguished themselves through good service. Heaven was thought of as a senate or a municipal council *(curia)*, where the apostles and martyrs were automatically inscribed in the membership lists, and holy men also had a chance of entering.[52]

Members of the curial class who competed for municipal office comprised the largest recruiting ground for the episcopate, as will be explained in greater detail below. These men were also acutely aware of their personal status of *honor*. The palpable importance of honor in defining a person's place in Roman society has been elucidated in a recent book by J. E. Lendon. Honor existed in the eye of the beholder, as the person of honor exuded it in his comportment. It could be confirmed or acquired through titles and offices, and it was affirmed through public acts of generosity. It comes as no surprise that to the status-conscious urban upper class of the later Roman Empire, the highest and most exclusive ecclesiastical office appeared as an additional source of honor.[53] John the Almsgiver, the early

48. Isidore of Pelusium, *Ep.* 2.127, *PG* 78, col. 568A.
49. Tertullian, *De corona* 13, p. 242, lines 2–3.
50. Origen, *Against Celsus* 8.75, p. 292, lines 1–8.
51. Jerome, *Commentary on Jesaiah* 2. 3.
52. L. Koep, *Das himmlische Buch in Antike und Christentum* (Bonn, 1952), 120–23, with further references.
53. Lendon, esp. 90–95.

seventh-century patriarch of Alexandria known for his spectacular deeds of charity, admitted that he himself was not above boastfulness and pride because of his appearance, wealth, and office: "I am puffed up and exalt myself over my brother if I am perhaps a little better-looking or richer or more distinguished or hold some public office *(eis archēn offikiou tinos)*."[54] Although the real intent of John's words was to bring excessively boastful laymen to compunction by his demonstrative self-incrimination, this can have been convincing only if his episcopate was indeed regarded as an *officium*.

The distinction attached to public service was advertised in laudatory speeches or honorific inscriptions. It is significant that the same vocabulary was used to celebrate magistrates, civic benefactors, and bishops.[55] Those who held positions of leadership, whether civic or ecclesiastical, were expected to display the same virtues of justice, respect for the laws, integrity, indifference to bribery, gentleness, and forgiveness. The same laudatory expressions were used by pagans, such as the rhetor Libanius, and Christians alike.[56] Guidelines on how to praise a governor were written down in the third century A.D. by Menander Rhetor, whose work was studied in classrooms throughout late antiquity and beyond. He advised that such a speech should highlight the virtues of the governor, such as wisdom, justice, temperance, and courage, whether real or hoped-for.[57] By the same token, late antique epigrams praise bishops for their wisdom or refer to their "throne" or seat of office in much the same way as is customary for provincial governors, as Charlotte Roueché has noted.[58] It would be extreme to interpret the common language of praise as an indication that bishops have been transformed into civil servants or were neatly absorbed into the operation of their municipalities. Indeed, it could be argued that a process of mutual approximation was under way that equally affected the language used in praise of civil servants: the Egyptian papyri from our period show that officials were frequently addressed with the same religiously inspired laudatory adjectives as men of the church *(eulabestatos*—most pious, *theophilestatos*—most God-beloved).[59] Since the church as an organization existed within the social and political framework of the empire, the two could not but share the same *mentalité*.

Another interesting parallel that deserves to be noted is the virtue known

---

54. *Life of John the Almsgiver* 42.

55. For the following, see C. Roueché, "The Functions of the Governor in Late Antiquity: Some Observations," *Antiquité Tardive* 6 (1998): 31–36.

56. P. Petit, *Libanius et la vie municipale à Antioche au IV^e siècle après J.-C.* (Paris, 1955), 271–72.

57. Menander Rhetor, *Treatise* 2 (10).415.

58. C. Roueché, "Benefactors in the Late Roman Period: The Eastern Empire," in *Actes du X^e Congrès International d'Épigraphie Grecque et Latine, Nimes, 4–9 Octobre 1992*, ed. M. Christol and O. Masson (Paris, 1997), 363.

59. O. Hornickel, *Ehren- und Rangprädikate in den Papyrusurkunden: Ein Beitrag zum römischen und byzantinischen Titelwesen* (Giessen, 1930).

in Greek as *praotēs* and in Latin as *clementia*, usually rendered in awkward and insufficient English as "meekness." A better translation would be "gentleness" (in the sense of "a true gentleman") with the further connotation of "consideration of others." This virtue is made evident especially in the care of those who have fallen on hard times, the poor and the sick.[60] It became particularly common in the vocabulary of civic praise in the late antique period. *Praotēs* was often invoked in the same context as *epieikeia*, another public virtue, which corresponds to the English "fairness" and was especially valued in those who had to make decisions and pass judgments.[61] *Praotēs* was expected of magistrates at all levels, and especially provincial governors, who were reminded of it by people who sought their favor. Basil of Caesarea deemed it useful to invoke the characteristic mildness of Modestus, the praetorian prefect of the Orient, before he launched into a request for tax exemptions for the clergy.[62] *Praotēs* was also the one virtue most commonly associated with Moses, who, as we have seen earlier, was considered the Old Testament prototype of the Christian bishop. Not surprisingly, it became the virtue most closely associated with the charitable work of bishops.

A last noteworthy commonality in the praise of bishops and leading citizens is the emphasis on the exemplarity of their conduct. Christian authors liked to think of the bishop as an exemplar of Christian virtue, as has already been discussed in detail. But a large number of Greek inscriptions from the imperial period also honor outstanding men and women in the community as "examples of virtue" (*hypodeigma aretēs*).[63]

Christian and civic virtues rested easily together as conversion became *en vogue* and ceased to require a radical reexamination of one's life prior to baptism or a strict adjustment of one's lifestyle afterwards. The Christians of the post-Constantinian period were no longer an exclusive group, but men and women of their times, participating in public life and expressing themselves in inscriptions and in literature in the traditional ways to which they were accustomed. An inscription of the sixth century on a bath in Smyrna, preserved in the *Greek Anthology*, illustrates this grafting of Christian ideals onto classical forms of expression. Cloaked in the traditional form of the verse epigram, it begins with great rhetorical flourish, continues with effusive praise for an upright magistrate, and ends with an invocation of Christ:

60. H. Bolkestein, *Wohltätigkeit und Armenpflege im vorchristlichen Altertum* (Utrecht, 1939), 108–9.
61. L. Robert, *Hellenica* 4 (1948): 14–27; id., *Hellenica* 13 (1965): 223–24. On *epieikeia*, see L. Robert, *Le martyre de Pionios prêtre de Smyrne*, ed. G. W. Bowersock and C. P. Jones (Washington, D.C., 1994), 63–64. For *clementia* as a public and politically desirable virtue, see K. Winkler, "Clementia," *RAC* 3 (1957): cols. 206–31.
62. Basil of Caesarea, *Ep.* 104.
63. Robert, *Hellenica* 13 (1965): 226–27.

Thou building, who of mortals made thee, who wast formerly dim, rich in light for bathers, and who, cleaning away the smoky grime that befouled thee, brightened thee thus? It was wise Theodorus who in this truly, as in everything, showed the cleanness of his heart. He being the treasurer of the possessions of the city and its father, did not stain his hands by gain derived from them. Mighty Christ, immortal God, keep by thy hand this patriot out of the reach of misfortune.[64]

This shared language of praise for men in positions of leadership, whether civic or ecclesiastical, alerts us to the possibility that the distinction between public roles in civic and ecclesiastical contexts was not always clearly drawn.

---

64. *Greek Anthology* 9.615. I slightly changed Paton's translation to convey the sense that Theodorus was, in all likelihood, involved in the financial administration of Smyrna as *patēr poleōs*, father of the city. On this title, see C. Roueché, "A New Inscription from Aphrodisias and the Title *patēr tēs poleōs*," *GRBS* 20 (1979): 173–85.

CHAPTER SIX

# Social Contexts

The public role of the bishop was greatly augmented as Christianity gained in importance and the church grew in numbers. The favors showered by Constantine and his successors on the Christian church contributed to making the new religion attractive to prospective converts.[1] The church soon became a considerable economic force as a result of the acquisition of property and income through regular contributions, imperial donations, and pious bequests, first allowed by Constantine in 321.[2] Ecclesiastical finances were put to use in providing charity to the needy and in the creation of a permanent ecclesiastical infrastructure, including building projects. Proportionate to this enlarged scope of church membership and Christian activities, the number of clergy attached to large sees increased. In the mid-third century, the church in Rome counted 46 priests, 7 deacons, 7 subdeacons, 42 acolytes, a combined total of 52 exorcists, readers, and doorkeepers, and more than 1,500 individuals on its poor roll.[3] Three centuries later, under Justinian, the staff attached to the Great Church in the Eastern capital of Constantinople was fixed at 60 priests, 100 deacons, 40 deaconesses, 90 subdeacons, 110 readers, 25 singers, and 100 doorkeepers.[4]

There was also an increase in the number of bishoprics. By the fifth century, all major cities had their own bishop, and additional bishops,

---

1. The relevant laws are listed by P.-P. Joannou, *La législation impériale et la christianisation de l'Empire romain*, OCA 192 (Rome, 1972). For an English translation of laws regarding the church until 535, see P. R. Coleman-Norton, *Roman State and Christian Church: A Collection of Legal Documents to A.D. 535*, 3 vols. (London, 1966).
2. CTh 16. 2. 4.
3. Eusebius, *HE* 6.43.11, p. 618, lines 14–18.
4. Nov. Just. 3.1 (535).

*chorepiskopoi,* were assigned to smaller rural settlements in remote areas. This means that there must have been a total of 2,000 bishops in the later Roman Empire.[5] It is possible to trace the explosive growth in the number of episcopal sees on a smaller scale, for the regions of Syria and Palestine. Syria had just fewer than 30 bishops at the time of the Council of Nicaea in 325, but more than 70 in the *Notitia Antiochena* of 570.[6] An even more dramatic jump in the number of sees occurred in Palestine, where there were 3 episcopal sees in 325 compared to about 50 during the reign of Justinian.[7]

As the episcopate was the single office at the top of the hierarchy of the ecclesiastical *cursus honorum,* and the bishop held a unique position of influence and power within his city, the distinction between the episcopate and a civil magistracy could become blurry. To continue the examination of the bishop's role within his urban context, it is therefore useful to take a closer look at the patterns of episcopal recruitment from the various levels of society in order to show the increasing dependence of episcopal appointments on the social criteria of family background, education, and wealth.[8]

### BISHOPS OF MODEST BACKGROUND

None of the normative texts of the church, neither the early church orders nor the canons of synods and councils, issued any specific recommendations for the social background or personal wealth of suitable candidates for the clergy, including the episcopate. A humble social background was thus never an official obstacle to appointment in the clergy, and we know of ecclesiastical officeholders who had been artisans, craftsmen, and laborers, even former slaves. But the evidence is patchy. First of all, the opacity of the sources leaves us guessing whether a *sacerdos* or *hiereus* of humble background had indeed acquired the rank of the episcopate. It will be argued below that such men tended to encounter a glass ceiling in promotion through the ecclesiastical ranks and became bishops only in exceptional cases. Second, the incidence of bishops of more modest background may be underreported in our sources. In fact, most of the evidence comes from imperial law.

---

5. W. Eck, "Der Einfluß der konstantinischen Wende auf die Auswahl der Bischöfe im 4. und 5. Jahrhundert," *Chiron* 8 (1978): 567.

6. T. Ulbert, "Bischof und Kathedrale (4.-7. Jh.): Archäologische Zeugnisse in Syrien," in *Actes du XI^e Congrès International d'Archéologie Chrétienne,* Studi di Antichità Cristiana 41 and Collection de l'École Française de Rome 123 (Vatican City and Rome, 1989), 1: 431.

7. M. Picirillo, "Gruppi episcopali nelle tre Palestine e in Arabia?" in *Actes du XI^e Congrès International d'Archéologie Chrétienne,* Studi di Antichità Cristiana 41 and Collection de l'École Française de Rome 123 (Vatican City and Rome, 1989), 1: 461.

8. See also C. Rapp, "Bishops in Late Antiquity: A New Social and Urban Elite?" in *Late Antiquity and Early Islam,* vol. 6, ed. J. Haldon and L. Conrad, 144–73 (forthcoming). This chapter expands on the latter article.

The authors of historical narratives tend to pay attention to bishops of humble background only when they wish to counterbalance a bishop's background with his extraordinary spiritual qualifications. This was the story of Alexander the Coal-burner, whose soot-stained and ragged appearance elicited the disgust of the people of Comana. Only after he had taken a bath and donned new clothes were they able to recognize the wisdom of Gregory the Wonder-worker in identifying him as their future bishop.[9] The humble background of bishops is also made an issue in works of polemical intent, with the intention of discrediting opponents. A good example are the snide remarks of Gregory of Nazianzus about the bishops who, in his mind, had necessitated his sudden retirement from the see of Constantinople:

> Some of them are the offspring of tax assessors, who think of nothing else but doctoring the accounts; some come from the tables of the money changers and the transactions there; some come from the plough and are parched by the sun; some come from the pitchfork and the hoe and have toiled the whole day. Others have left the oar or the army, smelling of bilgewater or bearing scars on their body, and now appear as the pilots and generals of the people and will not yield a bit. Others still have not yet completely washed away from their body the soot of their work at the fires; they are worthy of a whipping or of laboring in the mills.[10]

Such sentiments prevailed among men of means. In a letter in 376, Basil of Caesarea expressed his distaste for bishops who were poor men, calling them "slaves of slaves," a term coined by the ancient orator Demosthenes.[11] They had ousted Basil's brother Gregory from the see of Nyssa, appointing in his stead a slave whose worth, Basil sniggered, amounted to only a few obols. In addition, they had placed on the episcopal see of the town of Doara a domestic of orphans who had absconded from his masters.[12]

The church issued recommendations for the ordination of slaves, thus indirectly attesting that an entry into the ecclesiastical hierarchy was possible, provided that they were manumitted freedmen at the time of their ordination. Even then, their viable candidacy for the clergy depended on their former circumstances.[13] In 300, the Council of Elvira in Spain decreed that

9. *Life of Gregory the Wonder-worker, PG* 46, col. 936B–C.

10. Gregory of Nazianzus, *Carmen* 2.1.12 (my translation).

11. *oikotribōn oikotribas:* Demosthenes 13.24, ed. S. H. Butcher (Oxford, 1903), p.173, l. 8. This wordplay may be a display of erudition rather than an accurate family pedigree.

12. Basil of Caesarea, *Ep.* 239, p. 59.

13. The best treatment of the question of slaves and *coloni* and clerical office is E. J. Jonkers, "Das Verhalten der Alten Kirche hinsichtlich der Ernennung zum Priester von Sklaven, Freigelassenen und Curiales," *Mnemosyne* ser. 3, vol. 10 (1942): 286–302. See also

freedmen of pagan masters were barred from the clergy.[14] This specific requirement may well indicate that slaves were considered eligible for the clergy if they had formerly served in Christian households. About eighty years later, the *Apostolic Constitutions* indeed allowed this, provided the slaves had been properly manumitted and had physically left their master's household.[15] However, some cautious voices discouraged the ordination of freedmen, out of fear that problems would arise from their continued ties and obligations, whether moral or otherwise, to their former masters.[16] Still, men of formerly servile status are attested as bishops well into the fifth century and beyond. There is circumstantial evidence that Pius, the bishop of Rome in the mid-second century, was a former slave.[17] Callixtus, who later became bishop of Rome in 217, had begun his checkered career as a domestic slave whose master entrusted him with a moneylending business.[18] Basil the Elder had ordained a slave to the episcopate, a measure that later became a concern to Basil of Caesarea and Gregory of Nazianzus.[19] John Chrysostom had appointed several slaves as bishops during his tenure of the see of Constantinople. This would later be held against him in the list of accusations presented at the Synod of the Oak.[20] In 399, Jerome acknowledged that he had endorsed the ordination of a former slave, and reported that John, bishop of Jerusalem, had done the same.[21] A law of Valentinian III, issued in 452 and repeated by Justinian over a century later, acknowledged the possibility that slaves or men of servile status had attained the episcopate.[22] By the time of Justinian ordination to the clergy automatically made a slave into a freedman, provided that it had occurred with the knowledge and consent of his master.[23]

In the first half of the third century, as Georg Schöllgen has shown, a

---

W. Wischmeyer, *Von Golgatha zum Ponte Molle: Studien zur Sozialgeschichte der Kirche im dritten Jahrhundert* (Göttingen, 1992), 101–4.

14. Elvira (300), can. 80, H-L I/1, p. 263.

15. *Apostolic Constitutions* 8.47.82.

16. Boniface, bishop of Rome from 418 to 422, was reported to have prohibited the ordination of slaves to the clergy: *Liber pontificalis* 44.5. Cf. Jonkers, 292.

17. He was the brother of Hermas who identifies himself in the narrative as a freedman (*Shepherd of Hermas* 1.1). See Jonkers, 287.

18. This is the biased report by his contestant for the episcopate, Hippolytus: *Refutation of All Heresies* 9.12.1.

19. Gregory of Nazianzus, *Ep.* 79.

20. Photius, *Bibliotheca* 59.113–15. It must be noted, however, that the ostensible reason for the indignation of his detractors was not John's choice of candidates of low social status, but that these men lacked the formal legal and ethical qualifications for office: they did not belong to John, they had not yet been manumitted, and they had a bad reputation.

21. Jerome, *Ep.* 86.2 to Theophilus of Alexandria.

22. NVal 35.1.6 (452); Nov. Just. 123.4 (564).

23. Nov. Just.123.17 (546).

significant change occurred in the provisioning of the clergy.[24] Now for the first time each congregation was expected to provide funds for the livelihood of its clergy. This resulted in a "professionalization" of ecclesiastical office, in that joining the clergy became tantamount to taking up a profession. Those who benefited the most from this new custom were the clergymen who had depended on their own labor for the upkeep of their families—that is, farmers, craftsmen, and artisans—and who were now in a position to dedicate their work exclusively to the church. That this resulted in a greater influx of men from the lower middle class and the lower class into the clergy is a reasonable guess.[25]

Episcopal candidates who had earned their upkeep with manual labor were not uncommon in the first three centuries. This trend continued well into the fourth century and does not appear to have been affected by the reign of Constantine. The legislation of the fourth to sixth century listed a whole array of former professions of the clergy: slaves or men of servile status, *coloni,* merchants, pig dealers, bread makers, collectors of purple-dye fish, and other members of corporations.[26]

Even though accession to an office in the higher clergy assured the receipt of a regular stipend, many clergymen continued to engage in gainful pursuits, whether out of choice or out of necessity. This was a practice that church councils as well as imperial legislation attempted to regulate. Especially objectionable was moneylending for profit, prohibited by the Council of Elvira (ca. 300) and several subsequent councils throughout the fourth century.[27] Small commerce, on the other hand, was permitted, provided that the cleric did not expand his marketing network to other dioceses,[28] and as long as he generated only as much profit as was needed for

---

24. See above, p. 30.

25. For the social background of bishops, see also the general overview by A. H. M. Jones, *The Later Roman Empire, 284–602: A Social, Economic, and Administrative Survey* (Oxford, 1964; repr., 1986), 920–29.

26. Slaves and men of servile status: NVal 35 (452); Nov. Just. 123.4 (564); merchants: CTh 13.1.16 (399); pig dealers: CTh 14.4.8 (408); bread-makers: CTh 14.3.11 (365); "any slave, maidservant, decurion, public debtor, procurator, collector of purple dye fish, or anyone, finally, who is involved in public or private accounts": CTh 9.45.3 (398); guild members in Rome must be recalled from the clergy: NVal 20 (445); "No person of ignoble birth status, an inquilinus, a slave or a colonus . . . no guildsman of the City of Rome or of any other city whatsoever, no decurion, no ex-primate, no receiver of the gold tax, no citizen who is a sevir [*sic*] of a guild or a public slave": NVal 35.1.3 (452); *coloni:* NVal 13.8 (445); slaves should first be manumitted before joining the clergy: CJ I 3.36 (484).

27. Elvira (300), can. 20; reiterated at Arles (314), can. 13, Nicaea (325), can. 17, and Laodikeia (343? 381?), can. 4.

28. Elvira (300), can. 19.

the immediate needs of his household.[29] Already in the mid-third century, Cyprian lamented the indignities perpetrated by the clergy, and singled out commerce and moneylending as the most egregious of their economic activities:

> Not a few bishops who ought to furnish both exhortation and example to others, despising their divine charge, became agents in secular business, forsook their throne, deserted their people, wandered about over foreign provinces, hunted the markets for gainful merchandise, while brethren were starving in the Church. They sought to possess money in hoards, they seized estates by crafty deceits, they increased their gains by multiplying usuries.[30]

Although these sources refer to the clergy in general, without distinguishing between deacons, priests, and bishops, there is substantial anecdotal evidence that laborers of undistinguished background succeeded in attaining episcopal appointment during our period. Alexander of Comana, mentioned above, was a coal burner;[31] George, the Arian bishop of Alexandria, was born in the shop of a fuller;[32] Spyridon of Trimithous was a shepherd, and Zeno of Maiouma a linen weaver. They both continued in their professions even after their accession to the episcopate.[33] In sixth-century Italy, the deacon Andrew, who had until then worked as a groom of horses, was appointed to the see of Aquino; his successor Jovinus had been a fuller.[34]

Finally, a significant number of priests and bishops had been physicians.[35] Although practitioners of the medical profession in late antiquity were considered little more than skilled craftsmen, their work would have generated a large following of grateful clients and ensured their popularity as bishops. Some Christian physicians may have been thought to hold special healing powers, as was the case with Alexander, whose epitaph from Trastevere com-

29. CTh 16.2.8 (343): tax exemption for business of clerics designed to gain livelihood; this was revised in CTh 16.2.15 (360): no tax exemption for private enterprises by clerics; partially reinstated by CTh 16.2.36 (401): tax exemptions for clerical food merchants on a small scale.
30. Cyprian, *De lapsis* 6.
31. *Life of Gregory the Wonder-worker*, PG 46, col. 936B–C.
32. Ammianus Marcellinus, *Histories* 22.11.4.
33. Spyridon: Socrates, *HE* 1.12.1; Sozomen, *HE* 1.2.1; Rufinus, *HE* 10.5. Zeno: Sozomen *HE* 7.28.7.
34. Gregory the Great, *Dialogues* 3.8.2. The selection of these candidates, Gregory noted, occurred during a severe manpower shortage caused by the plague and the ravages of barbarian invasions.
35. See also A. Bigelmair, *Die Beteiligung der Christen am öffentlichen Leben in vorkonstantinischer Zeit: Ein Beitrag zur ältesten Kirchengeschichte* (Munich, 1902; repr., Aalen, 1970), 300–306. Nectarius, bishop of Constantinople, was eager to ordain his own physician and long-standing associate to the deaconate, but the latter refused: Sozomen, *HE* 7.10.1–3.

memorates him as "Christian and *pneumatikos*."[36] The checkered career of Gerontius illustrates the possibilities that were open to capable and ambitious physicians. His incompetence as a deacon under Ambrose led to his deposition and flight to Constantinople. In the Eastern capital, he managed to insinuate himself among influential men at the court. He received his episcopal see at Nicomedia in exchange for securing a post in the emperor's service for another bishop's son.[37] If we are to believe the surviving record, the reign of Constantine does not seem to have resulted in a diminution in the number of bishops who came from modest backgrounds. We must assume that, in addition to those cases listed above, this was especially true for bishops in smaller cities and in remote regions.[38]

To a large degree, the selection of the higher clergy was a direct result of the pool of available candidates. This led to significant regional variations. The correspondence between the social origin of the clergy and the general social demographics of a region can best be illustrated for Roman North Africa. Most of the 275 bishops listed in André Mandouze's *Prosopographie chrétienne du Bas-Empire* were of curial background. Only two, possibly three, bishops were senators: Cyprian of Carthage (a doubtful case), Petilianus, the Donatist bishop of Cirta, and Fulgentius of Ruspe. This is partly due to the relative paucity of senators in Africa, and partly due to the dense pattern of urbanization, which yielded large numbers of *curiales*. A further need for clergy in North Africa was occasioned by the existence of a parallel, Donatist hierarchy. As a result, the number of episcopal sees in North Africa amounted to at least 500, if not 1,000, at the end of the fourth and beginning of the fifth century. Not all these positions could be filled with candidates from the highest echelons of society.[39] In fact, quite a significant number of North African bishops came from the lower class of *coloni*, tenant farmers, whose education was little more than rudimentary.

## EDUCATION

The church did not make higher education a requirement for candidacy for the episcopate but was content with basic literacy among the higher clergy. *The Apostolic Constitutions* pay more attention to the character traits required

---

36. *CIG* 9792 (without date); Alexandros, *Prosopographie de l'Italie chrétienne*, p. 89 (dating the inscription to the fourth or fifth century).

37. Sozomen, *HE* 8.6.3–8.

38. This is certainly the case for the *chorepiskopoi*, the "country bishops" who served the rural backwaters of Cappadocia. See E. Kirsten, "Chorbischof," *RAC* 2 (1954): cols. 1105–14.

39. W. Eck, "Der Episkopat im spätantiken Afrika," *HZ* 236 (1983): 284. S. Lancel, "Évêchés et cités dans les provinces africaines (III$^e$–V$^e$ siècles)," in *L'Afrique dans l'occident romain*, 279–90 (Rome, 1990).

by a bishop than to his education: "Let him be educated *(pepaideumenos)*, if that is possible. But even if he is illiterate *(agrammatos)*, let him be experienced in scripture, having the proper age."[40] This text was compiled two generations after Constantine, around 380, when the public visibility of the church had become an undisputed fact. Even Justinian considered the piety and good reputation of a future clergyman the most important qualification for office, although he also stipulated basic literacy as indispensable for the proper and undisputed discharge of liturgical and pastoral duties.[41]

Beyond functional literacy, the church did not attribute much importance to the level of education of its bishops. Indeed, it did not foster the foundation of educational institutions, analogous to today's seminaries, with the specific purpose of training future clergy.[42] Spiritual qualifications were ranked above erudition, and the latter did not always pave the way to the episcopate. Malchion, for example, the head of a school of rhetoric in Antioch at the end of the third century, was only a priest. Eusebius mentions his educational credentials only in passing, while emphasizing that Malchion owed his appointment to the priesthood to "the surpassing sincerity of his faith in Christ."[43]

Christian schools did exist, but their students were not necessarily aiming for ecclesiastical office, neither were the *curricula* at these schools exclusively devoted to Christian learning. The catechetical school of Alexandria under its famous director Origen provided instruction in the liberal arts as well as in scriptural interpretation for all interested Christians, including women.[44] Its traces are lost after the end of the fourth century, just at the time when the need for competent clergy must have been greater than ever before. Neither did Antioch have a permanent establishment catering to the preparation of future clergy. Rather, individual teachers taught their pupils scriptural learning. Some of the students at the schools in Alexandria and Antioch later joined the clergy, but only a small number of those reached the episcopate. The most developed institutions of Christian learning that provided systematic instruction—partly, but not exclusively, with a view of training future clergy—were located on the Eastern fringe of the Roman

---

40. *Apostolic Constitutions* 2.1.2 (my translation).

41. Nov. Just. 6.4.

42. For the following, see H. R. Nelz, "Die theologischen Schulen der morgenländischen Kirchen während der sieben ersten christlichen Jahrhunderte in ihrer Bedeutung für die Ausbildung des Klerus," (Diss., Bonn, 1916). Very summary treatment in B. Kötting, "Klerikerbildung in der alten Kirche," in *Sacerdotium: Festschrift A. Francken* (Warendorf, 1948), repr. in his *Ecclesia peregrinans: Das Gottesvolk unterwegs*, vol. 1, Münsterische Beiträge zur Theologie 54/1 (Münster, 1988).

43. Eusebius, *HE* 7.29.2.

44. Ibid., 6.18.3–4 (classical curriculum); 6.4.3 (Herais); 6.5 (Potamiaena); 6.8.2 (women pupils).

Empire, in the Syriac-speaking cities of Edessa and Nisibis. Christian parents of noble status sent their sons there to be educated, thus narrowing the career options of their offspring to Christian clergy or scholarship, as was the case with Eusebius of Emesa, who seems to have led a migratory life devoted to his studies, including that of heretical theologians, and the practice of astronomy. Once he had been ordained bishop, Eusebius proved to be unpopular with congregations in Alexandria and Emesa, but the emperor Constantius liked him well enough to invite him to join a military campaign.[45]

At some Christian schools, scriptural learning was combined with guidance in the practice of Christian virtues and asceticism. The "school" of Diodorus, the future bishop of Tarsus, was thus called an *asketerion*.[46] Among its pupils were John Chrysostom and Theodore of Mopsuestia. The quasi-monastic households of prominent bishops also fall in this category. We need only think of the establishments of Eusebius of Vercelli and Augustine of Hippo, which provided exposure to ecclesiastical administration, combined with experience in communal living according to the monastic ideal. A gradual change may have been set into motion when, after the recommendation of the Council of Chalcedon in 451 that emphasized the importance of celibacy for bishops, monasteries became the preferred recruiting ground for the episcopate. Those bishops who had been monks from an early age may have received some education inside the monastery, with an emphasis on scripture and theology. But it would not be until 787 that candidates for the episcopate were required to pass a test about their knowledge of the scriptures and the canons.[47]

Although it was not a formal requirement, a good education in the classical tradition could contribute significantly to a bishop's successful discharge of his office. The importance of *paideia*, shared education and culture, that ran across the religious, regional, and social divisions in the later Roman Empire, has been highlighted in Peter Brown's book *Power and Persuasion*.[48] The ability of leaders of the Christian communities to "speak the same language" as their pagan peers carried greater weight than the fact that they represented a different set of beliefs. It facilitated communication and dialogue across the religious divide and ensured that bishops would find an open ear when they petitioned provincial governors and emperors on behalf of their communities. The vast majority of the bishops attested in the literary record of late antiquity, either through reports of their activities

45. Socrates, *HE* 2.9.1–10.
46. Ibid., 6.3.6. Sozomen, *HE* 8.2.6.
47. Nicaea II (787), can. 2.
48. P. L. R. Brown, *Power and Persuasion in Late Antiquity: Towards a Christian Empire* (Madison, 1992).

or through the treatises they composed, had enjoyed the privilege of the well-to-do to obtain a higher education. But this impression may stem from the nature of our sources, which are written by wealthy educated men with an acute interest in their peers or social superiors, rather than with the intention to provide an accurate reflection of the disposition of the episcopate as a whole. There are exceptions of uneducated bishops, of course, such as Martin of Tours, whose father had been a soldier, and some degree of variation may be expected depending on the location and importance of the episcopal see. The bishop of a large city like Antioch or Carthage would be faced with greater challenges than a bishop of a small town in a rural backwater would encounter. Such challenges would tax the urban bishop's ability of reasoning, his skill at public speaking, and his gift for persuasion. Still, erudition alone did not automatically set an individual on the path toward the episcopate. Learned Christian authors like Tertullian, Clement of Alexandria, Origen, Jerome, Rufinus of Aquileia, and John Cassian never rose above the level of the presbyterate. Erudite men of the caliber of Evagrius Ponticus could stagnate at the deaconate. And Lactantius, a professor of rhetoric, did not hold any rank in the clergy at all.

Education is an indicator of the prosperity of a family that was able to support its male offspring through years of study. While higher education was taken for granted as a status symbol for the very wealthy, for the curial class it was a gateway to upward social mobility. The multiplication of government posts resulting from the administrative reforms of Diocletian and Constantine provided greater opportunities for employment in the imperial service than ever before and consequently motivated many to pursue their education at the secondary level and above. Young *curiales* crowded the classrooms of rhetoricians and lawyers. The fourth-century rhetor Libanius at Antioch had no sons of senators among his pupils but taught a large number of students of the curial class. Forty-two of them succeeded in gaining higher positions; six of those even became senators in Constantinople, and three became bishops.[49]

Such education, however, was a costly enterprise, and families of the curial class—which, as we shall see, was the largest recruiting ground for the episcopal office—often had to strain their resources to fulfill their aspirations. Basil, the later bishop of Caesarea, studied at Constantinople and Athens but then took it upon himself to provide instruction for his younger brother Gregory at home. It is not unreasonable to think that the family finances only allowed for the oldest son to enjoy the privilege of studying abroad. John Chrysostom remembered fondly how his mother spared no effort to finance his education after the death of his father, who had been a

---

49. P. Petit, *Les étudiants de Libanius* (Paris, 1956), 118, 166–67.

civil servant in the office of the military governor of Syria.[50] Augustine's father, Patricius, was equally anxious to afford his son the education that would enable him to move up in the world and eventually to hold the chair of rhetoric in the imperial capital of Milan. But there was a one-year hiatus, early in Augustine's life, while his father was recouping his finances, during which he had to interrupt his studies and return to the family home.[51] Late in his life, Augustine would insist that he came from a poor family, calling himself "hominem pauperum, de pauperibus natum."[52]

Like the study of rhetoric, training in law was also highly coveted by young men of curial status as a ticket to upward social mobility. The court of a provincial governor in the early fifth century could have as many as 150 such positions, which carried the rank of *spectabilis*.[53] Not a few of them ended up as bishops. The *scholastici tēs agoras* were so much sought after for the administration of churches that they were often appointed directly to the episcopate.[54] This was the case with Nectarius, the successor of Gregory of Nazianzus in Constantinople, who was not even baptized at the time of his appointment. Several bishops had studied jurisprudence: Gregory the Wonder-worker, who later became bishop of Neocaesarea, had studied rhetoric, law, and Latin in Berytus.[55] The schooling of Basil of Caesarea and Gregory of Nazianzus prepared them for careers either as professors of rhetoric or as lawyers.[56] Alypius, Augustine's friend and future bishop of Thagaste, had studied law.[57] Triphyllius, the bishop of Ledri, had previously practiced law in Berytus.[58] Petilianus, the Donatist bishop of Cirta,[59] and Marculus, the Donatist bishop and martyr, were also former lawyers.[60]

The level of secular learning of a bishop was thus determined by his social status prior to his accession to the episcopate. It did not change after his ordination; neither did his theological erudition, unless he himself took the initiative to immerse himself in the study of scripture and the ecclesiastical tradition. Such study was strongly recommended in canon law

50. John Chrysostom, *On the Priesthood* 1.2.30–97.
51. P. Brown, *Augustine of Hippo: A Biography* (London, 1967; rev., Berkeley, 2000) 38.
52. Augustine, *Sermo* 356.13, *PL* 39, col. 1580.
53. Nov. Theod. 10.1.1 (439).
54. Sardica (347), can. 10. This is probably the same office as that of the *scholastikos phorou*, a professional judge. On this office, see O. Seeck, "Scholastikos," *RE* 2/3 (1921): cols. 624–25.
55. Gregory the Wonderworker, *Address of Thanksgiving to Origen* 5 (56–63). His brother Athenodorus had shared in his education in rhetoric and later also became a bishop in the Pontus region: 5 (65).
56. Socrates, *HE* 6.26.7.
57. Alypius, Mandouze, pp. 53–65.
58. Sozomen, *HE* 1.11.8.
59. Petilianus, *PLRE* 2: 861; Petilianus, Mandouze, pp. 855–68.
60. Marculus, Mandouze, pp. 696–97.

but was never made a formal requirement, nor was punishment threatened for its neglect.

### BISHOPS OF CURIAL BACKGROUND

Most bishops in late antiquity came from the municipal elite in the cities of the Roman Empire: the *curiales*.[61] These were landowning families, who passed their status on to their heirs along with their property. Their curial status was considered an honor, but this honor came at a price. The *curialis* was expected to be eligible and willing to run for municipal office, which involved great personal expense: the provision of games and entertainments, the heating of the baths, going on embassies. Personal status and honor were also displayed and reinforced through the tradition of private *euergeteia* in the form of building activity and other benefactions to the city. Moreover, in addition to the taxes each *curialis* had to pay on his own property, the *curia* collectively was held responsible for the collection of the tax money of the city and its territory in the amount that had been assessed by agents of the fisc.[62]

The Christianization of the *curiales* had proceeded at a particularly rapid pace in the course of the third and fourth centuries. During the persecutions of the second and third centuries, individual Christians were sometimes identified as being of curial or otherwise privileged status in the martyrs' *Acta*. This is particularly evident in North Africa and in the papyrus documentation from Egypt.[63] In Asia Minor entire cities were known to be Christian already in the pre-Constantinian period, one example being the (unnamed) city whose inhabitants, including the magistrates, were rounded up and burned in the Great Persecution.[64] After the end of the persecutions, cities with a Christian *curia* seized the opportunity to apply for favors to the emperor Constantine, whom they knew to be a coreligionist. This argument was successful in securing the rank of a *civitas* for the town of Orcistus in Phrygia Salutaris in 324–326,[65] and in the elevation of the town of Maiouma

---

61. D. Hunt, "The Church as a Public Institution," *The Cambridge Ancient History*, vol. 13, *The Late Empire, A.D. 337–425*, ed. A. Cameron and P. Garnsey (Cambridge, 1998), 264.

62. On the *curiales* in late antiquity, see Jones, *The Later Roman Empire*, 737–63; and the more contentious study by W. Langhammer, *Die rechtliche und soziale Stellung der Magistratus Municipales und der Decuriones in der Übergangsphase der Städte von sich selbst verwaltenden Gemeinden zu Vollzugsorganen des spätantiken Zwangsstaates (2.–4. Jahrhundert der römischen Kaiserzeit)* (Wiesbaden, 1973). For the Roman Empire, see F. F. Abbott and A. C. Johnson, *Municipal Administration in the Roman Empire* (Princeton, 1926).

63. Wischmeyer, *Von Golgatha zum Ponte Molle*, 63–77.

64. Eusebius, *HE* 8.11.1, and Lactantius, *Divine Institutes* 5.11.10.

65. A. Chastagnol, "L'inscription constantinienne d'Orcistus," *MEFRA* 93 (1981): 381–416. He suggests that Orcistus should be identified with the Phrygian city whose inhabitants were burned in the Great Persecution.

in Palestine to the status of a city, with the name of Constantia.[66] Conversely, the emperor Julian the Apostate was reported to have refused to receive delegations from Christian cities. He even declined any form of help to the city of Nisibis against Persian attacks unless they returned to paganism.[67] If entire cities in the Eastern part of the empire were identifiable as Christian in the fourth century, this must mean that the majority of the members of their city council—the representative body of self-administration—were adherents of the new religion. This is confirmed by the writings of the pagan author Libanius, which—according to Paul Petit—indicate that 80 percent of the *curiales* in Antioch were Christians.[68]

It has been estimated that there were 250,000 *curiales* in the late fourth century.[69] Merely in numerical terms, they thus constituted a large pool of potentially suitable candidates for the episcopate. The earliest bishop of curial status may well have been the father of Marcion, leader of the Marcionite heresy, who was born in Sinope on the Black Sea around 85.[70] Another pre-Constantinian bishop of curial rank is Marcus Julius Eugenius, the bishop of Laodiceia. According to a third-century inscription from Asia Minor, he came from a curial family and had previously served on the staff of the governor of Pisidia.[71]

The imperial legislation confirms that the *curiales* were the largest recruiting ground for the clergy at all levels, from deacon to bishop. Almost thirty laws in the Theodosian Code attempt to regulate the lateral or upward mobility of the *curiales,* who were eager to escape the obligations of their status—taxes and mandatory services *(munera)*—by claiming the exemptions that were granted as a privilege to those serving in the military and in the imperial administration or to those who held senatorial rank. Constantine had extended these privileges to the clergy, thus making an occupation in the service of the church attractive to *curiales* on merely financial grounds.[72] The great concern of subsequent imperial legislators was to en-

---

66. Sozomen, *HE* 5.3.6–7. Cf. Eusebius, *VC* 4.37.

67. Sozomen, *HE* 5.3.4–5.

68. P. Petit, *Libanius et la vie municipale à Antioche au IV$^e$ siècle après J.-C.* (Paris, 1955), 202.

69. A. H. M. Jones, "The Caste System of the Later Roman Empire," *Eirene* 8 (1970): 79–96.

70. We know that his father was a bishop (Epiphanius, *Panarion [Adversus haereses]* 42.1.4), and that he himself was a *ponticus nauclerus* (Tertullian, *De praescriptione haereticorum* 30.1). According to W. Wischmeyer, *Von Golgatha zum Ponte Molle,* 33, this is a *de facto* hereditary liturgy for men of curial status, which therefore Marcion's father the bishop must also have held.

71. P. Batiffol, "L'épitaphe d'Eugène, évêque de Laodicée," *Bulletin d'Ancienne Littérature et d'Archéologie Chrétiennes* 1 (1911): 25–34.

72. W. Schubert, "Die rechtliche Sonderstellung der Dekurionen (Kurialen) in der Kaisergesetzgebung des 4. Jhs.–6. Jhs.," *ZRG, Röm. Abt.* 86 (1969): 287–333; K. L. Noethlichs, "Zur Einflussnahme des Staates auf die Entwicklung eines christlichen Klerikerstandes: Schicht- und berufsspezifische Bestimmungen für den Klerus im 4. und 5. Jahrhundert in den spätantiken Rechtsquellen," *JAC* 15 (1972): 136–53.

sure that the property of these *curiales* remained at the disposal of their communities and accessible to the fisc, even if the *curiales* themselves moved on to positions that carried exemptions. By 439, Valentinian III demanded that "public losses must not be created by a general diminution of decurions, while the number of the clergy is being superabundantly augmented."[73] In 531, Justinian prohibited the ordination of men to the priesthood or the episcopate who had served actively on the *curia*. He ostensibly did so not for practical, but for moral reasons, noting that it would be wrong if those who had sullied themselves with the financial oppression of others were then called upon, as priests, to advocate philanthropy and poverty.[74]

While the fourth century did not spell the end for bishops of humble background, it did bring a significant increase in the number of bishops of curial status. Frank Gilliard concluded that of the sixty-eight bishops in the fourth century whose family background is identifiable, the vast majority were from the urban middle class.[75] From this time onward, curial bishops feature prominently in the literary sources. We are particularly well informed about their existence in late fourth-century Cappadocia, where not only the predecessor and the successor of Basil of Caesarea were, like him, of curial status, but also several of his relations who became bishops.[76] It is doubtful, to my mind, whether the indirect effect of Constantine's privileges for the clergy is the only reason why the evidence for bishops of curial rank becomes more plentiful in the fourth century. The relative density of information about bishops of curial status in the post-Constantinian period may in large part be a result of the explosion of sources, written by Christian authors who themselves came from a privileged background, that deal with matters of the church. It may also be the result of a general demographic trend in church membership, which was expanding in numbers and increasingly attracting people of higher social status.[77]

It is tempting to establish a simple syllogism: (1) *Curiales* were the most upwardly mobile class in the fourth century and later. (2) Most bishops at that time came from a curial background. Therefore (3), the episcopate was desired by ambitious *curiales* as a step up on the social ladder. This reasoning, however, is flawed for two reasons. First, it fails to take into account that, as a rule, anyone who became a bishop had previously spent a considerable

---

73. NVal 3.1 (439).
74. CJ 1.3.52. Cf. the similar prohibition in Nov. Just. 123.15 (546), which condemns the appointment of curial officeholders as *hybris*.
75. F. D. Gilliard, "The Social Origins of Bishops in the Fourth Century" (PhD diss., University of California, Berkeley, 1966).
76. T. A. Kopecek, "Curial Displacements and Flight in Later Fourth-Century Cappadocia," *Historia* 23 (1974): passim.
77. See the interesting observations by K. Hopkins, "Christian Number and Its Implications," *JECS* 6 (1998): 185–226; and earlier, Bigelmair, 213–20.

time as a priest and perhaps as a deacon. We should therefore assume that these more numerous positions in the clergy also enjoyed an influx of *curiales*. This raises the second issue, that of motivation. What was the intention of *curiales* who joined the clergy? Was it really to improve their social status by attaining the singular position of bishop?

In fact, two very different paths led *curiales* to the episcopate. The first is represented by those men who, after a long period in higher education, embarked on a career in the civil service and eventually, through various turns of fate, became bishops, a position that they held very late in life and often only briefly. Evagrius, a pupil of Libanius and a member of a prominent curial family in Antioch, is a good example of this progression. He succeeded in gaining a provincial governorship—thus escaping his curial obligations—and a subsequent promotion to a higher position. His efforts to shield the family fortune from the fisc came to an end when he was forced to pay a heavy fine for alleged maladministration. His rehabilitation in the subsequent year came too late. He had already joined the hierarchy of the church at Antioch, entering at the level of the priesthood. He eventually held the episcopate of this city, in succession of Paulinus, but only for a very brief period before his death.[78] For Evagrius and others like him, office in the clergy, culminating in the episcopate, came at the end of a life spent in public service. It was not a career choice, but an additional honor and distinction.

The second type of curial bishops is exemplified by five men from the late fourth century whose biographies follow the same pattern: Basil of Caesarea, Gregory of Nazianzus, John Chrysostom, Augustine, and his friend Alypius.[79] They commanded an impressive education yet opted to forgo the prospects of the career for which they had been trained and instead chose to withdraw from the world and to dedicate themselves to a period of Christian formation through asceticism and study. Eventually, they were ordained to the priesthood, thus making them viable future candidates for the episcopate once a see fell vacant. The timing of their ordination at this particular stage in their lives shows that it was conferred not only in the hope of securing their talent, but in large part as a confirmation of the credentials they had acquired through their monastic experience. Clearly, these men did not simply exchange a secular career for the distinction of being a bishop near the end of their lives, as Evagrius had done; rather, they were genuinely and from early adulthood dedicated to the service of the church. This sequence of education, withdrawal, and ministry followed the example established by Moses, the prototype of the perfect bishop.

78. Evagrius 6, *PLRE* 1: 285–86.
79. See above, pp. 133–36.

The episcopal office had not been the initial career goal of these five men during their student days. They came to it after dedicating their lives in earnest to the practice of Christianity and acquiring their ascetic credentials. Moreover, their ordination to the episcopate was preceded by many years in the rank and file of the clergy, as deacons or priests. Still, complaints by contemporaries about the appointment of unworthy, unprepared, and ambitious men are sufficiently frequent to let us suspect that the episcopate was indeed considered a desirable career option by some,[80] even though Christian authors and canon law insist that episcopal ordination should not be sought.

The exact status of prominent bishops, whether curial or senatorial, is not always easy to establish. It lies in the selective focus of our literary sources that they tend to concentrate on bishops whose activities—whether in local administration, religious disputes, or imperial politics—were worthy of note. The vast majority of these bishops had acquired their public eloquence and literary skill through a higher education that had been attained at considerable expense; thus we can safely assume that they hailed from well-to-do families. Since the sources are usually no more specific than to refer to someone's "good education" or "distinguished family," it is not always easy to establish with certainty if they belonged to the senatorial class or to the curial class of the landholding provincial aristocracy.[81]

This lack of specificity in the sources is further compounded by a gradual expansion of the meaning of *nobilitas*. Originally an indicator of senatorial class, it was by the sixth century also used to refer to men of curial status.[82] Moreover, Christian authors of late antiquity related the concept of *nobilitas* to virtue, specifically Christian virtue, and its social recognition, thus adding ethical overtones to an initially purely social term. The injection of Christian connotations into a traditional concept that was central to the identity of the Roman aristocracy allowed the higher echelons of society to embrace Christianity on terms that were familiar to them. In Christian literature, the traditional praise of an individual as "noble by birth, nobler still in mind *(nobilis natu, nobilior mente)*" was thus eventually

---

80. Ammianus Marcellinus (*Histories* 27.3.13) reports that in the bitter contest in 366 between Ursinus and Damasus for the episcopal see of Rome, 137 people lost their lives in a single day.
81. The family of Basil of Caesarea and his brother Gregory of Nyssa, for example, had long been thought to be of senatorial status, until T. A. Kopecek's detailed analysis of the larger family network demonstrated that they were of curial background: T. A. Kopecek, "The Senatorial Class of the Cappadocian Fathers," *Church History* 42 (1973): 453–66. The argument for Basil's nonsenatorial origin had already been made by S. Giet, "Basile, était-il sénateur?" *RHE* 60 (1965): 429–44.
82. F. D. Gilliard, "Senatorial Bishops in the Fourth Century," *Harv. Theol. Rev.* 77 (1984): 153–75.

rephrased as "noble by birth, nobler still through his religion *(natalibus nobilis, religione nobilior)*."[83]

## BISHOPS OF SENATORIAL BACKGROUND

The social stratification of the episcopate from the third to the sixth century expanded upward as the number of episcopal sees increased and Christianity gained greater prominence in society. While many bishops continued to hail from modest backgrounds, an additional influx of bishops of curial status has been observed beginning in the fourth century. The next addition were men of senatorial rank who joined the clergy. This trend began at the very end of the fourth century and came to full fruition in the fifth. The absolute number of senatorial bishops, however, remained significantly lower than that of curial bishops. This is not surprising, considering the fact that in the late fourth century there were only 2,000 senators throughout the empire, compared to 250,000 *curiales,* and the pool of potential candidates was therefore much smaller.[84]

The recruitment of bishops from the senatorial aristocracy followed the same chronological pattern as that of the Christianization of this group in general.[85] The senatorial families, especially the Italian families that prided themselves on their great ancestry, were the most traditionally minded and the most resistant to the new religion of Christianity. It was only in the late fourth century that members of senatorial families began to convert, when it had become clear that the process of Christianization would not be halted or reversed. This process was accelerated by imperial support for the new religion. There were real advantages to be reaped by those who adhered to the same religion as the imperial household. Under the Constantinian and

---

83. R. W. Mathisen, *Roman Aristocrats in Barbarian Gaul: Strategies for Survival in an Age of Transition* (Austin, 1993), 90–91, with n. 9. Cf. also G. Scheibelreiter, *Der Bischof in merovingischer Zeit* (Vienna, 1983), 21; F. D. Gilliard, "The Senators of Sixth-Century Gaul," *Speculum* 54 (1979): 685–97; B. Näf, *Senatorisches Standesbewußtsein in spätrömischer Zeit,* Paradosis 40 (Freiburg, 1995); M. R. Salzman, "Competing Claims to 'Nobilitas' in the Western Empire in the Fourth and Fifth Centuries," *JECS* 9/3 (2001): 359–85.

84. Jones, "Caste System."

85. P. L. R. Brown, "Aspects of the Christianization of the Roman Aristocracy," *JRS* 51 (1961): 1–11. Eck, "Der Einfluß der konstantinischen Wende," 572–75, gives further details, including on individuals whose senatorial rank is uncertain. See M. R. Salzman, "How the West was Won: The Christianization of the Roman Aristocracy in the West in the Years after Constantine," in *Studies in Latin Literature and Roman History,* vol. 6, ed. C. Deroux, Collection Latomus 217 (Brussels, 1992), 451–79; ead., "The Christianization of the Roman Aristocracy," *Historia* 42 (1993): 326–78, ead., *The Making of a Christian Aristocracy: Social and Religious Change in the Western Roman Empire* (Cambridge, Mass., 2002); C. R. Galvao-Sobrinho, "Funerary Epigraphy and the Spread of Christianity in the West," *Athenaeum* n.s. 83 (1995): 431–66.

Theodosian dynasties, as Raban von Haehling has shown, the highest administrative posts were given with preference to Christians, and this may well have been an incentive for conversion.[86] What had been practiced at imperial discretion became law in 415, when Theodosius II restricted posts in the imperial service to Christians only.[87]

The geographical distribution of bishops of the senatorial aristocracy is, of course, dependent on the presence of eligible senators in the different regions of the empire. As is to be expected, the highest concentration of senatorial bishops was in Italy and around Constantinople—one the heartland of the *imperium Romanum*, the other the new capital in the East—as well as in Gaul, where this trend was encouraged by particular historical circumstances that will be discussed below. Egypt had no bishops of senatorial background, although most Egyptian bishops came from prominent wealthy families.[88] North Africa had only two, possibly three: Cyprian of Carthage, who was martyred in 258, definitely came from a prosperous family, but that fact alone does not necessarily indicate senatorial rank.[89] Almost two centuries later, we encounter the first firmly attested senatorial bishop in Petilianus, the Donatist bishop of Constantina/Cirta (d. before 419/422). He was a *vir clarissimus* and well respected for his rhetorical skills. Originally a catechumen in the Catholic Church, he was baptized and ordained by force by the Donatists. A century later, Fulgentius of Ruspe (d. 533), the offspring of a senatorial family who had held the office of *ducenarius* (tax collector), spent a long period in the pursuit of the monastic life before he became bishop at the age of forty.[90]

As in the foregoing analysis of the motivation of bishops of curial status, it is important to take into account the career paths of senators who became bishops. Some made a direct transfer from a secular career to the episcopate, while others first devoted themselves to an intensified Christian

---

86. R. von Haehling, *Die Religionszugehörigkeit der hohen Amtsträger des römischen Reiches seit Constantins I Alleinherrschaft bis zum Ende der theodosianischen Dynastie (324–450 bzw. 455 n. Chr.)* (Bonn, 1978). The trend may have set in already under Constantius; see T. D. Barnes, "Statistics and the Conversion of the Roman Aristocracy," *JRS* 85 (1995): 135–47.
87. CTh 16.10.21 (415).
88. For a brief overview of the social stratification of the clergy in Egypt, see E. Wipszycka, "Le istituzioni ecclesiastiche in Egitto dalla fine del III all'inizio dell' VIII secolo," in *L'Egitto cristiano: Aspetti e problemi in età tardo-antica*, ed. A. Camplani, Studia Ephemeridis Augustinianum 56 (Rome, 1997), 248–60. For more detailed treatment, see ead., *Les ressources et les activités économiques des églises en Égypte du IVe au VIIIe siècle* (Brussels, 1972), 154–73.
89. H. Chadwick, "The Church of the Third Century in the West," in *The Roman West in the Third Century: Contributions from Archaeology and History*, BAR Intern. Series 109 (i), ed. A. King and M. Henig (Oxford, 1981), 7, asserts Cyprian's senatorial status. J. B. Rives, *Religion and Authority in Roman Carthage from Augustus to Constantine* (Oxford, 1995), 287, is more cautious.
90. Petilianus, Mandouze, pp. 855–68; Fulgentius 1, Mandouze, pp. 507–13.

lifestyle before they were recruited into the clergy. Ambrose exemplifies the former, Paulinus of Nola the latter.

Ambrose's appointment to the episcopal see of Milan in 374 set the precedent for senatorial bishops in Italy.[91] His father had been praetorian prefect of the Gauls in 339/340, and he himself had until then held the position of *consularis* of Aemilia and Liguria.[92] Ambrose represents the pattern of the senator who exchanged a high position in the imperial service for the highest office of the church.

Paulinus of Nola followed a different path. The son of a very distinguished family, he had held the governorship of Campania. But then he surprised his contemporaries with his decision to shun his brilliant career prospects, dispose of his substantial wealth, and pursue a life of asceticism. In 394, he was ordained to the priesthood, but it would not be until over a decade later that he was appointed bishop of Nola, a position he held for more than twenty years (409/410 to 431).[93] Jerome applauded Paulinus with a wordplay on the concept of *nobilitas:* "nobilem te ecclesia habeat, ut prius senatus habuit."[94]

The sequence of distinguished career, ascetic conversion, and gradual promotion through the ranks of the clergy, exemplified by Paulinus of Nola, is still in evidence in Italy in the sixth century. By this period, Christianity had firmly taken root, and many aristocratic families could proudly look back on their ancestors' impressive record in the service of the church. Gregory the Great is a case in point. He came from a prominent senatorial family, but his ancestry also boasted one, if not two bishops of Rome: his great-great-grandfather Felix, and perhaps Pope Agapetus as well. Gregory had advanced to the office of city prefect of Rome, but then, in his mid-thirties, withdrew from the public life to dedicate himself to the pursuit of monasticism. A few years later, he was ordained deacon and was soon sent as a papal legate to Constantinople. After his recall to Rome, he returned to his monastic life, until in 590, he was appointed bishop of Rome, a position held until his death in 604.[95]

Four lesser-known Italian bishops probably also came from senatorial families. Marcellus, whose brother Quintilius Laetus was a *clarissimus et illustris* and city prefect of Rome in 398/399, must have shared his brother's

---

91. For detailed information on the social background of bishops in Italy and the methodological problems involved, see C. Sotinel, "Le recrutement des évêques en Italie aux IVᵉ et Vᵉ siècles: Essai d'enquête prosopographique," in *Vescovi e pastori in epoca teodosiana*, 1 (Rome, 1997).

92. N. B. McLynn, *Ambrose of Milan: Church and Court in a Christian Capital* (Berkeley and Los Angeles, 1994), 32ff.

93. D. Trout, *Paulinus of Nola: Life, Letters, and Poems* (Berkeley and Los Angeles, 1999), passim.

94. Jerome, *Ep.* 58.11 to Paulinus.

95. Gregorius 5, *PLRE* 3A: 549–51.

senatorial rank. He is referred to in a letter by Ambrose as "sacerdos." This was the generic term for higher clergy, without distinguishing between bishops and priests, but in consideration of Marcellus's high social status it is likely that he was indeed a bishop.[96] Petronius, who became bishop of Bologna in 432, also came from a prominent senatorial family (his father had been praetorian prefect of Gaul) but had received a Christian formation since his youth.[97] Exsuperantius of Lucania and Julian of Eclanum should also be added to the list.[98] Despite the fact that Italy had a higher proportion of senatorial families than other regions of the empire and boasted the first bishop of senatorial rank, this did not translate into a large-scale social trend, as it did in Gaul.[99] According to the calculations of Claire Sotinel, the bishops of senatorial rank in Italy made up less than 3 percent of the total number of bishops between 350 and 450 whose background is known.[100]

In the East, senatorial bishops appeared at around the same time as in Italy. The senate in Constantinople was a relatively new creation, only as old as the new capital on the Bosporus itself, which had been inaugurated in 330. The number of senatorial bishops is correspondingly low; I have been able to identify only eight senators-turned-bishops until the sixth century. None of them came to the episcopate out of religious motivation and after an ascetic interlude, as Paulinus of Nola had done. For the Eastern bishops of senatorial rank, the episcopate was a kind of honorary retirement, which they took up after exhausting all other career opportunities in the imperial service or in the provincial administration. Like Ambrose, they all received their appointment *per saltum*, without prior experience in the clergy.

The eight bishops of senatorial rank in the East had previously held administrative posts in the administration of the Eastern capital or gained distinction in the higher levels of provincial administration. Leading the list is Nectarius, bishop of Constantinople in 381, who had been *praetor urbanus* of the capital and at the time of his ordination was only a catechumen.[101] His brother Arsacius eventually held the same office from 404 to 405—an indication of the potential importance of family associations also at the level of

96. See Marcellus 8, *PLRE* 1: 552, and Quintilius Laetus 2, *PLRE* I1: 492–93.
97. Petronius 3, *PLRE* 2: 863; for his father, see Petronius 1, *PLRE* 2: 862–63. He, or perhaps his father, is the author of a book on episcopal ordination mentioned in Gennadius's *Lives of Illustrious Men* 42.
98. Sotinel, "Le recrutement des évêques," 196. She mentions seven bishops of senatorial rank, but I am unable to identify more than six.
99. C. Pietri, "Aristocratie et société provinciale dans l'Italie chrétienne au temps d'Odoacre et de Théodoric," *MEFRA* 93 (1981): 432–36.
100. Sotinel, "Le recrutement des évêques," 196.
101. Nectarius 2, *PLRE* 1: 621.

senatorial bishops.[102] Chrysanthus was ordained bishop of the Novatians in Constantinople in 412, ostensibly against his will, although his father had held this office before him. He had retired to the capital after a long career as palatine official, consular governor in Italy, and vicar of Britain, entertaining hopes for an appointment as city prefect.[103] Thalassius became metropolitan of Caesarea in 439. He had been praetorian refect of Illyricum and was just about to be promoted to the prefecture of Oriens when his services were claimed for the church.[104] Cyrus was made bishop of Cotyaeum in Phrygia after a distinguished career as praetorian prefect of the Orient and city prefect of Constantinople. His ordination was a punitive, yet not entirely dishonorable measure after he had fallen into disfavor in 443. As soon as political circumstances permitted, he resigned from the clergy to resume his private life in Constantinople.[105] Irenaeus became bishop of Tyre in Palestine in 445. He had been *comes Orientis* from 431 to 435.[106] After a hiatus of nearly a century, we encounter two further senatorial bishops: Ephraem, who was patriarch of Antioch for nearly two decades (527–545), was a former *comes Orientis* and held an honorary consulate.[107] Isaiah, the bishop of Rhodes, had been *praefectus vigilium*. He was one of the victims of Justinian's crackdown on homosexuals in 529.[108] For these eight senators of the East, appointment to the episcopate was not a religiously motivated choice, nor was it a career option. Instead, it signaled their retirement from a life in politics, even if this retirement was—as in the case of Cyrus—involuntary.

In contrast to Italy and the East, where senatorial bishops were the exception, they developed into something of a pattern in the region of southern Gaul.[109] The extended sense in which late Latin authors used such words as

---

102. Arsacius 4, *PLRE* 1: 110.
103. Chrysanthus, *PLRE* 1: 203.
104. Thalassius 1, *PLRE* 2: 1060; Socrates, *HE* 7.48.4–5.
105. Cyrus 7, *PLRE* 2: 336–39.
106. Irenaeus 2, *PLRE* 2: 624–25. On the rank of *comes* and its senatorial privileges, see O. Seeck, "Comites," *RE* 4/1 (1900): cols. 635–36 and 659–61.
107. Ephrem (Ephraemius), *PLRE* 2: 394–96.
108. Isaiah, *PLRE* 2: 627. According to Jones, *The Later Roman Empire*, 106, with n. 64, the office of *praefectus vigilium* was one of the originally equestrian positions that were increasingly held by senators.
109. Mathisen, *Roman Aristocrats*, esp. 89–104. M. Heinzelmann, *Bischofsherrschaft in Gallien: Zur Kontinuität römischer Führungsschichten vom 4. bis zum 7. Jahrhundert: Soziale, prosopographische und bildungsgeschichtliche Aspekte* (Munich, 1976), 200–211. For a more detailed study, see H. Wieruszowski, "Die Zusammensetzung des gallischen und fränkischen Episkopats bis zum Vertrag von Verdun (843) mit besonderer Berücksichtigung der Nationalität und des Standes," *Bonner Jahrbücher* 127 (1922): esp. 44ff.; A. Rousselle, "Aspects sociaux du recrutement ecclésiastique au IVe siècle," in *Mélanges de l'École Française de Rome*, Antiquité 89 (Rome, 1977), 333–70; N. Gauthier, "Le réseau de pouvoirs de l'évêque dans la Gaule du haut moyen-âge," in *Towns and Their Territories between Late Antiquity and the Early Middle Ages*, ed. G. P. Broglio, N. Gauthier, and N. Christie, 195–199 (Leiden, 2000).

*nobilis* and *illustris* as general markers of social distinction, but not necessarily designating specifically senatorial rank, does not make it an easy task
to identify an individual as belonging to the senatorial class. The following
remarks therefore aim to bring into focus the most important patterns, but
make no claim to completeness. Since the breakdown of the Roman machinery of government at end of the fourth century as a result of immigra-
tion and intermittent warfare, men of senatorial background were appointed to the episcopate in ever-increasing numbers. By the fifth century,
this trend was well established. Deprived of access to the emperor as a
source of dispensation of honors and distinctions, these men found in the
episcopal office an opportunity to maintain their prominent role in local
society and to continue in activities that were associated with and expected
by their status, most particularly public benefactions through building
patronage and the provision of public entertainments, and the leisure to
engage in literary pursuits. This overlap of aristocratic markers of social eminence with Christian good works contributes to the development of the holy
bishop of noble background as a type in Latin hagiography.

Especially in the late fourth and fifth centuries, many bishops of senatorial background in Gaul attained their appointment, just like their colleagues in the *pars Orientis,* after many years in office in the civil administration. Often, the episcopate was conferred on them directly, without prior
experience in ecclesiastical office—confirmation of the ease with which social status could be translated into ecclesiastical rank. An early example of
a locally prominent senator-turned-bishop is Claudius Lupicinus, bishop of
Vienne. He had been a *vir consularis* in the 380s, and his civic benefactions
were commemorated in several honorific inscriptions.[110] This pattern continued in the fifth century. Sidonius Apollinaris's father and grandfather
had held the praetorian prefecture of the Gauls, and his wife was the daughter of the future emperor Avitus. Sidonius himself was city prefect of Rome
in 468. Soon thereafter, back in Gaul, he was ordained bishop of Clermont
in 470 and exercised his duties with great dedication and diligence until his
death in 487.[111] Germanus became bishop of Auxerre under circumstances
not too dissimilar from those that brought Ambrose to the episcopate.
While he was holding a high office, probably the governorship of the
province Lugdunensis Quarta, he was ordained to the priesthood and designated as the next successor to the episcopal see of that city, which he
would hold for thirty years, from 418 to 448.[112] The direct conferral of the
episcopal dignity on former officeholders honored and asserted their existing social status while shifting the arena in which they wielded their power.

---

110. Heinzelmann, *Bischofsherrschaft in Gallien,* 224–26.
111. J. Harries, *Sidonius Apollinaris and the Fall of Rome, AD 407–485* (Oxford, 1994), passim.
112. Germanus 1, *PLRE* 2: 504–5.

This could be used to good effect in order to neutralize enemies. The case of Cyrus, bishop of Cotyaeum, has already been mentioned. In the same manner, the short-lived Western emperor Avitus was deposed in 456 and made bishop of Piacenza,[113] and Glycerius's deposition after only one year as Western emperor was followed by his appointment to the episcopal see of Salona in 474. [114]

At the same time, however, the tradition of men who passed through the intermediary stage of monasticism before they became bishops continued on into the early fifth century, in Gaul as much as elsewhere. Eucherius of Lyon, the author of the monastic treatise *In Praise of the Desert*, for example, hailed from a senatorial family. Together with his wife and two daughters, he took up a monastic retreat on the island of Lérins, while entrusting the education of his two sons to the bishops Honoratus and Hilarius. He later became bishop of Lyon, probably in 434.[115]

Beginning with the last decades of the fifth century, a third pattern of episcopal recruitment from the senatorial aristocracy emerges. Until now, we have encountered the direct transition from secular to ecclesiastical career exemplified by Ambrose of Milan and the episcopal appointment preceded by monastic practice, as in the case of Paulinus of Nola and many of the fourth-century *curiales*. Now for the first time we encounter men of distinguished background whose careers evolved entirely within the context of the church.[116] Christianity had now permeated all aspects of Gallic society, and the region had politically become detached from Italy. Consequently, family traditions of gaining distinction through civic office or public benefactions found a new venue in the church as an institution. Men of prominent background who were appointed as bishops could thus enjoy a newly defined position of eminence, while at the same time continuing to bestow their patronage on their *civitas*. Gregory of Tours is a prime example of this pattern. He came from a senatorial family of great wealth. On his father's side, the family could trace its descent from the senator Vettius Epagathus, one of the martyrs of Lyon in 177. His father's uncle had been a priest, and his father's brother was a bishop. His mother's side of the family had in the last two generations produced one senator and at least five bishops. After obtaining the requisite secular education, Gregory opted for an ecclesiastical career, entering the ranks of the clergy as a deacon. After ten years, in 573, he became bishop of Tours and dedicated the last two decades of his life until his death in 594 to ecclesiastical administration and the composi-

---

113. Eparchius Avitus 5, *PLRE* 2: 196–98.
114. Glycerius 2, Pietri and Pietri, 1: 933–34; Glycerius, *PLRE* 2: 514.
115. Eucherius 3, *PLRE* 2: 405.
116. Mathisen, *Roman Aristocrats*, 91–93.

tion of literary works.[117] In his *Life of the Fathers*, Gregory mentions other men like himself, such as the priest Evodius, who was of senatorial status and harbored hopes for a bishopric.[118] Most telling perhaps is the curse of Bishop Quintinianus against the senator Hortensius that nobody of his family should ever become a bishop—a powerful social death sentence.[119]

This study of the social origin of the episcopate, patchy and incomplete though it may be, shows that the episcopal office increasingly mirrored the existing shape of society. Members of the established social elite were seeking a place in the elite of the ecclesiastical ministry. The trend set in with the noticeable influx of *curiales* in the fourth century and continued with the new addition of senatorial bishops, a development that began in the 380s and became very pronounced in the fifth century. The social stratification of the episcopate thus corresponded to the social stratification of church membership, and eventually—once Christianity had permeated the later Roman Empire—to the stratification of society as a whole. The church now complemented—and, in the case of Gaul, replaced—the empire as an outlet for the ambitions of the established social elite.

FAMILY TRADITIONS OF ECCLESIASTICAL OFFICEHOLDING

If the episcopate was regarded by some as an honor and distinction befitting their social status, then one would assume prominent men would make every effort to pass this on to their offspring or to share it with relatives. But here again, it is imperative to pay attention to motivation and individual biographies. If we look at individual cases, it soon becomes evident that a convenient distinction between either social ambition or religious dedication cannot be maintained. What we encounter instead is a genuine Christian motivation, combined with social ambition, in the service of the church.

Perhaps the earliest example of a family tradition of ecclesiastical service is Polycrates, who was bishop of Ephesus in the second century, at a time when the episcopal office was desirable only to the most dedicated of Christians. He proudly mentioned that he was the eighth member of his extended family to become bishop.[120] Extended familial networks of episcopal officeholding have been traced for fourth-century Cappadocia.[121] The fam-

---

117. Gregorius Florentius Gregorius 3, *PLRE* 3A, 548–49.
118. Gregory of Tours, *VP* 6.4.
119. Gregory of Tours, *VP* 4.3.
120. Eusebius, *HE* 5.24.6.
121. Gilliard, "The Social Origins of Bishops," 117–18. A further example is the son of Honorius, who succeeded his father when the latter was transferred to the larger see of Mauretanian Caesarea: Brown, *Power and Persuasion*, 101.

ily of Basil of Caesarea is a case in point. Both his brothers, Gregory and Peter, also became bishops, of Nyssa and Sebaste, respectively. Their uncle Gregory had also been a bishop, as was their relative Poemenius of Satala. Basil's closest friend and associate from his student days in Athens was Gregory, the future bishop of Nazianzus—another member of an episcopal family. Gregory was ordained to the priesthood by his father, Gregory the Elder, who was bishop of Nazianzus. He was eventually entrusted with the sees of the rural backwater of Sasima and later of the imperial capital of Constantinople, neither of which he held with much success. His uncle Eusebius was also a bishop, and his cousin Amphilochius bishop of Iconium.

Other instances where new bishops owed their appointment to the influence of family members who were also clergymen are Julian of Eclanum, whose father Memorius was a bishop, as was his father-in-law, Aemilius of Beneventum. Gelasius of Caesarea was appointed by his uncle Cyril of Jerusalem. Already in the third century, Origen noted with disapproval that episcopal sees were passed from father to son.[122] A century later, Jerome complained about personal favoritism of this kind in the appointment of clergymen: "As though they [the bishops] were distributing the offices of an earthly service, they give posts to their kindred and relations; or they listen to the dictates of wealth. And, worse than all, they give promotion to the clergy who besmear them with flattery."[123] The practice was widespread throughout the empire. In fifth-century Spain, bishoprics were passed on from father to son as if they were a piece of property.[124] The poet Prudentius commented on the family of the Valerii in Saragossa, who derived great pride in their ancestral tradition of ecclesiastical officeholding.[125] Once established, the trend of hereditary bishoprics was not likely to be reversed, as illustrated by the senatorial bishops in Gaul. This trend is also evident in the repeated attempts of church councils to restore the system of a free election from among a number of candidates. In 692, Canon 33 of the Council in Trullo inveighed heavily against the Armenian custom of appointing family members as successors.

At the same time, it was acknowledged that sons of the clergy did not always follow in their fathers' footsteps. Basil of Caesarea remarked on this when he asked that tax exemptions be granted in perpetuity to the clergy as a body, not to individual clergymen. This privilege should not become

---

122. Origen, *Homilies on Numbers* 22.4.
123. Jerome (*Commentary on the Letter to Titus* 1, *PL* 26, col. 562B), demands that "leadership of people should not be passed on through the qualification of blood ties, but of conduct," and complains that many bishops treat ecclesiastical office as a *beneficium*, appointing not the most capable but those whom they love. See also Jerome, *Against Jovinian* 1.43.
124. Hilarus, *Ep.* 15, p. 162.
125. Prudentius, *Peristephanon* 4.79–80.

attached to individuals, he argued, because the sons of the clergy may choose another career than their fathers.[126] Many of them in fact sought employment in the orbit of the imperial court. Basil's own brother had found a position in the imperial service and worked as a physician with connections to the court of Julian the Apostate, much to the dismay of his family, who were greatly embarrassed by the resulting gossip.[127] Bishop Helladius of Caesarea managed to obtain for his son a splendid position at the court of Arcadius, thanks to the good services of Gerontius, whose reward was the see of Nicomedia.[128] And a tombstone in Rome commemorates the *domesticus* Philipp, whose father was a priest in Galatia.[129]

The desire to perpetuate the status attached to ecclesiastical officeholding within the family was a powerful motivator. Yet it fails to explain family connections of ecclesiastical officeholding that leap one or more generations and/or bridge great geographical distances. In these instances, episcopal appointment cannot be attributed to the direct influence of a father or other relative who was also a bishop and who could thus exercise his influence on the election process. Rather, the fact that a candidate for the episcopate could point to a pedigree of ecclesiastical service among his relatives and ancestors must have been a source of pride and distinction for the individual, motivating him to uphold the family tradition, as had been in the case with Polycrates of Ephesus. Moreover, such a family background also contributed to a future bishop's qualifications for this ministry in the eyes of his contemporaries. This explains why ten of the fifty-five bishops in Italy from 350 to 450 came from families with a clerical tradition.[130] For example, the father of Damasus, who became bishop of Rome in 366, had been a deacon and perhaps a suburban bishop. Family traditions of serving in the clergy are also found elsewhere in the empire. The case of Gregory of Tours has already been mentioned. The grandfather of Bishop Severus of Antioch had been bishop of Sozopolis, but his father had been a *curialis*.[131] Philoxenus of Mabbug had a nephew of the same name who was bishop of Constantia in Cyprus, while he himself was located in Syria.[132] Gregory of Tours counted three bishops among his ancestry, and Gregory the Great's

126. Basil of Caesarea, *Ep.* 104.
127. Gregory of Nazianzus, *Ep.* 7.3 to Kaisarios (362).
128. Sozomen, *HE* 8.6.5.
129. Philippus 6, *PLRE* 1: 696, with further references. See W. Wischmeyer, *Griechische und lateinische Inschriften zur Sozialgeschichte der Alten Kirche* (Gütersloh, 1982), 83.
130. Sotinel, "Le recrutement des évêques," 199–200. See also C. Pietri, "Une aristocratie provinciale et la mission chrétienne: L'exemple de la *Venetia*," 901–49, repr. in his *Christiana respublica: Éléments d'une enquête sur le christianisme antique*, 2: 128 (Rome, 1997).
131. Zacharias Scholasticus, *Life of Severus* 11, ed. Kugener, p. 11.
132. Cf. C. Hadjipsaltis, "Un archévêque inconnu de Chypre: Philoxénos (VI^e siècle)," *Byzantion* 31 (1961): 215–16.

forebears included one, perhaps two bishops, but in both instances, their episcopal ancestors were at some chronological or geographical remove. Even sons of priests who had been ordained as a punitive measure, against their will, might become deacons, as was the case with the son of Apion, the scion of an important Egyptian landholding family.[133]

These examples point to the existence of family traditions, not primarily in holding the episcopal office, but in serving and supporting the church in a variety of positions, and often in regions at great distance from each other. Further examples of this pattern are easily found. A funerary inscription for the presbyter Nestorius from Isauria mentions three generations of clerics; his wife also came from a family of clergymen.[134] Descent from a clerical family was a source of pride and distinction that was noted also on the tombstones of women: for example, on the memorial erected by her children to Matrona "daughter of Bishop Mnesitheos."[135] Children of priests became bishops, nuns, and monks; the nephew of a deaconess became a bishop; and brothers became deacons and bishops.[136] The foundation of monasteries for one's relatives also belongs in this context, as it illustrates the establishment of family traditions in actively supporting the church.[137]

Family traditions of ecclesiastical service are, in sum, well attested, even if our documentation lacks geographical and chronological consistency. This practice, however, undermines the distinctive tenets of the episcopal office: its definition as a confirmation of personal virtue; its accessibility to anyone, regardless of prior social distinction; and its free conferral by the electorate.

---

133. Apion was entrusted with high office and achieved consular rank but then fell from grace. His goods were confiscated, and he was exiled to Nicaea. There, he was ordained to the priesthood against his will, but his son Heracleides was happy to become a deacon. It would be interesting to know if his father harbored hopes of establishing a family tradition. See J. Gascou, "Les grands domaines, la cité et l'état en Égypte byzantine," *TM* 9 (1985): 63.

134. Wischmeyer, *Griechische und lateinische Inschriften*, no. 42, pp. 67–69.

135. J. G. C. Anderson, "A Summer in Phrygia: II," *JHS* 18 (1898): p. 126, no. 88.

136. A few examples may suffice: Bishop Servus was the son of a priest who had been martyred by Donatists: Mandouze, 1066–67; Bishop Peter of Alexandria was the son of a *protopresbyteros*, according to the Coptic *encomium* by Bishop Alexander: trans. T. Vivian, *St. Peter of Alexandria: Bishop and Martyr* (Philadelphia, 1988), 79; Valens was a deacon in Hippo, and his brother was a subdeacon in Milevis: Augustine, *Sermo* 356.3. The son and the daughter of the priest Januarius had embraced the monastic life: Augustine, *Sermo* 355.3. The consecrated virgin Photeine was the daughter of Theoctistus, a priest in Laodicaea, and the deaconess Sabiniana in Antioch was an aunt of John Chrysostom: Palladius, *HL* 41.4. Evagrius Ponticus, who later became an important monastic figure in Egypt, was the son of a *chorepiscopus* and had been ordained lector by Basil of Caesarea, and deacon by Gregory of Nazianzus: Palladius, *HL* 38.2. Gilliard, "The Social Origins of Bishops," 117, mentions further pairs of brothers who were bishops: Auxentius of Mopsuestia and Theodore of Tarsus; Theodore of Mospuestia and Polychronius of Apamea; Zeno of Maiuma and Ajax of Botelion.

137. Leporius, a priest in Hippo, built a monastery for his family, on land that belonged to the church: Augustine, *Sermo* 356.10, *PL* 39, col. 1578.

For this reason, the practice of passing on episcopal office within the family was severely criticized by individual authors and prohibited by church councils. These voices of dissatisfaction are perhaps distorting the magnitude of the problem. For at the same time, as Gustave Bardy has shown, there is ample evidence for great geographical mobility when it came to episcopal appointments, a trend that runs counter to the establishment of regional family traditions.[138] Throughout the empire, it tended to be the important sees that welcomed foreigners as their bishops. Only half of the forty-eight bishops of Rome until the year 483 came from Rome itself; the rest were Greeks (nine), Italians (eight), Africans (two), and from Syria, Dalmatia, Spain, and Sardinia (one each). It seems that the Western regions of the empire, especially Italy and Britain, accepted greater numbers of bishops from abroad, especially from the East, than the more heavily Christianized regions of North Africa, Egypt, and Syria, where bishops were usually recruited from among the clergy in that region, although here, too, there were important exceptions. Most common is the appointment of outsiders, but often from within the same province, as compromise candidates in contested elections, or in times of increased need, as during the Arian controversy.

Family traditions of episcopal officeholding may thus not have been as dominant as their critics would make us believe. Nor did they always stem from entirely ulterior motives. More often than not, they were occasioned by a combination of a genuine religious motivation for serving in the Christian ministry, the desire to acquire distinction through ecclesiastical office, and the impetus to perpetuate within the family the social status that derived from both.

### THE CORRELATION OF WEALTH AND ECCLESIASTICAL OFFICE

Men of wealth, namely, those of the curial class and the senatorial aristocracy, stood a greater chance of attaining the episcopate than those of more modest means.[139] The episcopate is the pinnacle of the ecclesiastical *cursus honorum*, which progresses from lector to deacon, then to priest, and finally to bishop. It was predominantly the men of wealth and social status who made it through the bottleneck to the highest and singular position in the ecclesiastical hierarchy of their cities, while those of less distinguished background encountered a glass ceiling when it came to that last promotion.

Once Constantine had precipitated the growth of the church by signaling his support for Christianity, wealth, education, and the confident bearing and networking abilities that are the by-products of a privileged back-

---

138. G. Bardy, "Sur la patrie des évêques dans les premiers siècles," *RHE* 35 (1939): 217–42.
139. For the whole problematic, see L. W. Countryman, *The Rich Christian in the Church of the Early Empire: Contradictions and Accommodations* (New York and Toronto, 1980), 154–73.

ground became highly desirable qualifications for the episcopate more than ever before. In tandem with this opening up of the episcopate to a greater influx of men of the propertied classes, the concrete modalities of episcopal elections also changed. Whereas in the third century the entire congregation and its clergy were involved in the selection process, the selection of a candidate in the fourth century was determined by his future peers in the episcopal office, sometimes with the input of powerful civic leaders.[140]

The role of the bishop in securing the physical well-being of his flock was not very different from that of the wealthy public benefactor. Eusebius reported that Phileas was "outstanding" in his activities (politeia) on behalf of the city, performed liturgies, gave speeches, and composed works on philosophy. He did all this, Eusebius implied, while holding the see of the Egyptian city of Thmuis.[141] Not surprisingly, the city population often clamored to have as their bishops prominent men who were well known as civic leaders, effective mediators with the imperial government, and wealthy benefactors. As a consequence, John Chrysostom complained, "no one will look to the man who is really qualified, or make some test of his character."[142] Synesius was selected to be bishop of Cyrene mostly because he had successfully led several embassies to Constantinople, despite the fact that he insisted to keep his wife by his side and refused to give up his Neoplatonic ideas. In an increasingly Christianized empire, the public benefactions of a socially distinguished candidate also extended to the church. In 471, Simplicius was singled out by Sidonius Apollinaris for the see of Bourges in southern Gaul because he, too, had led embassies, in this instance to petition the Roman emperors and the Visigothic kings. But, in addition, his ancestors had a record of service both as prefects and as bishops, and Simplicius himself had constructed a church at his own expense.[143]

Personal wealth even made complete strangers to a community appear as attractive candidates for the clergy, especially if they were as fabulously rich as Pinianus. When he and his wife Melania the Younger stopped in Hippo on their way to the Holy Land, the congregation there demanded in a tumultuous scene that Pinianus be made a priest, probably anticipating that he would later become their bishop. Augustine was stunned and embarrassed by his congregation's clamoring, and it was only Pinianus's adamant, but diplomatically phrased refusal that settled the issue.[144] Pinianus and

140. R. Gryson, "Les élections épiscopales en orient au IVᵉ siècle," RHE 74 (1979): 301–45.
141. Eusebius, HE 8.9.7–8.10.1.
142. John Chrysostom, On the Priesthood 3.11.21–23.
143. Sidonius Apollinaris, Ep. 7.9.
144. Pinianus 2, PLRE 1: 702; C. Lepelley, Les cités de l'Afrique romaine au Bas-Empire (Paris, 1979), 1: 385–88. The episode is described in detail in F. van der Meer, Augustine the Bishop (London, 1961), 143–48; see also Brown, Augustine of Hippo, 294.

Melania belonged to the Roman senatorial aristocracy, and their wealth was stratospheric. The annual income from the properties they owned equaled $123 million, sufficient to provide subsistence living for approximately 24,000 families for a whole year.[145] But even at the more modest level of the property-owning provincial aristocracy, the imperial legislation of the fourth and fifth centuries shows a recurring concern that the appointment of *curiales* to the clergy would divert precious private resources from the public domain to the church.

Wealth could help in social climbing, in the church as much as elsewhere. Men of privileged background who had joined the lower orders of the clergy seem to have harbored more realistic expectations of promotion to the episcopate than their more humble colleagues. The appointment of Augustine's successor Heraclius, who was the wealthiest among the deacons of Hippo, will be discussed below. Ambitious deacons and priests who had the means could also help the election process along by greasing a few palms, as a law of Justinian implies.[146] Origen remarked that worthy men with the proper spiritual qualifications but lacking in social distinction often stagnated in their ecclesiastical careers.[147]

Those who came from less prosperous families could still position themselves as potential candidates for the episcopate by taking up the duties of the *oikonomos,* who was traditionally a deacon by rank. His task was the administration of the financial affairs of the church, in the process of which he would acquire significant skills in property management. The *oikonomos* assisted the bishop in administrative matters and was directly answerable to him. The close collaboration between the deacon-administrator with his bishop naturally transmuted into a situation of mentorship, which groomed the deacon to take his bishop's place at a future date. It was not uncommon for these deacon-administrators to be directly appointed to the episcopate, without an interim period in the priesthood. This was a prevalent pattern in the church in Rome. Pope Gregory the Great, for one, had been a high-level bureaucrat, a monk, a deacon, and a papal *apocrisiarius* in Constantinople, but not a priest, when he was made bishop of Rome. Instances in the East include Marathonius, who recommended himself for the episcopate at Nicomedia because he had, as a deacon, made a reputation for himself as administrator and supporter of the poor relief in his city.[148]

Priests who had served in the local clergy for a long time, especially if they were from a prominent and wealthy family, naturally anticipated their pro-

145. These figures are given by E. A. Clark, "The Lady Vanishes: Dilemmas of a Feminist Historian after the 'Linguistic Turn,'" *Church History* 67 (1998): 18.

146. Nov. Just. 6.1.9 (535).

147. Origen, *Homilies on Numbers* 2.1.

148. Sozomen, *HE* 4.20.2.

motion to the episcopate as soon as the see fell vacant. Their disappointment if they were passed over in favor of another candidate often found an outlet in threats or actual acts of violence. Cyprian, a relatively recent neophyte whose wealth and social standing were not unconnected to his appointment to the see of Carthage in 248, had to reckon with the hostility of clergy at whose head he had been placed *per saltum*. In the late fourth century, Epiphanius, a converted Jew and the son of a tenant farmer in Palestine, became the bishop of Salamis in Cyprus. The disgruntled clergy of his new see plotted to assassinate him by hiding a dagger on the episcopal throne.[149] In the early sixth century, Felix, who had served for many years as deacon and then priest of the see of Ruspe in North Africa, was thwarted in his ambitions and tried to prevent the ordination of Fulgentius to that see in 508. Felix could not stand up to Fulgentius's credentials, however, who brought to his office the ideal combination of the upbringing and education worthy of his senatorial family and several years spent in monastic pursuits.[150] Others were driven by ambition to the degree that they did not even want to wait for regular promotions and seized the opportunities to build a power base as soon as their position permitted. In Cappadocia at the end of the fourth century, Glycerius gathered a group of virgins around him as soon as he had become deacon, styling himself as their "patriarch" both in name and appearance. Basil of Caesarea, who was beleaguered by the girls' concerned parents, reports that Glycerius did so "not from any motive of obedience or of piety, but because he preferred this source of livelihood just as another man would chose one or another occupation."[151]

A privileged social background thus often translated into privileged access to the episcopal office. Men of means could expect direct appointment to the episcopate, *per saltum*, without following the ecclesiastical *cursus honorum*, merely on the basis of their social standing. Appointments of this kind were not uncommon. All the Eastern bishops of senatorial rank had, in fact, acquired the episcopate in this way. However, in some instances when appointment to the clergy served the punitive purpose of removing powerful men from the political arena, men of senatorial rank, such as Apion under Anastasius[152] and John the Cappadocian under Justinian, were not ordained as bishops, but only as priests, thus adding the insult of social demotion to the injury of loss of political power.[153]

149. *Life of Epiphanius of Salamis*, PG 41, col. 93C.
150. Felix 91, Mandouze, p. 441.
151. Basil of Caesarea, *Ep.* 169; cf. *Ep.* 170 and 171.
152. Apion 2, *PLRE* 2: 111–12. See also Gascou, "Les grands domaines," 61–63. Apion was ordained to the priesthood while in exile at Nicaea. He was recalled to Constantinople after the death of Anastasius and became praetorian prefect of the East.
153. Procopius, *Wars* 1.25 and 2.30.50. After his recall to Constantinople in 549, he was constrained to remain in the priesthood, even against his will.

Both ecclesiastical and imperial law made efforts to curb the practice of direct appointments to the higher clergy. Already the Council of Nicaea insisted that a suitable time must elapse between baptism and ordination to the priesthood or the episcopate. A few decades later, the Council of Sardica declared that wealthy men or men with extensive legal training, *scholastici tes agoras,* should not become bishops immediately but had to rise through the ecclesiastical ranks.[154] Still in the sixth century, Justinian found it necessary to endorse the observation of proper procedure in ecclesiastical appointments.[155] Nevertheless, when the need arose, ecclesiastical ritual could serve as a substitute for the proper interstices. Such was the case with Ambrose, who received baptism, "all the ecclesiastical offices," and ordination to the episcopate, all within the course of one week.[156] The preference for men with abundant worldly qualifications, but without a firm grounding in the faith or without much experience in ecclesiastical matters, did not go uncriticized. Jerome, for one, noted sarcastically: "Yesterday a catechumen, today a priest. Yesterday at the theatre, today in the church. In the evening at the chariot-races, the next morning at the altar. Recently a fan of actors, now a consecrator of holy virgins."[157]

## THE PERMEABILITY OF CIVIC AND ECCLESIASTICAL OFFICE

For many upwardly mobile *curiales,* the episcopate was the crowning glory of their public career. One such ambitious *curialis* was M. Iulius Eugenius, who died ca. 340 after twenty-five years as bishop of Laodiceia Combusta in Phrygia. To ensure that none of his proud accomplishments were forgotten, he composed the inscription for his tombstone himself. It deserves to be quoted in full:

> M. Iulios Eugenios, Son of Kyrillos Keler from Koussea, a *curialis;* he served in the office of the provincial governor of Pisidia and married Fl. Julia Flaviana, the daughter of the senator Gaios Nestorianos; and while he was serving with honor, in the meantime an order went forth under Maximinus that Christians had to offer sacrifice and were not allowed to leave the imperial service. So he suffered many trials under the Provincial Governor Diogenes, trying to give up his service while adhering to the faith of the Christians. Having spent a short time in the city of the Laodicaeans, he became bishop through the will of the omnipotent God, and for the duration of twenty-five years administered

154. Nicaea, can. 2; Serdica, can. 10.
155. Nov. Just. 6.1.2.
156. Paulinus, *Life of Ambrose* 9.
157. Jerome, *Ep.* 69.9 to Oceanus, *PL* 22, col. 663: "Heri catechumenus, hodie pontifex; heri in amphitheatro, hodie in ecclesia; vespere in circo, mane in altario; dudum fautor histrionum, nunc virginum consecrator."

the episcopate with much honor. And he built up the whole church from the foundations and [provided] all the adornments around it, namely the colonnades, the porticoes, paintings, mosaics, the fountain and the atrium, and outfitted it with all the works of the stonecutters and simply everything. And as I was about to depart from the life of men, I made for myself a lid [?] and a sarcophagus on which the foregoing was written at my behest, for the glory of the church and of my family.[158]

The offspring of a curial family, Iulius Eugenius explored all the opportunities for social advancement that were open to a man of his status. He was a proud officeholder in the provincial bureaucracy—an honorable distinction that sometimes entailed significant privileges, not least of which the option for further promotions. He made an advantageous marriage to the daughter of a senator. This must have been a source of special pride, for Julius Eugenius takes care to mention his father-in-law by name, an unusual feature in this kind of inscription. During the Great Persecution, Iulius Eugenius would have preferred to avoid conflict by resigning from his position but was not allowed to do so. His reference to the "trials" he endured as a result is too vague to give us any idea of the extent of his suffering. But it seems that his elevated social status protected him from physical harm, which he would surely have mentioned otherwise. After his tenure of office expired and he returned to the city of his origin (Koussea, where he was born, was a village belonging to the city territory of Laodiceia Combusta), it did not take long until he became bishop. He must have been a perfect candidate in all respects: a local son who had moved up in the world, a former civil servant with connections in high places, a dedicated Christian who could claim to have been a *confessor* during the Persecution, and a wealthy man who was able to build a lavishly appointed ecclesiastical complex for his city. The last lines of the inscription are testimony to the fusion of personal pride in his family, civic pride in his city, and pride in being a benefactor of the church—a mixture that would become more and more common over the course of the fourth century.

There was a surprising degree of permeability between service to the *civitas* and service in the *ecclesia*, starting in the fourth century. Transitions from a secular to an ecclesiastical career were not uncommon. Some of the bishops who were the target of Gregory of Nazianzus's scorn after his sudden demise from the see of Constantinople in 381 seem to have held prior posi-

158. *MAMA* 1 (1928): no. 170. For a detailed interpretation of the social significance of this inscription, which I follow here, see W. Wischmeyer, "M. Iulius Eugenius: Eine Fallstudie zum Thema Christen und Gesellschaft im 3. und 4. Jhdt.," *ZNW* 81 (1990): 225–46. See also S. Mitchell, *Anatolia: Land, Men, and Gods in Asia Minor* (Oxford, 1993), 82 and 102, suggesting that the Eugenius of the inscription is identical with the Novatian bishop of the same name.

tions as tax collectors or in the imperial service.[159] Another bishop who had distinguished himself in imperial service prior to his election was Eleusius of Cyzicus.[160] Then there were *curiales* who had been ordained rather prematurely to the episcopate by Neon, bishop of Seleucia. Apparently, they "had no inkling of either the scriptures or the canons of the church. After their ordination, they preferred the possession of their goods to the episcopate and declared in writing that they would rather hold liturgies with their possessions than the episcopate without them."[161] It seems that these *curiales* had agreed to become bishops without the knowledge that this would mean relinquishing access to their private property. Their resignation from the episcopate must have been successful, for only Neon, who had ordained them, was deposed by the Council of Constantinople in 360. In order to counteract this trend of immediate transition from a civil to an ecclesiastical office, canon law discouraged direct appointment to the episcopate and insisted that the proper ecclesiastical *cursus honorum* had to be observed and clergy had to move through the ranks of deacon and priest prior to becoming bishops. By the sixth century, Justinian barred former civil servants or *curiales* from access to the episcopate, unless they had already ruptured their ties to the world by entering the monastic order at a young age.[162] He even scornfully labeled direct appointments to the priesthood and then on to the episcopate as "pretend" or "fake" appointments.[163] Justinian's law would have affected people like the *curiales* and senators we encountered earlier, who treated the episcopate, to which they were appointed *per saltum,* as a retirement option at the end of their careers.

Even once a bishop was ordained, civic office was not entirely out of reach.[164] It seems that active ministers of the church sometimes attempted to join the secular administration. Paul of Samosata was not only bishop of Antioch from ca. 260 to 268 but possibly also held the office of *procurator ducenarius.* He certainly preferred to be treated as such.[165] Church councils saw the need to address the issue of clerics holding secular offices with grow-

159. Gregory of Nazianzus, *Carmen* 2.1.12, vv. 432–33.

160. Sozomen, *HE* 4.20.2.

161. Sozomen, *HE* 4.24.15 (my translation).

162. Nov. Just. 6.1.1 (535).

163. Ibid., 6.1.2 (535).

164. For interesting epigraphic evidence for high-ranking pagans acting as benefactors of Christian churches, see C. Lepelley, 'Évergetisme et épigraphie dans l'antiquité tardive: Les provinces de langue latine," in *Actes du X$^e$ Congrès International d'Épigraphie Grecque et Latine, Nîmes, 4–9 octobre 1992,* ed. M. Christol and O. Masson, 347–48 (Paris, 1997).

165. Eusebius, *HE* 7.30.8. There is some debate on whether Paul actually held the high-ranking office of *procurator ducenarius* (salaried tax collector), or whether he merely gave himself the air of being one. For the former view, see G. Bardy, *Paul de Samosate: Étude historique* (Louvain, 1929), 258–64; and F. Norris, "Paul of Samosata: Procurator Ducenarius,"

ing frequency. In some instances, as the *Apostolic Constitutions* show, bishops must have taken up public responsibilities after their ordination. In other instances, according to the same source, bishops, priests and deacons who had been engaged in imperial service intended to hold their new "priestly" rank without giving up their "Roman" one.[166] In 451, the Council of Chalcedon threatened excommunication unless these men abandoned their secular engagements.[167] Justinian was even harsher in his condemnation of clergy who had attained secular positions. They were to lose their belt of office, their honor, and their position and were compelled to return to serve on the *curia* of their hometown.[168] It is not too far-fetched to assume that many bishops traveled to the imperial capital in the hope of gaining influential allies who would eventually help them make the transition from the episcopate to service in the imperial administration. This is evident from the attempts to restrict episcopal travel and to prevent bishops from exploiting their friendships at the court for their own gain.[169] The targets of such chastisement must have been men of a certain station in society who maintained their friendships and continued to harbor worldly ambitions even after their accession to the episcopate.

Men of curial status who joined the clergy often returned to curial service at a later time in their lives. In other words, they treated clerical appointment like a magistracy that was not a profession, but an honor, to be held for a limited time. The transition from an ecclesiastical to a secular appointment was sometimes even condoned by the emperor. Dorotheus, a highly educated eunuch who had been a priest at Antioch, owed it to his friendship with the emperor Constantine that he was put in charge of the production of purple dye in Tyre, which was a state monopoly.[170] By the early fifth century, the practice of holding the episcopate only for a limited time seems to have become so common that efforts were made to curb it. In a letter of the year 402, Innocent, bishop of Rome, counseled against the

---

*JThS* 35 (1984): 50–70. Evidence for more bishops holding this office—not all of it convincing—is presented by T. Klauser, "Bischöfe als staatliche Prokuratoren im dritten Jahrhundert," *JAC* 14 (1971): 140–49. A more critical view is taken in F. Millar, "Paul of Samosata, Zenobia, and Aurelian: The Church, Local Culture, and Political Allegiance in Third-Century Syria," *JRS* 61 (1971): 1–17.

166. *Apostolic Constitutions* 81 and 83. On the correct interpretation of *strateia* in Canon 83 as "imperial service" (analogous to the Latin *militia*) rather than "military service," as Metzger translates it, see P. Batiffol, "L'incompatibilité de la strateia et de la cléricature," *Bulletin de la Société des Antiquaires de France*, 1911, 226–32.

167. Chalcedon (451), can. 7.

168. Nov. Just. 123.15 (546).

169. Sardica (347?), can. 9: the bishops may exploit their contacts by sending a letter, but this must be carried by a deacon. For Eudoxius, see Socrates, *HE* 2.37.9; and Sozomen, *HE* 4.12.3–4.

170. Eusebius, *HE* 7.32.2–3.

appointment of *curiales* to the clergy out of concern about the distress caused the church by the reflux of clergy into worldly affairs.[171] A few years later, in 408, a law of Arcadius and Honorius specified that priests who had either been deposed by the bishop or left the clergy *by their own volition* (my emphasis) immediately had to return to serve on the *curia* or in a guild, depending on their social origin, and that they would be barred from any office in the imperial service.[172] This law is intriguing in that it opens up the possibility that some Christians regarded the priesthood not as a lifelong vocation, but as an intermediate stage in their professional lives, with a position in the bureaucracy of the empire as their ultimate goal. All of this goes to prove that the Christian theologians had ample reason to remind their audience that the episcopate should not be regarded as an "honor" equivalent to municipal office.

171. Innocent, *Ep.* 4.3; *Ep.* 2.11, Mansi 3: 1035.
172. Sirm. 9 (408). The version of this law preserved at CTh 16.2.39 does not contain the passage referring to imperial service.

CHAPTER SEVEN

# Cities

The bishop of the late antique city came to belong to the urban elite. His social origin was, more often than not, among the urban upper class, and he usually had enjoyed the exclusive education to prove it. No wonder, then, that he displayed the same civic pride and social ambition as his peers. And little wonder that the episcopate appeared to many of those who attained it as a great distinction, a civic honor, unless they had come to it after a monastic interlude, as John Chrysostom and the Cappadocian fathers had done.

In order to understand the distinctive aspects of the bishop's role within the urban context, it is helpful to compare his activities to those of prominent citizens, on the one hand, and to those of holy men, on the other. This will locate the bishop at the the intersection of pragmatic authority and ascetic authority. His socioeconomic status is the source of the former, and his activities are to be motivated and propelled by the latter.

## THE BISHOP'S RESIDENCE

Since quite a few bishops seem to have entertained the notion that the episcopal dignity resembled a civic office, it is interesting to see to what degree the episcopal residences resembled the mansions of the rich and powerful. The episcopal residence or *episcopium* (Greek: *episkopeion*) was, next to the cathedral church, the place where the bishop interacted with his staff and with the people who sought his counsel and assistance. Some bishops, as has been noted before, lived together with their clergy, following a monastic regimen. The bishop's residence was also a monument to episcopal self-representation within the urban fabric. Only a very small number of episcopal residences from late antiquity have been found or identified as such. The most detailed study, by Wolfgang Müller-Wiener, has synthesized the archaeological findings for North Africa and the Eastern provinces.[1] The location of the bishops' residence within the city, its disposition of rooms, and its decorative scheme are emblematic of the way in which the Christian church grew into its new public role during this period. The church's need to adapt to the prevailing conditions finds concrete expression in the fact that the episcopal residence always inserts itself into the existing pattern of streets and neighboring buildings. The earliest identifiable bishops' residences date from the early fifth century. At this time, rather than asserting its authority by usurping a focal position at the city center, the bishop's residence was more often than not positioned on the periphery. Only in the late fifth century, as the number of Christians had grown and the church had become firmly entrenched in society, were the cathedral church and the episcopal residence relocated to a more prominent location in the center of the city, where they often replaced an earlier religious or public structure. This tendency has been noted in the eastern Mediterranean as well as in southern Gaul and may thus be regarded as an empire-wide phenomenon.[2]

The variations in the layout of the episcopal residences throughout the empire reflect both the universal aspects of the episcopal office and the concrete conditions of the individual sees. In contrast to church building, where liturgical demands dictated the dominance of the basilical shape, the arrangement of buildings within the episcopal complex could vary enormously. There are examples of a tightly clustered compound, built on a grid pattern, such as at Philippi in northern Greece, while other cities had a loose assemblage of buildings without any apparent overall plan, as was the case in Hippo in North Africa. Such variations depended on the history of the individual church, the size and shape of the available space, local architectural preferences, and the availability of funds and building materials. There was thus no fixed building type, but only an assemblage of structures with some characteristic features in common.

---

1. W. Müller-Wiener, "Riflessioni sulle caratteristiche dei palazzi episcopali," *Felix Ravenna* 125–126 (1983 [1984]); id., "Bischofsresidenzen des 4.–7.Jhs. im östlichen Mittelmeer-Raum," in *Actes du XI^e Congrès International d'Archéologie Chrétienne*, vol. 1, Studi di Antichità Cristiana 41 and Collection de l'École Française de Rome 123 (Vatican City and Rome, 1989), 651–709. In addition, this volume contains other valuable studies on specific regions. The late antique episcopal palaces throughout the Mediterranean are also discussed by D. I. Pallas, "Episkopion," in *Reallexikon zur byzantinischen Kunst*, vol. 2/11 (Stuttgart, 1968), cols. 335–71. For Italy, see now M. Miller, *The Bishop's Palace: Architecture and Authority in Medieval Italy* (Ithaca, N.Y., 2000). See also the forthcoming works by Barbara Polci and Yuri Marano.

2. S. Loseby, "Bishops and Cathedrals: Order and Diversity in the Fifth-Century Urban Landscape of Southern Gaul," in *Fifth-Century Gaul: A Crisis of Identity?* ed. J. Drinkwater and H. Elton (Cambridge, 1992), 144–55. Fulgentius of Ruspe built a new episcopal residence immediately adjacent to his church for the use of over forty "brothers": *Life of Fulgentius of Ruspe* 27.5.

The one distinctive feature shared by all episcopal complexes is the presence of a large rectangular room, sometimes with an apse or a triconch at its narrow end. This must have served for meetings, banquets, or judicial procedures. In fact, looked at in isolation, it is possible to mistake these halls for civic meeting spaces. Only relatively recently, when archaeologists began to turn their attention to the ensemble of buildings and their location within the cityscape were they clearly identified as ecclesiastical—further confirmation of the often interchangeable nature of ecclesiastical and civic activities. Next to the large meeting room were usually some smaller rooms that could be used for offices, record keeping, or storage. In addition to the cathedral church and its nearby or adjacent baptistery, the complex sometimes included a smaller chapel dedicated to a saint. Additional larger rooms must have provided storage for the agricultural and other goods administered by the church. The living quarters were probably on the upper floor. Many episcopal residences also featured a small, private bath—the only luxury in the entire setup, and one that was sometimes shared with the local clergy.[3] This is surprising in view of the vociferous condemnation by many church fathers of the widely enjoyed social practice of bathing.

The episcopal residences largely corresponded, albeit on a slightly more modest scale, to the mansions of the aristocracy, which also combined private living with public function. They followed the same basic outline as the residences of provincial governors or of other wealthy notables. The governor's living quarters had a large reception room for visitors who paid their respects in the morning, often featured a banqueting hall to entertain guests in the evening, and on occasion also boasted a private bathing structure. The governor's complex often also contained a religious shrine. The only feature of the private architecture of the nobility that was not shared by the episcopal palace was the atrium through which the stream of visitors was directed to the reception hall.[4] On the whole, the episcopal complex strove for functionality rather than ostentation. Conspicuously absent were the atrium courtyards with waterworks at their center that adorned the more glamorous private mansions. Simplicity prevailed also in the decorative schemes. Mosaic floors were common, but there were no expensive marble floors, and equally no marble revetments on the walls. Instead, a marbelized effect was achieved through skillful painting on plaster.

The archaeological record thus provides us with an important corrective

3. Agnellus of Ravenna, *Liber pontificalis* 25.66: Bishop Victor restored the episcopal baths in Ravenna and allowed the clergy of the city to use them twice a week free of charge.
4. R. Haensch, *Capita provinciarum: Statthaltersitze und Provinzialverwaltung in der römischen Kaiserzeit*, Kölner Forschungen 7 (Mainz, 1997), 374–76; L. Lavan, "The *praetoria* of Civil Governors in Late Antiquity," in *Recent Research in Late-Antique Urbanism*, ed. L. Lavan, JRA Suppl. 42 (Portsmouth, R.I., 2001).

to the literary sources. It shows that the great majority of bishops, those who remain unnamed in the literary or epigraphic sources, projected a public image of an efficient, functioning administration that inserted itself seamlessly into the existing urban structures, without drawing attention to itself. The outraged reports in the written sources about bishops who alienated the funds destined for the poor in order to engage in ambitious building projects should therefore be seen in the proper perspective, as isolated incidents, gleefully reported by detractors.

### BISHOPS AND WEALTH

The greatest distinction that separated the bishop from the holy man and placed him in proximity to the prominent citizen was his access to wealth. This wealth could have two sources: the private wealth of the bishop, and the wealth of the church that he was administering. These will be treated in turn.

### Private Wealth

Men of wealthy background had a greater chance to rise to the episcopate than others, and many prosperous Christians were eager to do so. It is a confirmation of our earlier observations about the episcopate as magistracy *and* honor that many aspiring bishops were prepared to make payments to secure their appointment. This is known as simony, the sin of Simon Magus. Bribing the electorate was not uncommon, and complaints about this practice can be found from an early date. In canon law, it was prohibited for the first time at the Council of Chalcedon,[5] and in imperial legislation soon thereafter, in a law of Leo I.[6] At around the same time, Isidore of Pelusium complained bitterly that some of his contemporaries had purchased the priesthood or the episcopate and were then offering ordination to others for sale.[7] By the time of Justinian, an extensive legislative effort was made to curb the excesses of this practice. Not only were such ordinations declared invalid, but those who had performed them were now also held accountable and fined.[8]

   In actual practice, it will have been difficult to differentiate the purchase of ordination from the customary payment that a bishop made at his acces-

---

5. Chalcedon (451), can. 2, H-L II/2, p. 772; again at the second council of Orléans (533), can. 3, 4, H-L II/1, p. 1133. It was declared a heresy at the council of Tours (567), can. 27, H-L III/1, p. 192.
6. CJ 1.3.30 (469) uses the pithy phrase "Non pretio, sed precibus ordinetur antistes" (The priest should be ordained not by [paying] a price but by [receiving] prayers).
7. Isidore of Pelusium *Ep.* 2.127, *PG* 78, col. 565C and 568D.
8. Nov. Just. 6.1.5 (535); Nov. Just. 6.1.9 (535).

sion to the individual members of the clergy of his church, in an amount proportionate to the annual income of his see. Georg Kolias notes that this so-called *synētheia* (custom) of newly appointed bishops was much higher than that paid by new provincial governors, probably because the bishop's appointment was not limited in time, and he thus had greater opportunity to recoup his initial outlay of expenses.[9] It is questionable whether the men of modest backgrounds who would have stood to benefit most from an episcopal appointment were able to pay extensive bribes or the "custom" gift that we are told passed hands on this occasion. To men who were already rich, on the other hand, the priesthood or the episcopate was attractive not necessarily because of the financial opportunities that ordination into the clergy had to offer, but, as Ewa Wipszycka suggests, because it served as a "proof of piety," "enhanced their position in the community," and thus became a "source of social prestige."[10] This must have been at least part of the motivation of the rich landowner in Alexandria whose offer of a very generous amount of grain and gold for the famine relief organized by John the Almsgiver was tied to the following request: "Only let me, unworthy though I am, enjoy the post of deacon under you, so that by standing beside my lord [i.e., you, John,] at the holy altar I may be cleansed from the profligacy of my sins."[11] John, however, was not only above bribery, he was also unwilling to bend the rules, since the man had been married twice and was thus disqualified from the clergy. The phrasing of the request is revealing. The rich man does not want to be deacon just anywhere, but "under" John, and he desires nothing more than to be seen every Sunday by the whole congregation standing "beside" the popular patriarch at the altar. Obviously, his hope was that some of the singular status of John would rub off on him.[12]

Christian custom and, later on, canon law and imperial law dictated that a man who entered the priesthood or the episcopate, just like the man who entered the monastic state, was not supposed to retain any private property. Yet the abandonment of property on the occasion of entry into the Christian ministry was not made an explicit requirement until the fourth

9. G. Kolias, *Ämter- und Würdenkauf im früh- und mittelbyzantinischen Reich* (Athens, 1939), 39–40 and 65–75.

10. E. Wipszycka, "Le istituzioni ecclesiastiche in Egitto dalla fine del III all'inizio dell'VIII secolo," in *L'Egitto cristiano: Aspetti e problemi in età tardo-antica*, edited by A. Camplani, Studia Ephemeridis Augustinianum 56 (Rome, 1997), 250, with reference to an (unidentified) letter of Severus of Antioch.

11. *Life of John the Almsgiver* 11.43–46.

12. The conventional interpretation of this episode ascribes the man's motivation to his desire to receive a salaried position within the church: V. Déroche, *Études sur Léontios de Néapolis*, Acta Universitatis Upsaliensis, Studia Byzantina Upsaliensia 3 (Uppsala, 1995), 148. But this seems doubtful in view of his significant wealth and the phrasing of his request.

century.[13] In theory, the bishop-elect was to relinquish all his rights to his family's property so that he entered the office unencumbered by personal financial interests. At most, a man was allowed to carry over into his religious state one third of his original private property.

There were three ways to give up one's private property, specifically land, for Christian causes: by making the property a gift to the church, by naming the church as the administrator and beneficiary of the income from it, while retaining the legal title of ownership, or by selling the property, thus commuting its value into cash. The owner could then dispense the money at his discretion and at his own pace to finance ecclesiastical or monastic building projects and charitable causes. In this way, the former owner was no longer liable to pay the land tax on his real estate, and his sudden reduction in landed wealth technically disqualified him from membership in the *curia* with all the obligations that entailed. This seems to have been the financial strategy employed by some of the wealthy Christians, like Basil of Caesarea or Paulinus of Nola, who abandoned their property in a single dramatic act when they embraced the monastic life, yet were able to dispense substantial amounts of money later in their lives for the construction of monasteries or for famine relief.[14] This method of commuting one's landed property into coin was probably the cause for the repeated concerns in imperial law that a future bishop's obligations to the fisc and to the *curia* should not simply vanish into thin air but must devolve on a designated replacement, usually his son. In actual fact, however, bishops often retained ownership of property. This is taken for granted in Canon 12 of the Council of Sardica, which allowed bishops to be absent from their see for a maximum of three weeks in order to collect income from property that still belonged to them, income that could benefit the charity of church.[15]

However, the offspring of bishops were not forced by their father's profession to live a life of reduced means themselves. Some sons of bishops were even in the position to sponsor public games. In 393 at the first council convened by Augustine as the new bishop of Hippo, generous gestures of public benefaction of this kind raised eyebrows and met with moral condemnation, because of the Christian disdain for public entertainments and their association with pagan practices.[16] Other sons of bishops aspired to positions in the imperial service and managed to obtain

13. L. W. Countryman, *The Rich Christian in the Church of the Early Empire: Contradictions and Accommodations* (New York and Toronto, 1980), 114–18.
14. B. Treucker, "Politische und sozialgeschichtliche Studien zu den Basilius-Briefen," (Diss., Frankfurt am Main, 1961), 22–26.
15. Sardica (347?), can. 12.
16. Council at Hippo (393), can. 15.

their posts through the extensive social networks of their fathers and their colleagues.[17]

Some insight into the personal finances of the descendant of a curial family is offered by the will that Gregory of Nazianzus drew up during his brief tenure as bishop of Constantinople. He had already made over most of his property to the church in Nazianzus, with the understanding that it was earmarked for the care of the poor. The goods that remained at his disposal were a few household slaves, all of whom were now manumitted, some land, which was deeded to relatives in need, and a large number of garments, which were evenly distributed among the clergy and close personal associates.[18]

The community in Hippo provides us with more detailed information about the relative wealth of the clergy in a large city. In 425, Augustine demanded a full disclosure of the private property held by the subdeacons, deacons, and priests who lived in the *monasterium clericorum* attached to his episcopal residence.[19] Since communal property and total dependence on church funds were one of the main requirements for all his clergy, Augustine wished to publicize this information to his congregation so as to avoid the suspicion of condoning hypocrisy.

The inquiry was occasioned by a dispute between the priest Januarius's daughter and son over the inheritance of his property. Two other priests also had property and disposable wealth that they used for church-related projects: Leporius had built a monastery for his family, but all his other investments benefited the church at Hippo: the construction of an inn for travelers, the rents from a small house, and a large contribution to the construction of a basilica. Barnabas had purchased a villa and then donated it to the monastery, but not without first making costly improvements. So that he could pay the debts for the expansion of the villa, Augustine allowed him to use the profits from his administration of a large property owned by the church. In Augustine's community, then, those who held the priesthood, and thus were candidates for the episcopate in Hippo or elsewhere, had firsthand experience in property ownership and property management.

The four deacons in Augustine's clergy were owners of or heirs to slaves and small amounts of land. Like the priests, they made their possessions available to the church. One deacon had purchased a house for the use of his mother and sister with financial support from "religious men." After setting aside equitable shares for their mothers and siblings, these deacons had

---

17. See above, p. 196.
18. Gregory of Nazianzus, *Testament, PG* 37, cols. 389–96. See R. van Dam, "Self-Representation in the Will of Gregory," *JThS* 46 (1995): 118–48.
19. Augustine, *Sermo* 356.3–11.

given or were intending to give the remainder to the church. This included their slaves, who were manumitted in a public ceremony, presided over by the bishop. The beneficiary was usually the church in the hometowns of these men, rather than the church at Hippo, where they were part of the clergy. The only deacon who made substantial contributions to the church at Hippo was Heraclius. He funded the construction of a chapel. With Augustine's encouragement, he retained legal ownership of a property to support his mother but deeded to the church a small house adjacent to the cathedral with the understanding that it would accommodate his mother if the need arose. His slaves who had been living with him were recently manumitted. With all these things arranged for the benefit of others, Augustine insisted—perhaps a little too vociferously—that "nobody should therefore say that he [Heraclius] is rich." It is perhaps no coincidence that only the following year Augustine ordained Heraclius to the priesthood and designated him as his successor to the episcopal see of Hippo.[20] When it came to promotions within the ecclesiastical hierarchy, the social status that was attached to personal wealth—even if that wealth had been placed in the legal ownership of the church—was clearly an advantage. This is confirmed by Augustine's remarks about the subdeacons who were poor. He insisted that they should not be regarded differently within the community of the clergy from those who were able to make financial contributions—an indirect admission that wealth did indeed translate into preferential treatment.

The church placed a high value on the voluntary poverty of its clergy but did not enforce it. Even a moral rigorist like Augustine encouraged his clergy to make provisions for family members rather than prematurely donate their property to the church in a grand, but ultimately empty gesture that might lead only to strife and litigation.

### Ecclesiastical Wealth

One of the bishop's responsibilities was the administration of the finances of his church. The church's finances were replenished and augmented from several sources. A steady flow of income came from the voluntary contributions, either in kind or in money, of the members of the church.[21] The size of these *oblationes* or *karpophoriai* remained at the discretion of each individual until the second half of the sixth century, when it seems that the biblical system of tithes was first applied systematically in Merovingian Gaul.[22] The clergy sometimes forgot the voluntary character of these donations and

20. Augustine, *Ep.* 213.
21. For the following, see A. H. M. Jones, *The Later Roman Empire, 284–602: A Social, Economic, and Administrative Survey* (Oxford, 1964; repr., 1986), 894–910.
22. Mâcon (585), can. 5, H-L III/1, p. 209.

began to exact them "like a tax" for their services of performing the eucharist or baptism, an abuse that an imperial law, probably by Anastasius, aimed to curb.[23]

More significant perhaps were the amounts that were added to the bishop's treasury through one-time donations. People who had enjoyed the hospitality of the church or who had been restored by the powers of spiritual or physical healing of a holy person showed their gratitude and appreciation in generous gifts. Others made over their inheritance, or part thereof, to the church. Wealthy women, in particular, were known to show their Christian piety by making substantial donations. Their generosity was actively pursued by clerics or holy men, whose zeal at fund-raising surely importuned the women themselves. Jerome derided these inheritance hunters as "ear ticklers." A law of 370 prohibited clergy and ascetic men from visiting women in the hopes of making financial gain.[24] In the fourth century especially, the church's wealth must also have increased greatly from the melting down of the pagan statues and the subsequent conversion of the gold and silver into coin.

Some churches in the fourth century were fortunate to attract donations from the imperial family. Real estate and the income it generated, church buildings, liturgical vessels and adornments made of gold and silver were liberally given to the church. The *Liber pontificalis,* a ninth-century compilation based partly on earlier sources, gives a detailed inventory of Constantine's gifts to the churches in Rome and elsewhere in Italy. These amounted to hundreds of pounds of gold and silver in chalices, patens, candlesticks, and other adornments, in addition to income from estates and commercial enterprises worth thousands of *solidi.*[25] Only in the late fifth century did the donations of aristocratic families surpass the imperial largesse.[26]

Traditionally, the incoming funds were divided into three parts: upkeep of the bishop, upkeep of the clergy, and works of charity.[27] The payment of a regular salary from church funds to bishops, priests, and deacons, which was common practice since the third century, alleviated the most dire

23. CJ 1.3.38.2.
24. CTh 16.2.20 (370).
25. *Liber pontificalis* 34–35.
26. C. Pietri, "Evérgetisme et richesses ecclésiastiques dans l'Italie du IVe à la fin du Ve siècle," *Ktema* 3 (1978): 317–37.
27. Different dispositions were made at Orléans (511), can. 14–15, H-L II/2, p. 1012: one-third or one-half of all offerings to the church belong to the bishop, depending on whether the offering is made in a parish or in his cathedral; and at Braga (563), can. 7, H-L III/1, p. 179: division of church property: one third each for bishop, rest of clergy, preparations, and illumination of the church. For the bishop's staff in the late antique West, see C. Sotinel, "Le personnel épiscopal: Enquête sur la puissance de l'évêque dans la cité," in *L'évêque dans la cité du IVe au Ve siècle: Image et autorité,* CEFR 248 (Rome, 1998).

financial needs of the clergy and thus reduced the likelihood of financial improprieties.[28]

Since charitable giving was considered a religious exercise that not only provided concrete support to the recipients but brought a spiritual reward for the donors, many authors of the period expressed their concern about defilement if the money for such purposes had been acquired by dishonest or disreputable means. The *Teaching of the Twelve Apostles*, for example, issues a stern warning:

> For they [the bishops] receive, forsooth, to administer for the nourishment of orphans and widows, from rich persons who keep men shut up in prison, or ill-treat their slaves, or behave with cruelty in their cities, or oppress the poor; or from the lewd, and those who abuse their bodies [i.e., actors and prostitutes]; or from evildoers; or from forgers; or from dishonest advocates, or false accusers; or from hypocritical lawyers; or from painters of pictures; or from makers of idols [i.e., pagan statues]; or from workers of gold and silver and bronze (who are) thieves; or from dishonest tax-gatherers; or from spectators of shows; or from those who alter weights or measures deceitfully; or from innkeepers who mingle water (with their wine); or from soldiers who act lawlessly; or from murderers; or from spies who procure condemnations; or from any Roman officials, who are defiled with wars and have shed innocent blood without trial: perverters of judgement who, in order to rob them, deal unjustly and deceitfully with the peasantry and with all the poor; and from idolaters; or from the unclean; or from those who practise usury, and extortioners.[29]

Bishops were not immune to greed and the alienation of church funds for private purposes, including the support of their family.[30] Justinian therefore demanded that only men without offspring should become bishops so that they might not be tempted by family concerns to siphon off church funds.[31] It is difficult to gauge the actual extent of the corruption of the clergy. Allowance must be made for the bias of our written sources. In fact, the most common accusation leveled against unpopular clergy was personal greed.[32] Especially vulnerable to such slander were bishops and other clergy

---

28. See above, p. 30.

29. R. . Connolly, *Didascalia Apostolorum: The Syriac Version Translated and Accompanied by the Verona Latin Fragments* (Oxford, 1929), chap. 18, p. 158.

30. Prohibitions of usury: Elvira (300?), can. 20; Nicaea (325), can. 17; Laodicaea (343? 381?), can. 4; strict separation between church property and private property of the bishop: Antioch (341), can. 17; prohibition of alienation of church property for nonecclesiastical causes: Antioch (341), can. 25; Orléans (511), can. 5; prohibition of accepting bribes: Tarragona (516), can. 10; prohibition of charging fees for ordinations and consecrations: Tours (567), can. 27; Braga (572), can. 3, 5, 7.

31. CJ 1.3.41 (528).

32. J. Roloff, "Themen und Traditionen urchristlicher Amtsträgerparänese," in *Neues Testament und Ethik: Festschrift R. Schnackenburg*, ed. H. Merklein (Freiburg, 1989).

who came from poor backgrounds or from outside the diocese. Still, complaints of this kind in the sources are so persistent, and they are voiced in general terms as well as against specific individuals, that we must accept that the greed of individual bishops was a genuine concern. An egregious case was Sophronius, bishop of Pompeiopolis, who had enriched himself from the offerings brought to his church and instead of heeding repeated summons to justify himself before other bishops had appealed to secular judges. He was deposed in 360.[33]

The greediness of the clergy or their deliberate inertia with regard to the demand of voluntary poverty was not, however, a new phenomenon in the fourth century. Theologians of the pre-Constantinian period, such as Tertullian, Cyprian, and Origen,[34] complained just as vociferously about these and other financial abuses as did their fourth-century counterparts. Later, Jerome had some choice phrases of condemnation for adversaries whom he accused of greed. He railed against John of Jerusalem for making a profit from "the piety of the whole world," insinuating that John was exploiting the pilgrims who came to the Holy City.[35] The secular historian Ammianus Marcellinus commented on the fierce contest between Damasus and Ursinus for the see in Rome in 366:

> Considering the ostentatious luxury of life in the city it is only natural that those who are ambitious of enjoying it should engage in the most strenuous competition to attain their goal. Once they have reached it [the episcopate] they are assured of rich gifts from ladies of quality; they can ride in carriages, dress splendidly, and outdo kings in the lavishness of their table.[36]

Even ambitious pagans were known to covet especially the important sees of large cities. The Roman consul Vettius Agorius Praetextatus, a staunch adherent of paganism, used to declare in jest to Damasus, who had won the episcopal throne of Rome: "Make me bishop of the city of Rome, and I will forthwith be a Christian."[37]

One safeguard against the abuse of church funds by bishops was the appointment of a financial administrator. To stem the rise of rumors about episcopal rapaciousness, the Council of Chalcedon decreed in 451 that the ecclesiastical finances had to be administered not by the bishop but, under his authority, by the *oikonomos*.[38] As the financial operations of each see

33. Sozomen, *HE* 4.24.14.
34. See A. von Harnack, *Der kirchengeschichtliche Ertrag der exegetischen Arbeiten des Origenes*, TU 42/3 (Leipzig, 1919), 2: 132 and 136–37.
35. Jerome, *Against John of Jerusalem* 14.
36. Ammianus Marcellinus, *Histories* 27.3.14.
37. Jerome, *Against John of Jerusalem* 8.
38. Chalcedon (451), can. 26.

became more and more extensive and complex, this had the additional advantage of relieving the bishop of an increasingly burdensome task that required constant attention and specialized knowledge. This measure may have had the desired effect of keeping the bishop clear of public scrutiny, but rather than eliminating the problem of financial abuse, this was now shifted to the *oikonomos,* who had all the opportunities for embezzlement and other improprieties.

The powerful position of the *oikonomos* even became the stuff of legend. A certain Theophilus, the story goes, was *oikonomos* of the church of Adana in Cilicia in the early decades of the seventh century.[39] He was a capable adminstrator of "all the different businesses and lands" of the church. "Everyone, from big to small, was grateful to him, for he provided generously for the needs of the orphans, the widows and the poor, especially for those whom he knew to have fallen from wealth into poverty." In other words, he was able to generate income, and he dispensed it wisely. After the death of the bishop of Adana, Theophilus was the favored candidate to become his successor. But he refused, out of humility, and a new bishop was appointed. Events took a turn for the worse when the new bishop gave in to slanderous rumors and relieved Theophilus of his office. To regain it, Theophilus made a pact with the devil from which he would eventually be released only through intercession to the Mother of God. In the meantime, however, he was not only reinstated as *oikonomos* but was given twice as much authority than before over all the financial affairs of the church and its properties, as well as over the city, its merchants, and its landowners. Before long, "he began to elevate himself over all, so that all obeyed him and served him with fear and trembling, and even the bishop was fearful and intimidated by him for a short time." This Byzantine precursor of the medieval legend of Doctor Faustus provides some insight into the extensive financial operation of an episcopal see and shows that the real power rested with the man who held the purse strings—in this case, the *oikonomos.*[40]

EPISCOPAL EXPENDITURE

The bishop's access to financial resources is the crucial distinction that set ✓ him apart from the holy man. But it was more a distinction of scale and of

39. L. Radermacher, "Griechische Quellen zur Faustsage," *SB Ak. Wiss. Vienna, Philos.-hist. Kl.* 206/4 (1927): 182 and 192. The version that I follow here is, according to Radermacher, a later and more detailed elaboration on an earlier tale. I am grateful to Wolfram Brandes for drawing my attention to this text.

40. Another example is Marathonius, who had been a deacon and overseer of the dwellings for poor men and women, before he was elevated directly to the see of Nicomedia: Sozomen *HE* 4.20.2.

means—money versus intercessory prayer—than of essence, for when it came to spending these resources, most of the bishop's expenditures were motivated by the same spirit of charity that also moved holy men to intervene on behalf of the needy. If his financial clout distinguished the bishop from the holy man, it placed him on a par with the leading men of his city. Many of the actions that the bishop undertook for the concrete benefit of his community were not the exclusive prerogative of his office but were also performed by other prominent individuals. In other words, the public functions of the bishop in his city could be exercised by any person who enjoyed general recognition, commanded a certain degree of authority, and had access to the necessary financial resources. The following pages will show bishops, holy men, and prominent citizens engaged in the same activities on behalf of the urban population.

A study by Rudolf Haensch shows that the provincial governors of the first to third century supported the life of their cities in much the same way as later bishops did.[41] First and foremost, provincial governors were patrons of construction, most commonly of temples and structures for the water supply, but also of city walls and road pavements. In times of need, they also helped to provision their city of residence with grain or wine and sometimes fixed the price of grain to counteract the effects of inflation during a shortage. Provincial governors also intervened with the imperial authorities on behalf of their city, or for the sake of groups or individuals among its citizens. In contrast to the provincial governor, who was usually a native of another region, without familial or ancestral ties to his city of residence, the bishop was, more often than not, recruited from among the local nobility and could thus tap into a well-established network of social relations in order to achieve his goals.

*Building Activity*

The erection of buildings was the most common and most popular form of public evergetism. Inscriptions from all parts of the empire abound recording contributions by prominent citizens and magistrates to construction of all kinds: walls, aqueducts, public baths, porticoes, theatres, and temples.

Since building patronage involved expense, it was not undertaken by holy men, who not only lived in demonstrative poverty, but who did not have access to wealth, unlike the bishops. However, holy men could exercise their power of intercession *(parrhēsia)* to gain support for a building project. In this manner, Porphyry of Gaza succeeded in securing from the imperial family money, building materials, and a workforce for the construction of a

41. Haensch, *Capita provinciarum*, esp. 380–89.

large basilica on the foundations of the old temple of Zeus Marnas. That Porphyry was a bishop was less important than that he had *parrhēsia* with God. The empress Eudoxia only gave her support to his project after his prayers that she would safely deliver a baby son had come true.[42] Another example of the construction of a church thanks to the power of persuasion, this time of a dead saint, comes from the Pontus region. A metric building inscription records that Theodore of Euchaita, "the athlete of Christ," 'citizen of the Heavens" and "protector of this city," had "persuaded" the emperor Anastasius to build this church, where Mamas presided over the liturgy.[43]

Bishops often directed their energies toward the construction of religious buildings. The funds for these projects occasionally came from imperial donations, sometimes out of the bishops' own pockets, and often were a result of successful fund-raising within the community, as the multiple donor inscriptions in the mosaic floors of churches in Italy and Palestine attest. The new churches proclaimed the power of the bishop who was able to get a large and beautiful building project off the ground. The bishop's building patronage often rivaled that of important citizens. In the dating system at the martyrion of Babylas, the bishop even eclipsed all others. His name appears in the inscription that dates the monument in the place where the eponymous magistrate is usually mentioned.[44] These new ecclesiastical structures not only served the community but also enhanced the public visibility of Christianity at a time when paganism still had its adherents. The inscription of Eugenius, mentioned above, which advertised the church he had built and described in loving detail all the adornments that he had provided, is emblematic of the combination of civic, familial, and episcopal pride that found its outlet in building patronage.

Building patronage was such a visible assertion of status within the city that some bishops went overboard. They lost their sense of propriety and proportion and diverted financial resources that ought to have benefited the needy to overly ambitious projects. Invariably, it was the detractors of these bishops who raised this charge. Antoninus, the bishop of Ephesus, was said to have taken the marbles from the entry to the baptistery and put them in his private bath. He also reportedly transferred the church columns that had been lying around unused for years to his private *triklinos,* his reception or dining hall. His offense was so egregious that he was deposed in 400.[45]

Episcopal interest in building was not limited to church-related struc-

42. Mark the Deacon, *Life of Porphyry of Gaza* 42–50.
43. C. M. Kaufmann, *Handbuch der altchristlichen Epigraphik* (Freiburg i. Br., 1917), 393.
44. G. Downey, "The Shrines of St. Babylas at Antioch and Daphne," in *Antioch-on-the-Orontes,* vol. 2, *The Excavations* (Princeton, 1934–), 39.
45. Palladius, *Dialogue on the Life of St. John Chrysostom* 13.163–67.

tures. Especially from the fifth century onward, bishops also collaborated and participated in public building. In the 430s, Theodoret of Cyrrhus boasted in a letter to the *patricius* and high functionary Anatolius that he had spent significant amounts of ecclesiastical revenue for the construction of porticoes, baths, bridges, and other structures of general use. His expenditure, he proudly declared, did not lag behind that of any civil magistrate.[46] In other locations, bishops contributed to the construction of walls, prisons, granaries, and aqueducts. They were involved in such projects with varying degrees of intensity, by petitioning the emperor for permission or funds, by contributing financially, by supervising the building activity, or by supporting it through their prayers.[47]

By the sixth century, the construction of new ecclesiastical structures had reached its peak, and attention turned to building maintenance. The only church canons that address episcopal oversight over buildings come from this period, and they are from the West. The Council of Tarragona (516) required bishops to make an annual round of inspection of the rural churches and to make available the regular income from the tithes for the necessary maintenance.[48] Similarly, the Council of Orléans in 538 required that the bishop ensure that the tithes that came from rural areas were directed to building maintenance or upkeep of the clergy in the same regions where they had been raised.[49]

The few imperial laws on church building also date from the same period. Justinian wanted to ensure that the bishops retained complete control and oversight over ecclesiastical building and therefore required that the construction of new chapels and monasteries could proceed only after the bishop had consecrated the site. Justinian also was concerned that all building or restoration projects be completed.[50] With regard to public works, Justinian gave their oversight to the leading citizens, the *principales*, of the city, including among them the bishop.[51] Building inscriptions on

---

46. Theodoret of Cyrrhus, *Ep.* 79. *Ep.* 81 mentions porticoes, two large bridges, and an aqueduct, all financed by the church.

47. A. Avramea, "Les constructions profanes de l'évêque d'après l'épigraphie et les textes d'Orient," in *Actes du XI^e Congrès International d'Archéologie Chrétienne*, vol. 1, Studi di Antichità Cristiana 41 and Collection de l'École Française de Rome 123 (Rome, 1989), 829–35; D. Feissel, "L'évêque, titres et fonctions d'après les inscriptions grecques jusqu'au VII^e siècle," in *Actes du XI^e Congrès International d'Archéologie Chrétienne*, vol. 1, Studi di Antichità Cristiana 41 and Collection de l'École Française de Rome 123 (Rome, 1989), 801–28; J. H. W. G. Liebeschuetz, "The Rise of the Bishop in the Christian Roman Empire and the Successor Kingdoms," (*Electrum* 1 1997): 120.

48. Tarragona (516), can. 8, H-L II/2, p. 1028.

49. Orléans (538), can. 5, H-L II/2, p. 1158.

50. Nov. Just. 131.7.

51. CJ 1.4.26.

public structures from the period record the bishop's participation "for the common good."[52] This is one, concrete indication of the way in which the bishop's care for the well-being of his flock was gradually extended from the members of his church to all the citizens of his city of residence as the numbers of Christians in any given municipality increased and Christianity became the dominant religion of the empire.

The participation of bishops in building activities shows the overlap of the civic role of bishops with that of prominent citizens. In the case of bishops who themselves hailed from leading families, the two roles coincided. In the case of bishops who came from lower social background or from outside the city, their assumption of these functions gained them the goodwill of the population and paved the way for their integration into the local elite. It is significant that building activity is not mentioned anywhere in the normative texts on the episcopate. In this regard, the bishops acted not as continuators of the priestly tradition of the Old Testament, nor as exemplars of Christian conduct, but as paragons of civic virtue. It was their social and economic clout that determined this aspect of their public role.

### Charitable Works

The crucial role of the bishop as a patron of the poor and needy and of widows and orphans can hardly be overestimated and has been the subject of important studies.[53] While the civic benefactors, the *euergetai,* of the classical world had been generous in their public donations and basked in the admiration for their good deeds that was often advertised in honorific inscriptions, the recipients of such munificence were primarily their peers. The bishop's largesse, by contrast, was destined for those who were off the radar of the "haves." The recipients of the charity of the church were the "have-nots," who did not even enjoy the same legal rights as the wealthy.

The Christian obligation to look after those community members who were in need, especially widows and orphans, has its roots in the Jewish tradition. But while the Jewish communities looked after their own, Christian teaching made it a religious duty to extend charity to all, even if they were not of the same religion. Care for those in need, the poor and the sick, had always been a major concern of the Christian communities, which distinguished them from their pagan surroundings and brought them many converts. The emperor Julian (361–363) recognized the powerful attraction of Christian charity in gaining converts. In his effort to revitalize Greco-Roman religion, he made resources available to pagan priests to do the same.

---

52. Avramea, 834.

53. E. Patlagean, *Pauvreté économique et pauvreté sociale à Byzance, 4ᵉ-7ᵉ siècles* (Paris, 1977); P. L. R. Brown, *Poverty and Leadership in the Later Roman Empire* (Hanover, N.H., 2002).

✓    The bishop's role as caretaker of the needy reaches back to the times before the development of the monepiscopate. It was such an integral part of his duties that there was hardly any reason to draw attention to it in the normative texts on the priesthood, the church canons, or imperial law. The *Didascalia* of the first half of the third century takes it for granted that the bishop provides for the upkeep, specifically food and firewood, of widows and also of orphans. The bishop is also charged with paying for the ransom of slaves, captives, and prisoners, as well as for those who have been sentenced to exile or to forced labor in the mines or in the gladiatorial games.[54] A bishop's administration of charity became a measure of his proper discharge of office. One of the most frequent, and most effective, criticisms that could be launched against an episcopal adversary was his misguided use for selfish or frivolous purposes of time, energy, and money that was earmarked for charity. The bishop who failed in his charitable works was a failure as a bishop.

Charity was also practiced by individuals, on a different scale, but with the same motivations. Not only had God commanded the care of the needy, but almsgiving was also considered one of the penitential practices, along with prayer and fasting, that could alleviate one's sins. The proper Christian attitude to worldly riches is illustrated in a charming story told by Palladius in his *Lausiac History*. A consecrated virgin in Alexandria, who also happened to be an heiress, had retained her haughty attitude and remained tightfisted with her possessions, wanting to pass them on to her adopted daughter. The priest Macarius, who was the head of the poorhouse for lepers, decided to teach her a lesson. He had been a stonecutter earlier in his life and thus approached her with the tempting offer to purchase some very precious stones, emeralds and aquamarines, which—he said—had come into his possession. Eager to seize this opportunity, the woman gave him 500 *nomismata*—a handsome amount of money. After a while, she demanded to see the jewels. Macarius then took her to his hospice and showed her the aquamarines (the women's quarters on the upper floor) and the emeralds (the men's quarters on the lower floor) that were her investment. It took the duped lady some time to acknowledge the spiritual benefit of Macarius's trickery.[55]

Holy men and ascetics, too, engaged in charitable deeds, with whatever means were available to them. The Galatian ascetic Philoromos, for example, lived a life of great austerity. He earned his upkeep as a scribe and then gave the surplus from his labors—250 *solidi* in total—to the poor.[56] An ascetic in fourth-century Egypt managed to give alms from his meagre daily income of two bronze coins *(keratia)*, after taking whatever he needed for his

54. Connolly, *Didascalia Apostolorum*, chap. 18, pp. 156–60.
55. Palladius, *HL* 6.1–9.
56. Palladius, *HL* 45.3.

own sparse nourishment.[57] Of course, the greater the extent of an ascetic's voluntary poverty, the less he had to give. But for the truly determined and resourceful ascetics, there was always the solution of selling themselves into slavery and giving the money from the sale to the poor, as did Serapion, who sold himself to a theatrical troupe.[58]

Yet there remains a distinction between private charitable deeds at the discretion of the individual and the regularized ministry to the needy required by the institutional church. While the former's actions were more or less spontaneous and on an ad hoc basis, the latter operated with a larger budget and could rely on an organizational machinery for the collection and distribution of funds on a regular basis.[59] The annual budget for the operation of the episcopal household of Theodore of Sykeon amounted to 365 *nomismata*, of which he used only 40 and gave the rest as alms.[60]

The importance of Christian charity in carving out a niche for the church within the social order of each city should not be underestimated. As a protector of the poor and disenfranchised, the bishop became the advocate of a large segment of the population.[61] The financial means and administrative expertise he had at his disposal enabled him to pursue charitable projects on a large enough scale to serve the whole city. In Caesarea in Cappadocia, a complex was built that included hospital facilities, an inn for travelers that was lavish enough to provide hospitality to the governor and his staff, and perhaps a poorhouse, in addition to residences for the church's staff.[62] It owed its existence to the initiative of Basil, who was then still a priest but soon became bishop of the city, which was called after him "Basileias" or else "new city."[63]

The important role of the bishop as administrator of ecclesiastical charity finds little reflection in imperial and canon law. Justinian placed bishops and their *oikonomoi* in charge of the administration of testaments that had been made for the benefit of captives and of the poor.[64] He later reiterated the role of the bishop in seeing such testamentary provisions carried out.

---

57. *Sayings of the Desert Fathers*, Pambo 2.
58. Palladius, *HL* 37.2.
59. A. H. M. Jones, "Church Finances in the Fifth and Sixth Centuries," *JThS* 11 (1960): 84–94.
60. *Life of Theodore of Sykeon* 78.
61. See P. L. R. Brown, *Power and Persuasion in Late Antiquity: Towards a Christian Empire* (Madison, 1992), chap. 3, "Poverty and Power," and now his *Poverty and Leadership*, passim.
62. Basil of Caesarea, *Ep.* 94.
63. See P. Rousseau, *Basil of Caesarea* (Berkeley and Los Angeles, 1994), 139–43, who suggests that the Basileias was built soon after the severe famine of 369; and B. E. Daley, S. J., "Building a New City: The Cappadocian Fathers and the Rhetoric of Philanthropy," *JECS* 7 (1999): 431–61.
64. CJ 1.3.55.

This time, it was assumed that the funds were intended for the construction of churches, hospices, or hospitals. The building activity was to be overseen by the bishop together with the civil magistrate, while it fell to the bishop alone to make sure that the donor's stipulations regarding the appointment of officers at the newly founded institution were carried out.[65] Church canons on the issue are equally obscure: the Council of Tours in 567 reinforced the bishops' role as advocates for the poor, threatening with excommunication those judges and powerful men who did not heed the bishops' warnings.[66] Fourteen years later, the Council of Lyon held the bishops responsible for providing food and clothing for the lepers in their cities so that they did not have to beg outside.[67]

### Care of Prisoners

One important aspect of Christian charity that became the responsibility of bishops was care for prisoners and captives. Christian communities had always given support to their imprisoned members awaiting execution and martyrdom, visiting them, providing them with food and other necessities, often bribing the prison guards to ameliorate their living conditions. Christian visitors to prisoners were so numerous and noticeable even in the early decades of the fourth century that one of Licinius's anti-Christian measures consisted of threatening them, too, with imprisonment.[68] But even the pagan emperor Julian urged that philanthropy be extended toward those in prison.[69]

It is perhaps because of this association with martyrdom that care for prisoners continued to be one of the main charitable activities after the peace of the church.[70] The Egyptian monasteries regularly contributed some of the surplus from their economic enterprises to help those in prison,[71] and many pious individuals put their inheritance to the same use or lent practi-

---

65. Nov. Just. 131.10.

66. Tours (567), can. 26, H-L III/1, p. 192.

67. Lyon (581), can. 6, H-L, p. 207.

68. Eusebius, *HE* 10.8.11.

69. Julian the Apostate, *Postquam Anciochiam advenit* 291, ed. J. Bidez, *L'empereur Julien: Oeuvres completes*, vol. 1/2 (Paris, 1924).

70. J.-U. Krause, *Gefängnisse im römischen Reich* (Stuttgart, 1996), 316–44, with extensive examples of Christian charity toward prisoners and captives; P. Koukoulès and R. Guilland, "Études sur la vie privée des Byzantins, I: Voleurs et prisons à Byzance," *REG* 61 (1948): 118–36.

71. John Cassian, *Institutes* 10.22: monks in Egypt distribute surplus food to prisoners; id., *Conferences* 18.7: true cenobites give of the surplus of their labor to prisons, hospitals, or the poor; Palladius, *HL* 32.9: one of the Pachomian monasteries gives the surplus from its labor to the women's monasteries and to prisons.

cal assistance.[72] Christian interest in prisoners took two forms, intercession on behalf of those who were suffering incarceration without just cause, and provisioning of prisoners with creature comforts. In the *Life of Pachomius,* Christians rushed to the local prison to bring food to the conscripts of Constantine's army—an act of charity that so impressed Pachomius that he sought conversion—and it seems that this was not the first time that they had done so.[73] Lasting and tangible support for prisoners was provided in a unique way by Bishop Paul of Gerasa. He constructed a prison especially for those awaiting trial so that they could remain separated from convicted criminals. His benefaction was recorded in an inscription, dated to November 539.[74] This was as much an act of Christian charity by a bishop as it was a gesture of public benefaction through building activity by a prominent citizen.

The clergy's care for prisoners is not reflected in imperial law until the early fifth century, when an obliquely phrased law indicates that the Christian clergy had taken it upon itself to provide food for people in prison and made it possible for the prisoners to go to the baths once a week. The bishops in particular were placed in charge of these ministrations.[75] The intent of this law was to instruct the civil judges that they had to allow the Christian clergy to look after prisoners. The legislator was not concerned with prescribing the scope and direction of Christian charitable activity, but rather with the creation of conditions in which it could be dispensed freely. Ten years later, priests or bishops *(sacerdotes)* were not only allowed to enter prisons and administer charity, but they were also encouraged to talk to prisoners so that they could make appeals in the case of those who were unjustly imprisoned.[76] With this law, care for the prisoner's physical condition became less of a concern than the bishops' intervention on behalf of those who had suffered an injustice. In the same spirit, a law of Justinian of 529 demanded that bishops visit the prisoners once a week, on a Wednesday or Friday, to find out the reasons for their incarceration and to report any "carelessness" to the authorities.[77] This law required bishops to act as a corrective and counterbalance to the civil authorities, a role that had previously been played by prominent citizens—Libanius is an example[78]—and into which the episcopate was being increasingly drawn under Justinian.

72. Palladius, *HL* 14.3: Paesius gives away his inheritance to ascetic establishments, churches, and prisons; *HL* 54.2: Melania supports churches, monasteries, the care of strangers, and prisons; *HL* 68.2: a monk lends concrete assistance to prisons and hospitals.
73. *Bohairic Life of Pachomius* 7.
74. P.-L. Gatier, "Nouvelles inscriptions de Gerasa," *Syria* 62 (1985): 297–307.
75. CTh 9.3.7 (409).
76. Sirm. 13 (419).
77. CJ 1.4.22 (529).
78. Libanius, *Autobiography* 232.

The literary sources confirm that bishops sometimes intervened with the authorities on behalf of those who were imprisoned without reason. Possidius devotes a whole chapter of the *Life of Augustine* to this intercession on behalf of the accused.[79] But bishops were not the only ones, and perhaps not the first ones, to do so. The first Christian to intercede at court on behalf of the imprisoned was the ascetic Eutychianus, shortly after 325. His visit to the local prison had miraculously caused all the fetters to break. He then went through the more conventional channel to obtain the release of an unjustly imprisoned man by traveling to Constantinople to petition the emperor.[80] A century later, the initiative of the monastic founder Euthymius led to the intervention of the bishop of Bostra for the release of the Saracen leader Terebos, who had fallen victim to a plot.[81] Intercession for the unjustly accused was almost regarded as a civic duty, especially if the men in question were of a social status that could not bear such insult to their personal liberty, to say nothing of the prospect of corporal punishment or judicial torture. It was in this spirit that Libanius called upon his fellow citizens to alleviate the condition of those who had been imprisoned on trumped-up charges.[82]

## Care of Captives

The episcopal duty to ransom captives concerned those who had fallen into misfortune at the hands of bandits, foreign raiding parties, or dealers in slaves and prostitutes. Unlike care for prisoners, it necessitated the raising of large amounts of money in a short period of time. How the collective responsibility for captured fellow-citizens was organized in the ancient world is described in lively detail by an inscription of the third century B.C. from the Ionian island of Teos, a significant number of whose inhabitants had fallen into the hands of pirates. The inscription announced how the required amount for the ransom was to be raised. Within the next twenty-three days, all citizens had to declare under oath the total value of their property in cash, precious metal, and clothes. Ten percent of this sum was then levied for the common fund for the purchase of the captives, although several benefactors had already given larger amounts.[83] Like these especially generous benefactors of Teos, wealthy individuals often took responsibility

---

79. Possidius, *Life of Augustine* 20.
80. Socrates, *HE* 1.13.4–10.
81. Cyril of Scythopolis, *Life of Euthymius* 34.
82. Libanius, *Or.* 45.34.
83. S. Sahin, "Piratenüberfall auf Teos: Volksbeschluss über die Finanzierung der Erpressungsgelder," *Epigraphica Anatolica* 23 (1994): 1–36.

for the ransoming of captives as an act of patronage for their family, friends, and associates.[84]

The use of funds from the church's community chest for the redemption of Christian captives, prisoners, or slaves was strongly recommended already in the first half of the third century in the *Didascalia*,[85] and repeated in the *Apostolic Constitutions* of the late fourth century.[86] The earliest detailed Christian endorsement of the redemption of captives as a particular virtue and obligation comes from a letter from Cyprian of Carthage to eight Numidian bishops, composed some time in the 250s. Cyprian gave several reasons: the need for the church to look after their own, as members of the one body of Christ; the recognition of all human beings, including and especially captives, as a temple of God; the imitation of Christ, who redeemed the world through his sacrificial death, by redeeming captives through a monetary sacrifice. Along with the letter, Cyprian sent 100,000 sesterces that he had been able to raise—a significant sum, sufficient to nourish twelve thousand people for a whole month. He also appended the names of the donors so that they could receive their reward through being remembered in the prayers of the beneficiaries.[87]

The earliest law on the ransoming of captives in the Theodosian Code dates from 343 and concerns not men, but women, who had fallen prey not to enemy activity, but to unscrupulous avarice at home. The law makes provisions that consecrated Christian women—namely, women belonging either to the order of virgins or to that of widows—who had been sold into prostitution be bought back. The law protected these women from further indignities by specifying that only members of the clergy or prominent Christians were to transact this "purchase."[88] It is significant that, rather than demanding that such a buyback occur, the law simply takes it for granted that individual Christians or the institutional church would want to engage in such an activity. In a law of 408, the provision of food and clothing and the redemption of captives are considered the task of the Christians and the *curiales* of the nearest municipality. The former in particular are expected to perform this duty motivated by their Christian beliefs: "It is Our will that Christians, who ought to be desirous of the redemption of such persons, shall be solicitous for the captives."[89] This is one of the many instances where the law lags significantly behind established Christian practice—in this case by well over a century.

84. Cicero, *De officiis* 2.16.55; Dionysius of Halicarnassus, *Roman Antiquities* 2.10.2.
85. *Didascalia apostolorum* 4.9.2.
86. *Apostolic Constitutions* 4.9.2.
87. Cyprian, *Ep.* 62, with commentary by Clarke, 3: 285.
88. CTh 15.8.1 (343).
89. CTh 5.7.2 (408), an abbreviated version of Sirm. 16 (408); repeated CJ 8.50.20.

Charitable motivations must have informed the practice of bequeathing a specified sum of money for the ransoming of captives. A law from the reign of Leo I demanded that if such a pious bequest has been made without naming a testator, the bishop of the birthplace of the bequeather was in charge of executing this will.[90] Justinian actively encouraged the church to engage in the ransoming of captives. He declared that all liturgical furnishings of a church, such as the silver vessels and chandeliers, or the embroidered and silken vestments, are inalienable and may be sold only by the bishop or his *skeuophylax* for the purpose of redeeming prisoners, "as it is praiseworthy for the souls of men to be preferred to any vessels or vestments whatsoever."[91] Justinian also allowed the church to pursue hitherto unclaimed bequests reaching back as far as a hundred years, especially if they were earmarked for the ransoming of captives.[92]

The customary responsibility of bishops for the ransoming of captives is reflected in canon law at a relatively late date, and only in the West. The Council of Orléans in 511 mentions the ransoming of captives along with care for the poor, upkeep of the clergy, and maintenance of churches as one of the legitimate expenditures for which the donations of the king to the church may be used.[93]

The safety and personal liberty of men and women were threatened not only by foreign military raids, but also by the activities of bands of brigands. The imperial government seems to have recognized the bishops' self-assumed role in combating the devastating effects of brigandage. According to an inscription from Asia Minor, the bishop received and authenticated a special imperial emissary who had been sent out to suppress local brigands.[94] It is conceivable that the appointment of this special agent was the result of an episcopal petition, which would explain why this officer was placed under the bishop's authority.

If the stories recorded in hagiographical and historical writing of the time are any indication, then the redemption of captives from brigands and enemies must have been one of the main activities of the bishops at a time when economic and social instability afflicted the empire from within and warfare threatened it from without. Ambrose in his *De officiis ministrorum* talks about it as one of the tasks of the clergy for which the melting down of church vessels is permitted.[95] At the beginning of his episcopate, Ambrose's

---

90. CJ 1.3.28 (468); cf. Nov. Just. 131.11.
91. CJ 1.2.21 (529).
92. CJ 1.2.23 (530).
93. Orléans (511), can. 5, H-L II/2, p. 1010. Mâcon (585), can. 5, H-L III/1, p. 209.
94. D. Feissel and I. Kaygusuz, "Un mandement impérial du VI$^e$ siècle dans une inscription d'Hadrianoupolis d'Honoriade," *TM* 9 (1985): 397–419.
95. Ambrose, *On the Duties of the Clergy* 2.15, 28, 70, and 142.

hagiographer reports, his care for captives and especially the poor was such that he gave all the gold and silver that he could have kept to the church and to the poor.[96] According to Ambrose's own report in his *De officiis*, the Arians in Milan made this act of charity a target of their criticism:

> So I once brought odium on myself because I broke up the sacred vessels to redeem captives—a fact that could displease the Arians. Not that it displeased them as an act, but as being a thing in which they could take hold of something for which to blame me. Who can be so hard, cruel, iron-hearted, as to be displeased because a man is redeemed from death, or a woman from barbarian impurities, things that are worse than death, or boys and girls and infants from the pollution of idols, whereby through fear of death they were defiled?[97]

Bands of brigands also terrorized North Africa at the time of Augustine. In a letter to his friend and co-bishop Alypius, he complained bitterly about the sad fate of those who were seized in raids or sold by their relatives into captivity, and expressed his despondency over the fact that the well-intentioned and persistent efforts of the church at Hippo and the individual members of his community who scraped together the ransom monies were not sufficient to eradicate this problem.[98] Just like Ambrose, Augustine, too, is commended by his hagiographer Possidius for melting down the church silver to provide assistance to captives and the poor.[99] In 455, a stream of captives arrived in Carthage after the sack of Rome by the Vandals. Bishop Deogratias melted down church vessels to pay for their ransom, then set up emergency shelter in two churches, and provided them with food.[100] Bishops along the Eastern frontier did the same. Some, like Acacius of Amida, even intervened on behalf of non-Christian captives. He used the church treasure to ransom from the Roman authorities the Persian captives who were in his city and returned them to the Persian king.[101] The Persians were so familiar with the role that bishops played in these transactions that on another occasion King Chosroes I was willing to accommodate Candidus, the bishop of Sergioupolis. He offered the bishop the captive prisoners of Sura at a high price but then agreed to a delayed payment.[102]

By his involvement in the ransoming of captives, the bishop was not assuming new responsibilities and claiming greater political prominence

---

96. Paulinus, *Life of Ambrose* 38.
97. Ambrose, *On the Duties of the Clergy* 2.28.136.
98. Augustine, *Ep.* 10*.
99. *Life of Augustine* 24.
100. Victor of Vita, *History of the Vandal Persecution* 1.25–26.
101. Socrates, *HE* 7.21.1–4.
102. Procopius, *Wars* 2.5.29–33.

but merely acted as a leader of his community, a shepherd of his flock, and patron of the faithful. Of course, in the hands of a politically astute bishop such as Caesarius of Arles (d. 542), such activity could become a means to assert territorial authority over neigboring regions, an opportunity to forge close links with rulers, and a vehicle to rally the community around himself in a massive financial undertaking.[103] But others, like John Chrysostom, who redeemed captives from Isaurian robbers while he was himself in exile after his deposition from the see of Constantinople, did not stand to gain anything but the divine reward for a good deed.[104]

### Food Provisioning

Another outlet for the bishop's charitable activities was his assistance in times of food shortage. None of the normative sources, neither church canons nor imperial laws, make any reference to direct episcopal involvement in the purchase or distribution of grain. Yet there is ample anecdotal evidence in the written sources that bishops actively engaged in the provisioning of their cities in times of shortage and famine. This aspect of episcopal activity should therefore be regarded simply as an ad hoc measure that bishops took upon themselves as the need arose. In fact, not only bishops but also prominent citizens and holy men intervened during food shortages, according to the means available to them.

In times of dire need, bishops even turned the precious fittings of their churches into coin to feed the hungry. This proved to be the undoing of Cyril of Jerusalem. When the poor appealed to him to help them in their need, he responded by selling the altar ornaments and other church decorations in order to purchase grain. One of the pieces that were sold had been given to the church as a pious donation. When the donor later recognized it as part of the outfit of an actress, he reported this to Acacius, the Arian contender to the episcopal see, who seized this opportunity to slander Cyril and bring about his deposition.[105]

One prominent citizen who helped his native city of Antioch on more than one occasion during a food shortage was the pagan rhetor Libanius. His interventions, however, were not of a material kind, but verbal. His prominent position as a rhetor allowed him to plead with the individuals who had the capability to restore the food supply.[106] The same strategy was

---

103. W. Klingshirn, "Caesarius of Arles and the Ransoming of Captives in Sub-Roman Gaul," *JRS* 75 (1985): 183–203.
104. Sozomen, *HE* 8.27.8.
105. Ibid., 4.25.3–4.
106. Libanius, *Autobiography* (Or. 1)126 (spokesman of the city council during a famine); 205–10 (intervention with civil authorities); 225–27 (stops a strike by the bakers).

used by the holy man Severinus of Noricum in the early fourth century, in a small town on the Danube River. Because of his gift of clairvoyance, he was able to rebuke a wealthy woman for hoarding grain during a famine, presumably to speculate for a higher price. Severinus's intervention alleviated a serious shortage just in the nick of time.[107] During the early Roman Empire, donations of grain by private individuals, as an act of public benefaction, are attested in Gaul, Spain, and North Africa. Such donations continued, enforced by Christian charitable motivations, in the late Roman Empire, for example, in Noricum in 453.[108]

Distinct from such crisis intervention on private initiative was the office of *sitōnēs* or *curator frumenti comparandi* (or *frumentarius*), which is attested in the late Roman Empire into the sixth century, especially in Asia Minor, Italy, and Sicily. This magistracy was usually held for one year, with a possibility for renewal. Since the *sitōnēs* was personally responsible with his own property for the grain provisioning of his city, only the wealthy landowners were eligible for this office. Beginning with the reign of Anastasius, the nominating committee for the *sitōnēs* consisted of the bishop along with the most prominent landowners of the city. In the event that the *sitōnēs* was unable to absorb himself any losses arising from his duty, the nominating committee had to step in and cover for him.[109] Unfortunately, the sources for this office are so patchy that scholars are not in agreeement on the question of whether the *sitōnia* was an annual office for the regularization of the grain supply,[110] or whether a *sitōnēs* was appointed only as an emergency measure in a time of famine.[111] Bishops were equally required to become involved in the regular grain provisioning outside the cities. A fragmentary law that probably dates from the beginning of the sixth century holds the bishops responsible for ensuring that the grain provisioning in the countryside is carried out by *officiales (taxeōtai)*.[112]

Monks or abbots of monasteries often became involved in the distribution of grain, among other charitable services.[113] If they were able to provide food, this was because they had amassed grain in storage or money in the

---

107. Eugippius, *Life of Severinus of Noricum* 3.2.
108. Cf. A. J. B. Sirks, P. J. Sijpesteijn, and K. A. Worp, *Ein frühbyzantinisches Szenario für die Amtswechslung der Sitonie*, Münchener Beiträge zur Papyrusforschung und antiken Rechtsgeschichte 86 (Munich, 1996), 99.
109. CJ 10.27.3. Cf. Nov. Just. 128.16 (545). Cf. Sirks, Sijpesteijn, and Worp, 102.
110. Detailed discussion by Sirks, Sijpesteijn, and Worp, 118–27.
111. H. Pavis d'Escurac, "À propos de l'approvisionement en blé des cités de l'Orient romain," in *Sociétés urbaines, sociétés rurales dans l'Asie Mineure et la Syrie hellénistiques et romaines*, ed. E. Frézouls, 117–30 (Strasburg, 1987).
112. CJ 10.27.4; cf. Sirks, Sijpesteijn, Worp, 100.
113. For Syria, see C. Villagomez, "The Fields, Flocks, and Finances of Monks: Economic Life at Nestorian Monasteries, 500–850" (PhD diss., UCLA, 1998).

chest as the result of the labor of the monks. Their help was thus of the same economic nature as that of the bishop.

Distinct from that is the assistance provided by holy men, as the example of Ephrem shows. During a severe famine in Edessa in 373, the rich men of the city were so distrustful of each other that they refused to donate money to any one party for organizing the relief of those who were starving. It took the intervention of an outsider to alleviate the situation. Ephrem, a deacon who had until then lived in ascetic seclusion, left his monastic cell and collected funds from the rich men of the city to set up an emergency ward for those who were dying of starvation and those who could be nourished back to health. After a year had gone by and he had fulfilled his mission, he returned to his cell, where he died the following month.[114] He would later become famous for his innovative religious poetry in the Syriac language. Ephrem may not have had direct access to finances, but he had the ascetic authority that commanded the respect of everyone and thus was able to rally the whole population of Edessa to the common cause of offering assistance to the hungry.

Mostly, it was the prayer of holy men that helped to alleviate famines. Since most ascetics lived on their own in the countryside, they were the first recourse for the rural population in need. There is hardly a hagiographical account of a rural saint that does not include at least one story of the holy man's prayers that restored the bounty of the earth. Holy men made rain or sunshine, ended infestations of vermin, locusts, and other harmful critters, and miraculously multiplied the food supply. In the final analysis, the prayers of holy men were much more effective than the organized relief efforts of bishops, for the intervention of holy men tackled the cause of the problem (namely, the climatic conditions), rather than merely alleviating its symptoms. In this spirit, Pachomius prayed not only for an end to the ongoing famine, but also for a timely swelling of the Nile to ensure a bountiful crop at the next harvest, and Banes prayed for an abundance of barley for the whole world.[115]

114. Palladius, *HL* 40. Cf. J. B. Segal, *Edessa, "The Blessed City"* (Oxford, 1970), 148.
115. Coptic apophthegma, translated in *Les sentences des pères du désert: Nouveau recueil,* 2d ed. (Solesmes, 1977), chap. 249, p. 281.

# CHAPTER EIGHT

# Empire

The first Roman emperor to put the accommodation and integration of Christians on his political agenda was Constantine. More than any other aspect of his reign, Constantine's religious policy has fueled the popular imagination and attracted the attention of scholars. Harold Drake's study firmly places Constantine's interaction with Christianity, in the form of his dealings with Christian bishops, in its historical context. Rather than following previous scholarship, which portrayed Constantine either as the pious ruler motivated by genuine conviction or the power-hungry exploiter of religious sentiment for his own political agenda, Drake depicts him as an "artful negotiator, patient consensus builder and ardent judicial reformer."[1] Conventional historical storytelling, in our classrooms and elsewhere, takes as a pivotal moment Constantine's vision of the cross, which promised him victory in a battle against all odds. The defeat of his competitor Maxentius at the Milvian Bridge outside of Rome in 312 made Constantine sole ruler over the West. In the following year, the so-called Edict of Milan declared an end to the Great Persecution of Christians, which Diocletian had begun in 303, ordered that restitution be made for property damage to churches and individual Christians, and granted official recognition to Christianity as a *religio licita*. In the twenty-five years until his death in 337, Constantine's involvement with Christianity remained strong, although the political purpose and religious motivation of his policies are still a matter of debate. He became involved in the settlement of doctrinal disputes and convened the First Ecumenical Council at Nicaea in 325. He and his family sponsored the construction of

---

1. H. A. Drake, *Constantine and the Bishops: The Politics of Intolerance* (Baltimore and London, 2000), 357.

churches in the old capital of Rome, in his newly founded capital of Constantinople, and in the Holy Land. And he cultivated personal connections to prominent Christians whom he attracted to his court. Constantine's sons and successors continued his legacy of supporting Christianity, with a brief interlude under Julian the Apostate (361–363), whose attempt to revitalize the traditional Greco-Roman religion was cut short by his premature death on a military campaign against Persia. With the court setting such an example, the Christianization of the Roman Empire, which already had snowballed since the second century, now proceeded at an accelerated pace, although scholars still disagree on its exact extent.[2]

## CONSTANTINE'S LEGACY

Constantine's actions on behalf of the clergy, and specifically the episcopate, have been subjected to much scrutiny, since they establish the parameters and set the precedent for all subsequent interaction of Christian emperors with the church. Did Constantine further elevate the bishops by granting them titles and privileges? Or did he simply give his stamp of approval to the status quo? Were his measures an attempt to absorb the episcopate into the imperial administrative apparatus, turning bishops into bureaucrats in the imperial service and raising their social status? Or did he recognize the independence of the administrative structure of the church, while ensuring that the bishops' work benefited the empire as a whole? Were bishops ambitious activists who seized the opportunities to gain greater power offered to them through the new system of imperial patronage? Or were they innocent dupes who were dragged into the political limelight by the clever politics of Constantine and his successors? Answers to these questions hinge largely on the interpretation of the legislation of Constantine and his fourth-century successors on bishops.

The arguments that have been brought forward in favor of Constantine's privileging the clergy with quasi-noble status are based on extracts from literary sources and on his legislation. They can be discounted easily by exploring a wider range of texts, and by setting the evidence in the larger context of the imperial treatment of the *collegia*,[3] and of representatives of other religions, particularly Judaism.

First, there is the titulature of bishops. Constantine on occasion addressed bishops with the adjectives *illustris* or *gloriosissimus*. This has been taken as evidence that he integrated the bishops into the hierarchical

---

2. See the reactions to R. Stark, *The Rise of Christianity: A Sociologist Reconsiders History* (Princeton, 1996) in *JECS* 6 (1998).

3. The most detailed study of the *collegia* in late antiquity is L. C. Ruggini, "Le associazioni professionali nel mondo romano-bizantino," *Settimane di Studi sull'Alto Medioevo* 18 (Spoleto, 1971).

stratification of the empire by treating them as *viri illustres*. Since this rank was the exclusive reserve of senators, this would have amounted to a de facto promotion of the vast majority of bishops, who came from curial and lesser backgrounds. Theodor Klauser was the main proponent of this thesis and coined the term *Nobilitierung* (ennobling) to describe this treatment of bishops.[4] A reevaluation of Klauser's evidence by Evangelos Chrysos casts serious doubt on the validity of this theory.[5] It was further deflated by Ernst Jerg's extensive study of the adjectives, epithets, and titles with which bishops are referred to in the written sources of late antiquity.[6] Jerg demonstrated in detail, as Santo Mazzarino had observed before him, that *gloriosissimus* was a frequent honorific designation acknowledging the bishops' spiritual and religious status in the same manner in which it was traditionally applied to martyrs and holy men.[7]

Next, is the permission to travel by imperial post, the *cursus publicus,* a privilege usually enjoyed only by imperial officials.[8] Constantine included this offer of free and fast transportation in his invitation to the bishops to gather at one specific event, the Council of Nicaea.[9] The impetus of Constantine's generous gesture was the speed of travel rather than the permanent granting of a privilege and the concomitant rise in social status. Two years later, it was the certified, but not entirely disgraced, heretic Arius who was urged by Constantine to visit him by this means of conveyance.[10] Constantius continued his father's custom. The frequency of synods during his reign generated such a heavy volume of episcopal travel, Ammianus Marcellinus remarks with some irony, that "by his attempts to impose conformity [in doctrinal matters] Constantius only succeeded in hamstringing the postal service."[11] It was not until 382 that this privilege was expressed in

---

4. T. Klauser, *Der Ursprung der bischöflichen Insignien und Ehrenrechte,* Bonner Akademische Reden 1 (Krefeld, 1949; 2d ed., 1953).

5. E. K. Chrysos, "Die angebliche 'Nobilitierung' des Klerus durch Kaiser Konstantin den Grossen," *Historia* 18 (1969): 119–29.

6. E. Jerg, *Vir venerabilis: Untersuchungen zur Titulatur der Bischöfe in den ausserkirchlichen Texten der Spätantike als Beitrag zur Deutung ihrer öffentlichen Stellung,* Wiener Beiträge zur Theologie 26 (Vienna, 1970); S. Mazzarino, "Costantino e l'episcopato," *Iura* 7 (1956): 345–52, repr. in his *Antico, tardoantico ed èra costantiniana,* vol. 1 (n.p., 1974).

7. Klauser further supported his thesis with reference to the ceremonial appearance of bishops, in particular their dress, shoes, staff, and throne, which he found paralleled in imperial court ceremonial. A critical and more sophisticated view was proposed by H. U. Instinsky, *Bischofsstuhl und Kaiserthron* (Munich, 1955).

8. Imperial ambassadors enjoyed this privilege: CTh 8.5.32 and 12.12.6.9.

9. Eusebius, *VC* 3.6, p. 79, ll. 28–30.

10. Socrates, *HE* 1.25.8. This privilege could also be claimed by influential men on behalf of their friends: Libanius had hoped to profit from just such an arrangement in order to travel to Athens: *Autobiography* (*Or.* 1) 14.

11. Ammianus Marcellinus, *Histories* 21.16.18. Cf. Theodoret of Cyrrhus, *HE* 2.16.17.

legal form, when the provincial governors were ordered to allow bishops to travel by imperial post to diocesan or provincial synods.[12] This was a tangible sign of imperial support for episcopal activities but did not indicate the integration of bishops into the imperial bureaucracy.

A third point are the exemptions for clergy of curial rank from the obligatory public duties *(munera)*.[13] This was a traditional privilege of pagan priests, and Constantine himself extended it to the religious leaders of the Jews.[14] The intention of such legislation was to free the priesthood from other obligations so that they could concentrate on their religious duties. In the spirit of equality, this privilege was also granted to Christians.

Finally, there was the right of the Christian clergy to be tried in internal matters before an ecclesiastical, rather than a civil, court. This measure, like the preceding one, merely placed the Christian church on the same level as the *collegia*, the pagan cult associations, and the Jews,[15] who also were allowed to take recourse to internal jurisdiction in matters that concerned violations of their own code of conduct or disputes between members.

It is important to note that Constantine's laws on internal jurisdiction and on the exemption from *munera* are addressed to *clerici* or to *sacerdotes*. In the absence of clear hierarchical distinctions in the legal language that continued well into the fifth century, it is not clear whether these laws singled out the bishops, or whether they were addressed to bishops, priests, and deacons alike. Their relevance in establishing the specific status of bishops must therefore remain doubtful.

Two further legislative initiatives of Constantine, addressed specifically to bishops, deserve to be treated in greater detail: the notarization of the manumission of slaves, and episcopal jurisdiction. They will be treated in sequence, with the addition of a third set of laws on ecclesiastical asylum, the earliest of which dates from 392. Two related questions will guide our analysis of these legal initiatives.[16] First, did the legislators create a novel situation,

---

12. CTh 12.12.9.

13. First mentioned in a letter to Anulinus, the proconsul of Africa, in 313: Eusebius, *HE* 10.7.2; and in the same year in CTh 16.2.1 and 16.2.2. See also C. Dupont, "Les privilèges des clercs sous Constantin," *RHE* 62 (1967): 729–52; T. G. Elliott, "The Tax Exemptions Granted to Clerics by Constantine and Constantius II," *Phoenix* 32 (1978): 326–36.

14. CTh 16.8.2 and 16.8.4 (both of 330). Cf. H.-J. Horstkotte, "Heidnische Priesterämter und Dekurionat im vierten Jahrhundert n. Chr.," in *Religion und Gesellschaft: Kolloquium zu Ehren von Friedrich Vittinghoff*, ed. W. Eck (Cologne and Vienna, 1989); A. Linder, *The Jews in Roman Imperial Legislation* (Detroit and Jerusalem, 1987), 72–73, and 132–38.

15. Linder, 71.

16. E. D. Hunt, "Christianizing the Roman Empire: The Evidence of the Code," in *The Theodosian Code: Studies in the Imperial Law of Late Antiquity*, ed. J. Harries and I. Wood (London, 1993), gives a succinct and levelheaded assessment of the legislation, concluding that "the laws . . . led the regiment of Christianizers from the rear" (158).

or did they simply confirm, and perhaps amplify, existing ecclesiastical practice? And second, were these measures intended to signal an integration of the bishops into the administrative machinery of the empire through endowing them with a specific portfolio of tasks?

In search of an answer to the latter, it is helpful to return to the interpretive categories developed in the earlier chapters. The bishops' exercise of the tasks required by their ministry—in other words, their pragmatic authority—did not occur by imperial dispensation. On the contrary, it will be shown that even those episcopal tasks that are regulated by imperial law—notarizing manumission, sitting in judgment, providing asylum— have their origin in the pastoral care and spiritual leadership inherent in the ideal of the episcopate. In many instances, as will be seen, holy men who embodied ascetic authority, but without the external veneer of representing an institution, performed exactly the same functions for the benefit of others as bishops did.

The following pages pose a methodological difficulty that cannot be resolved but must at least be acknowledged. Throughout this work, my preference is to proceed by induction. This does justice to the specificity of historical circumstance and allows for a fresh look at what individual bishops do, rather than postulating an artificial uniformity among the episcopate as a body of people. It also avoids an overly schematic treatment of the episcopal ministry, as if it were a set of well-defined tasks and competencies. My aim is to show that, with the important exception of the performance of ecclesiastical ritual, all the activities that bishops were expected to perform on behalf of others could also be performed by holy men—in other words, that these activities were firmly anchored in the religious nature of the episcopal position, rather than prescribed in a portfolio of episcopal duties. Too much attention to specificity, however, easily degenerates into endless strings of anecdotes. For the sake of clarity and succinctness, it has therefore been necessary to distill the evidence into broader statements, and to use anecdotes from literary sources, including hagiography, only for illustrative purposes.

### THE MANUMISSION OF SLAVES (MANUMISSIO IN ECCLESIA)

Only four years after he became emperor of the West, Constantine prescribed into law the bishop's ability to notarize the manumission of slaves. This law of 316 is not preserved in the Theodosian Code, but only in that of Justinian.[17] The intention of the lawgiver was not to prescribe a new custom or to add a new prerogative to the episcopal office, but simply to confirm the

---

17. CJ 1.13.1.

legal validity of a well-established existing custom: "*It has already been decided that masters can confer freedom upon their slaves in the Catholic Church*" (emphasis mine). Constantine repeated this episcopal prerogative again in 321—the earliest law on this issue contained in the Codex Theodosianus—confirming that manumission in a church has the same validity as that by traditional means. It is very likely that these two laws were given as imperial rescripts, in response to written inquiries by bishops.[18] Sozomen mentions a total of three Constantinian laws on this issue, but the third one is now lost.[19] Members of the clergy, however, were also able to grant freedom to their slaves in their will or by a simple declaration, without the need for witnesses.[20] John the Almsgiver in early seventh-century Alexandria seems to have availed himself of this possibility, making it a policy to purchase slaves who had been treated badly so that he could manumit them immediately.[21]

It would go too far to assume that this privilege placed the bishop on a par with the provincial governor, who held judicial and notarial authority and was usually of senatorial rank. A more plausible connection with the administrative system might be sought in the fact that since the mid-fourth century the state notaries who were traditionally in charge of authenticating the manumission of slaves disappear from the historical record. This may be more than just a chronological coincidence with the increased attestations of manumission in the church.

The thrust of these laws concerns slaves and the modalities of their manumission by Christian masters. Many Christians decided to liberate their slaves when they received baptism, when they joined the clergy, or on their deathbed.[22] The practice of manumission at baptism is perhaps the background for a law of 392, which prohibits all other legal action except manumission in the two weeks before Easter.[23] Easter was not only a feast of spiritual renewal for Christians; it was also the time when the catechumens received baptism, which would have been an occasion to manumit their slaves. Some manumitted their slaves at other turning points in their lives. Isaias of Scetis includes in his advice to monks the admonition to manumit their slaves, calling the failure to do so an "offence to the monastic habit."[24]

18. S. Corcoran, *The Empire of the Tetrarchs: Imperial Pronouncements and Government, AD 284–324*, rev. ed. (Oxford, 2000), 167.

19. Sozomen, *HE* 1.9.6.

20. CTh 4.7.1 (321). A great deal of material on *manumissio in ecclesia* has been assembled by H. Leclerq, "Affranchissement," *DACL* 1 (1924): cols. 554–76.

21. *Life of John the Almsgiver* 34.

22. E. Hermann, *Ecclesia in Re Publica: Die Entwicklung der Kirche von pseudostaatlicher zu staatlich-inkorporierter Existenz* (Frankfurt am Main, 1980), 142–49.

23. CJ 3.12.7 (392).

24. Abbé Isaie, *Recueil ascétique*, Logos 4. 49, intr. L. Regnault and trans. H. de Broc (Bellefontaine, 1970; 3d ed., 1985), 62.

Gregory of Nazianzus mentions in his *Testament,* which he drew up while bishop of Constantinople, that he had already manumitted two slaves, Gregory and Eustathius, who then became monks and deacons in his episcopal household. Other slaves, including Gregory's *notarius,* were to gain their liberty upon his death.[25] Several of Augustine's priests and deacons had manumitted their slaves when they entered the ministry. Augustine explained this in a sermon delivered in 425 that gives a full public account of the financial situation of his clergy. Two deacons, he added, were about to liberate their slaves on the same day, before the eyes of the congregation, and with a written entry in the records of the church.[26] In another sermon, Augustine described the modalities of the manumission in the church: the master leads the slave by the hand into the church, and his written statement is read out, followed by his own oral declaration.[27] Augustine's account of the public ceremony before the congregation gives us some idea of the concrete implementation of the Christian custom that Constantine's laws imbued with legal force.

Christians were not alone in associating religious devotion and manumission. A number of Greek inscriptions record the manumission of male and female slaves to pagan deities, including Artemis and Apollo. The inscriptions cover a wide geographical area, from Macedonia to Edessa, and several of them date from the third century A.D. Even more intriguing than the chronological coincidence is the fact that some of the former owners declare that they were acting at the specific command of the deity.[28] The religious component in the manumission of slaves carried over into Christian hagiography. The Syriac *Life of Symeon the Stylite* describes how masters manumitted their slaves by tearing up their documents in front of Symeon, who was perched atop his column. The owners must have preferred to have their act of piety witnessed by the holy man rather than by a bishop.[29] Constantine's law of 321 had indeed indicated that the religious status of the witnesses was of crucial importance in the act of manumission. This is also the interpretation of Constantine's legislation given by Sozomen: "Constantine therefore made three laws, enacting that all those individuals in the churches, *whose freedom should be attested by the priests,* should receive the freedom of Rome" (emphasis mine).[30] The manumission of slaves remained the full extent of the bishop's notarial authority for almost a century, until

25. Gregory of Nazianzus, *Testament, PG* 37, cols. 389–96.

26. Augustine, *Sermo* 356.6–7.

27. Augustine, *Sermo* 21.6.

28. A. Cameron, "Inscriptions Relating to Sacral Manumission and Confession," *Harv. Theol. Rev.* 32 (1939): 143–79; L. Robert, *Hellenica* I/12 (1940): 69–77.

29. *Syriac Life of Symeon the Stylite,* p. 159.

30. Sozomen, *HE* 1.9.6.

a law of 412 ordered that adoptions of foundling children must also be notarized by the bishop.[31] This was most likely motivated by the bishop's traditional obligation to care for orphans.

The actual implementation of *manumissio in ecclesia* in the different parts of the empire remains unclear. To the best of my knowledge, not a single papyrus from Egypt attests this practice, and it does not seem to have been exercised in Africa until 401. In that year, the fifth council of Carthage decided to petition the emperor specifically for the application of this privilege also to the Church of Africa.[32] On the other hand, only four decades later, the Council of Orange in Gaul reaffirmed the validity of the manumission of slaves that takes place in the church in words that seem to indicate a long-standing practice.[33] The second council of Mâcon, held in 585, ascribed to the bishop a moral responsibility for slaves who were manumitted in church, placing them under his protection.[34]

It is thus misleading to interpret Constantine's laws on *manumissio in ecclesia* as granting *general* notarial authority to the bishop, or to imply that the bishop was now in a position to establish his own access to the realm of secular law. The bishops' notarial authority was limited to the status of slaves and, later, of orphans and did not extend, for example, to marriage contracts or property transactions. These laws value the trustworthiness of clergy as witnesses of legal transactions, and they confirm that manumission could be a religiously motivated act.

## EPISCOPAL COURTS (EPISCOPALIS AUDIENTIA)

The laws on the judicial powers of bishops have become something of a touchstone in the evaluation of the relation between emperor and church during the period when Christianity was gaining public recognition. Although the evidence for the judicial activity of bishops consists of only a small handful of imperial laws, a few papyri, scattered references to the practice in literary sources, several mentions at local synods, and none in the canons of ecumenical councils, the secondary literature on the subject is disproportionately extensive.[35] To many scholars, Constantine's legislation and that of subse-

---

31. CTh 5.9.2 (412).
32. Carthage (401), can. 8 (64), H-L II/1, p. 126, repeated at the sixth council of Carthage, in the same year: can. 16, H-L II/1, p. 129.
33. Orange (441), can. 7, H-L II/1, pp. 439–40.
34. Mâcon, second council (585), can. 7, H-L III/1, p. 210.
35. See J. C. Lamoreaux, "Episcopal Courts in Late Antiquity," *JECS* 3 (1995): 143–67. This article illustrates the workings of episcopal courts but does not address the question of their relation to established forms of jurisdiction. More satisfying in this regard is W. Selb, "Episcopalis audientia von der Zeit Konstantins bis zur Novelle XXXV Valentinians III.," *Zs. d. Savigny-Stiftung f. Rechtsgeschichte, romanist. Abt.* 84 (1967): 162–217. See also the concise

quent Christian emperors have appeared as a conscious effort to lay the foundation of the caesaropapism that has traditionally been associated with the Byzantine Empire. Since the authority to administer justice at the local level had until then rested exclusively with provincial governors and local magistrates, Constantine's decision to extend judicial authority to bishops has often been interpreted as an imperial initiative to treat the bishops as officers of the state and to integrate them into the administrative structure of the empire. Constantine could thus be cast in the role of the shrewd politician who exploited and corrupted the hitherto pure and innocent episcopate by exposing it to the dirty business of everyday, urbane concerns.

The earliest law, of 318, allowed for pending cases to be transferred from the municipal to the episcopal court *(episcopale iudicium)*, provided that both parties agreed.[36] In 333, Constantine issued further specifications in response to a query of the praetorian prefect Ablabius regarding the judicial authority of bishops. This law, however, was not included in the Theodosian Code but only appears as part of the Sirmondian Constitutions, a separate, smaller collection of fourth-century laws that partially overlaps with the Theodosian compilation. The fact that Theodosius's compilers did not see the need to include this law, combined with the legislator's insistence that it merely reaffirms an earlier ruling, of which no trace has been found, has given rise to doubts about its authenticity. Nonetheless, it has become the most frequently repeated law on the subject of episcopal judicial authority. The Sirmondian Constitution 1 went further than the law of 318. It specifically allowed the transfer of a lawsuit from the municipal to the episcopal court at any time in the proceedings, and at the request of only one of the parties involved.[37] In concrete fact, this must have placed Christians at an advantage vis-à-vis their pagan neighbors, since they were now not only granted unhindered recourse to a judge of the same faith but could also subject their adversaries to the bishop's judgment against their will. The law also extended the validity of episcopal rulings by allowing no appeal.[38]

---

remarks by M. Kaser, *Das römische Zivilprozessrecht* (Munich, 1966), 526–29. The most exhaustive works are M. R. Cimma, *L' episcopalis audientia nelle costituzioni imperiali da Costantino à Giustiniano* (Turin, 1989), and G. Vismara, *L'audientia episcopalis* (Milan, 1995), a revised version of his 1937 monograph. See also Hermann, *Ecclesia in Re Publica*, 207–31. R. S. Bagnall, *Egypt in Late Antiquity* (Princeton, 1993), 225, emphatically denies that "the bishops had any formal powers of civil adjudication, enforced by the state." J. Harries, *Law and Empire in Late Antiquity* (Cambridge, 1999), 191–211, equally emphasizes the extra-judicial operation of the episcopal courts through arbitration.

36. CTh 1.27.1 (318?). The date of this law is problematic, as noted in F. Millar, *The Emperor in the Roman World (31 BC—AD 337)* (Ithaca, N.Y., 1977), 591 n. 7.

37. Sirm. 1 (333).

38. CTh 1.27.2 (408): *iudicium episcopale* is valid for those who agree to submit to it, and has the same force as a municipal court. NVal 35. 1 (452): the episcopal court may be sought by

After a hiatus of several decades, during which Julian apparently reversed Constantine's laws,[39] new legislation attempted to regularize the judicial activities of bishops. They were not to hear criminal cases,[40] but only those of religious import;[41] and the consent of both parties was again necessary to obtain episcopal arbitration.[42] A law of Arcadius and Honorius, given in 408, repeated that the consent of both parties was required, that no appeal was possible, and added that the bishop's ruling would be enforced by civil authorities.[43] The compilers of the Theodosian Code who paired this law with Constantine's initial law of 318 under the heading *De episcopali definitione* must have considered it to be either of historical interest or of enduring validity. The requirement of the agreement of both parties to submit to the bishop's ruling was reinforced by Valentinian III, in 452, even if one of the litigants was a cleric. The only exceptions were, as before, cases of strictly religious nature.[44]

The judicial activity of bishops was not a novelty. A tombstone in Phrygia commemorates Aquila, a Montanist bishop, who probably died in the Great Persecution, as "a chief of the people, who gave heed to the just precepts of the law."[45] The bishop's duty to conciliate and adjudicate within his community is highlighted in the *Apostolic Constitutions*, which were composed in 380, based in large part on the *Didascalia* of the first half of the third century.[46] The context in which episcopal judgment is first mentioned in the *Apostolic Constitutions* is that of the imposition of penance or, worse, of excommunication on members of the congregation who had violated the established rules of Christian conduct. Like a good physician, the bishop was called to restore the health of the whole body, if necessary by applying painful treatment to and even removal of the afflicted parts. Repeated reminders in the text about the importance of just and impartial judgment then provide the transition to the second set of issues that require episcopal

---

clerics and laymen if both parties consent: "Otherwise we do not allow the bishops to be judges, unless the wish of the disputants should precede." W. Waldstein, "Zur Stellung der episcopalis audientia im spätrömischen Prozeß," in *Festschrift M. Kaser* (Munich, 1976); Selb, 162ff.

39. As argued in Harries, *Law and Empire*, 199–200.

40. CTh 16.2.23 (376).

41. CTh 16.11.1 (399).

42. CJ 1.4.7 (398).

43. CTh 1.27.2.

44. NVal 35.1.1–2.

45. A. Petrie, "Epitaphs in Phrygian Greek," in *Studies in the History and Art of the Eastern Provinces of the Roman Empire,* ed. W. M. Ramsay, 125–26 (London, 1906); cf. also J. C. Anderson, "Paganism and Christianity in the Upper Tembris Valley," in *Studies in the History and Art of the Eastern Provinces of the Roman Empire,* 201–2.

46. *Apostolic Constitutions* 2.37–54. For the *Didaskalia,* see U. Mosiek, "Das altkirchliche Prozessrecht im Spiegel der Didaskalie," *Österreichisches Archiv für Kirchenrecht* 16 (1965): 183–206, This text, too, prefers reconciliation and arbitration to a formal trial.

intervention, namely, the need for reconciliation and the restoration of internal peace within the community. The Christian emphasis on the unity of spirit within the community also demanded forgiveness of one's brother, especially in anticipation of the weekly celebration of communion with Christ in the eucharist. For this reason, it was recommended that the bishops settle disputes on Mondays[47] so that the reconciliation would be complete by the following Sunday. These chapters in the *Apostolic Constitutions* interpret episcopal jurisdiction as an aspect of the bishop's roles as physician of souls and peacemaker, applied within the Christian community.[48]

It is not easy to define the exact nature of episcopal jurisdiction compared to that of provincial governors or other civil magistrates. The Roman judicial system depended on these elected or appointed magistrates to administer justice. They were considered qualified to dispense justice by the authority of their office as representatives of the emperor, and because men of their social status and education were believed to be attuned to a common value system. The governor of the province was the highest magistrate at the regional level who could dispense justice. Beyond that, only appeals to the praetorian prefects and, beyond them, to the emperor could result in reversal of a sentence. In order to enforce their judgment, the magistrates had at their disposal a whole array of sentences, from monetary fines to corporal punishment.

The bishop's role as a dispenser of justice departed from tradition in two important respects. First, in contrast to provincial governors, who were sent to their post for a very limited number of years, the bishop was usually firmly integrated into the social life of the city as a well-known and well-respected member of the local community. Moreover, where a magistrate was appointed for a limited amount of time, the bishop had been elected for life. His familiarity with local conditions must have been of great help in dispensing justice, and his social position must have ensured respect for his judgment. This explains why high-profile bishops like Ambrose and Augustine were swamped with legal work. Second, while the civil magistrate could dispense justice either by arbitration or by pronouncing a sentence, the bishop's court was either approached with the transfer of a pending case before a civil judge, in which case the bishop presumably pronounced a judgment, or the bishop's pronouncement was sought in a process of arbitration.[49] This last was by far the more common procedure. This has impor-

---

47. *Apostolic Constitutions* 2.47.1.

48. W. Hartmann, "Der Bischof als Richter nach den kirchenrechtlichen Quellen des 4. bis 7. Jahrhunderts," in *La giustizia nell'alto medioevo (secoli V–VIII)*, Settimane di Studio del Centro Italiano di Studi sull'Alto Medioevo 42 (Spoleto, 1995), 805–37, discusses the evidence from Western canon law, especially regarding the bishop's right to excommunicate offenders.

49. The predominant importance of arbitration in the *episcopale iudicium* is implied in the work of Lamoreaux and Harries.

tant implications for the interpretation of the status of the bishop in these proceedings, for while judgments could be pronounced only by an imperially appointed magistrate, anyone could act as an arbiter, provided that both parties agreed to submit to his ruling.[50]

The actual activities of episcopal courts can be gleaned from passages in Christian literature and a small handful of papyri, all assembled in an article by John Lamoreaux. Many bishops were known to spend a great amount of their time on judicial activities. Augustine chafed under the responsibility of this time-consuming task, which sometimes kept him past his dinnertime;[51] Ambrose, who had acquired relevant experience as a provincial governor, spent much time dispensing justice, and Epiphanius of Cyprus was so overwhelmed by the demands placed on him that he delegated this task to a deacon.[52] Episcopal courts, like their civil counterparts, used torture to extract testimony from witnesses of lower social status,[53] had the facilities to imprison the accused prior to trial,[54] and seem to have applied corporal punishment to those convicted of crimes, but their use of violence was relatively restrained. The cases brought before the bishop ranged from property disputes, marital quarrels, and charges of sexual misconduct to the legal guardianship of women and issues of personal liberty.

While the anecdotal evidence that can be culled from the literary sources, including autobiographical remarks by prominent bishops in their own letters, gives the impression that the bishop's judicial function was an important part of his ministry to the community and a time-consuming and thankless task, the papyrus evidence for the dispensation of justice by bishops is relatively small. The earliest relevant papyrus, from the fourth century, records the proceedings against the consecrated virgin Thaesis, who had been accused of stealing Christian books. The hearing was held in the atrium of the church, with Bishop Plousianos as arbiter, and in the presence of a magistrate, a deacon, and two other men.[55] Another fourth-century papyrus contains the complaint of a woman against her violent husband. He was a repeat offender. On an earlier occasion, he had sworn an oath in the presence of the bishop "and his brothers" that he would cease from insulting her, but had

50. For arbitration and mediation at work, see T. Gagos and P. van Minnen, *Settling a Dispute: Toward a Legal Anthropology of Late Antique Egypt* (Ann Arbor, 1997). Their list of forty-one papyri that record such settlements includes three cases that were initiated by clergy or monks and one that was settled by arbitration by a priest.

51. Possidius, *Life of Augustine* 19.

52. Polybius and John, *Life of Epiphanius, PG* 41, col. 93A.

53. T. D. Barnes, "The Crimes of Basil of Ancyra," *JThS* n.s. 47 (1996): 553–54.

54. J.-U. Krause, *Gefängnisse im römischen Reich* (Stuttgart, 1996), 54–55.

55. *PLips.* 43; cf. S. Elm, "An Alleged Book-Theft in Fourth-Century Egypt: *P. Lips.* 43," *Studia Patristica* 18/2 (1989).

soon reverted to his earlier behavior.[56] As Roger Bagnall notes, in adminis-tering the oath the bishop had acted as "reconciler, witness or guarantor of the reconciliation."[57] It is also important to note that he was assisted by oth-ers in this role, just as the hearing for the bookish nun involved several oth-ers. From the fifth century comes a complaint by Aurelia Nonna to the bishop of Oxyrhynchus regarding her nephew Alypius, who was a monk. He was also probably the legal guardian of Aurelia's daughter, whom he wanted to marry off to a relative—a union to which Aurelia objected. She also com-plained that Alypius had betrayed his monastic habit when their disagree-ment had ended in a physical altercation that had ruined her clothing.[58] These three cases are commonly cited as concrete examples of *episcopalis audientia* at work.[59] But this evidence is not as conclusive as one might wish. It is equally possible to assume that the case of the nun Thaesis and of the monk Alypius were brought before the bishop because of the monastic state of the defendants. In other words, the bishop may have been asked simply to exercise the *privilegium fori* (internal jurisdiction) of adjudicating cases involv-ing those in holy orders.[60] As for the case of the battered wife, we have no way of knowing the concrete circumstances of the oath that the husband is reported to have sworn in the presence of the bishop, whether this had taken place at the end of the formal arbitration process of the *episcopale iudicium,* or whether the bishop had merely intervened in this family crisis in a more informal way to foster reconciliation. These papyri thus serve as a reminder that the law codes contain guidelines and expressions of imperial intent, but that we know precious little about their actual implementation.

This is confirmed by two further papyri of judicial interest. The first, from 481, involves Bishop Cyrus and two presbyters, who were accused of stealing items of clothing and home-furnishing textiles. As a gesture of respect for the bishop, the accuser had refrained from bringing the case before the civil judge, but instead both parties agreed to accept the arbitration of Macarius,

---

56. *POxy.* 6.903.
57. Bagnall, *Egypt in Late Antiquity,* 195.
58. *PLond.* Inv. 2217; cf. H. I. Bell, "The *episcopalis audientia* in Byzantine Egypt," *Byzantion* 1 (1924): 139–44.
59. For example, W. Lammeyer, "Die 'audientia episcopalis' in Zivilsachen der Laien im römi-schen Kaiserrecht und in den Papryi," *Aegyptus* 13 (1933): 193–202. Thus also Lamoreaux.
60. The same argument can also be made for fourth- to sixth-century Gaul. The few cases where bishops act as judges involve at least one member of the clergy and may thus be consid-ered to fall under the general category of the internal jurisdiction of the church. Although her understanding of *episcopalis audientia* is flawed, the relevant examples are presented by N. Gauthier in "Le réseau de pouvoirs de l'évêque dans la Gaule du haut moyen-âge," in *Towns and Their Territories between Late Antiquity and the Early Middle Ages,* ed. G. P. Broglio, N. Gauthier, and N. Christie, 188–90 (Leiden, 2000).

the *ekdikos* of the Theban tax.[61] One would expect the accused bishop to insist on having his case tried before an ecclesiastical tribunal, but perhaps Macarius promised fast, sympathetic, and unbureaucratic help in ways that other judicial authorities did not. A papyrus letter from the sixth or seventh century provides further evidence that convenience, more than anything else, dictated the modus of judicial procedure. Abraam, the headman of a village, probably in the Fayum, had been approached with an unresolved dispute between two brothers and their sister-in-law. He sent this letter to the abba and archimandrite Seridos, asking him to either reconcile both parties or refer them back to Abraam for reconciliation. Here the broker of reconciliation is not a bishop, but the leader of a monastery. The second choice after the intervention of a religious authority, but only with the express endorsement of Abba Seridos, was reconciliation "according to the local custom" by Abraam, the most prominent person in the village.[62] These papyri show that caution is advised in the evaluation of the effect of Constantine's legislation on *episcopalis audientia* on the position of the bishop within late antique society. The bishop was not the only religious authority who could act as conciliator—archimandrites and holy men could do the same—nor was he the only judicial authority to whom the people had recourse—heads of village and *ekdikoi* of the Theban tax could assume the same function.

The bishop's judgment was based on common sense, custom, and the tenets of the Christian religion. Only rarely did a bishop like Augustine make an effort to familiarize himself with the precedent of imperial law or to seek counsel with legal experts.[63] Episcopal courts worked fast, efficiently, and without payment of hefty fees. They provided an accessible alternative at a time when the traditional system of jurisdiction by imperial officers seems to have been rife with corruption and delayed procedures.[64] Far from creating a new legal reality, Constantine's aim in legislating on the judgment of bishops was to facilitate access to dependable legal services by validating

---

61. H. B. Dewing, "A Dialysis of the Fifth Century A.D. in the Princeton Collection of Papyri," *TAPA* 53 (1922): 113–27.

62. L. Mitteis and U. Wilcken, *Grundzüge und Chrestomathie der Papyruskunde*, vol. 1/2 (Leipzig, 1912), no. 134, pp. 159–60 ( = *BGU* 103).

63. On Augustine's use of Roman legal terminology, and the difficulty of locating *episcopalis audientia* within the body of Roman law, see K. K. Raikas, "*Audientia episcopalis:* Problematik zwischen Staat und Kirche bei Augustin," *Augustinianum* 37 (1997): 459–81. On his awareness of Roman civil law, see also C. Lepelley, "Liberté, colonat et esclavage d'après la Lettre 24*: La juridiction épiscopale 'de liberali causa,'" in *Les lettres de saint Augustin découvertes par Johannes Divjak: Communications présentées au colloque des 20 et 21 Septembre 1982*, 329–42 (Paris, 1983).

64. On corruption of officials in Antioch, see P. Petit, *Libanius et la vie municipale à Antioche au IV^e siècle après J.-C.* (Paris, 1955), 258–60. Ecclesiastical courts, however, were also not above financial exploitation: Socrates, *HE* 7.37.17 .

the existing practice of episcopal courts. The greater dependability of bishops was recognized two centuries later by Justinian, who demanded that the bishops should act as the first instance of appeal against the judgment of provincial governors.[65]

Of special relevance to the present study is the connection between *episcopalis audientia* and the three issues of episcopal virtues, episcopal tutelage of widows, orphans and the oppressed, and reconciliation. A few observations may suffice. Constantine explained that it was the general expectations of the high moral and spiritual standard of the episcopate that prompted his legislation. The contrast between civil and episcopal judgment became almost proverbial. When Ambrose was appointed to the governorship of Liguria and Aemilia, the praetorian prefect reminded him: "Vade, age non ut iudex, sed ut episcopus (Go, act not like a judge, but like a bishop)."[66] It is in the context of the obligation to help others with whatever means possible that Ambrose mentioned judicial activity in his *On the Duties of the Clergy*, addressed to clerics in positions of responsibility. Of crucial importance for the discharge of this duty, Ambrose declared, was impartiality, combined with other virtues such as charity, compassion, and the immunity to bribery.[67]

*Episcopalis audientia* also aimed to plug into a bishop's charitable responsibility. Constantine's law of 333, as Drake has observed, was primarily concerned with giving minors legal recourse against their guardians.[68] In other words, it was intended to provide protection to orphans, who—along with widows and other unfortunates—were the recipients par excellence of Christian charity that was increasingly administered by bishops.

Finally, *episcopalis audientia* fits neatly into the context of reconciliation between quarreling parties. The emphasis in the imperial legislation on the bishop's dispensation of justice through arbitration, a process that required the initial consent of both parties to submit to the judgment of the arbiter, has already been observed. A papyrus, probably from the sixth century, illustrates the intimate connection between arbitration and reconciliation. Leontius, probably a bishop, informed a high-ranking *curialis* of his arbitration in a dispute between three men over the use of a number of tombs. He concluded his report: "And the three, John and Eusebios and Didymos, took thought of God and they left me compliantly and prayed for one another this very day, no one of them showing any signs of annoyance."[69] The importance of prayer in the process of conciliation was acknowledged

65. Nov. Just. 86 (539).
66. Paulinus, *Life of Ambrose* 8.
67. Ambrose, *On the Duties of the Clergy* 2.24.124–25.
68. Drake, 325–52.
69. J. G. Keenan, "A Christian Letter from the Michigan Collection," *ZPE* 75 (1988): 271.

also by Augustine, who had been called to restore peace among a badly divided priesthood: "We remedied [the situation] partly by reproof, partly by instruction, and partly by prayer."[70]

The bishop's role as arbiter is not all that dissimilar to the holy man's role as peacemaker. We need only recall how Daniel the Stylite, mentioned at the beginning of this book, reconciled the new emperor Basiliscus and the bishop Acacius in a stunning public ceremony in the Church of Saint Sophia. According to theologians of the fourth and fifth centuries, the ability to make peace and to bring reconciliation—with reference to Jesus's Sermon on the Mount ("Blessed are the peacemakers, for they will be called children of God," Matt. 5:9)—was strongly associated with a person's spiritual progress. The Syrian author Aphrahat, as well as Gregory of Nyssa, Ambrose, and Augustine, expresses the view that only the person who has made peace within himself by vanquishing his passions can also be a maker of peace between others.[71] Gregory of Nyssa finds occasion to exemplify this point in his encomium on Gregory the Wonder-worker, the disciple of Origen and bishop of Neocaeasarea who had died in the early 270s. Gregory's amazing self-control, in the manner of a true philosopher, so inspired the people of his city that "they did not suppose that when the disputes of daily life arose they had any more exalted court of appeal, but every judgement and every complicated entanglement was solved by his counsels."[72] Although Gregory had studied jurisprudence at Berytus in his youth, his method of conflict resolution as a bishop consisted—according to the examples given in the encomium—in a combination of common sense and miraculous powers.

Theodoret's *History of the Monks in Syria* contains several stories of ascetics who made sure that justice was served with the means that were at their disposal. During the reign of Constantine, James of Nisibis, a much-admired ascetic who later became a bishop, protested the unfair judgment of a Persian judge not in so many words, but by causing a large stone to shatter into a thousand pieces.[73] In a story that highlights both his power over demons and his clemency, Macedonius the Barley-eater (d. ca. 420), another well-known ascetic, was summoned by a distressed father to give testimony before court on behalf of his daughter, who had become the victim of a magic spell. "The judge," the story continues, "by taking his seat outside his residence, became not a judge but a spectator; the role of judges was performed by the great Macedonius, who used the power within him to order

70. Augustine, *Ep.* 62.1: "Partim objurgando, partim monendo, partim orando correximus."
71. W. Cramer, "Die Seligpreisung der Friedensstifter: Zur Rezeption der Bergpredigt bei Afrahat," in *Lingua restituta orientalis: Festgabe für Julius Assfalg*, ed. R. Schulz and M. Görg (Wiesbaden, 1990).
72. Gregory of Nyssa, *Life of Gregory the Wonder-worker* 49.
73. Theodoret of Cyrrhus, *HR* 1.6.

the demon to leave off his usual deceit and give a true account of the whole tragedy of the affair." That being done, and the culprit identified, Macedonius pleaded with the judge to spare the culprit's life and to give him a chance at repentance instead.[74] Symeon the Stylite, it is reported, gladly communicated with visitors of all kinds, preaching twice a day from atop his column, and then "judging and delivering verdicts that are right and just." Theodoret explains: "But after the ninth hour he first offers divine instruction to those present, and then, after receiving each man's request and working some cures, he resolves the strife of those in dispute."[75] This short sentence encapsulates the message that Symeon's conflict resolution is an integral part of his ministry of teaching and healing, first attending to the ailing bodies of individuals, then turning to remedy the fissures in the body politic. The same connection is made in a summary passage at the end of the *Life of Theodore of Sykeon* that talks first about his miraculous healing abilities, and then about his work as a physician of souls. It is in the latter context that the hagiographer explains:

> When men were at enmity with each other or had a grievance one against another he reconciled them, and those who were engaged in law-suits he sought to bring to a better mind counseling them not to wrong each other and to think nothing of temporal things but to prefer before all wealth the commandment of God which says: "Thou shalt love thy neighbour as thyself" for love, said he, worketh no ill to its neighbour and whosoever loveth his brother, loveth God.[76]

A hagiographical tale of the settlement of a marital dispute demonstrates how the gift of discernment and the mere physical appearance that are typical of the holy man can be fused with the bishop's role as administrator of oaths, protector of matrimony, and arbiter. The Arabic *Life* of Bishop Pisentius of Coptos (d. 631) contains the rather dramatic story of a dissolute woman who made a big display of appearing at the monastery where Bishop Pisentius lived, complaining that her husband had repudiated her and their five children. She demanded that the husband be summoned so that, in the presence of the bishop, he would either divorce her or they would be reconciled. The husband came before Pisentius and identified his wife's lover. The lover was also brought in and immediately crumbled under the effect of the holy man's gaze and stern admonition:

> And his [Pisentius's] eyes glowed upon him like a blazing fire when he looked at him and he knew what he had done sinfully with the unfaithful and dis-

solute woman. Now his face was pale and like the colour of saffron from fear
of what he saw in the countenance of the saint and righteous one, so that he
urinated along his legs.

The adulterer then made a full confession, which incriminated the
woman for having sworn a false oath to clear herself before her suspicious
husband. The proceedings continued inside the monastery. The adulterous
wife was brought in and asked to swear an oath on her innocence after
drinking holy oil. In her eagerness, she would have perjured herself again
had not Pisentius ordered her lover to repeat his confession in her presence. "And thereupon," the story concludes, "he [Pisentius] commanded
the woman to be beaten and driven from before him, and that they should
take her to the governor who would disgrace her and make her infamous
and cause her to be a warning to others."[77]
Just like the papyrus petition of the battered wife cited above, this story
takes it for granted that the bishop is capable of intervention in a marital
dispute, but without seeing the need to define the legal basis of his intervention. In neither instance did the bishop impose a sentence or punishment. Pisentius, in fact, turned the adulterous woman over to the governor
for this purpose after she had received a beating. In the papyrus as well as
in the hagiographical account, the bishop is called upon for his ability to
work reconciliation between quarreling parties and to administer oaths. A
bishop who, like Pisentius, was also a holy man was particularly effective in
that function, for he commanded special powers of intimidation and discernment that practically guaranteed the validity of any oath given before
him. The same combination of a holy man's powers of discernment and a
bishop's task to validate oaths is present in Gregory of Tours's description of
Bishop Nicetius of Trier (d. 566).[78] The bishop's role as an administrator of
oaths is an empire-wide phenomenon that deserves to be highlighted. Five
late antique papyri from Upper Egypt preserve the written confirmation of
oaths that were sworn with the unusual formula "by almighty God and the
prayers of NN the bishop."[79] Oaths were an integral part of legal proceedings, and, administered by a bishop who had the gifts of the spirit, they func-
tioned as a powerful spiritual lie-detector test.

---

77. De Lacy O'Leary, *The Arabic Life of S. Pisentius*, PO 22/3 (1930), 439–41. This story is
absent from the Coptic version of the *Life*, edited and translated by E. A. Wallis Budge in *Coptic
Apocrypha in the Dialect of Upper Egypt* (London, 1913; repr., 1977).
78. K. Uhalde, "Proof and Reproof: The Judicial Component of Episcopal Confrontation,"
*Early Medieval Europe* 8 (1999): 1–11.
79. *Bala'izah: Coptic Texts from deir el-Bala'izah in Upper Egypt*, ed. P. E. Kahle (London, 1974), 1:
46–47.

## ECCLESIASTICAL ASYLUM

Churches provided sanctuary to individuals, a custom that is first attested in 343 and from then on continuously into the Justinianic period and beyond. Refuge in churches was sought for a multitude of reasons: debtors wanted to escape their creditors, taxpayers ran away from fiscal oppression, condemned criminals became fugitives from the law, women were desperate to avoid forced marriage, and toppled politicians had to hide from their enemies. The pursuit of asylum seekers by civil forces could lead to a standoff with the bishop and sometimes even violent confrontation.

Modern scholarship has tended to see such confrontations as defining moments in the relationship between church and state, in which a bishop upheld the divinely sanctioned right of protection of the individual in defiance of the physical might of the secular authorities. The sacrality of the ecclesiastical space, the argument goes, made it exempt from the grasp of imperial law. A different, and certainly no less valid, approach that will be proposed here attributes the development of the right of asylum to the duty and obligation of the bishop to assist the poor and oppressed.[80]

It has been suggested that the Christian custom of seeking asylum in a church had its roots in the association of specific sites devoted to pagan deities with sanctuary, safety, and security—an association that was especially common in Egypt and the eastern Mediterranean.[81] In an inscription of the late third century A.D., the city of Perge in Pamphylia with its city goddess of Artemis proudly announced that it was the only city in the region that held the right of asylum.[82] However, it is difficult to posit a direct continuity between the pagan and the Christian practice of asylum beyond the most general religious sentiment of appreciation for the purity of holy places, and that is for two reasons. First, Christian asylum differed from the pagan practice in that it was supposed to apply to all churches, not just to specifically designated sites, and second, there does not seem to be evidence of any kind for ecclesiastical asylum before the fourth century,

---

80. For a comprehensive study that argues for an approach influenced by "histoire de mentalité," but with different conclusions from mine, see A. Ducloux, *Ad ecclesiam confugere: Naissance du droit d'asile dans les églises (IVe-milieu du Ve s.)* (Paris, 1994). For a brief overview of the right of asylum in antiquity, see L. Wenger, "Asylrecht," *RAC* 1 (1950): cols. 836–44; and id., "*Horoi asylias*," *Philologus* 86 (1931): 427–54.

81. F. von Woess, *Das Asylwesen Ägyptens in der Ptolemäerzeit und die spätere Entwicklung,* Münchener Beiträge zur Papyrusforschung und antiken Rechtsgeschichte 5 (Munich, 1923).

82. C. Roueché, "*Floreat Perge,*" in *Images of Authority: Papers Presented to Joyce Reynolds on the Occasion of Her Seventieth Birthday,* ed. M. M. Mackenzie and C. Roueché, Cambridge Philological Society Suppl. 16 (Cambridge, 1989).

well over a century after the last instance of traditional *asylia* at a pagan shrine.[83]

The earliest evidence for the practice of ecclesiastical asylum is Canon 8 of the Council of Sardica (343). The core issue of this canon was not asylum, however, but the regulation of episcopal intercession at the imperial court. Too many bishops, especially from Africa, had traveled to the court to petition on behalf of individuals, instead of intervening with administrators at a lower level on behalf of the poor, widows, and orphans. Hence, the council decided, bishops should travel to the court only upon express invitation by the emperor. However, if the need arose, they were allowed to travel at their own initiative in order to ask for a remission of the punishment for those individuals who had sought refuge in the church after being condemned to exile and banishment. The larger context of this canon is therefore not a delineation of the boundaries between the ecclesiastical and the imperial spheres of influence, but rather the *parrhēsia* of the bishop, his ability to intercede, that will concern us again below. For the duration of the bishop's journey to the court in order to entreat the emperor's clemency on behalf of the condemned, the latter found a safe haven in the church. An episode that occurred in Carthage in 311 and was recorded by Optatus of Milevis gives us some idea of this process. The deacon Felix, fearing for his life after he had been accused of composing seditious pamphlets against Maxentius, the ruler in Rome, sought refuge with Bishop Mensurius. Mensurius publicly refused to surrender him, and a report was sent on. The imperial response was to summon Mensurius to the court, unless he surrendered Felix. The bishop went and pleaded his case, successfully, it seems, for he was permitted to return but died on the journey back.[84] Although Optatus does not use the terminology associated with asylum, it seems clear that Felix was safe for as long as he was physically inside the church complex and that he was able to remain there for the duration of the appeal made by the bishop on his behalf.

What had begun as a collateral effect of the bishops' obligation to assist the oppressed, in subsequent decades and centuries became more and more attached to the physical location where the oppressed found shelter. Church councils became increasingly concerned with upholding the sanctity of the church buildings. According to the Council of Orange in 441, "whoever seeks refuge in a church may not be surrendered, but must be defended out of reverence for the [holy] place."[85] Fugitives to the church were again protected at the Council of Arles in 452.[86] The first Council of Orléans, con-

83. Ducloux, 253 n. 1.
84. Optatus of Milevis, 1.17.1–2.
85. Orange (441), can. 5, H-L II/1, p. 438.
86. Arles (452), can. 30, Mansi VII, col. 882.

vened by King Chlovis in 511, reported that murderers, adulterers, and thieves were seeking protection in the atrium of the church or in the episcopal palace.[87] In this canon, just as in a law of 431 in the Theodosian Code, not only the inner sanctum of the church and its altar space, but also the outlying building associated with the bishop, were considered immune from the arm of the civil authorities.[88] The right of asylum is reaffirmed by the second council of Mâcon, in 585.[89] It is striking that the church canons dealing with asylum all originate at councils held in the Latin-speaking West. The custom itself, however, is well attested in all areas of the empire.

Imperial legislation on ecclesiastical asylum begins at a time when the practice was already well established.[90] The issue of "those who take refuge in churches" by claiming the right of asylum constitutes a separate title of the Theodosian Code, consisting of five laws that span the period from 392 to 432. Three laws inform us that asylum was sought in churches by decurions and others, including Jews, who were desperate to escape responsibility for the debts that they owed either to the fisc or to individual debtors. Not infrequently, it seems, asylum seekers hoped to escape their fate by receiving ordination into the clergy, a privileged state that enjoyed exemptions from certain taxes and obligations.[91] Asylum was also sought by those who had been accused of criminal charges. The earliest three laws were promulgated in 392, 397, and 398, but their implementation and dissemination remains questionable, for in 399 a synod in Carthage felt the need to petition the emperor for a law that would protect those who had taken refuge in a church from being dragged away.[92]

The fourth law, of 431, is of special interest for its implicit definition of the boundaries of holy space: it protected the altar space and the inner sanctuary from defilement by prohibiting asylum seekers from eating or sleeping there. Their right of asylum was also honored within the perimeter of the ecclesiastical compound, including houses, cells, courtyards, colonnades, gardens, and baths. The ecclesiastical space that was protected from the reach of imperial authority thus extended beyond the strictly liturgical space to those structures where the clergy had its living quarters and where it came into direct and social contact with the laity.[93] That space, however,

87. Orléans (511), can. 1, H-L II/1, pp. 1007–8.
88. CTh 9.45.4.
89. Mâcon, second council (585), can. 8, H-L III/1, p. 210.
90. For a detailed overview, see F. Martoye, "L'asile et la législation impériale du IVe au VIe siècle," *Mémoires de la Société Nationale des Antiquaires de France* 75 (1919): 159–246.
91. CTh 9.45.1 (392); CTh 9.45.2 (397), repeated CJ 1.12.1; CTh 9.45.3 (398); cf. CJ 10.31.66.
92. H-L II/1, p. 121.
93. CTh 9.45.4 (431), repeated CJ 1.12.3. The original, longer Greek text of this law slipped into a collection of official documents associated with the Council of Ephesus. It was first edited by E. Schwartz, in Woess, 253–72.

was not inviolate. If the asylum seekers failed to abide by the custom, enforced by imperial law, of abandoning their arms, they were subject to eviction by the emperor's armed men, but only after the bishop had been consulted and informed: "They shall be given the assurance that they are defended by the name of religion better than by the protection of arms." This law should perhaps be seen as an expansion of a law of 419, contained in the Sirmondian Constitutions, which expanded the boundaries of the sanctuary for the purposes of asylum to fifty feet beyond the entrance to the church.[94] The fifth and last law contained in this section of the Theodosian Code, dating to 432, limited to one day the amount of time that runaway and unarmed slaves could spend as asylum seekers in the church. The bishops were placed in charge of reprimanding those who failed to implement this law.[95]

Further laws on asylum are scattered in other sections of the Theodosian Code and the Sirmondian Constitutions. A law of 398 allowed clerics and monks and *synoditae* to launch an appeal on behalf of those who had been unfairly condemned to punishment, but only within a specified period of time. After that, they were prohibited from sheltering these individuals.[96] The mention of clergy and monks as protectors and spokesmen on behalf of victims of the judicial system reinforces the point that ecclesiastical asylum was the spatial equivalent of an essentially religious obligation that fell to those who had the ability to intercede. Imperial legislation continued to preserve and reinforce the right of asylum. A law of 409 treated the violation of asylum as treason, a capital crime.[97] Subsequent legislation aimed to limit the application of the protection that the church could grant. The emperor Leo was concerned about those who had sought ecclesiastical asylum from the pursuit of their debtors, and assigned the legal authority over them to the bishop and his *oikonomos* or the *defensor ecclesiae*.[98] Finally, Justinian on several occasions denied the right of asylum to murderers, adulterers, and ravishers of virgins.[99] In addition, the first book of the Justinianic Code includes a title on ecclesiastical asylum, where three of the laws in the Theodosian Code are reiterated.[100]

The fact that ecclesiastical asylum is mentioned in canon law several decades before it appears in imperial legislation is significant. It indicates that in their legislation on asylum, as in so many other respects, the emper-

---

94. Sirm. 13 (419).
95. CTh 9.45.5 (432), repeated CJ 1.12.4.
96. CTh 9.40.16 (398); shorter version of the same law at CTh 11.30.57 (398).
97. CTh 16.8.19 (409), repeated CJ 1.12.2.
98. CJ 1.12.5 (466).
99. Just. Nov. 17.7.1 and Just. Nov. 37.10 (535), specifically relating to the church in Africa.
100. CTh 9.45.2 = CJ 1.12.1; CTh 9.45.4 = CJ 1.12.3; CTh 9.45.5 = CJ 1.12.4.

ors acknowledged and endorsed existing ecclesiastical practice. The imperial laws also confirmed the bishop in his role as the undisputed guarantor of the right of asylum, which helped him to exercise his function as the protector of the oppressed.

Like all imperial law, these laws were intended to be cited as precedent and applied to all churches throughout the empire. Nonetheless, several inscriptions from the eastern Mediterranean, all from the sixth century, show that specific churches had their right of asylum affirmed by imperial order. Such was the case in Miletus, where Justinian granted the right of asylum to a church at the request of Bishop Hyakinthos, probably around the year 536. The decree was to be carried out by the bishop together with the provincial governor of Caria, and it was the latter who publicized it in the inscription.[101] Two similar inscriptions, also from the sixth century, come from the region near Tyre on the coast of Palestine. One grants the right of asylum to the Church of Saint Zacharias near Tyre "according to the force of the holy canons."[102] The other, dating from ca. 578 to 582, records the petition that the presbyter Anastasius of the Church of the Martyr Irene addressed to the emperor Tiberius in order to obtain the right of asylum for this church.[103]

The practice of seeking asylum in a church was common in East and West by the second half of the fourth century and continued to be invoked rather frequently. Several of the laws implied that asylum was often sought under extreme financial pressure, and this is confirmed by the many cases that required Augustine's involvement.[104] Historical sources also mention men and women who sought the church's protection during political upheavals, especially changes of government.[105] In 399, John Chrysostom used the full weight of his position as bishop of Constantinople to protect the palace eunuch Eutropius after his sudden fall to disgrace from a position of great influence. While the congregation watched Eutropius clutching the altar, John gloated in a sermon that the *praepositus sacri cubiculi*, who had previously engaged in a licentious lifestyle and sponsored activities that were contrary to the teaching of the church, was now depending on protection that

101. H. Grégoire, *Recueil des inscriptions grecques chrétiennes d'Asie Mineure* (Paris, 1922), 1: 220 bis. For the date, see D. Feissel and I. Kaygusuz, "Un mandement impérial du VI$^e$ siècle dans une inscription d'Hadrianoupolis d'Honoriade," *TM* 9 (1985): 403.

102. *SEG* 8.18. The mention of "holy canons" need not necessarily refer to specific ecclesiastical canons but can also be taken as referring to ecclesiastical custom in general. See E. Herman, "Zum Asylrecht im byzantinischen Reich," *OCP* 1 (1935): 211.

103. *SEG* 7.327.

104. Ducloux, 170–206.

105. The examples from the late antique and Byzantine sources have been assembled by Herman, 204–38.

only the church could offer.[106] Other famous cases involve individuals who were seeking protection from oppressive civil authorities. Ammianus Marcellinus, in his history of the Roman Empire up to 378, describes how the charioteer Hilarinus, who had been convicted of the crime of sorcery, sought asylum in a church but was nonetheless dragged out and decapitated.[107] Gregory of Nazianzus in his funerary oration for Basil of Caesarea recalled how the latter stood up for a widow who had taken refuge at the altar of the church after the local magistrate attempted to force her into a second marriage. Basil's courage did not falter, Gregory said, even under the bullying and intimidation of the judge.[108] This last incident took place in Caesarea in Cappadocia in 372. It is the first written attestation of a connection between the altar space and protection, as Anne Ducloux noted.[109] The laws of 419 and 431, mentioned above, also attempt to delineate the spatial extent of asylum.[110]

It is worth considering that protection through asylum could also be conceived of as originating from the person of the bishop. This is suggested by the practice known from Egyptian papyri of the fourth century and later, and from scattered references in Greek literary texts, beginning with the sixth century, of issuing a *logos asylias*, a word of immunity. A substantial number of papyrus letters containing such *logoi* survive. They were written certificates issued by a bishop that served as a safe-conduct, usually for a specified period of time, for people who had sought asylum at a church but then had to travel back home on an urgent matter.[111] Sometimes, it was the provincial governors who issued *logoi asylias,* perhaps as a way of confirming inviolate the protection of sanctuary that the traveler had obtained from the bishop. These *logoi* thus constituted something like a "portable asylum" that could be granted by the bishop.

The widely recognized status of the bishop as the guarantor of asylum, and his ability to bestow *logoi asylias* on individuals, may well be related to the sense of security and unassailability that literally surrounded individuals by virtue of their personal sanctity. Numerous hagiographical stories relate how attempted attacks on holy men were thwarted, often through some

106. See especially John Chrysostom, *Hom. in Eutropium, PG* 52, cols. 391–96, A second homily was delivered after Eutropius had been captured outside the church, *Hom. in capt. Eutr., PG* 52, 393–414. The episode is made more complex by the report of the fifth-century church historian Sozomen (*HE* 8.7.1–4) that Eutropius had used his influence to persuade Arcadius to abolish ecclesiastical asylum. See Ducloux, 64–80 and 92–103.

107. Ammianus Marcellinus, *Histories* 26.3.3.

108. Gregory of Nazianzus, *Oratio* 43 *On Saint Basil the Great* 56.

109. Ducloux, 46–51.

110. Sirm. 13 (419). For the concept of sanctity of space, see also Ducloux, 210.

111. H. Liebesny, "Rechtsgeschichtliche Bemerkungen zu den koptischen Schutzbriefen," *Mitteilungen des deutschen Instituts für ägyptische Altertumskunde in Kairo* 8 (1939): 71–146.

kind of miraculous intervention. One example recorded in the *Life of Epiphanius* relates how a partially blind Saracen tribesman moved to strike Epiphanius with his sword but was immobilized by shock when he regained his eyesight at his approach to the saint.[112] The *Life of Ambrose* is particularly illuminating in this regard, because it associates the personal sanctity of an individual with the space around him. Its author Paulinus describes how a demon was rendered powerless for as long as his victim remained inside the city of Milan and near the person of Ambrose, but began to act up the moment the afflicted man stepped outside the city walls.[113] Here, the space around a holy bishop and indeed the whole urban space of his bishopric are unassailable by evil forces.

An extension of this concept of a person radiating unassailability can be traced to the Byzantine Empire, where priests were considered to represent a kind of "walking asylum" that placed them outside the reach of secular law. This was made explicit in a ruling by the patriarch of Constantinople Constantine III Leichoudes, in 1059, who argued that a priest who had encouraged his sons to participate in a murder had received sufficient punishment through his demotion to lay status. By way of explanation, the patriarch pointed out that while earlier lawgivers had granted the right of asylum to churches, the same also applies to consecrated priests, "because in some manner they are a temple of God, having been dedicated to him."[114] This indicates a spatial understanding of the security and immunity surrounding men of God in the same manner as it was applied to church buildings.

This investigation into the larger context of *manumissio in ecclesia, episcopalis audientia,* and ecclesiastical asylum has shown that the relevant laws of Constantine and his successors merely accorded imperial recognition to the already existing competence of the bishops within the church. The legislation on the legal capacities of the bishop did not create a new situation but rather affirmed and moderately expanded the status quo. Constantine, in short, was more a cautious emperor than a shrewd administrator or a devout revolutionary. It is worth repeating what the German scholar Bernhard Kötting had to say on this issue more than twenty-five years ago:

> That the church heaved a sigh of relief and warmly embraced the state after the so-called "Conversion of Constantine" is a fairy tale that had better disappear from serious scholarship on church history. The church and the faithful had been an integral part of the state for a long time before Constantine

---

112. Polybius and John, *Life of Epiphanius, PG* 41, col. 36.
113. Paulinus of Nola, *Life of Ambrose* 21.
114. *PG* 119, col. 856 B–C; cf. also V. Grumel, *Les regestes des actes du Patriarcat du Constantinople,* 2d ed. (Paris, 1972), 888.

granted it certain privileges. His privileges came too late to make Christianity an impressive force.[115]

### ACCESS TO THE EMPEROR: *PARRHĒSIA* OF BISHOPS AND HOLY MEN

The emperors were, on the whole, reactive rather than proactive in their legislation. Many of the laws discussed in the foregoing pages were issued as rescripts, in response to petitions. This raises the question of access to the emperor, either through letters or in a personal visit to his court, in order to obtain legal rulings and other favors. Traditionally, it was the foremost citizens who acted in this way, as the spokesmen of their cities. To be a member of an embassy to the court was considered a great honor that was granted to the prominent citizens whose financial resources allowed them to absorb the considerable costs involved in travel and a long absence. Bishops and holy men could also count on having the emperor's ear.

The general accessibility of the emperor was one of the characteristic features of late Roman government. Individuals or cities, more rarely also corporations, were able to approach him directly with their requests, and they did so with great frequency.[116] Between 354 and 388, for example, the city of Antioch sent at least twelve embassies to the court in Constantinople.[117] There was no limit to the content of these petitions. Bishops sometimes intervened on behalf of individuals to ask for a reversal of a judgment. This, as we have seen, was a likely source of the custom of ecclesiastical asylum. Cities often asked for an elevation of their status, which brought significant financial advantages. The people of Orcistus, for example, successfully petitioned Constantine to have their town recognized as a *civitas*, and then proudly set down Constantine's rescript of the year 331 in an inscription. The inhabitants had made the case that Orcistus boasted all the amenities of a city: a functioning city council, an advantageous location at the intersection of four roads, an ample supply of water to feed public and private baths and to operate water mills, a forum richly adorned with statues, and—last but not least—a large number of inhabitants with a Christian

---

115. "Das Märchen, daß die Kirche sich nach der sogenannten Konstantinischen Wende aufatmend der staatlichen Macht an die Brust geworfen habe, sollte allmählich aus soliden Darstellungen der Kirchengeschichte verschwinden. Die Kirche und die Gläubigen, die sich längst in das staatliche Gefüge eingegliedert hatten, privilegierte Konstantin, nicht erst durch seine Privilegierung ist sie die imponierende Größe geworden" (B. Kötting, "Dienstfunktion und Vollmacht kirchlicher Ämter in der Alten Kirche," in *Macht, Dienst, Herrschaft in Kirche und Gesellschaft*, ed. W. Weber, 79–80 [Freiburg im Breisgau, 1974]; my translation).

116. For the following, see the overview by Millar, *The Emperor in the Roman World*, 410–456 and 551–607.

117. Petit, *Libanius et la vie municipale*, 263.

majority.[118] In times of crisis, when cities found themselves unable to collect the taxes in the previously assessed amount because of famine, grain shortage, or warfare, they requested tax relief or tax remission from the emperor. The mission of Synesius of Cyrene to the court of Arcadius was to ask for an annulment of the taxes from previous years for which the region of Cyrenaica was still in arrears. Participation in such an embassy of the city to the court was considered a great honor and distinction for the individual. It was also a highly valued display of his service to the city, especially when the ambassador paid for his own expenses, as Synesius did. These could be considerable, as they involved not only travel and lodging during a prolonged absence, but also the various "fees" to open the doors to the imperial reception hall.

The great moment came when it was time to present one's case. This often became an occasion for the display of rhetorical fireworks, containing just the right mixture of flattery, information, and entreaty. Naturally, a city would select as its ambassadors its most eloquent men, those who had received ample formal training in rhetoric, to ensure the success of its mission. When travel and the personal presentation of a petition was not an option, the emperor could also be approached in writing. The success of any petition depended not only on the petitioner's rhetorical ability, but also on his connections at court. An extensive network of acquaintances in influential positions would open doors or, in the case of a written request, ensure that the petition actually made its way to the desk of the emperor without delay.

Christians, too, knew how to avail themselves of this channel to gain direct access to the emperor. The dramatic moment when Constantine saw the writing in the sky "In this you shall conquer" may have been the first time a Roman emperor came face-to-face with the message of the Christian God, as the imperial hagiographer Eusebius would have us believe, but it was not the first time that the imperial court was approached by Christians as a collective group.[119] In the second century, Christian apologists like Athenagoras or Tertullian used their eloquence to present the emperor with a positive view of Christianity.[120] It is not always clear whether what has been transmitted to us as apologetic "speeches" were in fact delivered before the emperor. But even if this pretense was merely a literary strategy, it underscores the belief that the possibility of approaching the emperor

118. A. Chastagnol, "L'inscription constantinienne d'Orcistus," *MEFRA* 93 (1981): 381–416.
119. On the presence of Christians in the social life of the Roman Empire, including court circles, in the second and third centuries, see W. Wischmeyer, *Von Golgatha zum Ponte Molle: Studien zur Sozialgeschichte der Kirche im dritten Jahrhundert* (Göttingen, 1992), 21–62.
120. W. R. Schroedel, "Apologetic Literature and Ambassadorial Activities," *Harv. Theol. Rev.* 82 (1989): 55–78.

directly was open to prominent Christian thinkers in the same measure as to their pagan contemporaries.

Episcopal intervention at court began several decades before Constantine showed his imperial favor toward bishops. According to Eusebius, the emperor Gallienus issued two rescripts in answer to requests by Christian bishops, granting them permission to recover churches and cemeteries that had fallen to other uses during the persecution of Valerian.[121] Not long thereafter, the emperor Aurelian was faced with the request to intervene in internal matters of the church. The issue at stake was the possession and use of the church building at Antioch, which Paul of Samosata had refused to relinquish, although he had been deposed from the see of Antioch, excommunicated by a synod of bishops, and a successor had been installed in his place. Aurelian's answer was to grant the use of the church building to the side that was in communion with the church in Italy and Rome, in other words to rule in favor of the majority party that had approached him.[122] At the beginning of the fourth century, petitions by Christians increased at a feverish pace. The intervention of Constantine was sought by the parties involved in the Donatist controversy in North Africa, in the Arian controversy that afflicted the Eastern provinces, and in the Meletian Schism in Egypt. Constantine's response usually consisted in referring the matter to a meeting of bishops, the decision of which he declared binding. This was the tactic he used for the Council of Nicaea in 325 in an attempt to settle the dispute over the teaching of Arius.

More common than episcopal requests for imperial intervention in doctrinal disputes were petitions on behalf of individuals (including the petitioners themselves), specific churches, or their city. Beginning in the fourth century, the bishops increasingly assumed the role of the prominent citizen in representing the city's concerns, either in letters or in person. The volume of their activity must have been considerable. Several rescripts in the Theodosian and the Justinianic codes are the direct result of episcopal intercession. The earliest dates from 369. It is evidence that not all episcopal appeals to the emperor were met with success. The emperor refused to overturn the condemnation of Bishop Chronopius by a council of seventy bishops. Not only that, because Chronopius had petitioned without a just cause, he was fined 50 pounds silver payable not to the fisc, but to the poor.[123] More successful was the bishops' request, in 398 (or perhaps 412), for the punishment and exile of the heretic Jovinian and his followers.[124] A law of 405 hints that it was not unusual for bishops who had been deposed

121. Eusebius, *HE* 7.13.
122. Ibid., 7.30.19.
123. CTh 11.36.20 (369).
124. CTh 16.5.53 (412; 398).

by their colleagues in a council to seek recourse by petitioning the emperor, as Chronopius had done.[125] In 419, Bishop Asclepiades of the Chersonese managed to obtain an imperial amnesty for a number of men who had been condemned for treason—an offense that carried capital punishment—because they had betrayed the secrets of shipbuilding to barbarians.[126] A rescript of 436 granted a special arrangement for the payment of taxes to "Cyrus, the Most Reverend Bishop of the City of Aphrodisium [sic], whose merits are so great that even contrary to the provisions of a general sanction of this kind, he shall not be prohibited from the full enjoyment of a special grant of imperial favor."[127] In 551, the inheritance laws for Samaritans were improved at the request of Sergius, metropolitan of Caesarea in Palestine.[128]

The great law codes of late antiquity, the Codex Theodosianus and the Codex Justinanus, dominate our knowledge of the legal process by privileging the imperial perspective. Legal codification was a selective means of preserving those laws that were considered relevant to the administration of justice (and the preservation of its history) throughout the empire. For this reason, imperial rescripts that were eliminated in the selection process by the compilers of the law codes are now accessible to us only in inscriptions, the medium in which imperial laws were publicized and preserved by the local communities.

By the sixth century, the bishops had assumed such prominence in the governance of their cities that they were involved in the dissemination of imperial orders. Justinian specifically requested their participation in publicizing imperial rescripts on inscriptions. He asked that all the archbishops and patriarchs addressed at the end of his Novella 8 should place the written copy in the sacristy for archival purposes and then advertise it publicly in an inscription:

> Your Highness will act even more advantageously for all persons in your jurisdiction if you should cause this law to be engraved upon marbles or stone, and placed at the portals of the holy church, as this measure will be beneficial by affording all persons the opportunity of reading it, and making themselves familiar with its contents.[129]

In an effort to curb the circulation of fraudulent documents, Justinian also placed the bishops, together with the foremost citizens, in charge of

---

125. Sirm. 2 (405); cf. CTh 16.2.35 (400).

126. CTh 9.40.24 (419).

127. CTh 11.1.37 (436).

128. Nov. Just. 129.1 (551). On the collaboration of bishops and monks of Palestine in soliciting imperial legislation, see P. Gray, "Palestine and Justinian's Legislation on Non-Christian Religions," in *Law, Politics, and Society in the Ancient Mediterranean World,* ed. B. Halpern and D. W. Hobson (Sheffield, 1993).

129. Nov. Just. 8, Edictum.

inspecting and then authenticating any orders issued from the court.[130] The concrete application of this process is known from an inscription of Hadrianopolis, dating from the second half of the sixth century. John, the *scribo* of the Great Palace, had been sent to that city on a special mission to reduce the threat of brigandage by armed horsemen. He first presented the imperial *commonitorium* to the bishop John. Only then was it announced to the local landowners, to whom it was addressed, and published in crude letters on three surfaces of a column base.[131]

Inscriptions recorded the imperial grants of asylum to specific churches that were often issued in response to episcopal requests, as has been noted. Other inscriptions of imperial rescripts to bishops concern administrative matters. An inscription from Corcyrus in Cilicia, from the reign of Anastasius, affirms in response to a query by Bishop Indakos that the bishop and the clergy should be involved in the appointment of the *defensor*.[132] An inscription in Ephesus records a pragmatic sanction by the emperor Justinian addressed to Archbishop Hypatius. It is too fragmentary to allow any further conclusions about its contents, beyond its encouragement to preserve the status quo.[133] A second, even more damaged inscription records a further rescript of the emperor to the archbishop.[134] In a third inscription, Hypatius of Ephesus himself announced the substance of Justinian's ruling in a dispute between the clergy of the churches of Saint Mary and of Saint John.[135] It is rare that the actual text of an episcopal petition to the emperor survives. One such precious document is a papyrus of the second quarter of the fifth century. It is probably the archival copy of a request of Bishop Appion of Syene for military help against the unruly tribes of the Blemmyes and Nobades; further, the bishop also asked that the soldiers be placed under his own command.[136] The outcome of this request is not known.

As the Christianization of the empire progressed at a more rapid pace from the fourth century on, the role of the bishop as pastor of his flock became more and more indistinguishable from his role as advocate for his city. In this regard, he takes up a position alongside the prominent citizens whose two great outlets for asserting and displaying their social standing were the sponsorship of public building activity and the intervention with

130. Nov. Just. 128.17.
131. Feissel and Kaygusuz.
132. *MAMA* 3: no. 197. This rescript is not contained in any of the law codes.
133. *I Ephesus* 7/2, 4133A, *Die Inschriften von Ephesos*, ed. R. Meriç, R. Merkelbach, J. Nollé, and S. Sahin (Bonn, 1981).
134. *I Ephesus* 7/2, 4133B.
135. *I Ephesus* 7/2, 4134.
136. *PLeid.* Z (Chrest. 1.6).

authorities on behalf of the *polis* or *civitas,* either by going on an embassy (as Synesius did) or by writing letters to people in power (as Libanius did). The bishops' pleas and petitions were not only directed to the imperial court; they also lobbied the civil authorities closer to home, most notably the provincial governor. And they asked their acquaintances in influential positions for favors and the support of worthy causes. A large portion of the letter collections of prominent bishops such as Theodoret of Cyrrhus or Gregory the Great is taken up with missives of this kind. Theodoret, for instance, was successful in obtaining tax relief for his city.[137] Those who had friends and acquaintances with influence at the court also tried to press their social network into service. The correspondence of Basil of Caesarea is particularly instructive in this regard.[138] He wrote to praetorian prefects, the master of offices, military generals, and provincial governors and asked for clemency in judicial proceedings, for leniency in financial matters, or for privileges of status. Obviously, a man's prior experience in activating his social network and conducting negotiations with rulers was a useful and desirable qualification for this aspect of his episcopate, whether he exercised it on behalf of individuals or on behalf of his city. This was one of the reasons why Synesius had been an attractive candidate for the see of Cyrene and why, at the other end of the empire, in Gaul, Sidonius Apollinaris recommended Simplicus for the episcopal see of Bourges, for the latter had already dealt with "skin-clad kings and purple-robed emperors."[139]

The amount of travel that late antique bishops undertook as spokesmen of their communities must have been considerable. The frequency of episcopal journeys reached such proportions that they became a cause for complaint. Hosius of Cordoba, for one, was concerned about the effects of prolonged absenteeism and the neglect of the bishop's charitable obligations at home. He knew that episcopal journeys were often undertaken without any real need, motivated merely by a desire for "worldly glories and business."[140] At Hosius's recommendation, the Council of Sardica restricted episcopal travel to appeals for the condemned who had sought the protection of the church. The same council also attempted to install an internal monitoring system: those bishops who provided hospitality to their colleagues who were on a journey to the court were to assure themselves of the legitimate nature of their visitors' mission before sending them on with letters of introduc-

137. Theodoret of Cyrrhus, *Ep.* 42–47.
138. See the brief remarks by B. Treucker, "A Note on Basil's Letters of Recommendation," in *Basil of Caesarea: Christian, Humanist, Ascetic: A Sixteen-Hundredth Anniversary Symposium,* ed. P. J. Fedwick, vol. 1 (Toronto, 1981).
139. Sidonius Apollinaris, *Ep.* 7.9.19.
140. Sardica (343–344), can. 7, H-L I/2, pp. 782–83.

tion.[141] Even heavier restrictions were imposed at the Council of Antioch in 341, which decided that a bishop was allowed to travel to petition the emperor only after obtaining the consent of all other bishops of the province, and a letter of approval from the metropolitan.[142] The synod of African bishops at Hippo in 393 likewise required the permission of the primate of the province for all episcopal travel abroad.[143]

Not long after the church itself had aimed to regulate episcopal travel, imperial legislation followed suit. Fraudulent petitions and appeals to the emperor by bishops who had been condemned by a synod were prohibited in laws of 369 and 405 respectively.[144] One illegitimate reason for travel is indicated in Canon 12 of the Council of Chalcedon in 451: bishops of lesser cities had apparently petitioned the emperor to grant their city the status of a metropolis, which would certainly have increased the status of the bishop but also placed him and his city in competition with the existing metropolis.[145] In a law of 528, Justinian asked the patriarch of Constantinople to instruct all the bishops under his care that they were prohibited from presenting a petition in person and at their own initiative. If necessary, one or two clerics should be sent as emissaries. This measure, the emperor explained, was intended to ensure the continued and proper celebration of the liturgy throughout the provinces and to spare the cities financial hardship, either as a result of the expense of the journey or through the lack of episcopal oversight in the administration of the diocese.[146]

With these restrictive regulations, the leadership of the church and the emperors aimed to keep the negative effect of prolonged absences and unnecessary travel to a minimum, while honoring the bishops' duty and ability to exercise their *parrhēsia* in petitioning the emperor. This was not merely an academic concern. The number of bishops in Constantinople who had come from the Eastern provinces on official or concocted business reached such proportions that they soon formed the *synodos endēmousa* (resident synod). This body is first attested in 448 but may well have been established earlier. It was an ever-changing group of those bishops who happened to be present in the capital. Its task was to advise and assist the patriarch in dogmatic, liturgical, and administrative matters.[147] The emperor sometimes also took counsel with the bishops present in the capital. A law of 360 that

141. Sardica (343), can. 21, H-L I/2, pp. 802–3.
142. Antioch (341), can. 11, H-L I/2, pp. 717–18.
143. Hippo (393), can. 31, H-L II/1, p. 88.
144. CTh 11.36.20 (369); Sirm. 2 (405).
145. Chalcedon (451), can. 12, H-L II/2, p. 800.
146. CJ 1.3.42.
147. A. Papadakis, "*Endemousa Synodos*," *Oxford Dictionary of Byzantium* (New York and Oxford, 1991), 1: 697.

increased the tax liability of the clergy tried to anticipate criticism by adding that "at the court of Our Tranquillity, other bishops who have come from sections of Italy and those also who have come from Spain and Africa, have esteemed that this regulation is very just."[148]

In addition to traveling to the capital, episcopal absenteeism could be created by journeys to attend regional synods, to participate in the ordination of new colleagues, and for a variety of other reasons. Aetius, the bishop of Thessalonike, complained to the Council of Sardica about the frequent and lengthy visits of clergy from the neighboring provinces to his see, especially because he was obliged to extend his hospitality to them.[149] And many funerary inscriptions commemorate bishops who died far away from home.[150]

In the later Roman Empire the approach of petitioners toward the emperor was increasingly associated with the term *parrhēsia*.[151] Eusebius of Nicomedia is said to have had *parrhēsia* with Constantine, for example, and thus was able to arrange an introduction at court for the representatives of the Meletian party, well-known ascetic leaders from Egypt who had traveled to Constantinople. Their group included the same Paphnutius who earlier illustrated for us the importance of intercessory prayer in generating followers and disciples.

The term *parrhēsia* derives from *pas* (all, everything) and *rhēsis* (saying, speech), literally "the ability to say anything."[152] It is often translated as "boldness of speech" or "freedom of access." In the context of the life of the classical Greek city, *parrhēsia* was the ability to raise one's voice freely. It was the sign of a free citizen.[153] But taking too much liberty in one's speeches could easily lead to unpleasant repercussions, as the caution exercised by Libanius in his rhetorical performances in Antioch shows. *Parrhēsia* therefore became increasingly the domain of philosophers. Their rhetorical training was offset by their strength of character and detachment from the world, which made them impervious to displays of power and threats of violence in response to the liberties they took in speaking. They were often called upon to act as advocates for individuals or cities before the powerful. Like the holy men who resemble them in many ways, the philosophers had

148. CTh 16.12.15.2 (360; 359); first part (taxation) repeated CJ 1.3.3, p. 30.

149. Sardica (347?), can. 16, H-L II/1, p. 799.

150. D. Feissel, "L'évêque, titres et fonctions d'après les inscriptions grecs jusqu'au VIIᵉ siècle," in *Actes du XIᵉ Congrès International d'Archéologie Chrétienne*, Studi di Antichità Cristiana 41 and Collection de l'École Française de Rome 123 (Rome, 1989), 1: 812–13.

151. Millar, *The Emperor in the Roman World*, 600.

152. There is an extensive literature on the topic. The following is largely based on G. Scarpat, *Parrhēsia: Storia del termine e delle sue traduzioni in Latino* (Brescia, 1964), and G. J. M. Bartelink, "*Parrhesia*," in *Graecitas et latinitas christianorum primaeva*, Suppl. 3 (Nimwegen, 1970).

153. For the following, see P. L. R. Brown, *Power and Persuasion in Late Antiquity: Towards a Christian Empire* (Madison, 1992), 61–70.

a trademark appearance—a distinctive cloak and a long beard. They persuaded through the force of their character and the effect of their words. But they lacked the powerful dimension of *parrhēsia* in prayer that Christian bishops and holy men could claim for themselves.

The term *parrhēsia* was adopted early on by Christians, who used it to refer to the individual's approach to the emperor in heaven. This Christian *parrhēsia* was acquired through baptism, which transformed men and women into sons and daughters of God who could then confidently address him as "Father." Beyond the *parrhēsia* acquired by all Christians through the grace of baptism, there was the *parrhēsia* of special individuals earned through personal effort. It is in this sense that Moses, who was admired as a "friend of God" by Philo and Origen, was said to have had *parrhēsia*. The stories of Christian martyrs are especially interesting in that they use both civic and religious frames of reference for *parrhēsia*. The martyrs displayed great boldness of speech in their loud and fearless confession of faith before the tribunal and later during their execution, while their suffering in imitation of Christ gained them the ability to intercede freely before God in their prayers. The boldness of speech displayed by the martyrs during their last days on earth thus resulted in their enduring *parrhēsia* in heaven.

The martyr tradition of effective prayer was carried on by the monastic movement. Through asceticism, penance, and the practice of virtues, ascetics strove to earn the same intercessory power of *parrhēsia* with God as the martyrs. The main obstacle to *parrhēsia* was the weight of one's sins, which could be alleviated through a sustained effort at penitential asceticism. Cyril of Scythopolis reports how Euthymius, one of the towering figures of Palestinian monasticism in the sixth century, rejected the desperate pleas of the people to pray for rain during a drought: "What are you seeking from a man who is a sinner? I, my children, because of the quantity of my offenses cannot pray over this with confidence of being heard *(meta parrhēsias)*."[154] On the other hand, extreme asceticism could bear fruit, as Theodoret of Cyrrhus says of James of Nisibis, who died in 337, the same year as Constantine: "And so his familiar access to God *(parrhēsia)* increased every day, and his requests for what he needed to ask from God were granted immediately."[155]

The bishops' status as "senators" of the church, as Jerome had called them, helped to earn them imperial recognition. The bishops in late antiquity, who were mostly of higher social status and thus had received rhetorical training, also relied on the eloquence of their speech and their social networks of acquaintances to influence the emperor in their favor. By virtue of their office, the bishops acted as representatives of their city in the old

154. Cyril of Scythopolis, *Life of Euthymius* 25.
155. Thedoret of Cyrus, *HR* 1.3.

style of prominent pagans, but their liturgical function as mediators of divine grace gave them the potential for *parrhēsia* in heaven. As will be seen below, the emperors placed a high prize on the prayers of the *sacerdotes* for the prosperity of the empire. In asking the emperor for a special favor, the bishop was able to display his *parrhēsia* of free speech and bold address to the emperor in the way pagan ambassadors would do. But beyond that, he became the mediator for the dispensation of divine favors for the emperor through his *parrhēsia* with God. These elements were present in all bishops, but especially in bishops who were revered for their asceticism. The two directions of the *parrhēsia* of the holy bishop, toward God and toward the emperor, are beautifully played out in the *Life of Theodore of Sykeon*. Theodore had prayed for the future success of Maurice, who was at that time a general leading his troops through Sykeon on his way to the Persian frontier. Once Maurice had become emperor, "remembering Theodore's words he sent him a letter asking him to pray for him and for his Empire that it might be preserved in peace and untroubled by enemies and bade him make any request he liked." Theodore later issued a modest request for food to support the poor who came to his monastery, which was answered by Maurice with great generosity. He sent an annual grant of 600 *modii* of grain, along with a gift of a chalice and a paten.[156] In the report of the hagiographer, Theodore's earlier successful intercessory *parrhēsia* before God on behalf of Maurice (who was then an ambitious general) put him in a position to exercise social *parrhēsia* on behalf of the poor with the new emperor.

The large-scale ambassadorial activities of bishops are well attested in imperial and canon law, as well as in other kinds of literature. For individual instances of holy men who acted in this function, we have to turn to the hagiographical record. The *parrhēsia* of holy men depended on the imperial recognition of their status as exemplars of holiness and their asceticism, although they, too, relied on social networking and introductions whenever they could.

Their status as holy men was advertised by their physical appearance. The *Life of Theodore of Sykeon* mentions a certain Antiochus who was passing through Sykeon on his return "to the East" after petitioning the emperor Maurice for assistance for a town that had suffered badly from a barbarian incursion. This man, of whose exact geographical origin the hagiographer seems unaware, could communicate only through an interpreter. Yet everything in his appearance bespoke his holiness and immediately instilled awe: "He had eyebrows that met each other and was an African by race, about

---

156. *Life of Theodore of Sykeon* 54. At this point in the story, Theodore had not yet been ordained to the episcopate.

one hundred years old, and the hair of his head was as white as wool, and hung down to his loins, and so too did his beard, and his nails were very long."[157] Although we are not told about the outcome of this man's intervention, it is safe to assume that the emperor honored his visible state of holiness by granting his requests.

The holy men's scruffiness was often dramatic to the point of being revolting, as in the case of the worm-eaten feet of Daniel the Stylite. It was a forceful declaration of disregard for the rules of comportment that governed the polite society of the world. By the same token, it was a visible and tangible announcement that the holy man followed a different code of conduct, one that prized ascetic perfection over aesthetic appearance. The distinctive ascetic "look"—the emaciated body, neglect of grooming, tattered garments—was an external manifestation of the internal progress of the soul. The true sign of spiritual perfection was written on the face of the holy man. Those who were in complete union with God were often described as wearing a luminous expression. The Coptic *Life* of Pisentius, who was bishop of Coptos in the late sixth and early seventh centuries, contains a charming description of Pisentius's appearance after he had encountered God in prayer. His eyes were "full of light"; they were shining like stars, and he had the cheerful glow of someone "who had been in a wine-shop."[158] Pisentius's transfigured facial expression and his penetrating gaze, it seems, had an immediate effect on the quality of his interaction with others. Those who stood in his presence proved unable to uphold pretenses or to tell lies; they gained a sharp and sudden awareness of their own shortcomings.[159] Whenever holy men of the caliber of Pisentius visited the imperial court, their ascetic detachment made them oblivious to the splendor of their surroundings and immune to the established protocol for approaching the emperor and his family. Their ascetic appearance announced the spiritual basis of their *parrhēsia* with worldly authority.

The visit of a holy man at the court in Constantinople generated more interest and received more attention than the trip of any bishop to the capital. Moreover, holy men were able to avoid controversies in ways that bishops could not. They were thus even able to petition on behalf of bishops. This is borne out in the contacts of Sabas, a leading figure in Palestinian monasticism in the early sixth century, with the court. According to his

---

157. *Life of Theodore of Sykeon* 73.

158. E. A. Wallis Budge, *Coptic Apocrypha in the Dialect of Upper Egypt* (London, 1913; repr., 1977), 290. The hagiographer's choice of words may also be connected with the context of this episode, which describes Pisentius's ability to go for a long time without any water, while his companion was already faint with dehydration.

159. The shepherd who came to receive a blessing from Pisentius was reminded by the holy man's presence that he had committed a rape that morning: Budge, p. 300.

hagiographer Cyril of Scythopolis, Sabas intervened on behalf of Bishop
Elias of Jerusalem, who had become entangled in a doctrinal dispute over
the Council of Chalcedon that threatened to divide the eastern churches.[160]
Hoping to calm the waves of this "fierce storm," Sabas traveled to the court
of Anastasius, the story continues, but was not received into the audience
hall immediately, for he had held himself aloof from the crowd of petitioners, and the doorkeepers had paid no heed to him, "since he looked like a
beggar and viler than all, when they saw him wearing dirty and much-
patched rags." A search eventually turned him out, standing in a corner and
reciting the psalms. When he was brought in, the emperor "saw an angelic
form leading the way for him." The audience ended with Anastasius's request for Sabas's prayers. The emperor also allowed him to spend the winter in the capital and to "enter the palace freely without being announced."
In the description of Cyril of Scythopolis, it was Sabas's outward appearance
and demeanor that singled him out among the throng of petitioners and
eventually gained him the attention of the emperor. In addition, his *parrhēsia*
with God, namely, his ability of intercessory prayer (which Anastasius requested), translated very concretely into free access and *parrhēsia* with the
emperor (which Anastasius granted). Sabas cashed in on this advantage in
the course of his second and third encounters with the emperor, obtaining
his assurance that Elias would not be deposed from the see of Jerusalem,
and his cancellation of a special tax that crushed the church of Jerusalem.

After the bloodshed and destruction of the Samaritan Revolt of 529 in
Palestine, Sabas made a second journey to Constantinople, this time to the
court of Justinian.[161] Again he acted not of his own accord, but as a spokesman for all the bishops of the region. Justinian's treatment of the holy man
was properly respectful and submissive. When he first set eyes on Sabas, the
emperor saw the holy man's head surrounded by a brilliant circle of light,
and then proceeded to kiss it. Sabas's head must have shown the signs of his
ascetic lifestyle, complete with a pale complexion, emaciated cheeks, and
the burn marks he had suffered on his chin during a journey across the hot
desert and its unpredictably blazing geysers near the Dead Sea.[162] Sabas did
not need to make a speech. His appearance and his prayers on behalf of the
emperor and his family were sufficient to obtain every single item on the
long wish list he had brought with him. It included funds for the rebuilding
of ecclesiastical structures damaged in the recent revolt, the construction of
a hospital and a church for the Holy Virgin in Jerusalem, a fort to protect
Sabas's monasteries from incursions across the Persian border, and reduced
taxation for the last two years in arrears. The hagiographer is careful to note

160. *Life of Sabas* 50–54.
161. Ibid., 71–74.
162. Ibid., 22.

the reciprocity of this arrangement: Sabas repaid Justinian's support with his prayers, which were instrumental in securing the capture of Gelimer in Africa and Witigis in Rome, and in convening the Fifth Ecumenical Council to end the recently flared-up dissent over Nestorian and Origenist teaching. As the story of Sabas shows, holy men may have been less willing than bishops to disrupt their lives by traveling, but if they did, their intervention before the emperor was guaranteed to be successful, for they could reciprocate the favor of money or privileges with a unique gift, their special intercession before God. Their appearance and comportment declared their ascetic authority, which, in turn, held the promise of their spiritual abilities of *parrhēsia* with God.

Gregory of Nazianzus's encounter with the emperor Theodosius I in 381 to ask for his dismissal from the see of Constantinople is a skillful and deliberate combination of venerable physical appearance, episcopal status, and rhetorical display. Gregory later recorded the event, in the way in which he wanted it to be remembered, in his autobiographical poem:

> How was it with the emperor? Did I bow down? Did I fall before him? Or clasp his right hand? Did I address him with words of entreaty? Did I send others from among my friends to represent my cause, especially those who were close to me among those in high office? Did I pour forth gold, that mighty power, in my desire to avoid falling from so high a throne? . . . No, I hastened to the purple robe, just as I was.

After this less than subtle hint at his own indifference to the pomp of the imperial palace, Gregory reports the content of his short speech before the emperor and in the process reveals to us the kinds of petitions most often made by bishops: he did not ask "for gold, for colourful mosaics, nor for rich cloths to cover the holy altar; nor that someone from my family might obtain a high position or even just serve at your side, you greatest of men." Once he had asked for permission to retire from his current position, Gregory's speech reached its high point: "'Demand of these grey hairs,' (and I pointed to them, together with the sweat I had poured out for God) 'that they persevere in suffering for the sake of the word. You know how unwilling I was when they set me on the throne.'"[163] Gregory was clearly anxious to remind the emperor (and the audience of his poem) that he could make a legitimate and outwardly visible claim to the holiness acquired through a long life in the service of God, and therefore deserved respect and admiration.

Prominent citizens, bishops, and holy men all acted as advocates for their

---

163. Gregory of Nazianzus, *Carmen* 2.1.11, vv. 1871–1901.

communities and petitioners before the emperor. Yet they had different means at their disposal to accomplish their goal. Prominent citizens depended on their status and role in society—what we have termed pragmatic authority, and holy men relied on the authority they commanded by virtue of their asceticism. Successful petitions by bishops were the result of a combination of their social status and episcopal role, on the the one hand, and their claim to ascetic authority, or at least their display thereof, on the other.

# CHAPTER NINE

# The Bishop as a
# New Urban Functionary

In the two centuries after Constantine, a new understanding of the episco-pate developed that privileged the bishop's pragmatic authority over his ascetic authority. This was the outcome of a gradual process in which a vari-ety of factors coalesced. The accelerated progress of Christianization and the recruitment of bishops predominantly from among the *curiales* com-bined to bring about the increasing identification of church and empire, on the one hand, and the bishop's de facto patronage of his city, on the other. Justinian's declaration, in 545, that canon law had the same legal force as imperial law is evidence of the extent to which Christianity came to perme-ate all aspects of civic life.[1]

While it is difficult to trace this progression in detail, it is possible to compare its early and late stages as they are reflected in the legal codifica-tions of Theodosius and Justinian. A selection of Constantine's laws, and those of his successors, is preserved in the Codex Theodosianus, which was compiled at the instigation of the emperor Theodosius II in 438.[2] New laws, or *novellae*, issued by emperors over the subsequent three decades also survive. An analogous effort at codification was made by the emperor Justinian a century later. His Codex Justinianus gathered all the laws up to 534 that were considered worth preserving. Toward the end of Justinian's reign, the laws that had been promulgated in the intervening period were published in a separate volume of Novels *(Novellae)*. The legal codifications of Theodosius and Justinian shed some light on the development of

---

1. Nov. Just. 131.1.

2. J. Harries and I. Wood, eds., *The Theodosian Code* (Ithaca, N.Y., 1993). On legal practice, see J. Harries, *Law and Empire in Late Antiquity* (Cambridge, 1999). On legal codification, see J. F. Matthews, *Laying Down the Law: A Study of the Theodosian Code* (New Haven and London, 2000).

the emperors' understanding of the bishops' role in society from the fourth to the sixth century.

The most obvious difference between these codes is noticeable right away, in the placement of regulations on the clergy. In the Theodosian Code, regulations on the clergy are included in book 16, the final book of the code, which deals with religion in the widest sense, including Judaism, paganism, heresy, and magic. Near the beginning it contains a group of forty-seven laws under the title "Bishops, Churches, and Clerics." Other laws of relevance to the clergy are scattered throughout the code, appearing in the context of the status of *curiales* or property issues. The compilers of the Theodosian Code did not single out Christianity and its representatives but integrated the laws pertaining to these matters into other contexts.

From this position of marginal concern in the early fifth century, legislation on the clergy is propelled to a singular place of prominence a century later. Book 1 of the Codex Justinianus allocates the first place to matters of faith, the church, and the clergy. After a brief treatment of non-Christian believers, it continues with several laws regarding petitions to the emperor, followed by details about the higher ranks in the imperial bureaucracy and some provincial offices. This progression of concerns—from ecclesiastical to imperial service—offers dramatic confirmation of the complete integration of the clergy into the fabric of the empire by the time of Justinian.

It is important to bear in mind the interpretive challenges posed by the very nature of these laws. As reflections of historical reality, they must be used with great caution. Most laws were issued as rescripts by the emperor, at a specific time, in response to a specific request (with bishops not rarely acting as petitioners, as has been noted) and addressed to a specific official. They were then supposed to have universal validity throughout the empire and could be cited as precedent in legal proceedings. Hence the importance of having the laws available in a *codex*. However, codification was not necessarily tantamount to acknowledging the enduring validity of a law. Some laws were simply incorporated into the codes because of their historical interest, even though their content had long become obsolete. It is therefore safest to treat each law as an expression of imperial will at the time when the law was issued.

## FROM MODEL CHRISTIANS TO MODEL CITIZENS

The imperial attitude toward bishops is reflected in a number of laws. Three areas in particular invite study: first, the internal operation of the church; second, the bishop's interaction with civil authorities; and third, the ideological underpinnings of the legal treatment of bishops.

In fourth-century legislation, especially that of Constantine, the clergy is treated as a corporate body without hierarchical stratification. The collective terms *sacerdos* and *antistēs* are frequently applied to the higher clergy in general, without distinguishing between priests and bishops.[3] This tendency is even more pronounced in the Christian literature of the time, where the distinction between priests and bishops begins to be made only in the fifth century. Until then, the internal operation of the church is not a concern to the legislation. The election and deposition of the clergy has not yet become an issue.

By the time of Justinian, the stratified hierarchy of the church was firmly in place. This is mirrored in the careful distinctions between bishops of cities, archbishops, metropolitans, and patriarchs in the Codex Justinianus. This view from the capital, as it is expressed in the laws, is confirmed at the provincial level in the inscriptions set up in and by local communities. As Denys Feissel has shown, the titles "metropolitan," "archbishop," and "patriarch" do not become common until the sixth century. Until then, and not infrequently even afterwards, inscriptions only employed the title "bishop," even for the holders of metropolitan and patriarchal sees.

Another noteworthy development is the introduction of imperial legislation on the deposition of bishops. This had been of no concern to Constantine. The earliest law that broached the topic dates from 373. Others followed in 400 and 405, respectively.[4] These laws merely endorsed the deposition of bishops that had been effected by a church council for reasons of doctrinal dissent, and declared that a deposed bishop had no means of appeal to the imperial court. A new reason for deposition is mentioned in 383.[5] Now for the first time, the legislators refer to the nexus of suitable conduct and ecclesiastical office. If the former is lacking, the cleric forfeits the latter. This particular law and others like it were intended to protect bishops and other clergy from false accusations, by requiring that their trials be conducted before an episcopal court.[6] The true concern of the legislators is made plain in Sirmondian Constitution 15: "If there is any fault in a minister of religion, he must be removed because of the pollution of his life, and he cannot participate in the sacred mysteries."[7] This emphasis on the personal virtues of the clergy as a precondition for the valid discharge of their liturgical duties is strongly reminiscent of the statements of the church fathers discussed earlier.

---

3. A. di Bernardino, "L'immagine del vescovo attraverso i suoi titoli nel codice teodosiano," in *L'évêque dans la cité du IV^e au V^e siècle: Image et autorité*, ed. E. Rebillard and C. Sotinel, Collection de l'École Française de Rome 248 (Rome, 1998), whose argument for the application of *sacerdos* exclusively to bishops is not entirely convincing.

4. CTh 16.6.1 (373); CJ 1.3.14 (400); CTh 16.2.35 (405); Sirm. 2 (405).

5. Sirm. 3.

6. CTh 16.2.41 (412).

7. Sirm. 15 (412).

Some later laws specify what, in the eyes of the imperial government, constituted the kind of unsuitable conduct that resulted in the immediate defrocking of clergy: the violation of tombs, presumably to gain access to building materials;[8] and the purchase of episcopal office.[9] Playing at dice and attending games merely resulted in a temporary suspension from office, and a penitential period of three years in a monastery.[10] These laws are indicative of a growing concern on the side of the emperors to hold the clergy, and especially the bishops, to a higher moral standard. This concern is also evident in the inclusion in the Codex Justinianus of a law of 469 regarding the proper selection and appointment of bishops, a process that should be free from simony.[11] Moreover, in 535, Justinian added his own regulations on the selection and appointment of bishops in his Novella 6.[12] That the emperors concerned themselves in this manner with episcopal appointments implies an approximation of the episcopate to any other office in the empire.

Justinian's interest in holding the episcopate to high moral standards should be seen in conjunction with his extensive and unprecedented dependence on bishops as reliable civic representatives. One of the distinctive features of his long reign was his effort to centralize government and to strengthen his direct grip on the provinces, while curbing the rampant financial abuses by provincial governors of the local population. The bishops, especially the metropolitans whose sees were located in the provincial capitals, were vital for the implementation of these goals. A number of laws may suffice to illustrate this. In absence of any other [!] civil or military official in the province, bishops were able to receive complaints by creditors on financial cases.[13] They were also specifically placed in charge of hearing complaints against the tax collection of provincial officials and were encouraged, if necessary, to petition the emperor directly.[14] Moreover, a provincial governor had to remain in the province for a period of fifty days after his retirement from his post so that the people could force him to return "everything which they may illegally have given him in the presence of the bishop."[15] By requiring the bishops to keep an eye on the civil administration, Justinian treated them, in effect, as his personal agents with direct and immediate access to his court.

8. NVal 23.1.5 (445).
9. Nov. Just. 6.1.9 (535).
10. Nov. Just. 123.10 (546).
11. CJ 1. 1.3.30 (469); Nov. Just. 6.1.9 (535).
12. Nov. Just. 6 (535).
13. CJ 1.4.21 (528).
14. Nov. Just. 8.8 (535).
15. Nov. Just. 8.9 (535).

What distinguished the clergy in the eyes of the legislators was their exceptional virtue. These were (or were supposed to be) men of outstanding integrity, bound by their own code of moral conduct, free of any self-interest in their actions, and hence above reproach and suspicion. In short, they were examples of the virtuous life. Flowery phrases reminded bishops of the superior code of conduct to which they were beholden. The "priests who serve God and who shine with the integrity of their divine priesthood offer their own lives not only as an adornment to themselves, but also as an example to the common people who are subject and obedient to them," one law says.[16] Another observes: "Chaste and humble bishops are selected, so that, wherever they may go, they will purify everything with the morality of their lives."[17] As in the case of imperial panegyric, this kind of flattery is as much a display of verbiage as it is a projection of wishful thinking. Even if the legislators were aware that many bishops fell short of the mark, they liked to think of them as being above reproach. Indeed, such complimentary remarks tend to occur as a counterpoint to severe criticism and threats of punishment for unworthy clergy.

Moreover, bishops also represented a link to the divine realm, as did the clergy in general. The emperors avowed that they depended on the clergy's prayers for their own welfare and for the prosperity of the empire as a whole. Constantius declared in 361: "We are aware that Our State is sustained more by religion than by official duties and physical toil and sweat."[18] The importance of the prayer of the clergy motivated Honorius in 411 to grant them exemptions from public duties, as he explained:

> The churches shall be free for the duties of divine preaching only, duties of which they are well aware, and they shall spend all the moments of all the hours in due devotion to prayer. They shall rejoice eternally in the protection of Our generosity, since We rejoice in their devotion to the worship of eternal piety.[19]

The famous preamble to Justinian's Novella 6, which advocates a "happy concord" between the church and the empire, unfailingly refers to the priests' duty of praying for the common good:

> Nothing . . . will be a greater matter of concern to the emperor than the dignity and honor of the clergy; the more as they offer prayers to God without ceasing on his behalf. For if the priesthood be in all respects without blame, and full of faith before God, and if the imperial authority rightly and duly

16. Sirm. 2 (405).
17. CJ 1.3.30.3 (469).
18. CTh 16.2.16 (361).
19. Sirm. 11 (412).

adorn the commonwealth committed to its charge, there will ensue a happy concord which will bring forth all good things for mankind.[20]

In the thoroughly Christianized society of the early Byzantine Empire, the intercessory prayer of the clergy was obviously considered essential for a general state of prosperity. Yet the clergy did not have a monopoly on intercessory prayer. Efficacious prayer was also an essential component in the interaction of holy men with the court, as we have noted before. By the time of Justinian, this function of individual holy men was taken up collectively, along with several others, by organized monasticism. Justinian in fact was much more eloquent and more exuberant when he extolled the good services of the monks in this regard:

> Where, however, these holy persons [the monks] pray to God for the prosperity of the government with pure hands, and souls free from every blemish, there is no doubt that Our armies will be victorious, and Our cities well governed; for where God is appeased and favorably disposed towards Us, why should We not enjoy universal peace and the devotion of Our subjects? The earth offers Us its fruits, the sea gives Us up its wealth, and the prayers of Our people will invoke the blessing of God upon the entire Empire. On the other hand, the monks will be entitled to more reverence; their lives will be still more exemplary; and they will shine in the brilliancy of their virtues. They will all have but one wish; all of them will strive to accomplish the same object; all wickedness will be banished as much as possible, more holy and better desires will be entertained; and recognizing these facts, We enact the present law, which We consider to be useful.[21]

By the sixth century, in the perception of the emperors, the clergy was not the only regular source of prayer for the common good. That same service could now also be performed by monks, and better so, for the monks were removed from the cares of the world, while bishops had become more and more involved in matters of civic government.

### BISHOPS AND THE CURIA

The legislators increasingly took for granted the bishops' participation in civic life. The good services that a bishop provided for his city could be extensive. They rivaled the benefactions of prominent citizens in scale and paralleled the public interventions of holy men in intent. The increased importance of bishops in civic life from ca. 350 to 600 has traditionally been

---

20. Nov. Just. 6 Pr., trans. D. J. Geanakoplos, *Byzantium: Church, Society, and Civilization Seen through Contemporary Eyes* (Chicago and London, 1984), 136.
21. Nov. Just. 133.5 (539), trans. Geanakoplos, 136–37.

explained with reference to a "power vacuum" in the cities that facilitated, or even necessitated, episcopal intervention. A great void somehow opened up as a result of the "decline of the *curiales*" and the "decline of the *curia*." These expressions may be pithy and convenient, but they are misleading. The following pages discuss the changes among the *curiales* as a social group, the reduction in the range of responsibilities of the *curia* as the body of municipal administration, and the growing public role of bishops.[22] Since all these developments are evident in the sources during the same time span, it is often assumed that the "rise of the bishop" occurs at the expense of civic self-governance. In fact, the most prominent citizens are joined by the bishop in providing leadership within the city.

"Everybody knows that the *curiales* are the nerves of the state and the sinews of the cities." Thus begins Novella 7 of Marcian, dated 458.[23] Without the city councils, the economic, social, and administrative life in the provinces would not have been able to function. The members of the city council constituted the local social elite and, taken together, the provincial aristocracy. *Curiales* and *politai*, citizens of the *polis*, were one and the same in the eyes of Libanius in the mid-fourth century.[24] Curial status was a desirable social distinction, as it carried certain honors and privileges, the most important being the immunity from torture and corporal punishment in judicial proceedings.[25] It was directly linked to the possession of land and was generally inherited through the father's side of the family, although some attempts were made to introduce the matrilineal principle as well.[26] To qualify for curial status, it was necessary to possess a certain amount of wealth,

---

22. For a good introduction, see A. H. M. Jones, *The Later Roman Empire, 284–602: A Social, Economic, and Administrative Survey* (Oxford, 1964; repr., 1986), 724–63. A levelheaded treatment critical of the notion of the "flight" of the *curiales* is F. Vittinghoff, "Zur Entwicklung der städtischen Selbstverwaltung: Einige kritische Anmerkungen," in *Stadt und Herrschaft: Römische Kaiserzeit und hohes Mittelalter*, ed. F. Vittinghoff, HZ Beihefte, N.F. 7 (Munich, 1982). See also the comprehensive treatment in J. H. W. G. Liebeschuetz, *The Decline and Fall of the Roman City* (Oxford, 2001), and id., "Oligarchies in the Cities of the Byzantine East," in *Integration und Herrschaft: Ethnische Identitäten und soziale Organisation im Frühmittelalter*, ed. W. Pohl and M. Diesenberger, Österr. Ak. Wiss., philos.-hist. Kl., Denkschriften 301 (Vienna, 2002). For North Africa, see C. Lepelley, "The Survival and Fall of the Classical City in Late Roman Africa" in the same volume. For the role of the *curiales*, especially from the fourth to the sixth century, see A. Laniado, *Recherches sur les notables municipaux dans l'Empire protobyzantin* (Paris, 2000). W. Langhammer, *Die rechtliche und soziale Stellung der Magistratus Municipales und der Decuriones in der Übergangsphase der Städte von sich selbst verwaltenden Gemeinden zu Vollzugsorganen des spätantiken Zwangsstaates (2.–4. Jahrhundert der römischen Kaiserzeit)* (Wiesbaden, 1973) deals primarily with the decline of the *curiales*.

23. Marcian, Nov. 7 (458).

24. P. Petit, *Libanius et la vie municipale à Antioche au IV^e siècle après J.-C.* (Paris, 1955), 25.

25. For a detailed treatment see P. Garnsey, "Aspects of the Decline of the Urban Aristocracy in the Empire," *ANRW* 2/1 (Berlin and New York, 1974).

26. Petit, *Libanius et la vie municipale*, 28.

usually landed property inherited through the family. The minimum required possession was 25 *iugera* of land.[27]

Those who had curial status qualified for active service on the *curia*, which was a lifelong obligation. One could also gain a seat in the *curia* of one's hometown after holding an office or as a consequence of receiving an imperial rank or title. Such distinctions were usually bestowed by the emperor on the socially privileged, who had the education and means to attract his attention. The *curiales* carried the full weight of the city's self-governance.[28] Not only did they constitute the pool from which public officers were elected, but they also were held responsible for collecting the taxes within the territory that belonged to the city.[29] Although higher social status in the Roman Empire usually translated into smaller tax obligations, the *curiales* were liable for some taxes. The public services that the *curiales* were expected to perform for the benefit of their city were manifold. Some required time and effort: participation in embassies; legal defense of the interests of the city; supervision of construction of public buildings, roads, bridges, and aqueducts; control of prices and general surveillance of the markets; acting as an *irenophylarchos* (guardian of the peace) and control of brigandage.[30] Other services involved substantial expense: the arrangement, organization, and payment of public spectacles in the theatre or the hippodrome and the provisioning of wood for the heating of the public baths in the city. In addition, there were the costly obligations demanded by the state: the requisition of animals for the public post, the supervision of the imperial arms factories, and the transportation of grain destined for the capitals or for the army stationed in the region. In addition, the *curiales* could be called upon to perform tasks or *munera* on behalf of the imperial government, such as making available a local workforce for the construction of roads and bridges or arranging for the billeting of soldiers. The size of the *curia* varied greatly. The *curiae* of the early Roman Empire usually had 100 members, but some were known to have as many as 1,000. Lists of local dignitaries are preserved on inscriptions from Spain and North Africa. The municipal album from Canusium for the year 223 contains 164 names, of which 100 were *curiales* on active duty; that of Timgad for the year 363–364 lists at least 168 names, including 11 *curiales* who were members of the Christian clergy.[31]

27. CTh 12.1.33 (342).

28. A. H. M. Jones, *The Greek City from Alexander to Justinian* (Oxford, 1940), 192–210.

29. For a detailed analysis and forceful (and not uncontested) reevaluation of the role of the *curiae* with regard to tax collection, see H.-J. Horstkotte, *Die "Steuerhaftung" im spätrömischen "Zwangsstaat,"* 2d ed. (Frankfurt am Main, 1988).

30. Petit, *Libanius et la vie municipale,* 46–49.

31. M. G. Jarrett, "Decurions and Priests," *AJPh* 92 (1971): 515; A. Chastagnol, *L'album municipal de Timgad,* Antiquitas 22 (Bonn, 1978), 33.

The concept of the decline of the *curiales* was popularized at the beginning of the twentieth century by the Russian social historian Michael Rostovtzeff and has become a dominating theme in the discussion of the social shifts in the later Roman Empire.[32] The situation of the *curiales* and the *curiae* was indeed a recurring concern in imperial legislation. This is evident in the large number of relevant laws, 192 in the Theodosian Code, most concentrated in book 12, and 180 in Justinian's *Corpus iuris civilis*.[33] These laws show that *curiales* attempted to escape the financial and other obligations attached to their status. They did so by striving to attain senatorial rank or by joining the military. Personal exemptions could also be obtained by petitioning the emperor directly. Some men asked to be excused because they were over fifty years old, were suffering from gout, or had thirteen children.[34] In 313, Constantine added a further escape route for the *curiales* when he granted exemptions from all compulsory public services to those in the clergy or in monastic life so that they would be unencumbered by any distractions.[35] He was later compelled to clarify and restrict these privileges. One of Augustine's thorns in the flesh was a certain Paulus who had become a bishop in order to escape his debt to the fisc, and who later brought the church of Hippo into discredit because of his inappropriate actions.[36]

But were these exemptions really the motivation that drove the *curiales* into the clergy? If we are to trust the legal sources, the *curiales* who switched careers already possessed considerable private wealth, and the legislators took great pains to prevent it from being siphoned off from public use to ecclesiastical purposes. The laws are largely concerned to ensure that this movement of the *curiales* to escape the burdens of their status, whether by joining the clergy or through other means, did not have any negative impact on the administrative functioning or financial well-being of the cities. The legislators demand that the *curiales* who intended to rid themselves of their obligations to the city council designate a stand-in, usually a son or close relative, for their administrative obligations. This person must also inherit most, if not all, of the property. These laws, it seems to me, show that the *curiales* were quick to respond to the incentives created by Constantine. They seized the opportunity to exploit this convenient loophole to maintain

---

32. M. Rostovtzeff, *The Social and Economic History of the Roman Empire* (Oxford, 1926), 502–41. On this issue, see especially C. Lepelley, "*Quot curiales, tot tyranni*: L'image du décurion oppresseur au Bas-Empire," in *Crise et redressement dans les provinces européennes de l'Empire (milieu du IIIᵉ-milieu du IVᵉ siècle ap. J.-C.): Actes du colloque de Strasbourg (décembre 1981)*, ed. E. Frézouls (Strasbourg, 1983), 143–45.

33. D. Claude, *Die byzantinische Stadt im 6. Jahrhundert* (Munich, 1969), 107.

34. CJ 10.32.13; CJ 10.33.24 (363). Only the latter request was granted.

35. CTh 16.2.2 (313, the correct date established by O. Seeck).

36. Paulus 4, Mandouze, p. 842.

their family fortune intact, away from the grasp of the fisc for as long as the legislation allowed them. Some must have engaged in veritable money-laundering schemes, while their curial colleagues and possibly the bishop, too, turned a blind eye. This is suggested by a law of 408, which imposes a heavy fine of two pounds gold on each of the "ten *curiales*" if they failed to compel a former colleague to return to curial service after he had escaped his obligations by joining the clergy, and had then been deposed by the bishop.[37] Such use of tax evasion does not necessarily indicate financial hardship among the *curiales,* but rather financial acumen. A law of 397 addressed to the proconsul of Africa implies that there was no lack in that region of *curiales* who had the means to perform public services.[38] Moreover, curial service was not universally shunned. Still in the early fifth century some men actively and voluntarily sought membership in the *curia,* as two laws of that period attest.[39]

Further evidence to illustrate the situation of the *curiales* can be extracted from the writings of Libanius.[40] His ancestors on both sides of the family had distinguished themselves as members of the *curia* of the city of Antioch. The many references to individual *curiales* in Libanius's correspondence show that there was little uniformity among them with regard to their personal wealth or their willingness to serve on the *curia.* Libanius had managed to escape his own obligations by virtue of his profession as a teacher of rhetoric and attempted to gain the same exemption for his illegitimate son Cimon. A large number of the fifty-eight *curiales* of Antioch whom Libanius mentions tried to do the same. The need to do so was more urgently felt among those who disposed of only moderate means. Two-thirds of the not-so-rich *curiales* attempted to escape (seven successfully, three unsuccessfully, out of a total of fifteen), while only three of a total of eleven rich *curiales* moved on to senatorial status, which carried with it the exemption from curial service.[41] But not everyone was eager to escape. In Antioch, as in other cities of the empire, about one-third of the *curiales* were known to be "poor," compared to those of middling and great wealth.[42] It is surprising, therefore, that merely less

---

37. Sirm. 9 (408), abbreviated in CTh 16.2.39.

38. CTh 12.5.3 (397).

39. CTh 12.1.172 (410); CTh 12.1.177 (413). Both laws were addressed to the praetorian prefect of Illyricum.

40. For the following, see Petit, *Libanius et la vie municipale,* 352–58. Petit cautions against the incomplete evidence assembled by R. Pack, "*Curiales* in the Correspondence of Libanius," *TAPA* 82 (1951): 176–92. According to Pack's count, six of the eighteen *curiales* who sought immunity were able to attain it. J. H. W. G. Liebeschuetz, *Antioch: City and Imperial Administration in the Later Roman Empire* (Oxford 1972), 179 n. 2, concludes that eleven out of twenty-two curiales who sought exemptions were successful.

41. I follow here the figures given by Petit, *Libanius et la vie municipale.*

42. Petit, *Libanius et la vie municipale,* 331.

than a quarter of the *curiales* claimed poverty to seek an exemption from curial service. Clearly, even at the time of Libanius, there must have been a number of Antiochene *curiales* of restricted means who considered curial service such a distinction and an honor that they were willing to stretch their limited resources in its pursuit.[43] Intellectual, religious, and political conservative that he was, Libanius noted with alarm the decline in civic-mindedness among his compatriots and heaped his praise on those who—unlike himself!—were conscientious members of the *curia*, gladly held municipal office, performed the required expensive liturgies, and went on embassies on behalf of their city. Despite Libanius's lamentations, the breakdown in civic patriotism was not complete: three *curiales* who had attained senatorial rank later supported the city of Antioch nonetheless.[44]

The letters and speeches of Synesius of Cyrene, like Libanius also a *curialis* who managed to obtain imperial exemption from his curial obligations, confirm that economic worries were not paramount among his peers. When Synesius expressed his concern on behalf of the *curiales*, he campaigned before the emperor and the provincial governor to ensure that the *curiales* were treated with the respect that the law accorded them, especially in judicial proceedings, but did not ask for an improvement of their economic burdens.[45] Being spared physical punishment was a traditional distinction of the *honestiores*, the better half of society; being subjected to it would have meant a painful reduction in status to that of the *humiliores*. The *curiales* of Libanius's acquaintance likewise no longer lived in the secure knowledge of their privilege of immunity from corporal punishment. Many of them were subject to beatings if they incurred the displeasure of the provincial governor.[46] A general brutalization of city life was the consequence, where the more powerful bullied those who had no means of recourse.

In addition to offering a less bleak picture of the economic situation of the *curiales* in the Eastern half of the empire in the late fourth century than the legal evidence alone would seem to evoke, Libanius refers to new developments within the curial structure that would be of lasting significance. In a much-repeated phrase, he quipped: "The *curia* which once counted 600 members, now only has 60."[47] This has often been interpreted literally, as a reduction of the membership of the Antiochene *curia* to 10 percent of its

43. For the continued tradition of public service by *curiales* in the later Roman Empire, see also J. E. Lendon, *Empire of Honour: The Art of Government in the Roman World* (Oxford, 1997), 84–89.

44. Liebeschuetz, *Antioch,* 179 n. 2.

45. C. H. Coster, "Synesius, a *curialis* of the Time of the Emperor Arcadius," *Byzantion* 15 (1940–41): 10–38.

46. Petit, *Libanius et la vie municipale,* 287.

47. Libanius, *Or.* 2.33; compare *Or.* 48.3–4 (where once there were 600 or even twice that many, now there are not even 60 *curiales*).

original size since the time of Diocletian. But in the same year, 388, Libanius also remarked that no more than a dozen men were serving on the *curia*.[48] Clearly, he is not talking about a reduction in absolute numbers of the *curiales*, but about a pyramid of importance within the *curia* with a small number of men now dominating proceedings. Libanius here hints at the increasing polarization within the municipal councils, a slow and gradual process that picked up momentum in the course of the fifth and sixth centuries.[49]

This was a largely economic development within the curial class, a scissor movement where the rich became richer and the poor became poorer.[50] It was probably just beginning in Libanius's Antioch. It was well under way in fifth-century Egypt, where the growth of large *latifundia* and the concomitant rise to prominence of very few families who dominated local and regional politics have been well documented.[51] Responsible for this development was the greed of the most wealthy members of the *curia* and their neglect of their poorer fellow citizens. They used all means available to them to enrich themselves, from speculation in land and grain prices to the assessment and collection of taxes, which the government had entrusted to them since the third century. These economic inequalities created a pecking order within the *curia* where, as Libanius observed, "those who have performed lavish liturgies [i.e., the very wealthy benefactors] are able to shut up those who want to speak."[52] Commenting on the scattered remarks to this effect in the letters and speeches of Libanius, Paul Petit dryly notes: "The greed of the *prōtoi* [the first men of the *curia*] does greater harm than the demands of the fisc."[53]

What Libanius alluded to had become an accepted reality in the fifth century, when the terminology for the institutions of municipal self-governance seems to have undergone a significant change.[54] Until then, imperial legis-

---

48. Libanius, *Or.* 49.8 (reduction from 12,000 to 12 [sic]).
49. Petit, *Libanius et la vie municipale*, 352–58, on the *principales curiae*; Liebeschuetz, *Decline and Fall*, 110–20. Libanius's statements are also the basis of A. F. Norman, "Gradations in Later Municipal Society," *JRS* 48 (1958): 79–85.
50. Petit, *Libanius et la vie municipale*, 335–38.
51. J. Gascou, "Les grands domaines, la cité et l'état en Égypte byzantine," *TM* 9 (1985): 1–89, passim.
52. Libanius, *Or.* 62.39. See also Petit, *Libanius et la vie municipale*, 323.
53. Petit, *Libanius et la vie municipale*, 175: "L'avidité des 'prôtoi' fait plus de mal que les exigences du fisc."
54. For this process of internal restructuring within the *curia*, see Jones, *The Later Roman Empire*, 731, 757; Claude, *Die byzantinische Stadt*, esp. 156–58; C. Lepelley, "La carrière municipale dans l'Afrique romaine sous l'Empire tardif," *Ktema* 6 (1981): 333–47. For Egypt and Palestine in the fifth century, see M. Blume, "La Vie de Porphyre et les papyrus: Quelques aspects de la vie municipale à la fin du IV^e et au début du V^e siècle," *Chronique d'Égypte* 66 (1991): 237–44.

lation focused on the *curia*, the city council, and the *decuriones*, the city councilors. In the fifth-century sources, there is mounting evidence that a small body of men, perhaps no more than a dozen or two, played the most active role in the governance of their cities.[55] From the reign of Anastasius onward, the individuals who formed the nominating committee for the magistracies and the pool of potential officeholders were no longer referred to as *decuriones* or *curiales*, but as *principales curiae* or *prōteuontes* (the first members of the *curia*) or as *possessores* or *ktētores* (landowners).[56]

The economic polarization within the *curiae* coincided with the loss of civic autonomy as a result of the administrative reforms of the fourth century, which encouraged a greater centralization of government at the imperial court.[57] As Claude Lepelley has shown, the distinctions between different types of urban settlements had vanished by the fourth century, and *civitas* became the blanket term where previously there had been *municipia*, *oppida*, and so forth. Moreover, where previously the cities had established their own laws, imperial law was now enforced throughout the empire, thus eradicating the individual differences between municipalities. A great deal of local autonomy of the municipalities had been derived from the fact that the *curia* was responsible for the collection of taxes within the territory that it administered. Under Anastasius, the collection of taxes was assigned to an imperial officer, the *vindex*, thus further reducing the scope of responsibilities of the *curia*.[58]

If it is true that the *curiae* in late antiquity underwent an internal process of polarization, we also have an implicit affirmation of the continued existence of the *curiae* (in whatever redefined form) throughout our period.[59] As municipal organizations, the *curiae* did not disappear for a long time. Admittedly, the white dress worn by the provincial magistrates was but a distant memory for John the Lydian, a high-level administrator under

---

55. According to A. J. B. Sirks, P. J. Sijpesteijn, and K. A. Worp, *Ein frühbyzantinisches Szenario für die Amtswechslung der Sitonie*, Münchener Beiträge zur Papyrusforschung und antiken Rechtsgeschichte 86 (Munich, 1996), 103–4: The sixth-century protocol for the election and inauguration of a new *sitonēs* contained in the Pommersfelden Papyri, which probably continued to be observed in South Italy and Sicily into the eighth century, makes a distinction between "the first of the landowners," who suggest a new candidate, and the meeting of all landowners, which approves this suggestion. But I am unable to see that distinction in the Greek text.

56. Sirks, Sijpesteijn, and Worp, 102–3.

57. C. Lepelley, "Vers la fin du 'privilège de la liberté': L'amoindrissement de l'autonomie des cités à l'aube du bas-empire." in *Splendidissima civitas,* ed. André Chastagnol et al. (Paris, 1996).

58. John the Lydian, *De magistratibus* 49. See also A. Chauvot, "Curiales et paysans en Orient à la fin du Ve et au début du VIe siècle: Note sur l'institution du *vindex,*" in *Sociétés urbaines, sociétés rurales dans l'Asie Mineure et la Syrie hellénistiques et romaines,* ed. E. Frézouls (Strasbourg, 1987).

59. M. Whittow, "Ruling the Late Roman and Early Byzantine City: A Continuous History," *Past and Present* 129 (1990): 3–29.

Justinian, who implied that the *curiae* had ceased to administer municipal affairs.[60] On the other hand, Justinian himself passed several laws regulating the affairs of city councils, some even in response to petitions from the concerned municipalities.[61] Civic institutions remained in operation well beyond the sixth century in Ravenna, where the *principales* dominated the *curia*.[62] In the seventh century, the *prōteuontes* still played a leading role in the Chersonese.[63] Individual *curiales* also continue to be attested at least into the seventh century.[64] It was not until the early ninth century that the *curiae* were officially declared to have become obsolete in the Byzantine Empire.[65]

The changes that affected the structure of city life in late antiquity are thus connected with a greater concentration of wealth and power in the hands of a few. It is therefore misleading to speak of a decline of the city councils, when in fact they experienced an internal restructuring. The *possessores* seized the positions of responsibility, while the less wealthy were devising new ways to escape the financial obligations that accompanied service on the city council. This restructuring ensured the continued vitality of city life, although it may have spelled the financial doom, or what was perceived as such, of formerly influential families. The complaints of Libanius may be read as the self-pitying remarks of an old man, who spoke for all his peers when he decried the disappearance of the good old days. The archaeological record certainly confirms that cities

60. John the Lydian, *De magistratibus* 28.
61. See Jones, *The Later Roman Empire*, 744ff.
62. The Ravenna papyri contain the names of forty-eight *curiales* for the period from 474 to 575. They have the notarial powers to register documents in the *gesta municipalia*. These entries continue into the seventh century. See F. Ausbüttel, "Die Curialen und Stadtmagistrate Ravennas im späten 5. und 6. Jahrhundert," *ZPE* 67 (1987): 207–14.
63. A. I. Romanchuk, "Die byzantinische Provinzstadt vom 7. Jahrhundert bis zur ersten Hälfte des 9. Jahrhunderts (auf Grund von Materialien aus Cherson)," in *Besonderheiten der byzantinischen Feudalentwicklung: Eine Sammlung von Beiträgen zu den frühen Jahrhunderten*, ed. H. Köpstein (Berlin, 1983), 62.
64. Jones, *The Later Roman Empire*, 759–63. For sixth-century Cilicia, see G. Dagron, "Two Documents Concerning Mid-Sixth-Century Mopsuestia," in *Charanis Studies: Essays in Honor of Peter Charanis*, ed. Angeliki E. Laiou-Thomadakis (New Brunswick, 1980), repr. in his *La romanité chrétienne en Orient* (London, 1984). Individual *curiales* are still mentioned in seals, letters, and hagiography in the seventh century: W. Brandes, "Byzantine Cities in the Seventh and Eighth Centuries—Different Sources, Different Histories?" in *The Idea and Ideal of the Town between Late Antiquity and the Early Middle Ages*, ed. G. P. Brogiolo and B. Ward-Perkins (Leiden, 1999), 30–31. The *curiae* of Angers and Tours in Gaul were still actively involved in judicial proceedings in the sixth and seventh centuries, as the compilation of their legal forms (*formulae*) made at the beginning of the Carolingian period shows: *MGH Legum, Sectio V, Formulae*. I am grateful to Ralph Mathisen for sharing this information with me.
65. Leo VI, Nov. 46, ed. and trans. P. Noailles and A. Dain, *Les novelles de Léon VI le Sage* (Paris, 1944), 182–85.

continued to prosper, especially in the eastern Mediterranean, well into the seventh century.[66]

Although the bishop was never integrated into the *curia* as just another member, with the beginning of the fifth century his participation in public activities is mentioned in the laws. Here he is most often encountered as operating in conjunction with the highest echelon of urban society: the *archōn* of the *curia*, the *potentiores*, or the *honorati*. The earliest law that demanded the involvement of the bishop in the public affairs of his city dates from 409. It stipulated that the bishop and his clergy, together with the *honorati*, *possessores*, and *curiales*, should select the *defensor civitatis*, an advocate for the socially disenfranchised.[67] After a hiatus of several decades, legislation of this kind resumed again under Anastasius and Justinian, this time with great intensity. A law of Anastasius specified that the nominating committee for the *sitōnēs*, an officer connected with the grain supply, should consist of the bishop and the first among the landowners *(prōteuontes tōn ktētorōn)*.[68] Anastasius also held the bishop, together with the *archōn* (chief magistrate)—or, in the latter's absence, the *defensor*—responsible for the distribution of the *annona naturalis*, provisions in kind, to the soldiers stationed in their territory.[69] In a law of 545, Justinian mentioned as members of a financial oversight committee the bishop and five of the first men in the city *(prōteuontes tēs poleōs)*. Farther on in the text, however, reference is made to the bishop and "the other landowners."[70] Justinian's most extensive law demanding the bishop's participation in municipal administration dates from 530. It required the bishop to participate in the annual audit of municipal expenditures, along with three of the leading citizens:

> Concerning civic incomes or revenues coming to cities in each year from public or private funds, either bequeathed to these by certain persons or donated or otherwise devised or acquired, whether allocated for works or for purchase of grain or for a public aqueduct or for heatings of baths or for harbours or for constructions of walls or of towers or for repair of bridges or for paving of roads or, simply, for the citizens' uses, whether from public or private causes (as has

---

66. Liebeschuetz, *Decline and Fall*, passim.

67. CJ 1.55.8 (409). A similar law of 505 lists the same electorate: CJ 1.4.19 (505). See also the inscription from Korykos in Cilicia Prima, probably from the reign of Anastasius, which contains an imperial rescript in response to a petition of the bishop, clergy, *ktētores kai oikētores*: MAMA 3: no. 197. On the office, see. E. Berneker, *"Defensor civitatis,"* RAC 3 (1957): cols. 649–56.

68. CJ 10.27.3.

69. CJ 1.4.18.

70. Nov. Just. 128.16. The exact identity of the "first of the city," "the first of the landowners," and "the first of the *curia*" has been some matter of debate. See Sirks, Sijpesteijn, and Worp(102 n. 42), who insist that "the first of the landowners" are not identical with "the first of the *curia*."

been said): we ordain that the most God-beloved bishop and three men of good repute and of the chief men in all respects in the several cities, assembling together, in each year should inspect the works performed and should provide that these should be surveyed and that the persons who administer or who have administered these should render accounts; and that in the constructing of the records it should be evident that the works have been completed or the funds for purchase of grain and for baths or concerning paving of roads or concerning an aqueduct or for any other such projects have been administered.[71]

This law implements the appointment of the bishop to a financial oversight committee. It is therefore often viewed as the capstone of the integration of bishops into municipal administration. However, the legislator's care in defining the nature of these financial resources should pique our interest. He mentions, *inter alia*, bequests and donations by private persons, some of which were earmarked for specific projects, others for the general benefit of the citizens—confirmation of the continued importance of private benefactions to the *civitas* in the sixth century. The underlying reason for the bishop's involvement in this committee may well have been that, as the highest religious representative, he was expected to keep an eye on the proper disposition of wills and bequests, especially if they were made for the common good. This would confirm that by the time of Justinian the regular participation of the bishop in civic self-governance had become a matter of fact, but this was often in recognition of his position of ecclesiastical and spiritual leadership, rather than in disregard of it.

The bishops thus did not simply replace the *curia* and its functions, nor were they absorbed into it. Rather, they stood alongside the small body of leading citizens that increasingly monopolized leadership in civic matters.[72]

The bishops' participation in the restructured *curiae* was the result of the general recognition that their leadership function, or what we have termed (pragmatic authority,) had received in the century and more since the reign of Constantine. They had become spokesmen of their cities, advocates for the concerns of the general population, community leaders with the ability to agitate the population into action. As the cities were increasingly Christianized, the roles of highest representative of the Christian community and of prominent leader of civic life fell into one.

---

71. CJ 1.4.26 (530).
72. See also the conclusions by M. Heinzelmann, "Bischof und Herrschaft vom spätantiken Gallien bis zu den karolingischen Hausmeiern: Die institutionellen Grundlagen," in *Herrschaft und Kirche: Beiträge zur Entstehung und Wirkungsweise episkopaler und monastischer Organisationsformen*, ed. F. Prinz, Monographien zur Geschichte des Mittelalters 33 (Stuttgart, 1988), 23–82; J. Durliat, "Les attributions civiles des évêques byzantins: L'exemple du diocèse d'Afrique (533–709)," *JÖB* 32/2 (1982): 73–83; Whittow, 1–29; V. Deroche, *Études sur Léontios de Néapolis*, Acta Universitatis Upsaliensis, Studia Byzantina Upsaliensia 3 (Uppsala, 1995), 143–46; Liebeschuetz, *Decline and Fall*, 137–68.

# Epilogue

The preceding pages have concentrated on the theory and practice of the episcopate within its late antique context. The theological and monastic literature examined in part 1 have revealed the importance of spiritual authority, which accounts for the ⌈potential congruity of bishops and holy men.⌋ Rather than being considered incompatible with or diametrically opposed to the ascetic or the monastic life, the episcopate was considered its culmination, a confirmation of personal virtues attained through an extended effort at *askēsis*. Holy men could and did become bishops, and bishops were expected to lead exemplary, holy lives. The historical and documentary sources that formed the basis of part 2 attest to the expansion of the public role of bishops. The patterns of the selection of candidates, the bishops' interaction with imperial power, and the bishops' position and activities in their cities reveal a gradual development in the role of bishops from model Christians to model citizens. The involvement of the bishops in civic matters was set into motion by the reign of Constantine but became a legislative reality only under the Theodosian dynasty. The pivotal moment may be identified as Theodosius's law of 408, in which bishops were charged with a task—participation in the election of the *defensor civitatis*—that they had not performed before and that was only indirectly connected with their pastoral duties, inasmuch as the concerns of the growing Christian community increasingly became one with those of the city. The process was completed during the reign of Justinian, which showed the bishop acting alongside the magistrates as a regular participant in municipal administration. This trend did not, however, completely mask or obliterate the earlier, spiritual understanding of the episcopate but rather in the manner of a slightly transparent curtain defined its outward appearance in the historical sources of the time, behind which the shadowy outlines of the bishop's spiritual authority are still discernible.

But what was the prevailing attitude and appreciation of the role of bishops in society in the centuries after Constantine? Here it is useful to turn to the commemoration of bishops after their death, which shows us how contemporaries and posterity liked to view individual bishops who were deemed remarkable enough to warrant the preservation of their memory, whether in funerary inscriptions, funerary eulogies, or saints' *Lives*.

Even in death, the bishop's public role paralleled that of other functionaries of the city. The celebration of the commemoration of the bishop's death thus became a source of civic pride and an affirmation of local identity. This local patriotism is still evident in the eulogies on bishops that were delivered at their sees and their place of burial, as in John Chrysostom's *Homily on Ignatius of Antioch* or Gregory of Nazianzus's *Funerary Oration on Basil of Caesarea*.

Funerary inscriptions on bishops are of particular relevance because they advertise the public position of the bishop within his city. Whether a bishop chose to compose his own eulogy—as Eugenius of Laodikeia did, celebrating his family, his building activity, and his career[1]—or whether his epitaph was written by others after his death, in either case his prominence as an important member of the community was announced to future generations, and this announcement was couched in the literary conventions of the day. Because of their brevity, funerary inscriptions condense into a few words what authors of eulogies and saints' *Lives* elaborate at great length with flowery language and lively anecdotes. Adjectives heavy with meaning are often just strung together, as in the following inscription: "Here lies the priest of God, divine, just, an ascetic, orthodox, apostolic, the bishop [Makedon]ios."[2]

More detailed is the inscription for another Makedonios, bishop of Apollonis in Lydia, who died probably after 378. He is known from other sources for his active involvement in protesting the extreme Arian position that the Son is "not similar" *(anhomoios)* to the Father. The inscription for this Makedonios follows:

> Having followed in the footsteps of the apostles, this man was a bishop in the flesh, but not according to the flesh, and in this way [as a bishop] he followed the path of the blessed and left here the bodily remains of a divine soul. He shone greatly in his asceticism, greatly also in his love, truly a holy bishop *(episkopos theios)*. He also took up the fight against all heresy, preserving the true faith of the fathers of the catholic church. This is Makedonios, who in the end is receiving a splendid funerary ornament and the fame of [having

---

1. See above, p. 203.
2. L. Robert, "Bulletin épigraphique," *REG* 85 (1972): 413. The name is uncertain, as is the date. Robert suggests Makedonios.

endured] many persecutions for the sake of Christ because of the demon of the *anhomoios*. [3]

Makedonios's episcopate is touted as the culmination and confirmation of his asceticism and Christian love. He was a follower of the apostles and defended the doctrinal unity of his flock. Makedonios is remembered as a "holy bishop" for his combination of asceticism, episcopal office, and steadfastness in the faith.

The most intriguing inscription is undoubtedly that of Aberkios, found in Hierapolis in Phrygia Salutaris. It dates to the last three decades of the second century.[4] Just like Eugenios of Laodikeia, Aberkios chose to compose his own epitaph, and in similar manner began by introducing himself as "the citizen of an outstanding city." Then he identifies himself as "the disciple of a pure shepherd," mentions his travels to Rome, throughout Syria, and to Nisibis in conjunction with his teaching, and makes opaque references to a "fish from the well" and a "chaste virgin." The meaning of this obscure inscription has generated much scholarly debate, but its Christian content now seems generally accepted. Wolfgang Wischmeyer has convincingly demonstrated that Aberkios employed expressions and phrases that were common in pagan and Christian epigraphy.[5] On the basis of this inscription, it seems, a local author of the fourth century, probably writing after the death of the emperor Julian in 363, composed a *Vita of Aberkios* that enjoyed great popularity in the Byzantine period. At the end of the *Vita*, the inscription is even quoted in the context of the description of Aberkios's death and burial.

The *Vita of Aberkios* provides us with wonderful insight into the mind and method of a fourth-century hagiographer as he was trying to imagine the life of his protagonist two centuries earlier, about whom he probably knew nothing more than the autobiographical statement of the inscription. It is worthy of note that the hagiographer simply assumes that Aberkios was a bishop. He is introduced as such immediately at the beginning of the *Vita*. The inscription, however, does not breathe a word about the clerical rank, if any, of Aberkios. Clearly, to a fourth-century hagiographer, it was unthinkable that a prominent citizen who went through the expense and trouble to erect his own funerary monument on which he

3. H. Grégoire, *Recueil des inscriptions grecques chrétiennes d'Asie Mineure* (Paris, 1922), 1: 118 (my translation). See also M. Guarducci, *Epigrafia greca*, vol. 4, *Epigrafi sacre pagane e cristiane* (Rome, 1978), 398–400, with detailed discussion.

4. On the epigram and its relation to the *Vita*, see R. Merkelbach, "Grabepigramm und Vita des Bischofs Aberkios von Hierapolis," *Epigraphica Anatolica* 28 (1997): 125–39, with reference to the earlier literature.

5. W. Wischmeyer, "Die Aberkiosinschrift als Grabepigramm," *JAC* 23 (1980): 22–47.

identified himself as a traveling teacher of the faith could have been anything else but a bishop.

If funerary inscriptions of bishops reinforce their social prominence among the leading citizens, their hagiographical commemoration depicts them as holy men in the spiritual and ascetic tradition. Bishops become an increasingly popular topic in the hagiography of late antiquity.[6] This is borne out by Paul Halsall's chronological survey of the individuals who were honored with hagiographical texts, as they are listed in the *Bibliotheca hagiographica graeca.*[7] Halsall subdivides his table into the categories of martyrs, monks, monastic leaders, and bishops.[8] In the first century, 27 percent of male saints were bishops, a relatively high number, as it includes all the apostles. In the second and third century, bishops constituted 12 and 13 percent of hagiographical commemoration respectively. During this time, the most numerous saints, including bishops, were those who had died a martyr's death. A slight increase in episcopal saints to 18 and 17 percent occurred in the fourth and fifth centuries. During this time, and especially in the fifth century, monastic saints and the founders of monastic establishments gained greater prominence. It is only in the sixth century that a significant jump occurred, with bishops accounting for 30 percent of all saints. The rising trend continued into the seventh century, with 44 percent, and then evened out in the eighth century, with 34 percent.

In the development of Christian literature, the hagiography of holy bishops thus occupies an important place. This trend has been recognized and studied for the Latin West, but not so much for the Greek East. Christian communities were in the habit of celebrating and commemorating the accomplishments in life and death of their most outstanding members, beginning with the martyrs. Accounts of martyrdoms were composed, often incorporating the original trial records, and shared with other communi-

---

6. Episcopal hagiography has in the last decade or so become a subject of intensified study: R. Lizzi, "Tra i classici e la Bibbia: L'otium come forma di santità episcopale," in *Modelli di santità e modelli di comportamento* (Turin, 1994); M. Forlin Patrucco, "Modelli di santità e santità episcopale nel IV secolo: L'elaborazion dei Padri cappadoci," in *Modelli di santità e modelli di comportamento;* E. Zocca, "La figura del santo vescovo in Africa da Ponzio a Possidio," in *Vescovi e pastori in epoca teodosiana* (Rome, 1997); E. Elm, *Die Macht der Weisheit: Das Bild des Bischofs in der Vita Augustini des Possidius und anderen spätantiken und frühmittelalterlichen Bischofsviten,* Studies in the History of Christian Thought 109 (Leiden and Boston, 2003). The following remarks are not intended to be an exhaustive treatment, but merely to point out significant trends in the hagiographical representations of bishops, predominantly in the East, inasmuch as they are relevant to the theme of this book.

7. Paul Halsall has very generously shared with me the results of chapter 4 of his dissertation, "Women's Bodies, Men's Souls: Sanctity and Gender in Byzantium" (PhD diss., Fordham University, 1999). The relevant table is found after p. 114.

8. These dates refer to the time of life of the saints in question. The hagiographical texts that commemorate them may be of considerably later date.

ties. The *Letter of the Churches of Lyons and Vienne* reported in Eusebius's *Church History* is one example.[9] During the persecutions, bishops often suffered a martyr's death. They did so either because the civic authorities recognized them as leaders of their communities and thus made them special targets, or because they themselves had the urge to come forward to prove their steadfastness in the faith and felt the obligation to set an example to their congregation. Examples are Polycarp of Smyrna and Cyprian of Carthage. After the peace of the church, bishops continued to confront paganism. But now they were harbingers of a triumphant Christianity rather than victims of persecution.[10] Acting as missionaries, they became mediators in a display of the superiority of the Christian religion over all worldly wisdom and over the pantheon of pagan deities.

After the end of the persecutions, it was the ascetic holy men who subjected their bodies to daily martyrdom that were celebrated in hagiographical accounts, a literary tradition that had its beginning with the *Life of Anthony*, composed shortly after his death in 356. Ascetics and monks who were appointed to episcopal sees eventually also became the subject of literary works, but it would take about a century for this development to take root. Holy bishops begin to be celebrated in hagiography in the fifth century, at the same time that the prominent role of bishops in civic life receives official recognition in imperial law. The earliest examples are the *Life of Martin of Tours* (d. 397) by his admirer Sulpicius Severus, the *Life of Ambrose of Milan* (d. 397) by his disciple Paulinus, the *Life of Augustine* (d. 430) by his disciple Possidius, the *Life of Epiphanius of Salamis* (d. 402) by his disciples John and Polybius, the *Life of Porphyry of Gaza* (d. 420), which claims to be the work of his disciple Mark the Deacon, and the Syriac *Life of Rabbula of Edessa* (d. 435) written by a close associate in the Edessene clergy.

The literary commemoration of bishops changed over time, reflecting both developments in the history of the church and hagiographical conventions that were established in response to those developments. The following remarks give a synthesis based on several dozens of *Lives* and funerary eulogies of bishops, spanning the period from the second to the early seventh century. They will show how the spiritual, ascetic, and pragmatic authority of bishops had taken hold of the popular imagination.

There is a twofold danger in concentrating on hagiographical writing. First, there is the possibility of becoming trapped in a circular argument. In the preceding pages, saints' *Lives* have been used selectively to prove and illustrate certain historical observations. It may seem risky to return now to hagiography in search of confirmation of these same historical points. But

9. Eusebius, *HE* 5.1.3–4, 2.

10. See E. Lucius, *Die Anfänge des Heiligenkults in der christlichen Kirche*, ed. G. Anrich (Tübingen, 1904), 410–19.

there is a difference in the kind of hagiographical texts employed in both instances. Whereas we previously made use of saints' *Lives* that are known for their reliable historical detail, we can now also draw on hagiographical texts that are plainly legendary, for it is exactly this distillation of the mash of historical tidbits and common perceptions that will reveal the essence of the popular appreciation of the episcopal role in society.

This brings us to the second problem, that of intention, authorship, and audience of hagiographical texts. Like panegyric and funerary eulogy, with which it shares a common occasion and stylistic similarities, hagiography was intended to praise its protagonist and often did so in a way that was not devoid of self-interest. Beyond their ostensible aim to edify and entertain, saints' *Lives* also pursue a multilayered agenda of a more concrete kind. They serve the apologetic purpose of presenting a whitewashed version of the life of a controversial figure;[11] they aim to create heroic figures or even martyrs for a common doctrinal cause;[12] they want to assert local identity by encouraging a cult, or they hope to establish an ecclesiastical or monastic tradition.[13] The feasts of local martyrs and the annual commemoration of deceased priests and bishops were crucial, for example, in preserving the independence of Gaza from the designs of the neighboring harbor city of Maiouma, as Sozomen, a native of the region, recalls.[14] Such festive occasions would not have been complete without a recital of relevant hagiographical stories.

Moreover, saints' *Lives* can be a vehicle for the hagiographer to claim his own stake in the sanctity of his story,[15] and they are usually intended to encourage the audience to remain loyal to the memory of the saint by showing their support for his shrine by frequent visits, by their readiness to experience miracles there, and—we must assume—by their willingness to honor it with financial donations. The posthumous miracles that make an obligatory appearance at the end of a *Vita* not only serve to confirm the intercessory powers of the saint after his death but also have the exhortatory function of encouraging the audience to seek his intercession.

11. This is the case in the *Life of Epiphanius,* where the author deems it necessary to address his audience directly with apologetic remarks regarding the saint's stance against John Chrysostom: *Life of Epiphanius, PG* 41, col. 105; and the *Life of Eutychius,* which uses the telltale expression *mē genoito* ("far from it") to clear the saint (who was patriarch of Constantinople under Justinian) from all suspicions of heretical leanings: Eustratius, *Life of Eutychius,* p. 79, l. 2472.
12. Examples are the *Life of Metrophanes and Alexander,* the dossier of Paul of Constantinople, and the *Martyrdom of the Holy Notaries Marcian and Martyrius.*
13. This tendency is evident in the *Life of Nicholas of Sion* and the *Life of Theodore of Sykeon.*
14. Sozomen, *HE* 5.3.8.
15. C. Rapp, "Storytelling as Spiritual Communication in Early Greek Hagiography: The Use of *Diegesis,*" *Journal of Early Christian Studies* 6 (1998): 431–48.

These issues are important in the study of individual hagiographical works but can be safely left aside for the present investigation into the common perceptions of the holy bishop as a hagiographical type in late antiquity. Two questions in particular merit closer scrutiny: In view of the fact that hagiographical conventions were first developed for martyrs, and then for ascetic holy men and monks, how does episcopal hagiography accommodate those earlier models of sanctity? What specific episcopal elements does the narrative contain that are not part of the hagiographical repertoire in the description of other kinds of saints?

One spiritual element that holy bishops share with martyrs and ascetic holy men is the gift of foreknowledge. Martyrs and ascetics often are said to have premonitory visions announcing the time and circumstance of their death. Holy bishops have the same. But, in addition, the appointment of a holy bishop to the episcopate is often preceded by a vision that announces this event, a vision experienced either by the future bishop himself or by someone else who communicates it to him.[16] Porphyry of Gaza is reported to have dreamt that he was going to be "married" to the church, as was Rabbula of Edessa.[17] In addition, the hagiographer can take advantage of hindsight and imbue an episode from the bishop's childhood with such premonitory significance. It was remembered about Ambrose, for example, that as a child he played at being a bishop, holding out his hand so that others should kiss it.[18] Similarly, the hagiographer of Eutychius of Constantinople knows that as a boy he had written "patriarch" as his career goal on the wall of the schoolyard.[19] The employment of visions or of significant anecdotes enables the hagiographer to assert that the ordination of the holy bishop was, in effect, divinely preordained. The hagiographers also love to tell stories of bishops-elect making a display of their rejection of office—a confirmation of the humility of the true ascetic, and thus ultimate proof of their worthiness for this office.[20] The hagiographer of Rabbula of Edessa, however, was unimpressed by such gestures. With disarming frankness he states that Rabbula, with calm confidence, immediately accepted his election, because he could see no sense in such false protestations.[21]

The monastic imprint on episcopal hagiography can take several forms.

16. *Life of Peter the Iberian*, p. 51 (the holy man Zeno has a premonition of Peter's ordination) and p. 85 (an "Old Man" in Arabia prophesied his future ordination while he was still very young); *Life of Nicholas of Sion* 67 (dream of a throne and priestly garment); *Life of Epiphanius*, *PG* 41, col. 57 (Paphnutius in Egypt foretells Epiphanius's episcopate in Cyprus) and col. 69 (the local bishop Pappos is directed in a vision to select Epiphanius for the vacant see).
17. Mark the Deacon, *Life of Porphyry of Gaza* 13; *Life of Rabbula*, p. 172.
18. Paulinus, *Life of Ambrose* 4.
19. Eustratius, *Life of Eutychius*, p. 11.
20. See above, pp. 143ff.
21. *Life of Rabbula*, p. 177.

On the literary plane, the prototype of an ascetic *Vita,* the *Life of Anthony,* provided the inspiration and blueprint for later hagiographical writing. This method was employed by the author of the *Life of Epiphanius,* bishop in Cyprus, who modeled his entire narrative on that by Athanasius, from the phrasing of his introduction down to the details of Epiphanius's age and dietary habits. On the historical plane, as has been noted before, many bishops had received a monastic formation earlier in their lives that served as a qualification for their later appointment. Some, like Martin of Tours, Pisentius of Coptos, and Theodore of Sykeon, made every effort so that they could continue to live in a monastic environment. Rabbula of Edessa, it was said, even surpassed the monks in his asceticism, because as a bishop he enjoyed a greater grace.[22] The hagiographers of these holy bishops thus had an easy task of describing (or inflating) the holy bishops' continued adherence to a regimen of fasting or moderate food intake and a regular rhythm of prayer vigils.

An interesting problem arises in the description of bishops who lacked any prior experience of asceticism. In that case, the hagiographers feel obliged to make a special point of emphasizing the moderate lifestyle that these men adopted after their ordination. Ambrose is said to have followed a strict regimen of only one meal per day, combined with frequent prayer vigils.[23] The same moderation in diet is reported of John the Almsgiver, the son of the governor of Cyprus and lifelong friend of the governor of Egypt, Nicetas. John the Almsgiver also insisted on simple bedding and is praised for "having surpassed monks."[24] Some hagiographers expended significant rhetorical skill to introduce a monastic element into their narrative. Gregory of Nazianzus finds sufficient evidence for the monastic credentials of Athanasius of Alexandria in his composition of the *Life of Anthony* and time in exile among the monks of Egypt. That Athanasius had to endure exile, Gregory explains, also makes him a martyr for the Orthodox cause.[25] Leontius of Neapolis praises John the Almsgiver for practicing a kind of vicarious monasticism by founding two monastic establishments in the city. As a result of this, "the life of the city under him was conducted almost after the fashion of a monastery."[26] Such anecdotes show that in the common perception of the episcopate (whether in the mind of the hagiographer or in the actual deeds of the bishop) a display of personal support for or—better yet—engagement in ascetic living was essential for the legitimation of the pragmatic authority of the bishop.

22. Ibid., p. 188.
23. Paulinus, *Life of Ambrose* 9.38.
24. Leontius of Neapolis, *Life of John the Almsgiver* 47.
25. Gregory of Nazianzus, *Or.* 21, *PG* 35, col. 1104 A–B.
26. Leontius of Neapolis, *Life of John the Almsgiver* 48.

The common currency of hagiography are, of course, miracles. This applies to holy bishops as much as to ascetic saints. While both perform miracles that display and advertise their powers over illness, demonic possession, and the adverse forces of nature, the consequences of the miracles worked by holy bishops are specific to their particular position in the church. The *Lives* of holy bishops who lived in the late fourth and fifth centuries abound with tales of miracles that led to conversion. In fact, it was after witnessing miracles that some of the future holy bishops were themselves converted. Rabbula of Edessa, whose father was a pagan priest, was set on the path to conversion after observing the miraculous healing of a paralyzed woman. His hagiographer is acutely aware of the function of miracles in attracting converts, as he notes: "Because signs are necessary for the unbelievers, the good Lord who cares for his servants prepared a bait for him [Rabbula] toward eternal life . . . through a minor miracle that captured him toward life."[27] The working of conversion-producing miracles is, of course, not restricted to holy bishops, but rather an ability they share with all holy men. Ascetic saints were also known to bring unbelievers to the faith. But bishops were uniquely equipped to perform this role in ways that were inaccessible to ascetic holy men, because only they had the liturgical competence to seal the conversion process by conferring baptism.

Miracles by bishops that lead to conversion fall into three general categories. The first is healings of individuals. This miracle results in the conversion and baptism of the individual and his or her household. It is especially effective if the healed convert comes from a prominent family and thus sets a trend that others in the community will feel compelled to follow. If the miracle occurs in public, the bystanders usually also seek baptism. At the sight of Aberkios's exorcism of three possessed men, the crowd falls silent like schoolchildren when their teacher approaches. No less than 500 receive baptism the next day.[28] A second form of public miracle that results in mass conversion is the bishop's display of his power over the forces of nature before a large group of observers. The rain miracle worked by Porphyry of Gaza during a drought brought 127 pagans to Christianity in one fell swoop.[29] Martin of Tours was able to cut down a tree that was sacred to the local pagans and made it fall in the other direction, a miracle that is also reported of Nicholas of Sion at the other end of the Mediterranean.[30]

---

27. *Life of Rabbula*, p. 168 (my translation from Bickell's German). Epiphanius of Salamis converted from Judaism after witnessing the divine recompense for an act of charity by a Christian who gave his coat to a beggar (possibly a literary reminiscence of the *Life of Martin of Tours*): *Life of Epiphanius, PG* 41, col. 29.

28. *Life of Aberkios*, ed. Nissen, pp. 7–16.

29. Mark the Deacon, *Life of Porphyry of Gaza* 20–21.

30. *Life of Nicholas of Sion* 16–19.

Martin's hagiographer declares triumphantly: "On that day salvation came to that region. For there was hardly anyone in that huge crowd of pagans who did not ask for the laying-on of hands."[31]

The third category of conversion-producing miracles concerns the imperial family. As this type of miracle usually results in the baptism of the imperial household by the miracle worker, it is exclusively performed by holy bishops, never by ascetic holy men.[32] The story follows a conventional pattern: a member of the imperial household, usually the daughter, son, or grandson of the emperor, falls ill or suffers from demonic possession. Pagan priests and experienced physicians declare their inability to find a cure. The holy bishop is invited to the court and immediately restores the health of the patient. The whole imperial household, if they are not already Christian, then asks to be baptized. Before the departure of the holy bishop, the emperor expresses his gratitude through generous gifts and the granting of whatever request the bishop may make.

As legendary as such tales may be, they reflect a few important facts about bishops that were common knowledge: bishops conferred baptism, they frequently traveled to the imperial court, and they usually returned home with gifts of money and other kinds of privileges for their city. This is, in other words, the hagiographical version of the bishops' *parrhēsia* before the emperors and their petitioning activity, which has been discussed above.

In the legendary *Martyrdom of Hypatius of Gangrai*, the holy bishop is called to Constantinople not in his function as a physician, but as a warrior to liberate the imperial treasury from a dangerous dragon that had taken possession of it. The outcome of this tale of violent confrontation is the same as that of stories of miraculous healing: conversion; baptism of the emperor, who takes the name Theodosius; return with generous gifts, including a grant of tax relief inscribed on a bronze column.[33] The hagiographers of Hypatius's *Vita* and *Martyrdom* treat his upbringing and youth in only the most superficial manner. It seems to have been unthinkable that a man of such powers did not hold the highest rank in the clergy, and thus he is made to rise through the offices of lector, deacon, and priest. This fact alone serves the hagiographer as a narrative substitute for anecdotes illustrating Hypatius's personal virtue, as he explains that "his diaconate and then the priesthood are testimony to his ascent in an exemplary life."[34] The same rhetorical device had been

---

31. Sulpicius Severus, *Life of Martin of Tours* 13.1–9.

32. Polybius and John, *Life of Epiphanius of Cyprus, PG* 41, cols. 84–89; a similar healing story, but in the Christian household of Theodosius, is reported in the *Life of Donatus of Euroia* 223–319.

33. *Life of Hypatius of Gangrae* 8–10; *Martyrdom of Hypatius of Gangrae* 9–12.

34. *Life of Hypatius of Gangrae*, chap. 1, p. 76.

applied in Pontius's *Life of Cyprian*, which affirmed that Cyprian's rapid rise to the episcopate was a confirmation of his good works.[35]

It is important to note that the hagiographical stories of imperial conversions to Christianity all concentrate on the house of Theodosius.[36] There is no contemporary Greek equivalent to the Latin legend of the baptism of the emperor Constantine by Saint Sylvester. Constantine's support of Christianity has found no reflection in the hagiographical narratives.[37] That privilege was reserved for Theodosius I and his successors. Theodosius I was known and celebrated for prohibiting the public performance of pagan cults. By this time, Christianity had survived the pagan revival attempted by Julian the Apostate, and orthodoxy had prevailed after several decades of wrangling over Arianism. The court of his grandson Theodosius II was said to resemble a monastery. The pious emperor was also rumored to wear a hairshirt under his purple robes in the manner of a true ascetic, and to burn the midnight oil poring over the scriptures, while spending the days in psalmody together with his courtiers.[38] The hagiographical focus on the imperial court at the end of the fourth and the beginning of the fifth century confirms our earlier findings that this was the crucial period in which the bishops gained certainty that their public role in their communities and within the empire had firmly taken root.

The bishop's missionary activity was not confined to unbelievers; it also extended to Christian adherents of different theological views. Here again, the hagiographical record shows holy bishops much more intensely engaged than ascetic holy men. They took part in staged public debates, attended councils and synods, addressed their flock in sermons and encyclical letters, and composed treatises in refutation of what they regarded as heresy. Peter the Iberian was celebrated by his hagiographer for his steadfast support of Nestorius, and a century later, Eutychius of Constantinople took a stand against the imperially supported doctrine of Aphthartodocetism.[39] In many cases, the steadfast bishops suffered punishment and exile. Thus the martyr's fight against the forces of evil in the form of the persecuting

35. Pontius the Deacon, *Life of Cyprian* 3.2–3.

36. The end of book 7 of Sozomen's *Church History* contains several chapters describing the holy bishops at that time: Ambrose of Milan, Donatus of Euroia, Theotimus of Tomi, Epiphanius of Salamis, Acacius of Beroia, and the brothers Zeno and Ajax of Gaza and Maiouma.

37. There is, however, a small cluster of hagiographical texts around the Arian controversy at the time of Constantine. These include the *Life of Metrophanes and Alexander* (Alexander was celebrated as the first bishop of Constantinople), the *Life of Paul* (Paul was Alexander's successor), and the *Martyrdom of the Holy Notaries* (Marcian and Martyrius were associates of Paul and were martyred at the hands of the Arians).

38. Socrates, *HE* 7.22.

39. Eustratius, *Life of Eutychius*, p. 32.

Roman officials became the bishop's fight against evil in the form of the absence of faith or, indeed, the absence of correct faith. The missionary activity of bishops continues to play a prominent role in episcopal hagiography until the mid-sixth century. After that, social justice within his city and its rural hinterland becomes the sole focus of the bishop's local activities.

The holy bishop is further distinguished from the ascetic holy man by his liturgical competence. In addition to the conferral of baptism, this is evident in his celebration of the eucharist. In hagiography, the bishops' liturgical prerogatives are reflected in the miraculous occurrences surrounding the holy bishops' celebration of the eucharistic liturgy. They had visions of, or were instrumental in, the miraculous transformation of the eucharistic elements: bread that oozed blood, lifted itself up, or gave off hot steam, for example. Theodore of Sykeon seems to have excelled at this kind of miracle.[40] The seventh-century *Life of John the Almsgiver* shows a very different approach to the bishop's role in the eucharistic celebration. Instead of the prayerful mediator of the awesome *mysterion* of the transformation of the bread and wine, the bishop appears as the powerful mediator of social peace. John instrumentalized the eucharistic event in order to force the reconciliation of enemies before they approached the altar. On occasion, he did so by publicly shaming them in front of the whole congregation, emerging from behind the altar, advancing toward them in the congregation, and admonishing them to make peace with their adversaries this very moment.[41] Eucharistic blackmail of this kind had its famous precedent in Ambrose's confrontation with the emperor Theodosius over the synagogue at Callinicum, but the *Life of John the Almsgiver* seems to be the first hagiographical record of such a successful episcopal manipulation of his liturgical role.

The use of hagiographical topoi in episcopal hagiography corroborates our earlier findings. Great emphasis is placed on the bishop's ascetic efforts, regardless of their intensity, which serve as a justification for his election and as legitimation of his position of authority. The bishop's spiritual authority is made evident in his miracles that are evidence of the efficacy of his intercessory prayer. The hagiographical reflection of the actual activities of bishops on behalf of their community—those that we have termed pragmatic authority—changes over time. Martyr-bishops were replaced by monk-bishops, and eventually bishops with a liturgical monopoly. The evolution over time of these popular tales reflects and confirms what has been observed with regard to the development of the public role of bishops: Constantine's legislation did not bring about a radical change but rather gave the imper-

---

40. *Life of Theodore of Sykeon* 80 (regular vision), 126 and 127 (miraculous transformation of the bread). *Peter the Iberian*, trans. Raabe, p. 57 (bread oozes blood), and pp. 127–28; *Epiphanius of Cyprus, PG* 41, col. 73 (visions at the consecration of the bread).
41. Leontius of Neapolis, *Life of John the Almsgiver* 41.

ial stamp of approval, as it were, to the existing episcopal activities that affected the lives of the faithful. Through his support of Christianity, Constantine set into motion the process that came to into full view only at the turn of the fifth century with the house of Theodosius. By the time of Justinian, the transformation of the bishop in public view from model Christian to model citizen was complete.

Beginning in the late sixth century, therefore, we encounter a new type of bishop commemorated as holy in hagiography, the career bishop. The first of this kind is Eutychius of Constantinople, whose *Vita* was composed by his disciple shortly after his death in 582. Eutychius had his eyes set on the patriarchal throne since he was a little boy sharing his dreams for the future with his friends in the schoolyard. He received his early education from his grandfather, who was a priest, and then went to Constantinople to complete his studies. When his name was mentioned as a candidate for a see in a rural backwater, he prayed—successfully—that he would be passed over, as he had his mind set on a higher goal. The hagiographer is not very successful in veiling these tales of ambition as expressions of premonition and piety. The second career bishop was John the Almsgiver, who died in his native Cyprus in 619 after conducting the affairs of the church in Alexandria for nearly a decade. Unlike Eutychius, he produced not a single healing miracle, or any other kind of miracle. He did, however, restore social justice to his city by his wise administrative measures. That these career bishops are depicted in the hagiographical medium confirms the enduring appeal of the spiritual and ascetic underpinnings of the episcopal role, even in a changing world.

# BIBLIOGRAPHY

## PRIMARY SOURCES

References in the notes to primary sources are to the works in Greek and Latin. Page numbers of the editions are given only when necessary for the identification of the passage in question. Translations into English, wherever available, are included below. Because the translations in the Ante-Nicene Fathers Series (ANF) and in the Nicene and Post-Nicene Fathers Series (NPNF) are conveniently accessible on the Web at www.ccel.org/fathers2/, the relevant volume numbers have also been indicated.

*Ad Novatianum.*
    Ed.: G. F. Diercks. *Novatiani opera.* CCL 4. Turnhout, 1972.
    Trans.: R. J. DeSimone. *Novatian.* FOTC 67. Washington, D.C., 1974.
Agnellus. *Liber pontificalis ecclesiae Ravennatis.*
    Ed.: O. Holder-Egger. MGH Scriptores rerum Langobardorum et Italicarum saec. VI–IX, 265–391. Hannover, 1878.
    Trans.: D. M. Deliyannis. *Agnellus of Ravenna, The Book of the Pontiffs of the Church of Ravenna.* Washington, D.C., 2004.
Ambrose. *Epistulae. [Ep.]*
    Ed.: M. Zelzer. CSEL 82. 3 vols. Vienna, 1968–82.
    Trans.: NPNF, ser. 2, vol. 10.
———. *Epistulae extra collectionem. [Ep.*]*
    Ed.: M. Zelzer. CSEL 82/83. Vienna, 1982.
———. *On Abraham.*
    Ed.: K. Schenkl. *Sancti Ambrosii opera.* Pt. 1. CSEL 32. Prague, 1897.
    Trans.: T. Tomkinson. *Ambrose, On Abraham.* Etna, Calif., 2000.
———. *On the Duties of the Clergy (De officiis ministrorum).*
    Ed.: M. Testard. *Saint Ambroise, Les devoirs.* 2 vols. Paris, 1984–92.
    Trans.: NPNF, ser. 2, vol. 10.
———. *Sermo 56.*
    Ed.: *PL* 17, cols. 743–45.

Ambrosiaster. *Commentary on the First Letter to Timothy.*
    Ed.: H. J. Vogels. *Ambrosiastri qui dicitur commentarius in epistulas Paulinas.* Pt. 3.
    CSEL 81. Vienna, 1969.
————. *Questions on the Old and New Testament.*
    Ed.: A. Souter. CSEL 50. Vienna and Leipzig, 1908.
Ammianus Marcellinus. *Histories.*
    Ed.: W. Seyfarth, with L. Jacob-Karau and I. Ulman. 2 vols. Leipzig, 1978.
    Trans.: J. C. Rolfe. Loeb ed. 3 vols. Cambridge, Mass., 1963–64.
Anastasius of Sinai. *Homilies on Psalm 6.*
    Ed.: *PG* 89, cols. 1116–44.
————. *Questions and Answers.*
    Ed.: *PG* 89, cols. 312–824.
————. *Viae dux.*
    Ed.: K.-H. Uthemann. CCG 8. Turnhout, 1981.
*Apocalypse of Paul.*
    Ed.: C. Carozzi. *Eschatologie et au-delà: Recherches sur l'apocalypse de Paul.* Aix-en-
    Provence, 1994.
    Trans.: M. R. James. *The Apocryphal New Testament,* 525–55. Oxford, 1924.
*Apostolic Constitutions.*
    Ed.: M. Metzger. *Les constitutions apostoliques.* SCh 320, 329, 336. Paris, 1985.
    Trans.: ANF, vol. 7.
*Apostolic Tradition.*
    Ed. and trans.: G. Dix and rev. H. Chadwick. *The Treatise on the Apostolic Tradition*
    *of St. Hippolytus of Rome.* London and Ridgefield, Conn., 1992. First published
    in 1937.
Athanasius of Alexandria. *Against the Arians* (*Orationes contra Arianos*).
    Ed.: *PG* 26, cols. 12–468.
    Trans.: NPNF, ser. 2, vol. 4.
————. *Defence of His Flight* (*Apologia de fuga sua*).
    Ed.: *PG* 25, cols. 644–80.
    Trans.: NPNF, ser. 1, vol. 4.
————. *Letter to Dracontius.*
    Ed.: *PG* 25, cols. 524–33.
    Trans.: NPNF, ser. 2, vol. 4.
————. *Life of Anthony.*
    Ed.: G. J. M. Bartelink. *Athanase d'Alexandrie, Vie d'Antoine.* SCh 400. Paris, 1994.
    Trans.: R. C. Gregg. *Athanasius, The Life of Anthony and the Letter to Marcellus.* New
    York, 1980.
Augustine. *City of God* (*De civitate Dei*).
    Ed.: B. Dombart and A. Kalb. 2 vols. CCL 47–48. Turnhout, 1955.
    Trans.: H. Bettenson. Harmondsworth, 1972.
————. *Confessions.*
    Ed.: J. J. O'Donnell. 3 vols. Oxford, 1992.
    Trans.: R. S. Pine-Coffin. Harmondsworth, 1961.
————. *Letters.*
    Ed.: A. Goldbacher. CSEL 44, 57. Vienna and Leipzig, 1904, 1911.
    J. Divjak. *Epistolae ex duobus codicibus nuper in lucem prolatae.* Vienna, 1981.

————. *Augustine, Lettres 1–29.* With French translation. Paris, 1987.
Trans.: R. Teske. *The Works of Saint Augustine: A Translation for the 21st Century.* Pt. 2, vol. 2. Hyde Park, 2001–3. [Letters 1–155]
————. *Sermons.*
Ed.: C. Lambot. CCL 41. Turnhout, 1961. [Sermons 1–50]
*PL* 38, col. 23–*PL* 39, col. 1638.
Trans.: E. Hill. *The Works of Saint Augustine: A Translation for the 21st Century.* Pt. 3, vols. 1–11. Brooklyn and New Rochelle, 1990–93.
*Bala'izah: Coptic Texts from deir el-Bala'izah in Upper Egypt.* Edited by P. E. Kahle. 2 vols. London, 1974.
Barsanuphius and John, *Letters.*
Ed.: F. Neyt and P. De Angelis-Noah. SCh 426, 427, 450, 451, 468. Paris, 1977–2002.
Trans.: D. J. Chitty. *Varsanuphius and John, Questions and Answers.* PO 31/3. Paris, 1966. [partial translation]
J. Chryssavgis. *Letters from the Desert: A Selection of Questions and Responses.* Crestwood, N.Y., 2003.
Basil of Caesarea. *An Ascetical Discourse (Sermo asceticus).*
Ed.: *PG* 31, cols. 869–82.
Trans.: M.M. Wagner. *Saint Basil, Ascetical Works.* FOTC 9: 207–15. New York, 1950.
————. *Constitutiones asceticae.*
Ed.: *PG* 31, cols. 1321–1428.
————. *Homilies on the Hexaemeron.*
Ed.: S. Giet. *Basile de Césarée, Homélies sur l'Hexaéméron.* SCh 26 bis. 2d ed. Paris, 1968.
Trans.: NPNF, ser. 2, vol. 8.
————. *Letters. [Ep.]*
Ed.: Y. Courtonne. *Saint Basile, Lettres.* 3 vols. Paris, 1957–66.
Trans.: NPNF, ser. 2, vol. 8.
R. J. Deferrari and M. R. Patrick. *Saint Basil, The Letters.* 4 vols. Loeb ed. London and Cambridge, Mass., 1926–34.
————. *Long Rules (Regulae fusius tractatae).*
Ed.: *PG* 31, cols. 889–1052.
Trans.: M. M. Wagner. *Saint Basil, Ascetical Works,* FOTC 9: 223–447. New York, 1950.
————. *On the Martyr Gordius.*
Ed.: *PG* 31, cols. 489–508.
Trans.: P. Allen. In *"Let Us Die That We May Live": Greek Homilies on Christian Martyrs from Asia Minor, Palestine, and Syria (c. A.D. 350–A.D. 450),* edited by J. Leemans, 56–66. London and New York, 2003.
————. *On the Martyr Mamas.*
Ed.: *PG* 31, cols. 589–600.
Bishop Alexander. *Encomium of Peter of Alexandria* (Coptic).
Trans.: T. Vivian. *St. Peter of Alexandria: Bishop and Martyr.* Philadelphia, 1988.
Cicero. *De officiis.*
Ed.: C. Atzert. Leipzig, 1958.
Trans.: P. G. Walsh. *On Obligations.* Oxford, 2000.

Clement of Alexandria. *Miscellanies* (*Stromata*).
Ed.: O. Stählin, rev. L. Früchtel, and add. U. Treu. *Clemens Alexandrinus*. Vol. 2. GCS. Berlin, 1960. [books 1–6]
———. *Clemens Alexandrinus*. Vol. 3, Stromata Buch VII und VIII. GCS. Berlin, 1970.
Trans.: J. Ferguson. *Clement of Alexandria, Stromateis, Books One to Three.* FOTC. Washington, D.C., 1991.
J. E. L. Oulton and H. Chadwick. *Alexandrian Christianity: Selected Translations of Clement and Origen.* The Library of Christian Classics, vol. 2. London, 1954. [selections]
ANF, vol. 12.
———. *On Virginity.*
Ed.: F. X. Funk and rev. F. Diekamp. *Patres apostolici.* Vol. 2. Tübingen, 1913.
———. *Paedagogus.*
Ed.: O. Stählin. *Clemens Alexandrinus.* Vol. 1, *Protrepticus und Paedagogus.* GCS. Berlin, 1972.
Trans.: S. P. Wood. *Christ the Educator.* FOTC 23. Washington, D.C., 1954.
———. *The Rich Man's Salvation* (*Quis dives salvetur*).
Ed.: O Stählin, L. Früchtel, and U. Treu. *Clemens Alexandrinus.* Vol. 3. GCS. Berlin, 1970.
Trans.: G. W. Butterworth. Loeb ed. Cambridge, Mass., 1919. Reprint, 1968.
(Ps.-)Clement. *Letter to James.*
Ed.: B. Rehm. *Die Pseudoklementinen.* Vol. 2, *Rekognitionen in Rufins Übersetzung.* GCS. Berlin, 1965.
Trans.: ANF, vol. 3.
Codex Justinianus. [CJ]
Ed.: P. Krueger. *Corpus iuris civilis.* Vol. 2. Berlin, 1877. Reprint, 1970.
Codex Theodosianus. [CTh]
Ed.: P. Krueger and T. Mommsen. *Theodosiani libri XVI cum constitutionibus Sirmondianis.* Vol. 1. 2d ed. Berlin, 1954. Reprint, 1962.
Trans.: C. Pharr. *The Theodosian Code and Novels, and the Sirmondian Constitutions.* Princeton, 1952.
*Conciles gaulois du IVe siècle.* Edited by C. Munier and translated and annotated by J. Gaudemet. SCh 241. Paris, 1977.
*Coptic Apocrypha in the Dialect of Upper Egypt.*
Trans.: E. A. Wallis Budge. London, 1913. Reprint, 1977.
*Corpus inscriptionum graecarum.* 4 vols. Berlin, 1828–77. [CIG]
Cyprian. *De lapsis.*
Ed.: W. Hartel. *Cyprian.* CSEL 3/1. Vienna, 1868.
Trans.: ANF, vol. 3.
———. *Letters.* [Ep.]
Ed.: W. Hartel. CSEL 3/2. Vienna, 1871.
Trans.: G. W. Clarke. *The Letters of St. Cyprian of Carthage.* 4 vols., FOTC 43, 44, 46, 47. New York, 1984–89.
Cyril of Scythopolis. *Life of Euthymius.*
Ed.: E. Schwartz. *Kyrillos von Skythopolis.* TU 49/2. Leipzig, 1939.

Trans.: R. M. Price. *Cyril of Scythopolis, Lives of the Monks of Palestine.* Kalamazoo, 1991.
———. *Life of Sabas.*
    Ed.: E. Schwartz. *Kyrillos von Skythopolis.* TU 49/2. Leipzig, 1939.
    Trans.: R. M. Price. Cyril of Scythopolis, Lives of the Monks of Palestine. Kalamazoo, 1991.
*Didache.*
    Ed.: A. von Harnack. *Die Lehre der zwölf Apostel.* Leipzig, 1884.
    Trans.: K. Lake. *The Apostolic Fathers.* Vol. 1. Loeb ed. Cambridge, Mass., 1912. Reprint, 1965.
*Didascalia apostolorum.*
    Ed.: F. X. Funk. *Didascalia et Constitutiones apostolorum.* Vol. 1. Paderborn, 1905.
    R. H. Connolly. *Didascalia apostolorum: The Syriac Version Translated and Accompanied by the Verona Latin Fragments.* Oxford, 1929.
Didymus the Blind. *Commentary on Ecclesiastes.*
    Ed.: M. Gronewald. *Didymos der Blinde, Kommentar zum Ecclesiastes (Tura-Papyrus).* Bonn, 1977.
———. *Commentary on the Psalms.*
    Ed.: L. Doutreleau, A. Gesché, and M. Gronewald. *Didymos der Blinde, Psalmenkommentar (Tura-Papyrus).* Vol.1. Bonn, 1969.
———. *Commentary on Zacharias.*
    Ed.: L. Doutreleau. *Didyme l'Aveugle, Sur Zacharie.* 3 vols. SCh 83–85. Paris, 1962.
*Die Inschriften von Ephesos, Teil VII,* 2. Edited by R. Meriç, R. Merkelbach, J. Nollé, and S. Sahin. Bonn, 1981.
*Die Septuaginta-Papyri und andere altchristliche Texte der Heidelberger Payrus-Sammlung.* Edited by A. Deissmann. Heidelberg, 1905.
Dionysius of Halicarnassus. *Roman Antiquities.*
    Ed.: K. Jacoby. *Dionysii Halicarnasei Antiquitatum romanarum quae supersunt.* 4 vols. Leipzig, 1885–1905. Reprint, 1967.
    Trans.: E. Cary. 7 vols. Loeb ed. Cambridge, Mass., and London, 1971–90.
Egeria. *Travels.*
    Ed.: P. Maraval. *Egerie, Journal de voyage.* SCh 296. Paris, 1997.
    Trans.: J. Wilkinson. *Egeria's Travels.* London, 1971.
Epiphanius. *Panarion.*
    Ed.: K. Holl. *Epiphanius.* Vol. 3, *Ancoratus und Panarion.* GCS. Leipzig, 1933. Rev. ed., J. Dummer. Berlin, 1980.
    Trans.: F. Williams. *The Panarion of Epiphanius of Salamis.* 2 vols. Leiden, 1987–94.
Eucherius of Lyons. *In Praise of the Desert (De laude eremi).*
    Ed.: *PL* 50, cols. 701–12.
    Trans.: C. Cummings. "In Praise of the Desert: A Letter to Hilary of Lérins by Eucher of Lyons." *Cistercian Studies* 11 (1976): 60–72.
Eugippius. *Life of Severinus of Noricum.*
    Ed. : P. Régerat. *Eugippe, Vie de saint Séverin.* SCh 374. Paris, 1991.
    Trans.: L. Bieler and L. Krestan. *Eugippius, The Life of Saint Severin.* FOTC 55. Washington, D.C., 1965.

Eusebius of Caesarea. *Church History*. [*HE*]
Ed.: E. Schwartz, T. Mommsen, and rev. F. Winkelmann. *Eusebius Werke*. Vol. 2.1–
3: *Die Kirchengeschichte*. GCS. Berlin, 1999.
K. Lake. *Eusebius, The Ecclesiastical History*. 2 vols. Loeb ed. Cambridge, Mass., and
London, 1926–32. Reprint, 1964–65. [complete translation]
NPNF, ser. 2, vol. 1.
———. *Commentary on Psalms 95.3–150*.
Ed.: *PG* 23, cols. 441–1369.
———. *Life of Constantine*. [*VC*]
Ed.: I. A. Heikel. *Eusebius Werke*. Vol. 1. GCS. Leipzig, 1902.
Trans.: A. Cameron and S. G. Hall. *Eusebius, Life of Constantine*. Oxford and New
York, 1999.
NPNF, ser. 2, vol. 1.
Eustratius. *Life of Eutychius*.
Ed.: C. Laga. *Eustratii presbyteri vita Eutychii patriarchae Constantinopolitani*. Turn-
hout and Louvain, 1992.
Trans.: A. Cameron. [forthcoming]
Evagrius Ponticus. *Gnostikos*.
Ed.: A. Guillaumont and C. Guillaumont. *Évagre le Pontique, Le gnostique*. SCh 356.
Paris, 1989.
———. *On Prayer*.
Ed.: *PG* 79, cols. 1165–1200.
Trans.: J. E. Bamberger. *Evagrius Ponticus, The Praktikos: Chapters on Prayer*. Kala-
mazoo, 1981.
———. *Praktikos*.
Ed.: A. Guillaumont and C. Guillaumont. *Évagre le Pontique, Traité pratique ou Le
moine*. SCh 171. Paris, 1971.
Trans.: J. E. Bamberger. *Evagrius Ponticus, The Praktikos: Chapters on Prayer*. Kala-
mazoo, 1981.
Evagrius Scholasticus. *Church History*. [*HE*]
Ed.: J. Bidez and L. Parmentier. *The Ecclesiastical History of Evagrius with the Scholia*.
London, 1898. Reprint, Amsterdam, 1964.
Trans.: M. Whitby. *The Ecclesiastical History of Evagrius Scholasticus*. TTH 33. Liver-
pool, 2000.
Feissel, D. *Recueil des inscriptions chrétiennes de Macédoine du III^e au IV^e siècle*. Paris,
1983.
Ferrandus of Carthage. *Life of Fulgentius of Ruspe*.
Ed.: *PL* 65, cols. 117–50.
Gennadius. *Lives of Illustrious Men (De viris illustribus)*.
Ed.: E. Richardson. TU 14/1. Leipzig, 1896.
Trans.: NPNF, ser. 2, vol. 3.
*Greek Anthology (Anthologia graeca)*.
Ed. and trans.: W. R. Paton. *The Greek Anthology*. 5 vols. Loeb ed. Cambridge,
Mass., and London, 1916–18. Reprint, 1958–63.
Gregory of Nazianzus. *Autobiography (Carmen 2)*.
Ed. and trans.: C. White. *Gregory of Nazianzus, Autobiographical Poems*. Cambridge,
1996.

Ed. and German trans.: Beno Meier. *Über die Bischöfe.* Paderborn, 1989.

———. *Homily 21 On Athanasius.*

Ed.: J. Mossay, with G. Lafontaine. *Grégoire de Nazianze, Discours 20–23.* SCh 270. Paris, 1980.

*PG* 35, cols. 1081–1128.

Trans.: C. G. Browne. NPNF, ser. 2, vol. 7. Reprint, Grand Rapids, 1952.

———. *Letters.* [*Ep.*]

Ed.: P. Gallay. *Gregor von Nazianz, Briefe.* GCS. Berlin, 1969.

Trans.: NPNF, ser. 2, vol. 7. [selection]

———. *Oratio 7 On His Brother Caesarius.*

Ed.: *PG* 35, cols. 755–88.

Trans.: L. P. McCauley. *Funeral Orations by Saint Gregory Nazianzen and Saint Ambrose.* FOTC 22. New York, 1953.

———. *On His Father (Oratio funebris in patrem).*

Ed.: *PG* 35, cols. 985–1044.

Trans.: L. P. McCauley. *Funeral Orations by Saint Gregory Nazianzen and Saint Ambrose.* FOTC 22. New York, 1953.

———. *Oratio 2 On His Flight.*

Ed.: J. Bernardi. *Grégoire de Nazianze, Discours 1–3.* SCh 247. Paris, 1978.

Trans.: NPNF, ser. 2, vol. 7.

———. *Oratio 39 On the Holy Lights.*

Ed.: *PG* 36, cols. 335–60.

Trans.: NPNF, ser. 2, vol. 7.

———. *Oratio 43 On Saint Basil the Great.*

Ed.: *PG* 36, cols. 493–606.

Trans.: L. P. McCauley. *Funeral Orations by Saint Gregory Nazianzen and Saint Ambrose.* FOTC 22. New York, 1953.

———. *Testament.*

Ed.: *PG* 37, cols. 389–96.

Gregory of Nyssa, *Encomium on Saint Stephen.*

Ed.: *PG* 46, cols. 701–21.

———. *Funerary Oration on Saint Basil (In laudem fratris Basilii).*

Ed. and trans.: Sister J. A. Stein. *Encomium of Saint Gregory, Bishop of Nyssa, on His Brother Saint Basil.* Catholic University of America. Patristic Studies 17. Washington, D.C., 1928.

———. *Life of Gregory the Wonder-worker.*

Ed.: *PG* 46, cols. 893–957.

Trans.: M. Slusser. *St. Gregory Thaumaturgus, Life and Works.* Washington, D.C., 1998.

———. *Life of Moses.*

Ed.: H. Musurillo. *Gregorii Nysseni opera.* Vol. 7/1. Leiden, 1964.

Trans.: A. J. Malherbe and E. Ferguson. *The Life of Moses.* New York, 1978.

———. *Life of Saint Macrina.*

Ed.: P. Maraval. *Grégoire de Nysse, Vie de Sainte Macrine.* SCh 178. Paris, 1971.

Trans.: V. Woods Callahan. *Saint Gregory of Nyssa, Ascetical Works.* FOTC 58. Washington, D.C., 1967.

———. *On Bishop Meletius (De Meletio episcopo).*

Ed.: *PG* 46, cols. 852–64.

Gregory of Tours. *Life of the Fathers (Liber vitae partum)*. [*VP*]
    Ed.: B. Krusch. *MGH SMer* 1/2. Hannover, 1895. Reprint, 1969.
    Trans.: E. Jones. *Gregory of Tours, Life of the Fathers*. TTH 1. Liverpool, 1991.
Gregory the Great. *Dialogues*.
    Ed. and French trans.: A. de Vogüé. *Grégoire le Grand, Dialogues*. 3 vols. SCh 251, 260, 265. Paris, 1978–80.
    Trans.: O. J. Zimmerman. FOTC 39. New York, 1959.
    ———. *Pastoral Care (Regula pastoralis)*.
    Ed.: F. Rommel. *Grégoire le Grand, Règle pastorale*. SCh 381. Paris, 1992.
    Trans.: H. Davis. ACW 11. Westminster, Md., 1950.
    ———. *Registrum epistularum*.
    Ed.: D. Norberg. 2 vols. CCL 140–140A. Turnhout, 1982.
Gregory the Wonder-worker. *Address of Thanksgiving to Origen*.
    Ed.: H. Crouzel. SCh 148. Paris, 1969.
    Trans.: M. Slusser. *St. Gregory Thaumaturgus, Life and Works*. Washington, D.C., 1998.
Hilarus. *Letters*. [*Ep.*]
    Ed.: A. Thiel. *Epistolae romanorum pontificum*. Braunsberg, 1868.
Hippolytus. *Refutation of All Heresies*.
    Ed.: M. Marcovich. Berlin and New York, 1986.
    Trans.: ANF, vol. 5.
*History of the Monks in Egypt (Historia monachorum)*. [*HM*]
    Ed.: E. Schulz-Flügel. *Tyrannius Rufinus, Historia monachorum sive De vita sanctorum patrum*. Patristische Texte und Studien 34. Berlin, 1990.
    Trans.: B. Ward. *The Lives of the Desert Fathers*. Oxford, 1980.
Honoratus of Marseilles. *Life of Hilarius of Arles*.
    Ed.: P.-A. Jacob. *Honorat de Marseille, La vie d'Hilaire d'Arles*. SCh 404. Paris, 1995.
Ignatius of Antioch. *Letters*.
    Ed.: F. X. Funk and rev. K. Bihlmeyer. *Die Apostolischen Väter*. Tübingen, 1956.
    Trans.: K. Lake. *The Apostolic Fathers*. Vol. 1. Loeb ed. Cambridge, Mass., and London, 1912. Reprint, 1965.
    ANF, vol. 1.
    ———. *Spurious Letters*.
    Ed.: F. X. Funk and F. Diekamp. *Apostolic Fathers*. 2d ed. Tübingen, 1906.
    Trans.: ANF, vol. 1.
*Inscriptiones christianae urbis Romae*. Vol. 1–. Rome, 1922–.
Irenaeus of Lyons. *Five Books against Heresies*.
    Ed.: W. W. Harvey. 2 vols. Cambridge, 1857.
    Trans.: ANF, vol. 1.
Isaias of Scetis, *Asketikon*.
    Ed.: *PG* 40, cols. 1105–1206.
    Trans.: H. de Broc. *Abbé Isaie, Recueil ascétique*. Bellefontaine, 1970. 3d ed., 1985.
Isidore of Pelusium. *Letters*. [*Ep.*]
    Ed.: *PG* 78, cols. 177–1645.
    P. Evieux. *Isidore de Péluse, Lettres*. SCh 422, 454. Paris, 1977–2000. [letters 1214–1700]

Isidore of Seville. *De ecclesiasticis officiis.*
    Ed.: C. M. Lawson. CCL 113. Turnhout, 1989.
Jerome. *Against John of Jerusalem.*
    Ed.: *PL* 23, cols. 355–96.
———. *Against Jovinian.*
    Ed.: *PL* 23, cols. 211–338.
    Trans.: NPNF, ser. 2, vol. 6.
———. *Apology (Against Rufinus).*
    Ed.: P. Lardet. CCL 79. Turnhout, 1982.
    Trans.: NPNF, ser. 2, vol. 3.
———. *Chronicle.*
    Ed.: R. Helm. *Eusebius Werke.* Vol. 7, *Die Chronik des Hieronymus.* GCS. 2d ed.
    Berlin, 1956.
———. *Commentary on Jesaiah.*
    Ed.: R. Gryson, P.-A. Deproost, et al. *Commentaires de Jérome sur le prophète Isaie.* 5
    vols. Freiburg, 1993–99.
———. *Commentary on the Letter to Titus.*
    Ed.: *PL* 26, cols. 589–635.
———. *Letters.* [*Ep.*]
    Ed.: I. Hilberg. CSEL 54–56. Vienna, 1910–18.
    Trans.: NPNF, ser. 2, vol. 6.
———. *Lives of Illustrious Men (De viris illustribus).*
    Ed.: E. Richardson. TU 14/1. Leipzig, 1896.
    Trans.: NPNF, ser. 2, vol. 3.
*Jews and Christians in Egypt: The Jewish Troubles in Alexandria and the Athanasian Con-
    troversy.* Edited and translated by H. I. Bell. London, 1924. [PJews]
John Cassian. *Conferences.*
    Ed.: M. Petschenig. *Iohannis Cassiani opera.* Vol. 2. CSEL 13. Vienna, 1886.
    Trans.: C. Luibheid. New York, 1985.
    NPNF, ser. 2, vol. 9.
———. *Institutes.*
    Ed.: M. Petschenig. *Iohannis Cassiani opera.* Vol. 1. CSEL 17. Vienna, 1888.
    Trans.: NPNF, ser. 2, vol. 9.
John Chrysostom, *Against the Anhomoeans.*
    Ed.: *PG* 48, cols. 795–802.
———. *Against the Enemies of the Monastic Life (Adversus oppugnatores vitae monasticae).*
    Ed.: *PG* 47, cols. 319–86.
———. *De compunctione ad Demetrium.*
    Ed.: *PG* 47, cols. 393–410.
———. *De compunctione ad Stelechium.*
    Ed.: *PG* 47, cols. 411–22.
———. *De nativitate Ioannis Baptistae.*
    Ed.: *PG* 61, cols. 757–62.
———. *De non iudicando proximo.*
    Ed.: *PG* 60, cols. 763–66.

————. *Homilies on 1 Thessalonians.*
　　Ed.: *PG* 62, cols. 391–468.
　　Trans.: NPNF, ser. 1, vol. 13.
————. *Homilies on 1 Timothy 3.*
　　Ed.: *PG* 62, cols. 501–600.
　　Trans.: NPNF, ser. 1, vol. 13.
————. *Homilies on Eutropius.*
　　Ed.: *PG* 52, cols. 391–96.
　　Trans.: NPNF, ser. 1, vol. 9.
————. *Homily 3 on Acts.*
　　Ed.: *PG* 62, cols. 33–42.
　　Trans.: NPNF, ser. 1, vol. 11.
————. *Homily 3 on Colossians 1:15.*
　　Ed.: *PG* 62, cols. 317–24.
　　Trans.: NPNF, ser. 1, vol. 13.
————. *Homily on Meletius of Antioch.*
　　Ed.: *PG* 50, cols. 515–20.
————. *Homily on Saint Babylas.*
　　Ed.: *PG* 50, cols. 527–34.
　　Trans.: NPNF, ser. 1, vol. 9.
————. *On Diodorus of Tarsus.*
　　Ed.: *PG* 52, cols. 761–66.
————. *On His Return (De regressu).*
　　Ed.: W. Wenger. "L'homélie de saint Jean Chrysostome 'A son retour d'Asie.'"
　　*Revue des Études Byzantines* 19 (1961): 110–23.
————. *On the Priesthood.*
　　Ed.: A.-M. Malingrey. *Jean Chrysostome, Sur le sacerdoce.* SCh 272. Paris, 1980.
　　Trans.: NPNF, ser. 1, vol. 9. [with different chapter divisions than the edition]
————. *On Providence (Ad eos qui scandalizati sunt).*
　　Ed.: A.-M. Malingrey. *Jean Chrysostome, Sur la providence de Dieu.* SCh 79. Paris,
　　　1961.
————. *Panegyrics on Saint Paul.*
　　Ed.: A. Piédnagel. *Panégyriques de S. Paul.* SCh 300. Paris, 1982.
John Climacus. *Ladder of Divine Ascent.*
　　Ed.: *PG* 88, cols. 631–1164.
　　Trans.: C. Luibheid and N. Russell. *John Climacus, The Ladder of Divine Ascent.* New
　　　York, 1982.
John the Lydian. *De magistratibus.*
　　Ed. and trans.: A. C. Bandy. *Ioannes Lydus, On Powers or The Magistracies of the
　　　Roman State.* Philadelphia, 1983.
John Moschos. *Spiritual Meadow (Pratum spirituale).*
　　Ed.: *PG* 87/3, cols. 2852–3112.
　　Trans.: J. Wortley. *The Spiritual Meadow.* Kalamazoo, 1992.
Joshua the Stylite. *Chronicle.*
　　Ed.: I.-B. Chabot. *Incerti auctoris Chronicon anonymum Pseudo-Dionysianum vulgo dic-
　　　tum.* CSCO 91, 104, 121. Paris, 1927–.

Trans.: F. R. Trombley and J. W. Watt. *The Chronicle of Pseudo-Joshua the Stylite*. TTH 32. Liverpool, 2000.

Julianus Pomerius. *The Contemplative Life.*
    Ed.: *PL* 59, cols. 415–520.
    Trans.: M. J. Suelzer. ACW 4. Westminster, Md., 1947.

Justinian. Novellae. [Nov. Just.]
    Ed.: R. Schoell and G. Kroll. *Corpus iuris civilis.* Vol. 3. 7th ed. Berlin, 1959.

Lactantius. *Divine institutes.*
    Ed.: P. Monat. 2 vols. SCh 204–5. Paris, 1973.
    Trans.: ANF, vol. 7.

Leontius of Neapolis. *Life of John the Almsgiver.*
    Ed.: A. J. Festugière. L. Rydèn, *Léontios de Néapolis, Vie de Syméon le Fou, Vie de Jean de Chypre.* Paris, 1974.
    Trans.: E. Dawes and N. H. Baynes. *Three Byzantine Saints.* Oxford, 1977. [first published in 1948, with different chapter divisions than the edition]
    ———. *Life of Symeon the Fool.*
    Ed.: A. J. Festugière. L. Rydèn, *Léontios de Néapolis, Vie de Syméon le Fou, Vie de Jean de Chypre.* Paris, 1974.
    Trans.: D. Krueger. *Symeon the Holy Fool: Leontius' Life and the Late Antique City.* Berkeley, 1996.

Libanius. *Autobiography (Or. 1).*
    Ed.: R. Foerster. *Libanii opera.* Vol. 1/1. Leipzig, 1903.
    Trans.: A. F. Norman. *Libanius, Autobiography and Selected Letters.* Vol. 1. Loeb ed. Cambridge, Mass., and London, 1992.

*Liber pontificalis.*
    Ed.: L. Duchesne. 2 vols. Paris, 1955.
    Trans.: A. Davis. *The Book of Pontiffs (Liber pontificalis): The Ancient Biographies of the First Ninety Roman Bishops to A.D. 715.* TTH 6. Liverpool, 1989. Rev. ed., 2000.

*Life of Aberkios.*
    Ed.: T. Nissen. *S. Abercii vita.* Leipzig, 1902.

*Life of Abraham of Qidun* (Syriac).
    Trans.: S. P. Brock and S. Ashbrook Harvey. *Holy Women of the Syrian Orient.* Berkeley, 1987.

*Life of Daniel the Stylite.*
    Ed.: H. Delehaye. *Les saints stylites.* Subs. hag. 14. Brussels and Paris, 1923.
    Trans.:E. Dawes and N. H. Baynes. *Three Byzantine Saints.* London and Oxford, 1948. Reprint, 1977.

*Life of Hypatius of Gangrae.*
    Ed.: S. Ferri. "Il Bios e il Martyrion di Hypatios di Gangrai." *Studi Bizantini e Neoellenici* 3 (1931): 69–103.

*Life of Irene of Chrysobalanton.*
    Ed. and trans.: O. Rosenqvist. *The Life of Irene, Abbess of Chrysobalanton.* Uppsala, 1986.

*Life of Metrophanes and Alexander.*
    Ed.: F. Winkelmann. "Vita Metrophanis et Alexandri (BHG 1279)." *AB* 100 (1982): 147–83.

*Life of Nicholas of Sion.*
   Ed. and trans.: I. Sevcenko and N. Sevcenko. Brookline, 1984.
*Life of Pachomius* (Bohairic).
   Trans.: A. Veilleux. *Pachomian Koinonia*. Vol. 1. Kalamazoo, 1980.
*Life of Pachomius (Vita prima).*
   Ed.: F. Halkin. *Sancti Pachomii vitae graecae*. Subs. hag. 19. Brussels, 1932.
   Trans.: A. Veilleux. *Pachomian Koinonia*. Vol. 1. Kalamazoo, 1980.
*Life of Paul of Constantinople.*
   Ed.: Photius. *Bibliotheke*, cod. 257. [summary]
*Life of Peter the Iberian* (Syriac).
   Trans. in German: R. Raabe. *Petrus der Iberer: Ein Charakterbild zur Kirchen- und Sittengeschichte des fünften Jahrhunderts*. Leipzig, 1895.
*Life of Pisentius of Coptus* (Arabic).
   Trans.: *The Arabic Life of S. Pisentius*. Edited by De Lacy O'Leary. PO 22/3 (1930).
   Trans.: E. A. Wallis Budge. *Coptic Apocrypha in the Dialect of Upper Egypt*. London, 1913. Reprint, 1917.
*Life of Rabbula* (Syriac).
   Trans. in German: G. Bickell. *Ausgewählte Schriften der syrischen Kirchenväter Aphraates, Rabulas und Isaak v. Ninive, zum ersten Male aus dem Syrischen übersetzt.* Kempten, 1874.
*Life of St. Mary of Egypt.*
   Ed.: *PG* 87, cols. 3697–3726.
   Trans.: M. Kouli. In *Holy Women of Byzantium*, edited by A.-M. Talbot. Washington, D.C., 1996.
*Life of Stephen the Younger.*
   Ed.: M.-F. Auzépy. *La vie d' Étienne le Jeune par Étienne le Diacre*. Birmingham Byzantine and Ottoman Monographs 3. Aldershot, 1997.
   Trans.: A.-M. Talbot. *Byzantine Defenders of Images*. Washington, D.C., 1998.
*Life of Symeon the Stylite.*
   Ed.: H. Lietzmann. *Das Leben des heiligen Symeon Stylites*. TU 32/4. Leipzig, 1908.
   Trans.: R. Doran. *The Lives of Simeon Stylites*. Kalamazoo, 1992.
*Life of Symeon the Younger.*
   Ed. and French trans.: P. van den Ven. *La vie ancienne de saint Symeon Stylite le Jeune (521–592)*. 2 vols. Subs. hag. 32. Brussels, 1962–70.
*Life of Theodore of Sykeon.*
   Ed.: A.-J. Festugière. *Vie de Théodore de Sykéôn*. 2 vols. Subs. hag. 48. Brussels, 1970.
   Trans.: E. Dawes and N. H. Baynes. *Three Byzantine Saints*. Oxford, 1977. First published in 1948. [partial translation]
Mansi, G. D. *Sacrorum conciliorum nova et amplissima collectio*. 54 vols. Paris, 1901–27. First published in 1759–98. [Mansi]
Mark the Deacon. *Life of Porphyry of Gaza.*
   Ed.: H. Grégoire and M.-A. Kugener. *Marc le Diacre, Vie de Porphyre*. Paris, 1930.
   Trans.: G. F. Hill. *The Life of Porphyry, Bishop of Gaza*. Oxford, 1913.
*Martyrdom of the Holy Notaries Marcian and Martyrius.*
   Ed.: P. Franchi de Cavalieri. *AB* 64 (1946): 169–75.

*Martyrdom of Hypatius of Gangrae.*
Ed.: S. Ferri. "Il Bios e il Martyrion di Hypatios di Gangrai." *Studi Bizantini e Neoellenici* 3 (1931): 69–103.
*Martyrdom of Pionius.*
Ed. and French trans.: L. Robert. *Le martyre de Pionios prêtre de Smyrne.* Edited by G. W. Bowersock and C. P. Jones. Washington, D.C., 1994.
Maximus Confessor. *Diversa capita.*
Ed.: *PG* 90, cols. 1177–1389.
———. *Quaestiones ad Thalassium.*
Ed.: C. Laga and C. G. Steel. *Maximi confessoris quaestiones ad Thalassium, una cum Latina interpretatione Ioannis Scotti Eriugenae iuxta posita.* 2 vols. CCG 7, 22. Turnhout, 1980–90.
[Maximus of Turin]. *Sermons* 22–23.
Ed.: *PL* 57, cols. 889–94.
Menander Rhetor.
Ed. and trans.: D. A. Russell and N. G. Wilson. Oxford, 1981.
*Monumenta Asiae Minoris antiqua.* Vols. 1–. Manchester and London, 1928–. [*MAMA*]
Nilus of Ancyra. *Liber de monastica exercitatione.*
Ed.: *PG* 79, cols. 720–809.
Nilus the Hermit (Syriac).
Ed.: B. Bettiolo. *Gli scritti siriaci di Nilo il Solitario.* Publications de l'Institut Orientaliste de Louvain 30. Louvain, 1993.
Novellae.
Ed.: T. Mommsen and P. M. Meyer. *Leges novellae ad Theodosianum pertinentes.* 2d ed., Berlin, 1954. Reprint, 1962.
*Novels of Leo VI.*
Ed.: P. Noailles and A. Dain. *Les novelles de Léon VI le Sage.* Paris, 1944.
"On Hermits and Desert Dwellers." In *Ascetic Behavior in Greco-Roman Antiquity: A Sourcebook,* translated by J. P. Amar and edited by V. L. Wimbush. Fortress Press, 1990.
Optatus of Milevis. *Against the Donatists.*
Ed.: M. Labrousse. *Traité contre les donatistes.* SCh 412–13. Paris, 1995–96.
Trans.: M. Edwards. *Optatus, Against the Donatists.* TTH 27. Liverpool, 1997.
Origen. *Against Celsus* (*Contra Celsum*).
Ed.: P. Koetschau. *Origenes Werke.* Vols. 1–2. GCS. Leipzig, 1899.
Trans.: H. Chadwick. Cambridge, 1953.
———. *Commentary on Matthew.*
Ed.: E, Klostermann, E. Benz, and rev. U. Treu. *Origenes Werke.* Vol. 11, *Origenes Matthäuserklärung,* pt. 2. GCS. Berlin, 1976.
Trans.: ANF, vol. 9.
———. *Commentary on Romans.*
Ed.: T. Heither. *Origenes, Römerbriefkommentar, siebtes und achtes Buch.* Freiburg, 1994.
Trans.: T. P. Scheck. *Origen, Commentary on the Epistle to the Romans.* 2 vols. FOTC 103–4. Washington, D.C., 2001–2.

————. *Homilies on Jeremiah.*
　Ed.: P. Nautin. *Origène, Homélies sur Jérémie.* 2 vols. SCh, 232, 238. Paris, 1976–77.
　Trans.: J. C. Smith. *Origen, Homilies on Jeremiah.* FOTC 97. Washington, D.C., 1998.
————. *Homilies on Joshua.*
　Ed.: W. A. Baehrens. *Origenes Werke.* Vol. 7, *Homilien zum Hexateuch in Rufins Übersetzung,* pt. 2. GCS. Leipzig, 1921.
　Trans.: B. J. Bruce and C. White. *Origen, Homilies on Joshua.* FOTC 105. Washington, D.C., 2002.
————. *Homilies on Numbers.*
　Ed.: W. A. Baehrens. *Origenes Werke.* Vol. 7, *Homilien zum Hexateuch in Rufins Übersetzung,* pt. 2. GCS. Leipzig, 1921.
————. *Homily on Leviticus.*
　Ed.: W. A. Baehrens. *Origenes Werke.* Vol. 6, *Homilien zum Hexateuch in Rufins Übersetzung,* pt. 1. GCS. Leipzig, 1920.
　Trans.: G. W. Barkley. *Origen, Homilies on Leviticus 1–16.* FOTC 83. Washington, D.C., 1990.
————. *On Prayer (De oratione).*
　Ed.: P. Koetschau. *Origenes Werke.* Vol. 2. GCS. Leipzig, 1899.
　Trans.: R. A. Greer. *Origen.* New York, 1979.
Orosius. *Against the Pagans.*
　Ed.:. C. Zangemeister. CSEL 5. Vienna, 1882.
　Trans.: R. J. Deferrari. *The Seven Books of History against the Pagans.* FOTC 50. Washington, D.C., 1964.
*The Oxyrhynchus Papyri.* Edited by B. P. Grenfell and A. S. Hunt. Vols. 1–. London, 1898–. [*POxy*]
Palladius of Helenopolis. *Dialogue on the Life of St. John Chrysostom.*
　Ed.: A.-M. Malingrey. *Palladios, Dialogue sur la vie de Jean Chrysostome.* 2 vols. SCh 341, 342. Paris, 1988.
　Trans.: R. T. Meyer. *Dialogue on the Life of St. John Chrysostom.* New York, 1985.
————. *Lausiac History (Historia Lausiaca).* [*HL*]
　Ed.: G. J. M. Bartelink. Milan, 1974.
　Trans.: R. T. Meyer. ACW 34. London, 1965.
*Papyri from Hermopolis.* Edited by B. R. Rees. London, 1964.
*Passio of Perpetua and Felicity.*
　Ed.: J. Amat. *Passion de Perpétue et de Félicité.* SCh 417. Paris, 1996.
　Trans.: ANF, vol. 3.
Paulinus. *Life of Ambrose.*
　Ed.: M. S. Kaniecka. *Paulinus, Vita sancti Ambrosii.* Catholic University of America, Patristic Studies 16. Washington, D.C., 1928.
　Trans.: R. J. Deferrari. *Early Christian Biographies.* FOTC 15. Washington, D.C., 1952.
Philo of Alexandria. *De decalogo.*
　Ed.: L. Cohn. *Philonis Alexandrini opera quae supersunt.* Vol. 4. Berlin, 1902.
————. *De vita contemplativa.*
　Ed.: L. Cohn and S. Reiter. *Philonis Alexandrini opera quae supersunt.* Vol. 6. Berlin, 1915.

———. *Life of Moses.*
Ed.: L. Cohn. *Philonis Alexandrini opera que supersunt.* Vol. 4. Berlin, 1902.
Trans.: F. H. Colson. *Philo.* Vol. 6. Loeb ed. Cambridge, Mass., and London, 1959.
First published in 1935.
Philostorgius. *Church History.* [*HE*]
Ed.: J. Bidez and rev. F. Winkelmann. *Philostorgius, Historia ecclesiastica.* Berlin, 1981.
Photius. *Bibliotheca.*
Ed.: R. Henry. *Photius, Bibliothèque.* 8 vols. Paris, 1959–77.
Polybius and John. *Life of Epiphanius of Cyprus.*
Ed.: *PG* 41, cols. 23–113.
Pontius the Deacon. *Life of Cyprian.*
Ed.: W. Hartel CSEL 3/3. Vienna, 1871.
A. Bastiaensen. *Vite dei santi.* Vol. 3. Milan, 1975.
Trans.: R. J. Deferrari. *Early Christian Biographies.* FOTC 15. Washington, D.C., 1952.
Possidius. *Life of Augustine.*
Ed.: H. T. Weiskotten. *Sancti Augustini vita scripta a Possidio episcope.* Princeton, 1919.
Trans.: R. J. Deferrari. *Early Christian Biographies.* FOTC 15. Washington, D.C., 1952.
Procopius. *Wars.*
Ed.: J. Hauryand G. Wirth. 2 vols. Leipzig, 1962–63.
Trans.: H. B. Dewing. *Procopius.* Vols. 1–5. Loeb ed. Cambridge, Mass., and London, 1954.
Prudentius. *Peristephanon.*
Ed.: CCL 126. Turnhout, 1966.
Ps.-Dionysius Areopagita. *Ecclesiastical Hierarchy.*
Ed.: *PG* 3, cols. 369–569.
Trans.: T. L. Campbell. Lanham, Md., and London, 1981.
Pseudo-Macarius. *Homilies.*
Ed.: H. Berthold. *Makarios/Symeon, Reden und Briefe: Die Sammlung 1 des Vaticanus Graecus 694 (B).* Vol. 1. Berlin, 1973.
H. Dörries, E. Klostermann, and M. Kroeger. *Die 50 geistlichen Homilien des Makarios.* Berlin, 1964.
Trans.: G. A. Maloney. *Pseudo-Macarius, The Fifty Spiritual Homilies and the Great Letter.* New York, 1992.
*Recueil des inscriptions grecques chrétiennes d'Asie Mineure.* Edited by H. Grégoire. Vol. 1. Paris, 1922.
Rufinus. *Church History.* [*HE*]
Ed.: T. Mommsen. In *Eusebius Werke,* edited by E. Schwartz and T. Mommsen and revised by F. Winkelmann. Vol. 2.2, *Die Kirchengeschichte.* Berlin, 1999.
Trans.: P. R. Amidon. *The Church History of Rufinus of Aquileia, Books 10 and 11.* New York, 1997.
*Sayings of the Desert Fathers (Apophthegmata patrum).* Alphabetic Collection.
Ed.: *PG* 65, cols. 72–456.
Trans.: B. Ward. *The Sayings of the Desert Fathers.* Oxford, 1975.
*Sayings of the Desert Fathers (Apophthegmata patrum).* Coptic.
Trans. (French): *Les sentences des pères du desert: Nouveau recueil.* 2d ed. Solesmes, 1977.

*Sayings of the Desert Fathers* (*Apophthegmata patrum*). Systematic Collection (Anonymous Series).
    Ed.: J. Guy. *Les apophthegmes des pères: Collection systematique.* SCh 387. Paris, 1993.
    Trans.: B. Ward. *The Wisdom of the Desert Fathers.* Oxford, 1975.
*Sayings of Macarius the Egyptian* (*Apophthegmata sancti Macarii Aegyptii*).
    Ed.: *PG* 34, cols. 232–64.
*Shepherd of Hermas.*
    Ed.: M. Whittaker. *Die Apostolischen Väter: Der Hirt des Hermas.* Berlin, 1967.
    Trans.: K. Lake. *The Apostolic Fathers.* Vol. 2. Loeb ed. Cambridge, Mass., and London, 1913. Reprint, 1965.
Sidonius Apollinaris. *Letters.* [*Ep.*]
    Ed.: A. Loyen. *Sidoine Apollinaire, Lettres.* 3 vols. Paris, 1970.
Socrates. *Historia ecclesiastica.* [*HE*]
    Ed.: G. C. Hansen. GCS. Berlin, 1995.
    Trans.: NPNF, ser. 2, vol. 2.
Sozomen. *Historia ecclesiastica.* [*HE*]
    Ed.: J. Bidez and rev. C. Hansen. GCS. Berlin, 1960.
    Trans.: NPNF, ser. 2, vol. 2.
*St. Peter of Alexandria: Bishop and Martyr.* Trans. T. Vivian. Philadelphia, 1988.
Sulpicius Severus. *Chronicle.*
    Ed.: C. Halm. *Sulpicii Severi libri qui supersunt.* CSEL 1. Vienna, 1866. Reprint, Hildesheim, 1983.
    Trans.: NPNF, ser. 2, vol. 11.
———. *Life of Martin of Tours.*
    Ed.: J. Fontaine. *Sulpice Sevère, Vie de saint Martin.* 3 vols. SCh 133–35. Paris, 1967.
    Trans.: C. White. *Early Christian Lives.* Harmondsworth, 1998.
*Supplementum epigraphicum graecum.* Vols. 1–. Amsterdam, 1923–. [*SEG*]
Synesius of Cyrene. *Letters.* [*Ep.*]
    Ed.: A. Garzya. *Synesii Cyrenensis epistolae.* Rome, 1979.
    Trans.: A. Fitzgerald. *The Letters of Synesius of Cyrene.* Oxford and London, 1926.
Tertullian. *Against Marcion.*
    Ed.: E. Kroymann. *Tertulliani opera.* Vol. 3. CSEL 47. Vienna and Leipzig, 1906.
    Trans.: ANF, vol. 3.
———. *De corona.*
    Ed.: J. Fontaine. *Q. Septimi Florentis Tertulliani De corona.* Paris, 1966.
    Trans.: ANF, vol. 3.
———. *De praescriptione haereticorum.*
    Ed.: E. Kroymann. *Tertulliani opera.* Vol. 10. CSEL 70. Vienna and Leipzig, 1942.
———. *Exhortation to Chastity.*
    Ed.: A. Gerlo. *Tertulliani opera.* Pt. 2. CCL 2. Turnhout, 1954.
    Trans.: W. P. Le Saint. *Tertullian, Treatises on Marriage and Remarriage.* ACW 13. Westminster, Md., 1951.
———. *On Modesty* (*De pudicitia*).
    Ed.: C. Munier and C. Micaelli. *Tertullien, La pudicité.* SCh 394–95. Paris, 1993.
———. *On Monogamy.*
    Ed.: V. Bulhart. *Tertulliani opera.* Pt. 4. CSEL 76. Vienna, 1957.

Trans.: W. P. Le Saint. *Tertullian, Treatises on Marriage and Remarriage.* ACW 13. Westminster, Md., 1951.

———. *On Penitence.*

Ed.: P. Borleffs. CSEL 76. Vienna, 1957.

Trans.: W. P. Le Saint. *Tertullian, Treatises on Penance.* ACW 28. Westminster, Md., 1959.

———. *On the Soul.*

Ed.: A. Gerlo. *Tertulliani opera.* Pt. 2. CCL 2. Turnhout, 1954.

*Testament of Our Lord* (*Testamentum Domini*).

Ed. and trans.: A. Vööbus. *The Synodicon in the West Syrian Tradition.* CSCO, Scriptores Syri, 162. Louvain, 1975.

Theodore of Mopsuestia. *Commentary on 1 Timothy.*

Ed.: H. B. Swete. *Theodori Episcopi Mopsuesteni in epistolas b. Pauli commentarii: The Latin Version with the Greek Fragments.* Vol. 2. Cambridge, 1882.

———. *In epistulam priorem Pauli ad Timotheum commentarii fragmenta.*

Ed.: *PG* 66, cols. 935–44.

Theodore. *Laudatio on the Deceased Pachomius.*

Ed.: E. Amélineau. *Monuments pour servir à l'histoire de l'Égypte chrétienne au IV siècle: Histoire de saint Pakhôme et de ses communautés.* Annales du Musée Guimet 17/2. Paris, 1889.

Theodoret of Cyrrhus. *Church History.* [*HE*]

Ed.: L. Parmentier. *Theodoret, Kirchengeschichte.* GCS 19. Leipzig, 1911.

Trans.: E. Walford. *History of the Church . . . by Theodoret, Bishop of Cyrus and . . . by Evagrius.* London, 1854.

———. *Historia religiosa.* [*HR*]

Ed.: P. Canivet and A. Leroy-Molinghen. *Théodoret de Cyr, Histoire des moines de Syrie.* 2 vols. SCh 234, 257. Paris, 1977 and 1979.

Trans.: R. M. Price. *A History of the Monks in Syria.* Kalamazoo, 1985.

———. *Letters.* [*Ep.*]

Ed.: Y. Azéma. *Théodoret de Cyr, Correspondance.* 4 vols. SCh 40, 98, 111, 429. Paris, 1955–98.

Trans.: NPNF, ser. 2, vol. 3.

Victor of Vita. *Historia persecutionis Africae provinciae.*

Ed.: C. Halm. *MGH, Auct. ant.* 2. Berlin, 1879.

Trans.: J. Moorhead. *Victor of Vita, History of the Vandal Persecution.* TTH 10. Liverpool, 1992.

Zacharias Scholasticus. *Life of Severus of Antioch* (Syriac).

Ed. and French trans.: M.-A. Kugener. PO 2/1. Turnhout, 1904. Reprint, 1971.

## SECONDARY LITERATURE

Abbott, F. F., and Johnson, A. C. *Municipal Administration in the Roman Empire.* Princeton, 1926.

Allenbach, J., et al., eds. *Biblia patristica: Index des citations et allusions bibliques dans la literature patristique.* 6 vols. Paris, 1975–87.

Anderson, J. C. "Paganism and Christianity in the Upper Tembris Valley." In *Studies in the History and Art of the Eastern Provinces of the Roman Empire*, edited by W. M. Ramsay. London, 1906.

Arnaldi, G. "Gregorio magno e la giustizia." In *La giustizia nell' alto medioevo (secoli V–VIII)*, 2 vols. XLII Settimane di Studio del Centro Italiano di Studi sull'Alto Medioevo. Spoleto, 1995.

Ausbüttel, F. "Die Curialen und Stadtmagistrate Ravennas im späten 5. und 6. Jahrhundert." *ZPE* 67 (1987): 207–14.

Avramea, A. "Les constructions profanes de l'évêque d'après l'épigraphie et les textes d'Orient." In *Actes du XI^e Congrès International d' Archéologie Chrétienne*, vol. 1. Studi di Antichità Cristiana 41 and Collection de l'École Française de Rome 123. Rome, 1989.

Bacht, H. "Die Rolle des orientalischen Mönchtums in den kirchenpolitischen Auseinandersetzungen um Chalkedon (431–519)." In *Das Konzil von Chalkedon*, edited by A. Grillmeier and H. Bacht, vol. 2. Würzburg, 1953.

Bagnall, R. S. *Egypt in Late Antiquity*. Princeton, 1993.

———. "Fourth-Century Prices: New Evidence and Further Thoughts." *ZPE* 76 (1989): 69–76.

Bardy, G. *Paul de Samosate: Étude historique*. Louvain, 1929.

———. "Sur la patrie des évêques dans les premiers siècles." *RHE* 35 (1939): 217–42.

Barnes, T. D. *Athanasius and Constantius: Theology and Politics in the Constantinian Empire*. Cambridge, Mass., 1993.

———. *Constantine and Eusebius*. Cambridge, Mass., and London, 1981.

———. "The Crimes of Basil of Ancyra." *JThS* n.s. 47 (1996): 550–54.

———. "Statistics and the Conversion of the Roman Aristocracy." *JRS* 85 (1995): 135–47.

Bartelink, G. J. M. "Les oxymores *desertum civitas* and *desertum floribus vernans*." *Studia Monastica* 15 (1973): 7–15.

———. "*Parrhesia*." In *Graecitas et latinitas christianorum primaeva*, Suppl. 3. Nimwegen, 1970.

Batiffol, P. "L'épitaphe d'Eugène, évêque de Laodicée." *Bulletin d' Ancienne Littérature et d' Archéologie Chrétiennes* 1 (1911): 25–34.

———. "L'incompatibilité de la strateia et de la cléricature." *Bulletin de la Société des Antiquaires de France*, 1911, 226–32.

Bayer, H. "*Vita in deserto:* Kassians Askese der Einöde und die mittelalterliche Frauenmystik." *Zeitschrift für Kirchengeschichte* 98 (1987): 1–27.

Bell, H. I. "The *episcopalis audientia* in Byzantine Egypt." *Byzantion* 1 (1924): 139–44.

Béranger, J. "Le refus du pouvoir." In his *Principatus: Études de notions et d' histoire politiques dans l' antiquité gréco-romaine*, edited with the collaboration of F. Paschoud and P. Ducrey. Geneva, 1973.

Berneker, E. "*Defensor civitatis.*" *RAC* 3 (1957): cols. 649–56.

Beyer, H. W., and H. Karpp. "Bischof." *RAC* 2 (1954): cols. 394–407.

Bieler, L. *THEIOS ANĒR: Das Bild des göttlichen Menschen in Spätantike und Frühchristentum*. Darmstadt, 1967. First published in two volumes, Vienna, 1935–36.

Bigelmair, A. *Die Beteiligung der Christen am öffentlichen Leben in vorkonstantinischer Zeit: Ein Beitrag zur ältesten Kirchengeschichte*. Munich, 1902. Reprint, Aalen, 1970.

Blume, M. "La Vie de Porphyre et les papyrus: Quelques aspects de la vie municipale à la fin du IV^e et au début du V^e siècle." *Chronique d'Égypte* 66 (1991): 237–44.

Bolkestein, H. *Wohltätigkeit und Armenpflege im vorchristlichen Altertum.* Utrecht, 1939.

Bosl, K. "*Erēmos-Eremus:* Begriffsgeschichtliche Bemerkungen zum historischen Problem der Entfremdung und Vereinsamung des Menschen." *ByzForsch* 2 (1967): 73–90 ( = *Polychordia: Festschrift Franz Dölger,* vol. 2, edited by P. Wirth).

Brakke, D. *Athanasius and the Politics of Asceticism.* Oxford, 1995.

Brandes, W. "Byzantine Cities in the Seventh and Eighth Centuries—Different Sources, Different Histories?" In *The Idea and Ideal of the Town between Late Antiquity and the Early Middle Ages,* edited by G. P. Brogiolo and B. Ward-Perkins. Leiden, 1999.

———. *Die Städte Kleinasiens im 7. und 8. Jahrhundert.* Berlin, 1989.

Bregman, A. J. *Synesius of Cyrene: Philosopher and Bishop.* Berkeley and Los Angeles, 1982.

Brightman, F. E. "The *Historia Mystagogica* and Other Greek Commentaries on the Byzantine Liturgy." *JThS* n.s. 9 (1907–8): 248–67.

Brock, S. P. *The Syriac Fathers on Prayer and the Spiritual Life.* Kalamazoo, 1987.

Brown, P. L. R. "Aspects of the Christianization of the Roman Aristocracy." *JRS* 51 (1961): 1–11.

———. *Augustine of Hippo: A Biography.* London, 1967. Rev. ed., Berkeley, 2000.

———. "The Philosopher and Society in Late Antiquity." In *Protocol of the Thirty-Fourth Colloquy of the Center for Hermeneutical Studies in Hellenistic and Modern Culture.* Berkeley, 1980.

———. *Poverty and Leadership in the Later Roman Empire.* Hanover, N.H., 2002.

———. *Power and Persuasion in Late Antiquity: Towards a Christian Empire.* Madison, 1992.

———. "The Rise and Function of the Holy Man in Late Antiquity." *JRS* 61 (1971): 80–101. Reprinted in his *Society and the Holy* (Berkeley and Los Angeles, 1982).

———. "The Rise and Function of the Holy Man in Late Antiquity, 1971–1997." *JECS* 6 (1998): 353–76.

———. "The Saint as Exemplar in Late Antiquity." *Representations* 1 (1983): 1–25.

Bruns, J. E. "The 'Agreement of Moses and Jesus' in the 'Demonstratio Evangelica' of Eusebius." *VigChrist* 31 (1977): 117–25.

Budge, E. A. Wallis. *Coptic Apocrypha in the Dialect of Upper Egypt.* London, 1913. Reprint, 1977.

Burton-Christie, D. *The Word in the Desert: Scripture and the Quest for Holiness in Early Christian Monasticism.* New York, 1993.

Buxton, R. *Imaginary Greece: The Contexts of Mythology.* Cambridge, 1994.

Cameron, A. "Inscriptions Relating to Sacral Manumission and Confession." *Harv. Theol. Rev.* 32 (1939): 143–79.

Cameron, A., J. Long, with L. Sherry. *Barbarians and Politics at the Court of Arcadius.* Berkeley, 1993.

Campenhausen, H. von. *Kirchliches Amt und geistliche Vollmacht in den ersten drei Jahrhunderten.* Göttingen, 1953. Translated as *Ecclesiastical Authority and Spiritual Power in the Church of the First Three Centuries* (London, 1969).

Caner, D. "Nilus of Ancyra and the Promotion of a Monastic Elite." *Arethusa* 33 (2000), 401–10.

Chadwick, H. "Bishops and Monks." *Studia Patristica* 24 (1993): 45–61.

———. "The Church of the Third Century in the West." In *The Roman West in the Third Century: Contributions from Archaeology and History.* BAR Intern. Series 109 (i), edited by A. King and M. Henig. Oxford, 1981.

Chastagnol, A. *L'album municipal de Timgad.* Antiquitas 22. Bonn, 1978.

———. "L'inscription constantinienne d'Orcistus." *MEFRA* 93 (1981): 381–416.

Chauvot, A. "Curiales et paysans en Orient à la fin du V$^e$ et au début du VI$^e$ siècle: Note sur l'institution du *vindex.*" In *Sociétés urbaines, sociétés rurales dans l'Asie Mineure et la Syrie hellénistiques et romaines,* edited by E. Frézouls. Strasbourg, 1987.

Cherubini, R. "Ammonas di Sketis (+ 375 ca): Un esempio di influsso monastico in un vescovo egiziano del IV sec." In *Vescovi e pastori in epoca teodosiana,* 2. Rome, 1997.

Chitty, D. H. *The Desert a City: An Introduction to the Study of Egyptian and Palestinian Monasticism under the Christian Empire.* Oxford, 1966.

Chrysos, E. K. "Die angebliche 'Nobilitierung' des Klerus durch Kaiser Konstantin den Grossen." *Historia* 18 (1969): 119–29.

Chryssavgis, J. *Soul Mending: The Art of Spiritual Direction.* Brookline, 2000.

Cimma, M. R. *L'episcopalis audientia nelle costituzioni imperiali da Costantino à Giustiniano.* Turin, 1989.

Clark, E. A. "The Lady Vanishes: Dilemmas of a Feminist Historian after the 'Linguistic Turn.'" *Church History* 67 (1998): 1–31.

Claude, D. *Die byzantinische Stadt im 6. Jahrhundert.* Munich, 1969.

Coleman-Norton, P. R. *Roman State and Christian Church: A Collection of Legal Documents to A.D. 535.* 3 vols. London, 1966.

Consolino, F. E., *Ascesi e mondanità nella Gallia tardoantica: Studi sulla figura del vescovo nei secoli IV–VI.* Naples, 1979.

Constable, G. "The Ceremonies and Symbolism of Entering Religious Life and Taking the Monastic Habit, from the Fourth to the Twelfth Century." In *Segni e riti nella chiesa altomedievale occidentale.* Settimane di Studio del Centro Italiano di Studi sull'Alto Medioevo. Spoleto, 1987.

Corcoran, S. *The Empire of the Tetrarchs: Imperial Pronouncements and Government, A.D. 284–324.* Rev. ed. Oxford, 2000.

Coster, C. H. "Synesius, a *curialis* of the Time of the Emperor Arcadius." *Byzantion* 15 (1940–41): 10–38.

Countryman, L. W. *The Rich Christian in the Church of the Early Empire: Contradictions and Accommodations.* New York and Toronto, 1980.

Cracco Ruggini, L. "Le associazioni professionali nel mondo romano-bizantino." In *Artigianato e technica nella società dell'alto medioevo occidentale.* Settimane di Studio del Centro Italiano di Studi sull'Alto Medioevo 18. Spoleto, 1971.

Cramer, W. "Die Seligpreisung der Friedensstifter: Zur Rezeption der Bergpredigt bei Afrahat." In *Lingua restituta orientalis: Festgabe für Julius Assfalg,* edited by R. Schulz and M. Görg. Wiesbaden, 1990.

Cristiani, L. "Eucher (saint), évêque de Lyon." *DSp* 4 (1961): cols. 1653–60.

Cummings, C. "In Praise of the Desert. A Letter to Hilary of Lérins by Eucher of Lyons." *Cistercian Studies* 11 (1976): 60–72.

Dagemark, S. "Prayer as Hagiographic Motif in *Vita Martini* and *Vita Augustini.*" In *La preghiera nel tardo antico dalle origini ad Agostino, XXVII Incontro di Studiosi dell'Antichità Cristiana, Roma, 7–9 maggio 1998.* Rome, 1999.

Dagron, G. *Emperor and Priest: The Imperial Office in Byzantium.* Cambridge and New York, 2003. First published in French (1996).

———. "Two Documents Concerning Mid-Sixth-Century Mopsuestia." In *Charanis Studies: Essays in Honor of Peter Charanis,* edited by Angeliki E. Laiou-Thomadakis. New Brunswick, 1980. Reprinted in his *La romanité chrétienne en Orient* (London, 1984).

Daley, B. E. "Building a New City: The Cappadocian Fathers and the Rhetoric of Philanthropy." *JECS* 7 (1999): 431–61.

Daniélou, J. "Moses bei Gregor von Nyssa: Vorbild und Gestalt." In *Moses in Schrift und Überlieferung.* Düsseldorf, 1963. First published in French (1954).

Dassmann, E. *Sündenvergebung durch Taufe, Busse und Martyrerfürbitte in den Zeugnissen frühchristlicher Frömmigkeit und Kunst.* Münster, 1973.

de Decker, D., and G. Dupuis-Masay. "L' 'épiscopat' de l'empereur Constantin." *Byzantion* 50 (1980): 118–57.

Demacopoulos, G. "A Monk in Shepherd's Clothing: Pope Gregory I and the Asceticizing of Pastoral Direction." Ph.D. diss., University of North Carolina, Chapel Hill, 2001.

Déroche, V. *Études sur Léontios de Néapolis.* Acta Universitatis Upsaliensis. Studia Byzantina Upsaliensia 3. Uppsala, 1995.

Dewing, H. B. "A Dialysis of the Fifth Century A.D. in the Princeton Collection of Papyri." *TAPA* 53 (1922): 113–27.

di Bernardino, A. "L'immagine del vescovo attraverso i suoi titoli nel codice teodosiano." In *L'évêque dans la cité du IVᵉ au Vᵉ siècle: Image et autorité,* edited by E. Rebillard and C. Sotinel. Collection de l'École Française de Rome 248. Rome, 1998.

Dörries, H. "Erneuerung des kirchlichen Amts im vierten Jahrhundert: Die Schrift *De sacerdotio* des Johannes Chrysostomus und ihre Vorlage, die *Oratio de fuga sua* des Gregor von Nazianz." In *Bleibendes im Wandel der Kirchengeschichte,* edited by B. Moeller and G. Ruhbach. Tübingen, 1973.

Drake, H. A. *Constantine and the Bishops: The Politics of Intolerance.* Baltimore and London, 2000.

Ducloux, A. *Ad ecclesiam confugere: Naissance du droit d'asile dans les églises (IVᵉ-milieu du Vᵉ s.).* Paris, 1994.

Dunn, M. *The Emergence of Monasticism: From the Desert Fathers to the Early Middle Ages.* Oxford, 2000.

Dupont, C. "Les privilèges des clercs sous Constantin." *RHE* 62 (1967): 729–52.

Durliat, J. "Les attributions civiles des évêques byzantins: L'exemple du diocèse d'Afrique (533–709)." *JÖB* 32/2 (1982): 73–83.

Eck, W. "Der Einfluß der konstantinischen Wende auf die Auswahl der Bischöfe im 4. und 5. Jahrhundert." *Chiron* 8 (1978): 561–85.

———. "Der Episkopat im spätantiken Afrika." *Historische Zeitschrift* 236 (1983): 265–95.

Eisenstadt, S. N., ed. *Max Weber on Charisma and Institution Building: Selected Papers.* Chicago and London, 1968.

Elliott, T. G. "The Tax Exemptions Granted to Clerics by Constantine and Constantius II." *Phoenix* 32 (1978): 326–36.

Elm, E. *Die Macht der Weisheit: Das Bild des Bischofs in der* Vita Augustini *des Possidius und anderen spätantiken und frühmittelalterlichen Bischofsviten.* Studies in the History of Christian Thought 109. Leiden and Boston, 2003.

Elm, S. "An Alleged Book-Theft in Fourth-Century Egypt: *P. Lips.* 43." In *Studia Patristica* 18/2. Kalamazoo and Louvain, 1989.

———. "The Diagnostic Gaze: Gregory of Nazianzus' Theory of Orthodox Priesthood in His Orations 6 *De pace* and 2 *Apologia de fuga sua.*" In *Orthodoxie, Christianisme, Histoire/Orthodoxy, Christianity, History,* edited by S. Elm, E. Rebillard, and A. Romano. Collection de l'École Française de Rome 270. Rome, 2000.

———. *Virgins of God: The Making of Asceticism in Late Antiquity.* Oxford and New York, 1994.

Escolan, P. *Monachisme et église: Le monachisme syrien du IV^e au VII^e siècle, un ministère charismatique.* Théologie Historique 109. Paris, 1999.

Faivre, A. *Naissance d'une hiérarchie.* Théologie Historique 40. Paris, 1977.

Faraggiana di Sarzana, C. "*Apophthegmata Patrum:* Some Crucial Points of Their Textual Transmission and the Problem of a Critical Edition." In *Studia Patristica* 29. Louvain, 1997.

———. "Il *Paterikon Vat. Gr.* 2592, già di Mezzoiuso, e il suo rapporto testuale con lo *Hieros. S. Sepulchri gr.* 113." *Bollettino della Badia Greca di Grottaferrata* 47 (1993): 76–96.

Feissel, D. "L'évêque, titres et fonctions d'après les inscriptions grecs jusqu'au VII^e siècle." In *Actes du XI^e Congrès International d'Archéologie Chrétienne,* vol. 1. Studi di Antichità Cristiana 41 and Collection de l'École Française de Rome 123. Rome, 1989.

Feissel, D., and I. Kaygusuz. "Un mandement impérial du VI^e siècle dans une inscription d'Hadrianoupolis d'Honoriade." *TM* 9 (1985): 397–419.

Fontaine, J. "Valeurs antiques et valeurs chrétiennes dans la spiritualité des grands propriétaires terriens à la fin du IV^e siècle occidental." In *Epektasis: Mélanges patristiques offerts au Cardinal Daniélou,* edited by J. Fontaine and C. Kannengiesser. Paris, 1972.

Forlin Patrucco, M. "Modelli di santità e santità episcopale nel IV secolo: L'elaborazione dei Padri cappadoci." In *Modelli di santità e modelli di comportamento.* Turin, 1994.

Frank, K. S. *Aggelikos Bios: Begriffsanalytische und begriffsgeschichtliche Untersuchung zum "engelgleichen Leben" im frühen Mönchtum.* Beiträge zur Geschichte des alten Mönchtums und des Benediktinerordens 26. Münster, 1964.

Frend, W. H. C. *The Donatist Church: A Movement of Protest in Roman North Africa.* Oxford, 1952. Reprint, 1985.

———. *The Rise of the Monophysite Movement: Chapters in the History of the Church in the Fifth and Six Centuries.* London, 1972.

Gagos, T., and P. van Minnen. *Settling a Dispute: Toward a Legal Anthropology of Late Antique Egypt.* Ann Arbor, 1997.

Galvao-Sobrinho, C. R. "Funerary Epigraphy and the Spread of Christianity in the West." *Athenaeum* n.s. 83 (1995): 431–66.

Garnsey, P. "Aspects of the Decline of the Urban Aristocracy in the Empire." In *ANRW* 2/1: 229–52. Berlin and New York, 1974.

Gascou, J. "Les grands domaines, la cité et l'état en Égypte byzantine." *TM* 9 (1985): 1–89.

———. "Metanoia." *Coptic Encyclopedia* 5 (1991): 1608–11.

Gaudemet, J. *Église et cité: Histoire du droit canonique.* Paris, 1994.

———. *L'église et l'état au IV^e siècle.* Milan, 1981.

Gauthier, N. "Le réseau de pouvoirs de l'évêque dans la Gaule du haut moyen-âge." In *Towns and Their Territories between Late Antiquity and the Early Middle Ages,* edited by G. P. Broglio, N. Gauthier, and N. Christie. Leiden, 2000.

Giet, S. "Basile, était-il sénateur?" *RHE* 60 (1965): 429–44.

Gilliard, F. D. "Senatorial Bishops in the Fourth Century." *Harv. Theol. Rev.* 77 (1984): 153–75.

———. "The Senators of Sixth-Century Gaul." *Speculum* 54 (1979): 685–97.

———. "The Social Origins of Bishops in the Fourth Century." PhD diss., University of California, Berkeley, 1966.

Goddart-Eliott, A. *Roads to Paradise: Reading the Lives of the Early Saints.* Hanover, N.H., 1987.

Goehring, J. E. *Ascetics, Society, and the Desert: Studies in Early Egyptian Monasticism.* Harrisburg, 1999.

———. "The Encroaching Desert: Literary Production and Ascetic Space in Early Christian Egypt." *JECS* 1 (1993): 281–96. Reprinted in his *Ascetics, Society, and the Desert: Studies in Early Egyptian Monasticism* (Harrisburg, 1999).

Gorday, P., ed. *Ancient Christian Commentary on Scripture: New Testament.* Vol. 9, *Colossians 1–2 Thessalonians, 1–2 Timothy, Titus, Philemon.* Downers Grove, Ill., 2000.

Gould, G. *The Desert Fathers on Monastic Community.* Oxford and New York, 1993.

Graffigna, P. "Il vescovo tardoantico tra philosophia e prostasia: Sinesio di Cirene." In *Vescovi e pastori in epoca teodosiana,* 2. Rome, 1997.

Gray, P. "Palestine and Justinian's Legislation on Non-Christian Religions." In *Law, Politics, and Society in the Ancient Mediterranean World,* edited by B. Halpern and D. W. Hobson. Sheffield, 1993.

Gryson, R. "Les élections épiscopales en orient au IV^e siècle." *RHE* 74 (1979): 301–45.

Guarducci, M. *Epigrafia greca.* Vol. 4, *Epigrafi sacre pagane e cristiane.* Rome, 1978.

Guillaumont, A. "La conception du désert chez les moines d'Égypte." *Revue de l'Histoire des Religions* 188 (1975): 3–21. Reprinted in his *Aux origines du monachisme chrétien: Pour une phénoménologie du monachisme,* Spiritualité Orientale 30 (Begrolles-en-Mauges, 1979).

Guillou, A. "L'évêque dans la société méditerranéenne des VI^e–VII^e siècles: Un modèle." *Bibliothèque de l'École des Chartes* 131 (1973): 5–19. Reprinted in his *Culture et société en Italie Byzantine (VI^e-XI^e s.)* (London, 1978).

Guinot, J.-N. "L'apport des panégyriques de Jean Chrysostome à une définition de l'évêque modèle." In *Vescovi e pastori in epoca teodosiana,* 2. Rome, 1997.

Haas, C. *Alexandria in Late Antiquity: Topography and Social Conflict.* Baltimore and London, 1997.

Hadjipsaltis, C. "Un archévêque inconnu de Chypre: Philoxénos (VI^e siècle)." *Byzantion* 31 (1961): 215–16.

Hadot, P. "The Spiritual Guide." In *Classical Mediterranean Spirituality*, edited by A.H. Armstrong. New York, 1986.

Haehling, R. von. *Die Religionszugehörigkeit der hohen Amtsträger des römischen Reiches seit Constantins I. Alleinherrschaft bis zum Ende der theodosianischen Dynastie (324–450 bzw. 455 n. Chr.).* Bonn, 1978.

Haensch, R. *Capita provinciarum: Statthaltersitze und Provinzialverwaltung in der römischen Kaiserzeit.* Kölner Forschungen 7. Mainz, 1997.

Halsall, P. "Women's Bodies, Men's Souls: Sanctity and Gender in Byzantium." PhD diss., Fordham University, 1999.

Harl, M. "Moise figure de l'évêque dans l'éloge de Basile de Grégoire de Nysse (381)." In *The Biographical Works of Gregory of Nyssa: Proceedings of the Fifth International Colloquium on Gregory of Nyssa (Mainz, 6–10 September 1982)*, edited by A. Spira. Cambridge, Mass., 1984.

———. "Les trois quarantaines de la vie de Moise, schéma idéal de la vie du moine-évêque chez les Pères Cappadociens." *Rev. ét. gr.* 80 (1967): 407–12.

Harnack, A. von. *Der kirchengeschichtliche Ertrag der exegetischen Arbeiten des Origenes.* Vol. 2. TU 42/3. Leipzig, 1919.

———. *The Mission and Expansion of Christianity in the First Three Centuries.* Gloucester, Mass., 1972. First published in German as *Mission und Ausbreitung des Christentums in den ersten drei Jahrhunderten* (Leipzig, 1915).

Harries, J. *Law and Empire in Late Antiquity.* Cambridge, 1999.

———. *Sidonius Apollinaris and the Fall of Rome, A.D. 407–485.* Oxford, 1994.

Harries, J., and I. Wood, eds. *The Theodosian Code.* Ithaca, N.Y., 1993.

Hartmann, W. "Der Bischof als Richter nach den kirchenrechtlichen Quellen des 4. bis 7. Jahrhunderts." In *La giustizia nell' alto medioevo (secoli V–VIII).* Settimane di Studio del Centro Italiano di Studi sull'Alto Medioevo 42. Spoleto, 1995.

Hausherr, H. *Penthos: The Doctrine of Compunction in the Christian East.* Kalamazoo, 1982. First published in French (1944).

Hausherr, I. *Spiritual Direction in the Early Christian East.* Kalamazoo, 1990. First published in French as *Direction spirituelle en Orient autrefois*, OCA 144 (Rome, 1955).

Heather, P. "New Men for New Constantines? Creating an Imperial Elite in the Eastern Mediterranean." In *New Constantines: The Rhythm of Imperial Renewal in Byzantium, 4th–13th Centuries*, edited by P. Magdalino. Aldershot, 1994.

———. "Senators and Senates." In *The Cambridge Ancient History*, vol.13, *The Late Empire, A.D. 337–425*, edited by A. Cameron and P. Garnsey. Cambridge, 1998.

Hefele, C. J., and H. Leclerq. *Histoire des conciles d'après les documents originaux.* 11 vols. Paris, 1907–52. [H-L]

Heim, F. "L'expérience mystique des pèlerins occidentaux en Terre Sainte aux alentours de 400." *Ktema* 10 (1985): 193–208.

Heinzelmann, M. *Bischofsherrschaft in Gallien: Zur Kontinuität römischer Führungsschichten vom 4. bis zum 7. Jahrhundert: Soziale, prosopographische und bildungsgeschichtliche Aspekte.* Munich, 1976.

———. "Bischof und Herrschaft vom spätantiken Gallien bis zu den karolingischen Hausmeiern: Die institutionellen Grundlagen." In *Herrschaft und Kirche: Beiträge zur Entstehung und Wirkungsweise episkopaler und monastischer Organisationsformen*, edited by F. Prinz. Monographien zur Geschichte des Mittelalters 33. Stuttgart, 1988.

Herman, E. "Zum Asylrecht im byzantinischen Reich." *OCP* 1 (1935): 204–38.

Herrmann, E. *Ecclesia in Re Publica: Die Entwicklung der Kirche von pseudostaatlicher zu staatlich inkorporierter Existenz.* Frankfurt am Main, 1980.

Heussi, K. *Der Ursprung des Mönchtums.* Tübingen, 1936. Reprint, Aalen, 1981.

Hohlweg, A. "Bischof und Stadtherr im frühen Byzanz." *JÖB* 20 (1971): 51–62.

Holl, K. *Enthusiasmus und Bussgewalt beim griechischen Mönchtum: Eine Studie zu Symeon dem Neuen Theologen.* Leipzig, 1898. Reprint, Hildesheim, 1969.

Hollerich, M. "The Comparison of Moses and Constantine in Eusebius of Caesarea's *Life of Constantine.*" In *Studia Patristica* 19. Louvain, 1989.

———. "Religion and Politics in the Writings of Eusebius: Reassessing the First 'Court Theologian.'" *Church History* 59 (1990): 309–25.

Hopkins, K. "Christian Number and Its Implications." *JECS* 6 (1998): 185–226.

———. "Elite Mobility in the Roman Empire." *P&P* 32 (1965): 12–26.

Hörmann, J. *Untersuchungen zur griechischen Laienbeicht: Ein Beitrag zur allgemeinen Bussgeschichte.* Donauwörth, 1913.

Hornickel, O. *Ehren- und Rangprädikate in den Papyrusurkunden: Ein Beitrag zum römischen und byzantinischen Titelwesen.* Giessen, 1930.

Hornung, E. "Seth: Geschichte und Bedeutung eines ägyptischen Gottes." *Symbolon* n.s. 2 (1974): 43–63.

Horstkotte, H.-J. "Heidnische Priesterämter und Dekurionat im vierten Jahrhundert n. Chr." In *Religion und Gesellschaft: Kolloquium zu Ehren von Friedrich Vittinghoff,* edited by W. Eck. Cologne and Vienna, 1989.

———. *Die "Steuerhaftung" im spätrömischen "Zwangsstaat."* 2d ed. Frankfurt am Main, 1988.

Hummel, E. L. *The Concept of Martyrdom According to St. Cyprian of Carthage.* The Catholic University of America, Studies in Christian Antiquity 9. Washington, D.C., 1946.

Hunt, E. D. "Christianizing the Roman Empire: The Evidence of the Code." In *The Theodosian Code: Studies in the Imperial Law of Late Antiquity,* edited by J. Harries and I. Wood. London, 1993.

———. "The Church as a Public Institution." In *The Cambridge Ancient History,* vol. 13: *The Late Empire,* A.D. *337–425,* edited by A. Cameron and P. Garnsey. Cambridge, 1998.

Instinsky, H. U. *Bischofsstuhl und Kaiserthron.* Munich, 1955.

Jarrett, M. G. "Decurions and Priests." *AJPh* 92 (1971): 513–18.

Jerg, E. *Vir venerabilis: Untersuchungen zur Titulatur der Bischöfe in den ausserkirchlichen Texten der Spätantike als Beitrag zur Deutung ihrer öffentlichen Stellung.* Wiener Beiträge zur Theologie 26. Vienna, 1970.

Joannou, P.-P. *La législation impériale et la christianisation de l'Empire romain.* OCA 192. Rome, 1972.

Jones, A. H. M. "The Caste System of the Later Roman Empire." *Eirene* 8 (1970): 79–96.

———. "Church Finances in the Fifth and Sixth Centuries." *JThS* 11 (1960): 84–94.

———. *The Greek City from Alexander to Justinian.* Oxford, 1940.

———. *The Later Roman Empire, 284–602: A Social, Economic, and Administrative Survey.* 2 vols. Oxford, 1964. Reprint, 1986.

Jones, A. H. M., J. Martindale, and J. Morris, eds. *The Prosopography of the Later Roman Empire.* 3 vols. London, 1971–92. [*PLRE*]

Jonkers, E. J. "Das Verhalten der Alten Kirche hinsichtlich der Ernennung zum Priester von Sklaven, Freigelassenen und Curiales." *Mnemosyne* ser. 3, vol. 10 (1942): 286–302.

Jussen, B. "Liturgie und Legitimation, oder Wie die Gallo-Romanen das römische Reich beendeten." In *Institutionen und Ereignis: Über historische Praktiken und Vorstellungen gesellschaftlichen Ordnens,* edited by R. Blänkner and B. Jussen. Göttingen, 1998.

———. "Über 'Bischofsherrschaften' und die Prozeduren politisch-sozialer Umordnung in Gallien zwischen 'Antike' und 'Mittelalter.'" *Historische Zeitschrift* 260 (1995): 673–718.

Kaegi, W. E., Jr. "New Evidence on the Early Reign of Heraclius." *BZ* 66 (1973): 308–30. Reprinted in his *Army, Society, and Religion in Byzantium* (London, 1982).

Kaiser, R. "Bischofsstadt." In *Lexikon des Mittelalters* (Munich and Zurich, 1983), 2: cols. 239–45.

Karpp, H. *Die Busse: Quellen zur Entstehung des altkirchlichen Busswesens.* Traditio Christiana 1. Zurich, 1969.

Kaser, M. *Das römische Zivilprozessrecht.* Munich, 1966.

Kaufmann, C. M. *Handbuch der altchristlichen Epigraphik.* Freiburg i. Br., 1917.

Keenan, J. G. "A Christian Letter from the Michigan Collection." *ZPE* 75 (1988): 267–71.

Kirsten, E. "Chorbishof." *RAC* 2 (1954): cols. 1105–14.

Klauser, T. "Bischöfe als staatliche Prokuratoren im dritten Jahrhundert." *JAC* 14 (1971): 140–49.

———. *Der Ursprung der bischöflichen Insignien und Ehrenrechte.* Bonner Akademische Reden 1. Krefeld, 1949. 2d ed., 1953.

Klingshirn, W. E. *Caesarius of Arles: The Making of a Christian Community in Late Antique Gaul.* Cambridge and New York, 1994.

———. "Caesarius of Arles and the Ransoming of Captives in Sub-Roman Gaul." *JRS* 75 (1985): 183–203.

Kneller, C. A. "Moses und Petrus." *Stimmen aus Maria-Laach* 60 (1901): 237–57.

Koep, L. *Das himmlische Buch in Antike und Christentum.* Bonn, 1952.

Kolias, G. *Ämter- und Würdenkauf im früh- und mittelbyzantinischen Reich.* Athens, 1939.

Kopecek, T. A. "Curial Displacements and Flight in Later Fourth-Century Cappadocia." *Historia* 23 (1974): 319–42.

———. "The Senatorial Class of the Cappadocian Fathers." *Church History* 42 (1973): 453–66.

Koschorke, K. *Spuren der alten Liebe: Studien zum Kirchenbegriff des Basilius von Caesarea.* Paradosis 32. Freiburg, Switzerland, 1991.

Koskenniemi, H. *Studien zur Geschichte und Phraseologie des griechischen Briefes bis 400 n. Chr.* Helsinki, 1956.

Kötting, B. "Dienstfunktion und Vollmacht kirchlicher Ämter in der Alten Kirche." In *Macht, Dienst, Herrschaft in Kirche und Gesellschaft,* edited by W. Weber. Freiburg im Breisgau, 1974.

———. "Die Stellung des Konfessors in der Alten Kirche." *JAC* 19 (1976): 7–23.

———. "Klerikerbildung in der alten Kirche." In *Sacerdotium: Festschrift A. Francken.*

Warendorf, 1948. Reprinted in his *Ecclesia peregrinans: Das Gottesvolk unterwegs,* vol. 1, Münsterische Beiträge zur Theologie 54/1 (Münster, 1988).

Koukoulès, P., and R. Guilland. "Études sur la vie privée des Byzantins, I: Voleurs et prisons à Byzance." *REG* 61 (1948): 118–36.

Kramer, B., J. C. Shelton, and G. M. Browne. *Das Archiv des Nepheros und verwandte Texte.* Mainz, 1987.

Krause, J.-U. *Gefängnisse im römischen Reich.* Stuttgart, 1996.

Ladner, G. B. *The Idea of Reform: Its Impact on Christian Thought and Action in the Age of the Fathers.* Cambridge, Mass., 1959.

Lafontaine, P.-H. *Les conditions positives de l'accession aux ordres dans la première législation ecclésiastique (300–492).* Ottawa, 1963.

Lammeyer, W. "Die 'audientia episcopalis' in Zivilsachen der Laien im römischen Kaiserrecht und in den Papryi." *Aegyptus* 13 (1933): 193–202.

Lamoreaux, J. C. "Episcopal Courts in Late Antiquity." *JECS* 3 (1995): 143–67.

Lancel, S. "Évêchés et cités dans les provinces africaines (III$^e$-V$^e$ siècles)." In *L'Afrique dans l'occident romain.* Rome, 1990.

Langhammer, W. *Die rechtliche und soziale Stellung der Magistratus Municipales und der Decuriones in der Übergangsphase der Städte von sich selbst verwaltenden Gemeinden zu Vollzugsorganen des spätantiken Zwangsstaates (2.–4. Jahrhundert) der römischen Kaiserzeit.* Wiesbaden, 1973.

Laniado, A. *Recherches sur les notables municipaux dans l'empire protobyzantin.* Paris, 2002.

Lavan, L. "The *praetoria* of Civil Governors in Late Antiquity." In *Recent Research in Late-Antique Urbanism,* edited by L. Lavan. JRA Suppl. 42. Portsmouth, R.I., 2001.

Leclerq, H. "Affranchissement." *DACL* 1 (1924): cols. 554–76.

Lendon, J.E. *Empire of Honour: The Art of Government in the Roman World.* Oxford, 1997.

Lepelley, C. "La carrière municipale dans l'Afrique romaine sous l'Empire tardif." *Ktema* 6 (1981): 333–47.

———. *Les cités de l'Afrique romaine au Bas-Empire.* 2 vols. Paris, 1979–81.

———. "Évergetisme et épigraphie dans l'antiquité tardive: Les provinces de langue latine." In *Actes du X$^e$ Congrès International d'Épigraphie Grecque et Latine, Nîmes, 4–9 octobre 1992,* edited by M. Christol and O. Masson. Paris, 1997.

———. "Liberté, colonat et esclavage d'après la Lettre 24*: La juridiction épiscopale 'de liberali causa.'" In *Les lettres de saint Augustin découvertes par Johannes Divjak: Communications présentées au colloque des 20 et 21 Septembre 1982.* Paris, 1983.

———. "*Quot curiales, tot tyranni:* L'image du décurion oppresseur au Bas-Empire." In *Crise et redressement dans les provinces européennes de l'Empire (milieu du III$^e$-milieu du IV$^e$ siècle ap. J.-C.): Actes du colloque de Strasbourg (décembre 1981),* ed. E. Frézouls. Strasbourg, 1983.

———. "The Survival and Fall of the Classical City in Late Roman Africa." In *Integration and Herrschaft: Ethnische Identitäten und soziale Organisation im Frühmittelalter,* edited by W. Pohl and M. Diesenberger. Österr. Ak. Wiss., Philos.-hist. Kl., Denkschriften 301. Vienna, 2002.

———. "Vers la fin du 'privilège de la liberté': L'amoindrissement de l'autonomie des cités à l'aube du bas-empire." In *Splendidissima civitas,* edited by André Chastagnol et al. Paris, 1996.

Leyser, C. *Authority and Asceticism from Augustine to Gregory the Great.* Oxford, 2000.

Liebeschuetz, J. H. W. G. *Antioch: City and Imperial Administration in the Later Roman Empire.* Oxford 1972.

———. *The Decline and Fall of the Roman City.* Oxford, 2001.

———. "Oligarchies in the Cities of the Byzantine East." In *Integration und Herrschaft: Ethnische Identitäten und soziale Organisation im Frühmittelalter,* edited by W. Pohl and M. Diesenberger, Österr. Ak. Wiss., Philos.-hist. Kl., Denkschriften 301. Vienna, 2002.

———. "The Rise of the Bishop in the Christian Roman Empire and the Successor Kingdoms." *Electrum* 1 (1997): 113–25.

———. "Synesius and Municipal Politics of Cyrenaica in the 5th Century A.D." *Byzantion* 55 (1985): 146–64.

———. "Why Did Synesius Become Bishop of Ptolemais?" *Byzantion* 56 (1986): 180–95.

Liebesny, H. "Rechtsgeschichtliche Bemerkungen zu den koptischen Schutzbriefen." *Mitteilungen des deutschen Instituts für ägyptische Altertumskunde in Kairo* 8 (1939): 71–146.

Lienhard, J. T. "Patristic Sermons on Eusebius of Vercelli and Their Relation to His Monasticism." *Revue Bénédictine* 87 (1977): 164–72.

Linder, A. *The Jews in Roman Imperial Legislation.* Detroit and Jerusalem, 1987.

Lizzi, R., *Il potere episcopale nell'Oriente romano: Rappresentazione ideologica e realtà politica (IV–V sec. d. C.).* Rome, 1987.

———. "I vescovi e i potentes della terra: Definizione e limite del ruolo episcopale nelle due *partes imperii* fra IV e V secolo d.C." In *L'évêque dans la cité du IV^e au V^e siècle: Image et autorité,* edited by E. Rebillard and C. Sotinel. Collection de l'École Française de Rome 248. Rome, 1998.

———. "Tra i classici e la Bibbia: L'otium come forma di santità episcopale." In *Modelli di santità e modelli di comportamento.* Turin, 1994.

———. *Vescovi e strutture ecclesiastiche nella città tardoantica: L'Italia Annonaria nel IV–V secolo d.C.* Como, 1989.

Lochbrunner, M. *Über das Priestertum: Historische und systematische Untersuchung zum Priesterbild des Johannes Chrysostomus.* Bonn, 1993.

Loseby, S. "Bishops and Cathedrals: Order and Diversity in the Fifth-Century Urban Landscape of Southern Gaul." In *Fifth-Century Gaul: A Crisis of Identity?* edited by J. Drinkwater and H. Elton. Cambridge, 1992.

Louf, A. "Spiritual Fatherhood in the Literature of the Desert." In *Abba: Guides to Wholeness and Holiness East and West,* edited by J. R. Sommerfeldt. Cistercian Studies Series 38. Kalamazoo, 1982.

Louth, A. "St. Gregory Nazianzen on Bishops and the Episcopate." In *Vescovi e pastori in epoca teodosiana,* 2. Rome, 1997.

Lucius, E. *Die Anfänge des Heiligenkults in der christlichen Kirche.* Edited by G. Anrich. Tübingen, 1904.

Lyman, J. R. "Ascetics and Bishops: Epiphanius on Orthodoxy." In *Orthodoxie, Christianisme, Histoire/Orthodoxy, Christianity, History,* edited by S. Elm, E. Rebillard, and A. Romano. Collection de l'École Française de Rome 270. Rome, 2000.

Malone, E. *The Monk and the Martyr: The Monk as Successor of the Martyr.* Catholic University of America, Studies in Christian Antiquity 12. Washington, D.C., 1950.

Mandouze, A. *Prosopographie chrétienne du Bas-Empire: Prosopographie de l'Afrique chrétienne (303–533)*. Paris, 1982.

Maraval, P. "Synésius de Cyrène." *DSp* 14 (1990): cols. 1422–29.

Markus, R. A. *Gregory the Great and His World*. Cambridge, 1997.

Martin, A. *Athanase d'Alexandrie et l'église d'Égypte au IV^e siècle (328–373)*. Collection de l'École Française de Rome 216. Rome, 1996.

Martoye, F. "L'asile et la législation impériale du IV^e au VI^e siècle." *Mémoires de la Société Nationale des Antiquaires de France* 75 (1919): 159–246.

Mathisen, R. W. *Roman Aristocrats in Barbarian Gaul: Strategies for Survival in an Age of Transition*. Austin, 1993.

Matthews, J. F. *Laying Down the Law: A Study of the Theodosian Code*. New Haven and London, 2000.

Mazzarino, S. "Costantino e l'episcopato." *Iura* 7 (1956): 345–52. Reprinted in his *Antico, tardoantico ed èra costantiniana*, vol. 1 (n.p., 1974).

McCoull, L. S. B. "Paul of Tamma and the Monastic Priesthood." *VigChrist* 54 (1999): 316–20.

McGinn, B. "Ocean and Desert as Symbols of Mystical Absorption in the Christian Tradition." *Journal of Religion* 74 (1994): 155–81.

McLynn, N. B. *Ambrose of Milan: Church and Court in a Christian Capital*. Berkeley and Los Angeles, 1994.

———. "A Self-Made Holy Man: The Case of Gregory Nazianzen." *JECS* 6 (1998): 463–83.

Merkelbach, R. "Grabepigramm und Vita des Bischofs Aberkios von Hierapolis." *Epigraphica Anatolica* 28 (1997): 125–39.

Meyer, L. "Perfection chrétienne et vie solitaire dans la pensée de S. Jean Chrysostome." *Revue d'Ascetique et de Mystique* 14 (1933): 232–62.

Meyer, R. T. "Holy Orders in the Eastern Church in the Early Fifth Century as Seen in Palladius." In *Studia Patristica* 16/2. TU 129. Berlin, 1985.

Millar, F. *The Emperor in the Roman World (31 B.C.–A.D. 337)*. Ithaca, N.Y., 1977.

———. "Paul of Samosata, Zenobia, and Aurelian: The Church, Local Culture, and Political Allegiance in Third-Century Syria." *JRS* 61 (1971): 1–17.

Miller, M. *The Bishop's Palace: Architecture and Authority in Medieval Italy*. Ithaca, N.Y., 2000.

Miquel, P. *Lexique du désert: Étude de quelques mot-clés du vocabulaire monastique grec ancien*. Spiritualité Orientale 44. Bégrolles-en-Mauges, 1986.

Mitchell, S. *Anatolia: Land, Men, and Gods in Asia Minor*. Vol. 2, *The Rise of the Church*. Oxford, 1993.

Mitteis, L., and U. Wilcken. *Grundzüge und Chrestomathie der Papyruskunde*. Vol. 1/2. Leipzig, 1912.

Mohrmann, C. "Episkopos—Speculator." In *Études sur le latin des chrétiens*, vol. 4. Rome, 1977.

*The Monastery of Epiphanius at Thebes*. Pt. 1, *The Archaeological Material*, by H. E. Winlock. Pt. 2, *Coptic Ostraka and Papyri*, by W. E. Crum, and *Greek Ostraka and Papyri*, by H. G. Evelyn White. New York, 1926. Reprint, 1973.

Morris, R. L. B. "Bishops in the Papyri." In *Proceedings of the 20^th International Congress of Papyrologists, Copenhagen, 23–29 August, 1992*. Copenhagen, 1994.

Mosiek, U. "Das altkirchliche Prozessrecht im Spiegel der Didaskalie." *Österreichisches Archiv für Kirchenrecht* 16 (1965): 183–206.

Müller-Wiener, W. "Bischofsresidenzen des 4.–7.Jhs. im östlichen Mittelmeer-Raum." In *Actes du XI^e Congrès International d' Archéologie Chrétienne*, vol. 1. Studi di Antichità Cristiana 41 and Collection de l'École Française de Rome 123. Vatican City and Rome, 1989.

———. "Riflessioni sulle caratteristiche dei palazzi episcopali." *Felix Ravenna* 125–126 (1983 [1984]).

Näf, B. *Senatorisches Standesbewußtsein in spätrömischer Zeit.* Paradosis 40. Freiburg, 1995.

Nagel, P. *Die Motivierung der Askese in der alten Kirche und der Ursprung des Mönchtums.* Berlin, 1966.

Naldini, M. *Il Cristianesimo in Egitto: Lettere private nei papiri dei secoli II–IV.* Florence, 1968.

Nelz, H. R. "Die theologischen Schulen der morgenländischen Kirchen während der sieben ersten christlichen Jahrhunderte in ihrer Bedeutung für die Ausbildung des Klerus." Diss., Bonn, 1916.

Niederwimmer, K. *Die Didache.* Göttingen, 1989.

Noethlichs, K. "Zur Einflussnahme des Staates auf die Entwicklung eines christlichen Klerikerstandes: Schicht- und berufsspezifische Bestimmmungen für den Klerus im 4. und 5. Jahrhundert in den spätantiken Rechtsquellen." *JAC* 15 (1972): 136–53.

———. "Materialien zum Bischafsbild aus den spätantiken Rechtsquellen." *JAC* 16 (1973): 28–59.

Norman, A. F. "Gradations in Later Municipal Society." *JRS* 48 (1958): 79–85.

Norris, F. "Paul of Samosata: Procurator Ducenarius." *JThS* 35 (1984): 50–70.

Nürnberg, R. *Askese als sozialer Impuls: Monastisch-asketische Spiritualität als Wurzel und Triebfeder sozialer Ideen und Aktivitäten der Kirche in Südgallien im 5. Jahrhundert.* Bonn, 1988.

Opelt, I. "Zur literarischen Eigenart von Eucherius' Schrift *De laude eremi.*" *VigChrist* 22 (1968): 198–208.

Oppenheim, P. "Mönchsweihe und Taufritus: Ein Kommentar zur Auslegung bei Dionysius dem Areopagiten." In *Miscellanea liturgica in honorem L. Cuniberti Mohlberg*, vol. 1. Rome, 1948.

Pack, R. "*Curiales* in the Correspondence of Libanius." *TAPA* 82 (1951): 176–92.

Pallas, D. I. "Episkopion." In *Reallexikon zur byzantinischen Kunst,* 2/11: 335–71. Stuttgart, 1968.

Papadakis, A. "Endemousa Synodos." In *Oxford Dictionary of Byzantium*, 1: 697. New York and Oxford, 1991.

Patlagean, E. *Pauvreté économique et pauvreté sociale à Byzance, 4^e-7^e siècles.* Paris, 1977.

Pavis d'Escurac, H. "À propos de l'approvisionement en blé des cités de l'Orient romain." In *Sociétés urbaines, sociétés rurales dans l'Asie Mineure et la Syrie hellénistiques et romaines,* edited by E. Frézouls. Strasbourg, 1987.

Petit, P. *Les étudiants de Libanius.* Paris, 1956.

———. *Libanius et la vie municipale à Antioche au IV^e siècle après J.-C.* Paris, 1955.

Petrie, A. "Epitaphs in Phrygian Greek." In *Studies in the History and Art of the Eastern Provinces of the Roman Empire,* edited by W. M. Ramsay. London, 1906.

Picirillo, M. "Gruppi episcopali nelle tre Palestine e in Arabia?" In *Actes du XI<sup>e</sup> Congrès International d' Archéologie Chrétienne*, vol. 1. Studi di Antichità Cristiana 41 and Collection de l'École Française de Rome 123. Vatican City and Rome, 1989.

Pietri, C. "Aristocratie et société provinciale dans l'Italie chrétienne au temps d'Odoacre et de Théodoric." *MEFRA* 93 (1981): 417–67.

———. "Evérgetisme et richesses ecclésiastiques dans l'Italie du IV<sup>e</sup> à la fin du V<sup>e</sup> siècle." *Ktema* 3 (1978): 317–37.

———. "L'évolution du culte des saints aux premiers siècles chrétiens: du témoin à l'intercesseur." In *Les fonctions des saints dans le monde occidental (III<sup>e</sup>-XIII<sup>e</sup> siècle)*. Collection de l'École Française de Rome 149. Rome, 1991.

———. "Une aristocratie provinciale et la mission chrétienne: L'exemple de la *Venetia*." Reprinted in his *Christiana respublica: Éléments d' une enquête sur le christianisme antique*, vol. 2 (Rome, 1997).

Pietri, C., and L. Pietri, eds. *Prosopographie chrétienne du Bas-Empire: Italie (303–604)*. 2 vols. Rome, 2000.

Plumpe, J. C. "Pomeriana." *VigChrist* 1 (1947): 227–39.

Poschmann, B. *Paenitentia secunda: Die kirchliche Busse im ältesten Christentum bis Cyprian und Origenes*. Theophaneia 1. Bonn, 1940. Reprint, 1960.

Pouchet, J.-R. "Athanase d'Alexandrie, modèle de l'évêque, selon Grégoire de Nazianze, Discours 21." In *Vescovi e pastori in epoca teodosiana*, 2. Rome, 1997.

Prinz, F. "Die bischöfliche Stadtherrschaft im Frankenreich vom 5. bis 7. Jahrhundert." *Historische Zeitschrift* 217 (1973): 1–35.

Quasten, J. "Mysterium tremendum: Eucharistische Frömmigkeitsauffassungen des vierten Jahrhunderts." In *Vom christlichen Mysterium: Gesammelte Arbeiten zum Gedächtnis von Odo Casel OSB*, edited by A. Mayer, J. Quasten, and B. Neunheuser. Düsseldorf, 1951.

Quibell, J. E., ed. *Excavations at Saqqara*. 6 vols. Cairo, 1907–23.

Radermacher, L. "Griechische Quellen zur Faustsage." *SB Ak. Wiss. Vienna, Philos.-hist. Kl.* 206/4 (Vienna, 1927).

Raikas, K. K. "*Audientia episcopalis:* Problematik zwischen Staat und Kirche bei Augustin." *Augustinianum* 37 (1997): 459–81.

Ramsay, W. M. *The Cities and Bishoprics of Phrygia*. Vol. 1. Oxford, 1895.

Rapp, C. "Bishops in Late Antiquity: A New Social and Urban Elite?" In *Late Antiquity and Early Islam*, vol. 6, edited by J. Haldon, and L. Conrad, 144–73. Forthcoming.

———. "Comparison, Paradigm, and the Case of Moses in Panegyric and Hagiography." In *The Propaganda of Power: The Role of Panegyric in Late Antiquity*, edited by Mary Whitby. Leiden, 1998.

———. "The Elite Status of Bishops in Late Antiquity in the Ecclesiastical, Spiritual, and Social Contexts." *Arethusa* 33 (2000): 379–99.

———. " 'For Next to God, You Are My Salvation': Reflections on the Rise of the Holy Man in Late Antiquity." In *The Cult of Saints in Late Antiquity and the Middle Ages: Essays on the Contribution of Peter Brown*, edited by J. Howard-Johnston and P. A. Hayward. Oxford, 1999.

———. "Imperial Ideology in the Making: Eusebius of Caesarea on Constantine as 'Bishop.' " *JThS* 49 (1998): 685–95.

———. "Storytelling as Spiritual Communication in Early Greek Hagiography: The Use of *Diegesis*." *JECS* 6 (1998): 431–48.

Rebillard, E., and C. Sotinel, eds. *L'évêque dans la cité du IV^e au V^e siècle: Image et autorité.* Collection de l'École Française de Rome 248. Rome, 1998.

Reinhold, M. "Usurpation of Status and Status Symbols in the Roman Empire." *Historia* 20 (1971): 275–302.

Reitzenstein, R. *Historia Monachorum und Historia Lausiaca: Eine Studie zur Geschichte des Mönchtums und der frühchristlichen Begriffe Gnostiker und Pneumatiker.* Göttingen, 1916.

Rice, M. "*CIG* 4142—A Forgotten Confession-Inscription from North-West Phrygia." *Epigraphica Anatolica* 29 (1997): 35–43.

Rich, J., ed. *The City in Late Antiquity.* London, 1992.

Richards, J. *Consul of God: The Life and Times of Gregory the Great.* London and Boston, 1980.

Ritter, A. M. *Charisma im Verständnis des Joannes Chrysostomos und seiner Zeit: Ein Beitrag zur Erforschung der griechisch-orientalischen Ekklesiologie in der Frühzeit der Reichskirche.* Göttingen, 1972.

Rives, J. B. *Religion and Authority in Roman Carthage from Augustus to Constantine.* Oxford, 1995.

Robert, L. "Bulletin épigraphique." *REG* 85 (1972).

———. *Hellenica* 1/12 (1940); 4 (1948); 13 (1965).

———. *Le martyre de Pionios prêtre de Smyrne.* Edited by G. W. Bowersock and C. P. Jones. Washington, D.C., 1994.

Roloff, J. "Themen und Traditionen urchristlicher Amtsträgerparänese." In *Neues Testament und Ethik: Festschrift R. Schnackenburg,* edited by H. Merklein. Freiburg, 1989.

Romanchuk, A. I. "Die byzantinische Provinzstadt vom 7. Jahrhundert bis zur ersten Hälfte des 9. Jahrhunderts (auf Grund von Materialien aus Cherson)." In *Besonderheiten der byzantinischen Feudalentwicklung: Eine Sammlung von Beiträgen zu den frühen Jahrhunderten,* edited by H. Köpstein. Berlin, 1983.

Romilly, J. de. *La douceur dans la pensée grecque.* Paris, 1979.

Roques, D. *Synésius de Cyrène et la Cyrénaïque du Bas-Empire.* Paris, 1987.

Roueché, C. *Aphrodisias in Late Antiquity: The Late Roman and Byzantine Inscriptions.* London, 1989.

———. "Benefactors in the Late Roman Period: The Eastern Empire." In *Actes du X^e Congrès International d'Épigraphie Grecque et Latine, Nimes, 4–9 Octobre 1992,* edited by M. Christol and O. Masson. Paris, 1997.

———. "Floreat Perge." In *Images of Authority: Papers Presented to Joyce Reynolds on the Occasion of Her Seventieth Birthday,* edited by M. M. Mackenzie and C. Roueché. Cambridge Philological Society Suppl. 16. Cambridge, 1989.

———. "The Functions of the Governor in Late Antiquity: Some Observations." *Antiquité Tardive* 6 (1998): 31–36.

———. "A New Inscription from Aphrodisias and the Title *patēr tēs poleōs.*" *GRBS* 20 (1979): 173–85.

Rousseau, P. *Ascetics, Authority, and the Church in the Age of Jerome and Cassian.* Oxford, 1978.

———. *Basil of Caesarea.* Berkeley and Los Angeles, 1994.

———. "Eccentrics and Coenobites in the Late Roman East." *ByzForsch* 24 (1997): 35–50.

————. "The Spiritual Authority of the 'Monk-Bishop': Eastern Elements in Some Western Hagiography of the Fourth and Fifth Centuries." *JThS* 22 (1971): 380–419.

Rousselle, A. "Aspects sociaux du recrutement ecclésiastique au IVᵉ siècle." In *Mélanges de l'École Française de Rome*. Antiquité 89. 1977.

Sahin, S. "Piratenüberfall auf Teos: Volksbeschluss über die Finanzierung der Erpressungsgelder." *Epigraphica Anatolica* 23 (1994): 1–36.

Saller, S. J. *The Memorial of Moses on Mount Nebo*. Vol. 1. Jerusalem, 1941.

Salzman, M. R. "The Christianization of the Roman Aristocracy." *Historia* 42 (1993): 326–78.

————. "Competing Claims to 'Nobilitas' in the Western Empire in the Fourth and Fifth Centuries." *JECS* 9/3 (2001): 359–85.

————. "How the West was Won: The Christianization of the Roman Aristocracy in the West in the Years after Constantine." In *Studies in Latin Literature and Roman History*, edited by C. Deroux, 6: 451–79. Collection Latomus 217. Brussels, 1992.

————. *The Making of a Christian Aristocracy: Social and Religious Change in the Western Roman Empire*. Cambridge, Mass., 2002.

Sansterre, J.-M. "Eusèbe de Césarée et la naissance de la théorie 'césaropapiste.'" *Byzantion* 42 (1972): 131–95.

Saxer, V. "Institution et charisme dans les textes canonico-liturgiques et autres du IIIᵉ siècle." In *Miscellanea historiae ecclesiasticae VIII*, edited by B. Vogler. Bibliothèque de la Revue d'Histoire Ecclésiastique 72. Brussels and Louvain, 1987.

Scarpat, G. *Parrhēsia: Storia del termine e delle sue traduzioni in Latino*. Brescia, 1964.

Scheibelreiter, G. *Der Bischof in merowingischer Zeit*. Vienna, 1983.

Schiwietz, S. *Das morgenländische Mönchtum*. Vol. 1, *Das Ascetentum der drei ersten christl. Jahrhunderte und das egyptische Mönchtum im vierten Jahrhundert*. Vol. 2, *Das Mönchtum auf Sinai und in Palästina im vierten Jahrhundert*. Mainz, 1904–13.

Schöllgen, G. *Die Anfänge der Professionalisierung des Klerus und das kirchliche Amt in der syrischen Didaskalie*. JAC Ergänzungsband 26. Münster, 1988.

Schroedel, W. R. "Apologetic Literature and Ambassadorial Activities." *Harv. Theol. Rev.* 82 (1989): 55–78.

Schubert, W. "Die rechtliche Sonderstellung der Dekurionen (Kurialen) in der Kaisergesetzgebung des 4. Jhs.–6. Jhs." *ZRG, Röm. Abt.* 86 (1969): 287–333.

Schwartz, E. "*Basilikos nomos peri tōn prospheugontōn en ekklēsia*." In *Das Asylwesen Ägyptens in der Ptolemäerzeit und die spätere Entwicklung*, edited by F. von Woess. Münchener Beiträge zur Papyrusforschung und antiken Rechtsgeschichte 5. Munich, 1923.

Seeck, O. "Comites." *RE* 4/1 (1900): cols. 622–79.

————. "Scholastikos." *RE* 2/3 (1921): cols. 624–25.

Segal, J. B. *Edessa, "The Blessed City."* Oxford, 1970.

Selb, W. "Episcopalis audientia von der Zeit Konstantins bis zur Novelle XXXV Valentinians III." *Zs. d. Savigy-Stiftung f. Rechstgeschichte, romanist. Abt.* 84 (1967): 162–217.

Shaw, T. "Askesis and the Appearance of Holiness." *JECS* 6 (1998): 485–99.

Sirks, A. J. B., P. J. Sijpesteijn, and , K. A. Worp. *Ein frühbyzantinisches Szenario für die Amtswechslung der Sitonie*. Münchener Beiträge zur Papyrusforschung und antiken Rechtsgeschichte 86. Munich, 1996.

Solignac, A. "Julien Pomère." *DSp* 8 (1974): cols. 1594–1600.

Sotinel, C. "Le personnel épiscopal: Enquête sur la puissance de l'évêque dans la cité." In *L'évêque dans la cité du IV^e au V^e siècle: Image et autorité*, edited by E. Rebillard and C. Sotinel. Collection de l'École Française de Rome 248. Rome, 1998.

———. "Le recrutement des évêques en Italie aux IV^e et V^e siècles: Essai d'enquête prosopographique." In *Vescovi e pastori in epoca teodosiana*, 1. Rome, 1997.

Stancliffe, C. *St. Martin and His Hagiographer: History and Miracle in Sulpicius Severus.* Oxford and New York, 1983.

Steinleitner, F. S. *Die Beicht im Zusammenhange mit der sakralen Rechtspflege in der Antike.* Munich, 1913.

Sterk, A. "On Basil, Moses, and the Model Bishop: The Cappadocian Legacy of Leadership." *Church History* 67 (1998): 227–53.

———. *Renouncing the World Yet Leading the Church: The Monk-Bishop in Late Antiquity.* Cambridge, Mass., and London, 2004.

Stockmeier, P. "Aspekte zur Ausbildung des Klerus in der Spätantike." *Münchener Theologische Zeitschrift* 27 (1976): 217–32.

Straw, C. E. *Gregory the Great: Perfection in Imperfection.* Berkeley and Los Angeles, 1988.

Sundwall, J. *Weströmische Studien.* Berlin, 1915.

Treucker, B. "A Note on Basil's Letters of Recommendation." In *Basil of Caesarea: Christian, Humanist, Ascetic: A Sixteen-Hundredth Anniversary Symposium*, edited by P. J. Fedwick, vol. 1. Toronto, 1981.

———. "Politische und sozialgeschichtliche Studien zu den Basilius-Briefen." Diss., Frankfurt am Main, 1961.

Trout, D. *Paulinus of Nola: Life, Letters, and Poems.* Berkeley and Los Angeles, 1999.

Uhalde, K. "Proof and Reproof: The Judicial Component of Episcopal Confrontation." *Early Medieval Europe* 8 (1999): 1–11.

Ulbert, T. "Bischof und Kathedrale (4.-7. Jh.): Archäologische Zeugnisse in Syrien." In *Actes du XI^e Congrès International d'Archéologie Chrétienne*, vol. 1. Studi di Antichità Cristiana 41 and Collection de l'École Française de Rome 123. Vatican City and Rome, 1989.

van Dam, R. *Families and Friends in Late Roman Cappadocia.* Philadelphia, 2003.

———. *Kingdom of Snow: Roman Rule and Greek Culture in Cappadocia.* Philadelphia, 2002.

———. *Leadership and Community in Late Antique Gaul.* Berkeley, 1985.

———. "Self-Representation in the Will of Gregory." *JThS* 46 (1995): 118–48.

van der Meer, F. *Augustine the Bishop.* London, 1961.

van Deun, P. "Euchē distingue de proseuchē: Un essay de précision terminologique chez les pères grecs et les écrivains byzantins." In *The Impact of Scripture in Early Christianity*, edited by J. den Boeft and M. L. van Poll-van de Lisdonk. Vigiliae Christianae Suppl. 44. Leiden, 1999.

*Vescovi e pastori in epoca teodosiana: XXV Incontro di Studiosi dell'Antichità Cristiana, Roma, 8–11 maggio 1996.* 2 vols. Studia Ephemeridis Augustinianum 58. Rome, 1997.

Villagomez, C. "The Fields, Flocks, and Finances of Monks: Economic Life at Nestorian Monasteries, 500–850." PhD diss., University of California, Los Angeles, 1998.

Vismara, G. *L'audientia episcopalis.* Milan, 1995.

Vittinghoff, F. "Zur Entwicklung der städtischen Selbstverwaltung: Einige kritische Anmerkungen." In *Stadt und Herrschaft: Römische Kaiserzeit und hohes Mittelalter,* edited by F. Vittinghoff. Historische Zeitschrift Beihefte, Neue Folge 7. Munich, 1982.

Vivian, T. *Histories of the Monks of Upper Egypt and the Life of Onnophrius by Paphnutius.* Kalamazoo, 1993.

―――. "Monks, Middle Egypt, and Metanoia: The Life of Phib by Papohe the Steward (Translation and Introduction)." *JECS* 7 (1999): 547–71.

―――. *St. Peter of Alexandria: Bishop and Martyr.* Philadelphia, 1988.

Vogel, C. *Le pécheur et la pénitence dans l'église ancienne.* Paris, 1966.

Vogt, H. J. *Coetus sanctorum: Der Kirchenbegriff des Novatian und die Geschichte seiner Sonderkirche.* Bonn, 1968.

Vogüé, A. de. Foreword to *Pachomian Koinonia,* vol. 1. Kalamazoo, 1980.

Völker, W. *Das Vollkommenheitsideal des Origenes: Eine Untersuchung zur Geschichte der Frömmigkeit und zu den Anfängen christlicher Mystik.* Tübingen, 1931.

Vollenweider, S. "Synesius von Cyrene." In *Lexikon der antiken christlichen Literatur,* 578–80. Freiburg, 1998.

Vööbus, A. *A History of Asceticism in the Syrian Orient: A Contribution to the History of Culture in the Near East.* CSCO Subsidia 14, 17, 81. Louvain, 1958–88.

Waldstein, W. "Zur Stellung der episcopalis audientia im spätrömischen Prozeß." In *Festschrift M. Kaser.* Munich, 1976.

Walker, J. "In Search of St. Theodore in Central Anatolia: Archaeological Survey of Late Roman Galatia." In *Abstracts of Papers, Twenty-fourth Annual Byzantine Studies Conference, Lexington, Kentucky, October 20–22, 1998.*

Ware, K. T. "The Spiritual Father in St. John Climacus and St. Symeon the New Theologian." In *Studia Patristica* XVIII/2, *Papers of the 1983 Oxford Patristics Conference,* edited by E. A. Livingstone. Kalamazoo and Louvain, 1989.

Watkins, O. D. *A History of Penance.* London, 1920. New York, 1961.

Wenger, L. "Asylrecht." *RAC* 1 (1950): cols. 836–44.

―――. "Horoi asylias." *Philologus* 86 (1931): 427–54.

Whittow, M. "Ruling the Late Roman and Early Byzantine City: A Continuous History." *Past and Present* 129 (1990): 3–29.

Wickert, L. "Princeps." *RE* 22/2 (1954): cols. 2258–64.

Wieruszowski, H. "Die Zusammensetzung des gallischen und fränkischen Episkopats bis zum Vertrag von Verdun (843) mit besonderer Berücksichtigung der Nationalität und des Standes." *Bonner Jahrbücher* 127 (1922): 1–83.

Wild, R. "I Am in the Desert." *Studies in Formative Spirituality* 1/2 (1980): 207–16.

Williams, G. H. *Wilderness and Paradise in Christian Thought: The Biblical Experience in the History of Christianity and the Paradise Theme in the Theological Idea of the University.* New York, 1962.

Wilson, A. "Biographical Models: The Constantinian Period and Beyond." In *Constantine: History, Historiography, and Legend,* edited by S. N. C. Lieu and D. Montserrat. London and New York, 1998.

Winkler, K. "Clementia." *RAC* 3 (1957): cols. 206–31.

Wipszycka, E. "Le istituzioni ecclesiastiche in Egitto dalla fine del III all'inizio dell'VIII secolo." In *L'Egitto cristiano: Aspetti e problemi in età tardo-antica,* edited by A. Camplani. Studia Ephemeridis Augustinianum 56. Rome, 1997.

————. "Les clercs dans les communautés monastiques d'Égypte." *The Journal of Juristic Papyrology* 26 (1996): 135–66.

————. *Les ressources et les activités économiques des églises en Égypte du IV$^e$ au VIII$^e$ siècle.* Brussels, 1972.

Wischmeyer, W. "Die Aberkiosinschrift als Grabepigramm." *JAC* 23 (1980): 22–47.

————. *Griechische und lateinische Inschriften zur Sozialgeschichte der Alten Kirche.* Gütersloh, 1982.

————. "M. Iulius Eugenius: Eine Fallstudie zum Thema 'Christen und Gesellschaft im 3. und 4. Jahrhundert.'" *ZNW* 81 (1990): 225–46.

————. *Von Golgatha zum Ponte Molle: Studien zur Sozialgeschichte der Kirche im dritten Jahrhundert.* Göttingen, 1992.

Woess, F. von. *Das Asylwesen Ägyptens in der Ptolemäerzeit und die spätere Entwicklung.* Münchener Beiträge zur Papyrusforschung und antiken Rechtsgeschichte 5. Munich, 1923.

Ysebaert, J. *Die Amtsterminologie im Neuen Testament und in der Alten Kirche: Eine lexikographische Untersuchung.* Breda, 1994.

Zocca, E. "La figura del santo vescovo in Africa da Ponzio a Possidio." In *Vescovi e pastori in epoca teodosiana.* Rome, 1997.

# INDEX

Aaron, brother of Moses, 131–32
Aberkios, inscription and *Life* of, 292, 298
Abraam, head of village in Egypt, 248
Abraham, bishop of Qidun, 85
Acacius, bishop of Constantinople, 4, 5, 250
Acacius, bishop of Amida, 231, 232
Acepsimas, hermit and priest, 140
Aemilius, bishop of Beneventum, 190
Aetius, 267
Alexander, bishop and physician, 177–78
Alexander, bishop of Comana, 174, 177
Alypius, bishop of Thagaste, 182, 186
Ambrose of Milan, 10–11, 132, 145, 203, 246, 249, 296; on combining monasticism and clerical life, 149, 150, 297; *Letters*, 36, 150, 191; *Life of*, 18, 259; *On the Duties of the Clergy*, 48–50, 230–31, 249; as senatorial bishop, 190
Ambrosiaster, 40
Ammianus Marcellinus, 187n80, 218, 237, 258
Ammonius, monk in Egypt, 144
Amoun, monk in Egypt, 115
Amphilochius, bishop of Iconium, 196
Anastasius, emperor, 216, 233, 264, 271, 286, 288
Anastasius, presbyter, 257
Anastasius Sinaites, 80
Andrew, bishop of Aquino, 177
Anthony, Saint, 61, 103, 109, 115, 120; battle with demons of, 110–11; "daily martyrdom," of 75; refusal to leave seclusion of monastery of, 143

Antoninus, bishop of Ephesus, 221
Aphrahat, 250
Aphthonius, bishop, 148
Apion, 202
*Apocalypse of Paul*, 112
apostasy, 88–90, 98
*Apostolic Constitutions*, 32, 94, 131, 175, 178–79, 206, 229; on episcopal judgment, 244–45
*Apostolic Tradition*, 28–29, 30, 32, 34, 90–91, 94
Apphy, bishop of Oxyrhynchus, 143
Appion, bishop of Syene, 264
Aquila, Montanist bishop, 244
Arcadius, emperor, 157, 207, 244, 261
Arianism, 12, 237
Arsacius, bishop of Constantinople, 191
ascetics/asceticism, 75–76, 101–2; hagiography of bishops and, 296–97; *parrhēsia* and, 268; penitential practices and, 79, 102; teaching and, 102–3. *See also* holy men
Asclepiades, bishop of the Chersonese, 263
asylum, ecclesiastical, 253–60
Athanasius of Alexandria, 12, 59, 144; appointment of monks as bishops by, 147; on bishop's office as opportunity for sinning, 143; compares himself with Moses, 128; *Life of Anthony*, 103, 109–10, 112, 124–25, 294; praised by Gregory of Nazianzus, 40, 126–27, 139
Athenagoras, 261
Athenodorus, bishop in Pontus, 182n55

Eutychius of Constantinople, patriarch, 296, 300, 302
Evagrius, bishop of Antioch, 186
Evagrius Ponticus, 181; *Gnostikos,* 64–65; on evil thoughts, 138; on sin and the intellect, 117–18; as Spirit-bearer, 59; on tears, 80–81
excommunication, 93. *See also* penance
*exemplarion,* 27–28
*exemplum,* 126–27
Exsuperantius, bishop of Lucania, 191

Felix, deacon in Carthage, 254
Felix, deacon in Ruspe, 202
Fulgentius of Ruspe, 178, 189, 202

Gallienus, emperor, 262
Gelasius, abbot in Nilopolis, 124
Gelasius, bishop of Caesarea, 196
Gennadius, bishop on Constantinople, 4
George, bishop of Alexandria, 177
Gerasimos, hermit, 115
Germanus, bishop of Auxerre, 11, 193
Gerontius, bishop of Nicomedia, 178
Gilliard, F., 185
Glycerius, deacon, 202
Glycerius, emperor, 194
Goehring, J. E., 121
Great Persecution, 86, 183, 204, 235
*Greek Anthology,* 170–71
Gregory of Nazianzus, 60, 95, 196, 204; *Autobiography,* 121, 131, 146; biographical trajectory of, 134, 182, 186, 272; on bishops of humble background, 174; *In Defence of His Flight,* 40, 42–44, 45; on monasticism, 121; *Oration on Athanasius of Alexandria,* 126–27, 297; *Oration on Basil of Caesarea,* 127, 258, 291; on penance as a form of baptism, 80; personal wealth of, 214, 241
Gregory of Nyssa, 60, 80, 129, 181, 187n81, 196; *Encomium on Saint Stephen,* 60; *Funerary Oration on Saint Basil,* 127; *Life of Gregory the Wonder-worker,* 250; *Life of Macrina,* 122; *Life of Moses,* 126
Gregory the Elder, father of Gregory of Nazianzus, 196
Gregory the Great, 11, 197–98, 265; career path of, 190, 201; *Pastoral Care,* 53–55
Gregory of Tours, 194–95, 197, 252

Gregory the Wonder-worker, 65–66, 129, 141–42, 182, 250

Hadot, P., 76
Haehling, R. von, 189
Haensch, R., 220
hagiographical writing: on bishops, 11, 18–19, 21–22, 293–302; intent of, 295; origin of, 103
Halsall, P., 293
Harl, M., 132
Hausherr, I., 79
Helladius, bishop of Caesarea, 197
Helle, monk in Egypt, 115
Heraclius, bishop of Hippo, 201, 215
Hermas, 59
Heussi, K., 103, 137
Hilarinus, charioteer, 258
Hippolytus of Rome, 28
Holl, K., 15
holy men, 15–16; as "bearers of Christ," 71; as bishops, 140; correspondence with followers of, 67–73; efforts during famine by, 234; as exemplars, 155; Justinian on, 279; Moses as model for, 126–27; *parrhēsia* of, 67, 220, 269, 270, 271; as *patronus,* 15, 155–56; as peacemakers of, 250; physical appearance of, 269–70; visits to court by, 270–72
Holy Spirit, 56, 57; ordination and the, 29, 104
Honoratus of Marseilles, 123n99
Honorius, emperor, 207, 244, 278
Hörmann, J., 84
Hosius of Cordoba, 265
Hunt, E. D., 238n16
Hyakinthos, bishop of Miletus, 257
Hypatia, philosopher in Alexandria, 157, 165
Hypatius, bishop of Ephesus, 264

Ignatius of Antioch, 7, 26–28, 59, 60
Indakos, bishop of Corcyrus, 264
Innocent, bishop of Rome, 206–7
Instinsky, H. U., 8
Irenaeus, bishop of Tyre, 192
Irene of Chrysobalanton, 79
Isaiah, 115
Isaiah, bishop of Rhodes, 192
Isaias of Scetis, 240

| | |
|---:|:---|
| Compositor: | BookMatters, Berkeley |
| Text: | 10/13 Baskerville |
| Display: | Baskerville |
| Printer and binder: | Friesens Corporation |